The PMOSIG Program Management Office Handbook

EDITED BY

Craig Letavec, PMP, PgMP and Dennis Bolles, PMP

Copyright © 2011 by PMI® Program Management Office Specific Interest Group

ISBN: 978-1-60427-044-0

Printed and bound in the U.S.A. Printed on acid-free paper
10 9 8 7 6 5 4 3 2 1

Library of Congress Cataloging-in-Publication Data

The PMOSIG program management office handbook : strategic and tactical insights for improving results / edited by Craig Letavec and Dennis Bolles.
　　p. cm.
　Includes bibliographical references and index.
　ISBN 978-1-60427-044-0 (hbk. : alk. paper)
　1. Project management.　I. Letavec, Craig J., 1970–　II. Bolles, Dennis.
　HD69.P75P586 2010
　658.4'04—dc22

　　　　　　　　　　　　　　　　　　　　　　　　2010037242

"PMI", "PMP", "PgMP" and "OPM3" are marks or registered marks of the Project Management Institute, Inc. which are registered in the United States and other nations.

Direct all inquiries to J. Ross Publishing, Inc., 5765 N. Andrews Way, Fort Lauderdale, FL 33309.

Phone: (954) 727-9333
Fax: (561) 892-0700
Web: www.jrosspub.com

Contents

Section I: PMO Governance

Chapters 1-3 include roles in organizational governance, portfolio management, and organizational change management.

Section II: PMO Strategy & Tactics

Chapters 4-8 include examples of how PMOs have participated in the strategic and tactical management of programs and projects to achieve business benefits.

Section III: PMO Strategy & Tactics

Chapters 9 and 10 include development and management of governance policies and procedures, standards, methodologies and processes, education and training programs, and tools and templates. Also covered are PMO technical systems, and program manager, project manager and portfolio manager assignments.

Section IV: PMO Strategy & Tactics

Chapters 11-14 include best practices and case studies for successfully aligning new PMOs to business objectives, delivering benefits/ROI, and managing and expanding the PMO's scope of services.

Section V: PMO Strategy & Tactics

Chapters 15-18 include key performance indicators and processes used to manage the identification, recording, and analysis of PMO data. Also covered are PMO maturity and driving excellence that enhances the PMO's long-term sustainability as a business function.

**Chapter 19   The PMO Maturity Cube: A Project Management
Office Maturity Model** **383**

**Epilogue   The Role of the PMO as a Portfolio Management
Office** **403**

Foreword

From their origins in project controls and project support functions, project management offices (PMOs), in their many forms and fashions, have evolved to be at the forefront of operational effectiveness. Today we even see enterprise versions that are focused on portfolio and program management in a more strategic capacity assisting organizations to map performance more effectively. However, many commentators feel that there is more that should be achieved by PMOs, and those who work within them, to continue adding value to their organization's endeavors.

From the moment I first heard of the initiative to put together this book, I knew that it would be a comprehensive source of all things PMO for all people. That is exactly what the book achieves, and I applaud this initiative.

Packed full of information, data, and how-to tips and techniques from recognized global experts and leaders, this book does not offer just another theory or one-dimensional viewpoint but rather features in-depth perspectives from seasoned and experienced practitioners and thought leaders who have practiced program and project management and have been associated with PMOs in various forms across a full range of sectors and geographies. It is simply *the* complete source for all things PMO.

The structure and depth of the content should assist organizations and individuals alike to achieve the desired and anticipated levels of success and sustainability because of its significant content in each of the various chapters that are built around three core domains of:

- Governance, including portfolio management and execution management
- Organizational leadership & alignment, including organizational change management
- PMO operations, including structure, roles, and set-up

This coverage ensures that the global community can have confidence in using this book as a guide and trusted advisor that is equally applicable for large, publically listed corporations and government departments, as well as small-to-medium enterprises.

This book is the most comprehensive source available for all things PMO be it portfolio, program, or project. I encourage everyone to read this book to gain valuable knowledge and insights from the contributing authors. Finally, make sure that your organization's library has at least one copy on its shelves!

Iain Fraser, PMP, PMI Fellow, Fellow PMINZ
PMI Past Chair

Preface

The PMI® Program Management Office Specific Interest Group (PMOSIG), consistent with its vision to be the leading professional community providing innovation and thought leadership in the area of the PMO and related subjects, has created this book to achieve its mission to return direct value to the PMO community. This PMO handbook contains chapters submitted by more than 20 notable authors, subject matter experts, experienced practitioners, and thought leaders with a variety of backgrounds and experiences. These contributions provide insight into practices that successful PMOs have employed to return direct value to the organizations that they serve.

As an edited work, this book provides realistic strategies, methods, insights, and case examples to serve the needs of organizations, PMO practitioners, and the project management community as a whole worldwide. It features practical guidance on a variety of PMO-related topics in the areas of:

- **PMO governance**—Covers roles in organizational governance, portfolio management, and organizational change management
- **PMO strategic and tactical aspects**—Includes examples of how PMOs have participated in strategic and tactical management, as well as in the management of programs and projects, to achieve business benefits
- **PMO services**—Covers the development and management of governance policies and procedures, standards, methodologies and processes, education and training programs, tools and templates, PMO technical systems, and program manager, project manager and portfolio assignments
- **PMO setup and execution**—Includes best practices and case studies for successfully aligning new PMOs with business objectives, delivering benefits and ROI, and managing and expanding the PMO's scope of services
- **PMO performance and maturity**—Describes the processes used to drive excellence that enhances the PMO's long-term sustainability as a business function

It is our hope that this book provides content that will help you enhance your PMO, whether just starting out or as part of the ongoing process of delivering additional value through the PMO. It is exciting to see how the contributions to this book vary even with something as simple as a description of what a PMO really is. The variety of techniques and approaches presented for PMO setup, establishing and maintaining sponsorship, expanding PMO services, and maturing the PMO demonstrate that we have learned a lot since the PMO concept was initially established and that we seem to agree that flexibility is one key to success as no two PMOs will be exactly alike. We are still a long way from a common understanding of the PMO and its role in the project and organizational context, but clarity is starting to emerge regarding the factors that are likely to lead to PMO success—reflected on in numerous places within this book. The PMI PMOSIG welcomes the opportunity to help further drive the PMO community forward, and hopes that this book is another step toward enhancing knowledge in PMO theory and practice. Whether you're just starting a new PMO, focused on re-establishing a PMO in your company, or have a successful PMO that is expanding its scope of services, you are on an exciting journey. Let the experience of the contributors to this book help be your guide.

About the Editors

Craig Letavec, MSP, IPMA-B, PMP, PgMP, has led large program efforts in a diverse range of large, global companies in a variety of industries including consumer products, new venture start-ups, information technology services, and information technology consulting. He has served as an active speaker and author on a range of topics, including program management, implementing effective change management, and establishing, managing, and building the value of the program management office (PMO) in organizations. He is the author of *The Program Management Office*, a noted text in the project management community specifically focused on PMO implementation and development, as well as a co-author of *Program Management Professional* and a contributor to *99 Things Every Project Manager Should Know*.

Throughout his professional career, Craig has studied the role of project and program management in organizations, the process of formalizing project and program management practices in organizations, and the many challenges that face organizations and program managers alike. This practical analysis, combined with academic research in the field, has led him to a number of conclusions regarding how organizations can best exploit program management to improve business results.

Craig holds a Bachelor of Science degree from the University of Dayton (Go Flyers!) and a Master of Science in project management from The George Washington University. As an active teacher who enjoys educating future project and program managers and business professionals alike, he has served as an adjunct lecturer in project management in the master of business administration program at Wright State University in Dayton, Ohio and as an adjunct instructor at the University of Dayton. Craig also serves as vice chair of the global Project Management Institute (PMI®) Program Management Office Specific Interest Group (PMOSIG) and as general conference chair for *PMO Symposium*, the largest focused international conference for PMO practitioners.

 **Dennis Bolles**, PMP, has more than 40 years experience providing business, project management, and PMO services. He has been a member of PMI since 1985, received his PMP® certification in 1986 (#81), and is a founder of PMI's Western Michigan Chapter, serving on its Board of Directors in several positions since its inception in 1993. He has been serving on the PMI PMOSIG board of directors as vice chair of public relations since June 2009.

Dennis is president of DLB Associates, whose primary focus is working with organizations to establish PMOs, formulate project business management processes, develop and enhance enterprise project management centers of excellence, create project management methodologies, and plan organizational project management training programs. Dennis is the PMI standards project manager who led the project core team to a successful completion and on-time delivery of the *PMBOK® Guide—Third Edition* in 2004. He is a published author of many project management articles; a congress, symposium, and chapter professional development day speaker; and author of *Building Project Management Centers of Excellence* and co-author of *The Power of Enterprise-Wide Project Management*.

PMOSIG History

The concept of a Specific Interest Group (SIG) dedicated to the needs of the Program Management Office (PMO) community was initially formulated in 1998. Subsequently, an initiative was undertaken to establish the group as a PMOSIG under the global body of the Project Management Institute (PMI®). The initiative was led by David Griffith and Rommy Musch. David assumed the responsibilities of PMOSIG (Potential) Board Chairman. Along with a multi-talented Board, he led the way for the PMOSIG to structure a knowledge base of PMO best practices and established the forum for the broad discussion of PMO concerns, techniques, and lessons learned.

The PMOSIG finalized its charter and bylaws in August 2001 and started its charter under the leadership of Robert Johnston, Executive Chair of the PMOSIG Board of Directors. Robert joined Rommy Musch, PMOSIG Principal Chair, in establishing the PMOSIG within the wider PM community.

The PMOSIG set out to establish a knowledge base of best practices and lessons learned for the PMO community and to provide a network for program and project managers from a variety of industries and interest areas. PMOSIG membership is worldwide (has no geographical boundaries) and gives members the opportunity to network with peers who have similar interests.

Throughout the evolution of the PMOSIG, the Board of Directors (past and present) have worked together on initiatives that contribute to the delivery of the values outlined in the vision and mission statements.

Vision statement:

> "To be the leading professional community that develops insights and opportunities to advance the Program Management Office through innovation and thought leadership."

Mission statement:

> "To provide value to our community by:
> - enabling the sharing of knowledge and experience
> - creating professional development opportunities for individuals and teams
> - leveraging relationships to access additional resources and innovative thinking
> - facilitating community through active participation and contribution
> - fostering innovation and competency through collaboration."

With the contributions of its Board and members, the PMOSIG will continue to evolve and provide its unique global community with the opportunity to network and learn.

Membership

The PMOSIG membership represents more than 3000 professionals worldwide. Membership has remained strong throughout the SIG's history, and it continues to be one of the largest specific interest groups within PMI.

Members by Region	03/09	04/09	05/09	06/09	07/09	08/09	09/09
North America	3216	3160	3083	3019	2984	2939	2894
Latin America	117	114	119	114	115	115	117
EMEA	537	527	527	511	494	485	487
Asia Pacific	307	298	286	287	281	273	271

Members by Region (continued)	10/09	11/09	12/09	01/10	02/10	03/10
North America	2854	2830	2843	2886	2866	2893
Latin America	120	124	125	124	128	128
EMEA	497	495	480	494	498	506
Asia Pacific	269	264	271	279	283	279

Timeline and Milestones

Major milestones in the SIG's history have included:

- Launching a well-received global local interest group initiative
- Establishing the *PMO Symposium*, the premiere international conference for PMO professionals
- Publishing the *PMO Accord*, a practitioner-led publication that addresses recommended PMO practices
- Partnering to present the PMO of the Year award

A brief timeline of major SIG activities can be seen in Figure 1.

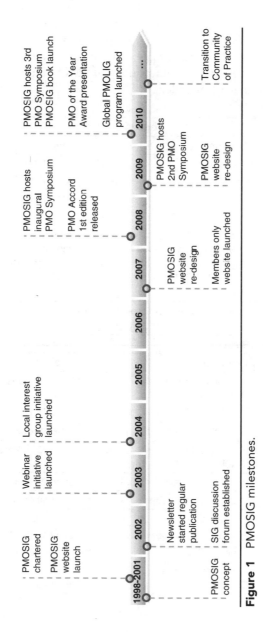

Figure 1 PMOSIG milestones.

Board of Directors–Past and Present

Throughout its existence the PMOSIG has been managed by a dedicated group of volunteer leaders who have given their time and talents to support the advancement of the PMOSIG. From the initial founders to the current members of the Board of Directors, these individuals worked to serve the needs of the PMO community and to foster a global community of PMO practitioners. Members of the Board of Directors have included:

Founders		
Name	**Position**	**Tenure**
David Griffith	Co-founder	June 1998
	Potential SIG Chair	June 1998–Dec 1999
Rommy Musch	Co-founder	June 1998
	Potential SIG Chair	June 1998–May 2001
	Principal Chair	June 2001–December 2003
	Vice Chair, Governance	January 2004–March 2009
	Executive Chair	April 2009–**Present**

Board of Directors 2010 (as of July 2010)		
Name	**Position**	**Tenure**
Art Brody	Vice Chair, Finance	December 2003–**Present**
Craig Letavec	Vice Chair, Professional Development	May 2005–May 2007
	Vice Chair, Operations	June 2007–**Present**
	PMO Symposium Chair	2008–**Present**
Darlene Fladager	Vice Chair, Professional Development	April 2010–**Present**
Dennis Bolles	Vice Chair, Public Relations	June 2009–**Present**
Frederic Casagrande	Vice Chair, Membership	November 2009–**Present**
Rommy Musch	Co-founder	June 1998
	Potential SIG Chair	June 1998–May 2001
	Principal Chair Vice	June 2001–December 2003
	Chair, Governance	January 2004–March 2009
	Executive Chair	April 2009–**Present**

Past members of the Board of Directors

Name	Tenure
Art Drake	September 2001–April 2009
	(Executive Chair October 2003–April 2009)
Cyndie Canzoneri	June 2001–December 2003
Derry Simmel	April 2004–October 2009
Jennifer Graham	May 2004–December 2008
Jim Carras	August 2008–February 2009
Kenneth Bunzel	November 2002–December 2003
Lindsay Chamberlain	June 2007–April 2010
Richard Schwarz	June 2001–December 2001
Robert Johnston	January 2001–November 2003
	(Executive Chair, June 2001–November 2003)
Robert Lofthouse	September 2001–September 2007
Robin Black	January 2006–July 2008
Robin Jenkins	July 1999–July 2000
Steve Taylor	June 2001–November 2003
Thomas McCabe	June 2001–October 2003
Wendy King	November 2001–December 2002

About the PMOSIG Executive Chair

Rommy G. Musch has more than 20 years of experience in the information technology sector. Her major emphasis is in project and program management, two areas in which she has extensive knowledge and experience. Rommy is a recognized leader in the establishment and operation of program and project offices and has been consistently successful in the delivery of large, complex projects.

Rommy is currently employed with Orange Business Services, an affiliate of France Telecom. At Orange, Rommy manages the Business PMO within the Global Services division that focuses on the delivery of business critical and sensitive projects and programs. She has developed and implemented the methodology and project disciplines that are being applied globally throughout the Professional Services organization.

Other key accomplishments with Orange include: the development of the training methodology used to instruct some 540+ project managers globally;

presales activities on large opportunities involving the composition of the PM value proposition, pricing, and customer presentations; set-up of project offices for large global projects; project recovery on failing projects; management of all PM requirements in the Asia Pacific region; and development and implementation of continuous improvements to the methodology and processes across the global PM community.

Prior to her role with Orange, Rommy was the Manager of the Project Office for The National Bank of New Zealand. This position included the development of the project management methodology, disciplines, and reporting used to conduct the successful merger of Countrywide Bank with The National Bank. Her role also comprised 15 months as the Enterprise Plan Coordinator.

Rommy is based in Wellington, New Zealand.

Web
Added
Value™

This book has free material available for download from the
Web Added Value™ resource center at **www.jrosspub.com**

At J. Ross Publishing we are committed to providing today's professional with practical, hands-on tools that enhance the learning experience and give readers an opportunity to apply what they have learned. That is why we offer free ancillary materials available for download on this book and all participating Web Added Value™ publications. These online resources may include interactive versions of material that appears in the book or supplemental templates, worksheets, models, plans, case studies, proposals, spreadsheets and assessment tools, among other things. Whenever you see the WAV™ symbol in any of our publications, it means bonus materials accompany the book and are available from the Web Added Value Download Resource Center at www.jrosspub.com.

Downloads available for *The PMOSIG Program Management Office Handbook: Strategic and Tactical Insights for Improving Results* consist of a collection of easy-to-adapt templates for PMO leaders, including resources to support, establish, and enhance the PMO.

1

The PMO Role in Project Portfolio Governance

Shyamprakash Agrawal, PMP

Introduction

An effective project management office (PMO) assists in the decision-making process to identify, select, and monitor the projects managed in the portfolio. The PMO plays a key role in meeting the organization's objectives to contribute to the success of the projects in the portfolio by ensuring that projects:

- Have appropriate project governance
- Align with organization strategy
- Practice project management methodology and processes
- Utilize project management tools
- Perform resource management
- Perform risk management
- Conduct project reviews
- Produce management reporting

Project Governance

From a corporate governance perspective, it is essential that the performing organization deploys enterprise-wide minimum standards for project management to demonstrate that consistent and robust controls are in place, and to ensure that results can be forecasted with a certain degree of accuracy. As the organization maturates pertaining to project execution, the precision increases and the forecasting more accurately predicts actual performance. Corporate governance plays an important role by providing decision support for project sponsors, decision makers, and stakeholders involved in the program, organization, and enterprise. Documenting governance decisions and tracking action items for future governance sessions provides the administrative support needed for effective decision making.

Tracking actual expenditures and forecasting future costs while navigating an organization's internal billing and reconciliation procedures can often be a full-time role within the PMO. Reporting cost variances and adjusting program forecasts based on change control is a critical function for fiscal success.

The most ambitious set of roles gives it responsibility for any number of project governance functions. For example, the PMO might be centrally involved in the approval process by evaluating the strength and benefits of project proposals. Additionally, it might be involved in business case development, aligning project proposals with core business objectives and strategic goals, and weighing costs, risks, and return on investment.

The next few sections discuss several of the primary roles of the PMO in the project governance context, including project authorization and maintaining a responsibility matrix.

Project Authorization Levels

The expected expenditure of a project determines what level of governance and authorization or approval is required at both the project initiation stage as well as at later approval stages within the project lifecycle. The level of expected expenditure may also determine into which category a project falls for reporting purposes. Projects may be categorized according to total project cost or by utilizing other relevant organizational factors.

Role and Responsibility Matrix

The PMO is responsible for creating, maintaining, and enhancing the responsibility matrix for all roles related to project management for uniform implementation across the organization. Examples of some common roles and responsibilities are described in this section.

Project Sponsor

The project sponsor should be identified at the outset of the project and is responsible for the initiation and approval of documentation and subsequent delivery of the project in line with the identified performance standards for the project. Individual responsibility for project sponsorship may change throughout the project lifecycle, but the role must always remain fulfilled. Day-to-day management of the project will be delegated to a project manager, although it is recognized that a project manager may not be identified until project approval has been granted.

The project sponsor has overall accountability for ensuring that project objectives are met. As the project champion, he is often accountable to management for the development and delivery of the approved business case for the project.

Another responsibility of the project sponsor is accountability for the major planned benefits from the project. Therefore, he must insure that the delivery of the benefits is coordinated as specified in the project's benefit realization plan or business case, as well as manage changes impacting the realization of benefits throughout the project lifecycle.

A crucial role of the project sponsor is ensuring continued strategic alignment and monitoring the ongoing viability of the project throughout the project lifecycle. As an individual whose seniority (as determined by the management) is commensurate with the size, scope, and risk of the particular project, he provides the necessary directional and decision-making support to the project manager. The project sponsor and management are responsible for ensuring that the project is managed throughout the project lifecycle in line with organization-wide project management minimum standards and other relevant standards.

The sponsor is accountable for securing the internal resources throughout the project, and for ensuring that the project is adequately staffed. In addition, the project sponsor is responsible for ensuring that the overall process of project organization and governance incorporates a robust and clearly defined approach to risk management. He is ultimately accountable for insuring that major project risks are clearly identified and that a realistic assessment of the potential impact is made at each phase of the project lifecycle.

In some cases, the project sponsor may find it appropriate to serve as the executive sponsor and to appoint a deputy as project sponsor to undertake some of the more detailed day-to-day responsibilities. These responsibilities may include managing initial-level issue resolution to allow time for the executive sponsor to handle the overall responsibilities.

Project Steering Committee

The project steering committee responsibilities include:

- Championing the project at a senior level
- Providing strategic input to the project to ensure that the project still fits within the strategic direction
- Assessing and approving (subject to management approval, if required) any changes to the approved project scope and ensuring that the project sponsor is in a position to make informed decisions
- Setting and monitoring the priorities for the project
- Reviewing major deliverables (i.e., performing a quality assurance role)
- Resolving project issues escalated by the project manager

- Monitoring progress and comparing it to the plan
- Ensuring that an appropriate risk management approach is in place that covers all elements of risk, including operational, market, strategic, credit, regulatory, and event losses for each project

Project Manager

The project manager is accountable to the project sponsor and has the authority to run the project on a day-to-day basis on behalf of the sponsor. Her primary responsibility is to ensure that the project is delivered in line with the timelines, cost, and scope that are detailed in the approved project charter and project plan, and in accordance with the organization-wide project management standards.

The complexity, risk, execution efforts, and strategic nature of the project will influence the selection of the project manager. For example, if 80 percent of the project's efforts are with the organization's information technology (IT) department, then a manager should be selected from the IT department, but will be responsible for successfully executing the remaining 20 percent of the non-IT project efforts as well.

The project manager is responsible for defining and establishing the risk management approach that will be adopted during the project and, where appropriate, assigning ongoing management responsibility of the process within the project team in conjunction with any specialist risk teams. The project manager must ensure that any events due to a failure of people, process, systems, or external influences are managed and, if necessary, reported to the sponsor.

It is the responsibility of the individual project manager to ensure that project documents are retained in line with organization policy. When the project is complete, the responsibility for maintenance and retrieval should lie with the relevant division or business area.

For each project, an overall (or lead) project manager must be appointed. She is responsible for overall project management and delivery. The project manager must ensure that the deliverables are transitioned to the appropriate operation teams after project completion. She also has to ensure that all required training and other transition activities to make the project operational occur.

Project Management Office

The responsibilities of the PMO include:

- *Identifying and solving problems*—The PMO performs assessments or evaluations of the overall state of project management. The first assessment is performed during the business case creation process, and the results are reported in a business case template. Additional assessments are performed as needed, such as in the project planning phase. In addition, the PMO may review and audit individual projects to identify any problems, and then take specific actions to resolve them.

- *Providing ongoing services to ensure that resolved problems do not recur*—Because new projects are always starting, it is insufficient to simply solve the problems in current projects. The PMO must offer a suite of services to meet the needs of current as well as future projects. These services fall into four distinct categories:
    - General: Disseminate project status information and reduce costs through standardization
    - Support: Provide the training and support to help project managers succeed on their projects
    - Control: Assess and review the status of project management and projects to define problems and recommend corrective action
    - Direct: Manage projects directly
- *Reducing costs through efficient, centralized services*—The PMO can increase project efficiency through the centralization of services, including staff, supplier, customer, and equipment management. Centralizing these services also standardizes how they are implemented, thereby reducing the costs incurred by using other methods on different projects.
- *Making sure that stakeholders have up-to-date, accurate information*—The PMO will update plans and produce status reports for projects, programs, and portfolios.
- *Supporting ongoing improvement in project management*—Organizations and their projects are constantly changing, and the project manager must change with them. When current problems are solved, new problems or opportunities are identified. Ongoing improvement in project management can then be supported by the PMO.

Defining the exact role begins in the first step of project initiation, and that role is given its initial definition in the project charter. The process of defining the PMO's role is ongoing; it continues through the project planning process and is revisited during the processes of performing assessments and process improvement.

It is essential that the role of a PMO is well defined and thoroughly understood by everyone in the organization. When its role is poorly defined, either some jobs will not get done or there will be a duplication of effort. A poorly defined role will result in an organizational perception that the PMO is either overextending its mandate or failing to perform. When this happens, its effectiveness is severely compromised.

Alignment with Organization Strategy

For the longer term, the PMO undertakes a greater role in business analysis and project portfolio management. Ideally, projects are approved not as isolated proposals, but as assets in a project portfolio. If there is a finite budget, how does the organization decide, for example, to continue Project A but terminate Project B?

Some PMOs are limited to making sure that the executive leaders have all the information they need to make informed decisions. In other companies, it gets involved in analyzing, comparing, and making recommendations for projects. Somewhere in between, many PMOs are responsible for defining the methodology of project approval. Additional roles include:

- Providing a structure for selecting appropriate projects and avoiding or eliminating inappropriate ones
- Allocating resources to the correct projects, thus reducing wasteful spending
- Aligning portfolio decisions with strategic business goals
- Basing portfolio decisions on logic, reason, and objectivity
- Creating ownership among staff by being involved at the appropriate levels
- Establishing avenues for which people can identify opportunities and obtain support
- Helping project teams understand the value of their contributions

The PMO often determines the optimal mix and sequencing of proposed projects to best achieve the organization's overall goals. These are typically expressed in terms of hard economic measures and business or technical strategy goals, while honoring constraints imposed by management or external real-world factors. Expected attributes for a project's total expected cost include: consumption of scarce resources (human or otherwise); expected timeline and schedule of investment; expected nature, magnitude, and timing of the benefits to be realized; and relationship or interdependencies with other projects in the portfolio.

An ongoing analysis of the project portfolio so that each investment can be monitored for its relative contribution to business goals versus other portfolio investments is also undertaken by the PMO. If a project is either performing below expectations (e.g., due to cost overruns or benefit erosion) or is no longer aligned to business objectives (such as with a change in natural market and statutory evolution), management can choose to stop a project thus stemming further investment. Resources are then redirected toward other projects that better fit the business objectives. This analysis typically can be performed on a periodic basis to refresh the portfolio for optimal business performance. In this way, both new and existing projects are continually monitored for their contributions to overall portfolio health.

Project Selection and Prioritization

The selection of projects is an important organizational aspect. They need to align with the long- and short-term strategic goals of the performing organization. Whereas a particular business case may seem attractive, to ensure the best value for the money invested it is important to compare it with other business cases. They all may not be worthy. Likewise, it may not be feasible to implement every worthy business proposal.

Benefit Management

Managing project benefits involves these activities:

- Benefits must be placed at the center of the project selection criteria and investment appraisal processes. Funding should be linked to benefits forecasts, and key stakeholders should be clear about what benefits they are buying.
- Benefits realization starts with the business case. It is critical to ensure that the business case includes all activities and costs required to realize the forecast benefits.
- Funding allocations should be incremental, and continued funding should be directly linked to the latest benefits forecast. Regular checkpoints should be built in so that if benefits fall away, budgets can be adjusted accordingly.
- Benefits should be booked early by cutting budgets, limiting the headcount, targeting unit costs, and by including them in divisional and individual performance targets where possible.
- Benefits tend to be overstated and are rarely more than unsubstantiated assumptions. Such claims must be robustly scrutinized and challenged.
- Benefits should be validated wherever possible to ensure that they are attainable.
- Benefits need to be actively managed to ensure that forecasted benefits are realized (this is especially important when benefits depend on business change) and to capture benefits that were unanticipated at the business case stage.
- Benefits realization planning and managing should be from a business rather than a project perspective. Benefits are usually dependent on business change, often going unrealized until project deployment is complete and the project team is disbanded.
- Utilize summary documentation and leverage the Pareto principle. Short summary documents (business cases and benefits reports, for example) convey the salient facts far more effectively than do extensive documents.

To govern projects, the organization should establish a project approval and prioritization board (PAPB), having full authority and accountability for:

- Ensuring that the project approach satisfies an organization's project management standards
- Establishing a consistent approach to governance and management of projects with an expected expenditure
- Authorizing project proposals
- Approving business cases
- Agreeing on tolerance levels for costs, benefits, scope, and delivery timescales beyond which any material change must be referred back to PAPB for approval

- Prioritizing departmental or business projects and resolving resource and budget conflicts
- Ensuring that an appropriate level of risk has been considered for each project based on the documentation submitted for authorization and approval, and that acceptable approaches to risk management are in place

The PAPB should be led by a chief or senior executive with appropriate authority, and its members need to represent key stakeholders (finance, technology, strategy, and business), also with the appropriate seniority, to ensure effective control. Regional PAPBs can be created to make decisions on proposals with predetermined maximum value limits, whereas higher-value proposals can be referred to a central PAPB with recommendations. The PAPB should meet as required, often no more than once each month. The PMO can play an important administrative role to brief the board and put forth the agenda items for discussion and decision.

The PAPB should include appropriate floating or ad hoc members to ensure proper representation of the projects under consideration of a specific agenda, if any. A standing agenda item for each PAPB should be the monitoring of all projects for:

- Authorizing project proposals
- Deciding inclusion of authorized project proposals waiting in quarterly forecasts or in business plans
- Approving business cases
- Prioritizing projects, considering the available resources
- Terminating the scope of projects that are not expected to meet predetermined objectives
- Approving or rejecting changes requested by the projects that exceed predefined limits
- Agreeing on the tolerance levels for costs, benefits, scope, and delivery timescales beyond which any material change must be referred back to PAPB for approval

The PMO plays an important role in ensuring that proposals are aligned with strategy. Specifically it helps to ensure that:

- All business cases are countersigned by the relevant finance organization, confirming their input to:
  - Review financial assumptions.
  - Quantify business benefits.
  - Prepare costing for the proposal.
  - Assess the impact on existing budgets and plans.
  - Model cash flow and conduct sensitivity analysis.
  - Calculate NPV, IRR, and the discounted payback period.
  - Assess the impact on the profit and loss account (by year).
  - Assess the impact on the balance sheet (where material).

- All proposals received by various agencies (provided they have a relevant business case) are assessed for feasibility (technology, financial, and functional).
- Proposals are listed in an annual plan, or special approval is obtained.
- Proposals are properly classified and aligned with strategy.
- Estimates of required resources and corresponding availability timelines are made available.
- Recommendations are made to management to terminate a project when it is not expected to meet a stated objective or benefit.

Project proposals can be classified into key categories as part of the review process:

- *Strategic focus*—Initiatives that strengthen core business activities
- *Revenue generation*—Show a revenue increase for the organization
- *Operational efficiency*—Cause productivity to increase, indirectly increasing an organization's revenue or reducing its costs
- *Risk mitigation*—Mitigate risks
- *Compliance*—Address regulatory compliance requirements
- *Customer service improvements*—Support improved customer service
- *Environmental protection*—Support environmental protection efforts
- *Corporate social responsibility*—Funded by the organization to meet corporate social responsibilities

As the PMO drives the project management culture of a business, it becomes part of the very fabric of the business—it is how you get projects done. It will continue to add value as long as its framework has inherent flexibility and the leadership team is committed to the PMO as a critical business asset.

Project Management Methodology and Processes

Standard methodology and processes play an important role in ensuring project success. The methods and processes need to be appropriate and, often, it is insufficient to simply follow textbook examples. From a corporate governance perspective, it is essential that a performing organization deploys organization-wide minimum standards for key processes such as project portfolio management. Standards provide a common framework for the initiation, planning, execution, and for monitoring, controlling, and closing processes. PMOs champion the development of project management minimum standards and deploy, maintain, and enhance them to improve the probability of success. These reusable components save time by allowing projects to start more quickly and with minimal effort.

The project management minimum standards under the five process phases of a project management lifecycle are shown in Figure 1.1. Checkpoints play an important role in making go-no-go decisions (see Table 1.1).

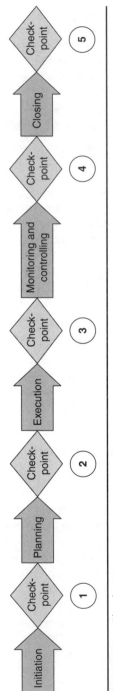

Figure 1.1 Checkpoints.

Table 1.1 Checkpoint processes detail

Checkpoint	Activity description
Initiation	Defines and authorizes the project or a project phase. After project initiation commences, the project proceeds to the planning phase.
Planning	Defines and refines objectives and plans the course of action that is required to attain the objectives and scope that the project was undertaken to address.
Execution	Integrates people and other resources and carries out the project management plan for the project.
Monitoring and controlling	Regularly measures and monitors progress to identify variances from the project management plan so that corrective action can be taken when necessary to keep the project in line with the objectives.
Closing	Formalizes acceptance of the product, service, or result and brings the project or a project phase to an orderly end.

There is a need to develop templates, processes, and forms for projects. It is also important to have a different set of templates to match the rigor of the project to avoid unnecessary process overhead. Considering project specific requirements, templates need to be developed and customized so that they are appropriate for the project.

The PMO ensures all projects operate using similar best practices, ensuring that the overall project success rate increases and project cost decreases. When it performs its core activities, the PMO improves both the organization's effectiveness and its efficiency in project management. Its role for process assurance is a quality management function. Project managers should recognize the PMO's responsibility to audit project deliverables. It is not a malicious entity bent on inhibiting project progress by deciding not to sign off on a deliverable. However, it is the PMO's role to ensure that the process is followed.

Knowledge Database

Historical data, reference information, lessons learned, and any best practices followed in previous projects are important inputs for planning similar projects or proposals. Using a predefined format, information is collected and stored in a central database to prepare future estimates or projections, trend analyses, and various other aspects. In addition, information gleaned from projects or information obtained from industry-associated trade publications may be included.

Potentially, serving as a central repository of information (project successes, failures, best practices, and lessons learned) is a key role for the PMO. It might assume responsibility for capturing all relevant information and applying it to revamp the project management methodology, change templates, or make other changes in project-related processes.

Project Management Tools

The contribution of appropriate project management tools that are based on specific needs is vital to the success of the project. The PMO plays an important role in selecting, implementing, and arranging training for users. It ensures that the tools selected can be integrated, that data entry is not duplicated, and that vital project information is not left out. Some of the tools are related to integrated project management, scheduling and tracking, effort and cost estimation, project status reporting, and risk management.

Responsibility for a number of software tools within the organization, including tools for project management, resource management and tracking, time tracking, and others falls on the PMO. Its staff needs to understand how the tools work and what they contribute to the organization's functioning. As with methodology, if the tools are off-the-shelf software packages, demands on the PMO staff's expertise will be minimal. If the tools are developed in-house, the staff will need a deeper knowledge of them.

It is also important for a PMO to continuously look for upgrades and new tools to keep up with advancements in project management. Organizations and their project needs are constantly changing and the PMO must change with them.

Resource Management

Although managing project-specific resources lies with the respective project manager, the PMO can play a role in acquisition, deployment, redeployment, training, appraisal, and the release of resources. In addition to providing resources for the projects, it can enhance project efficiency through the centralization of services such as staff, supplier, customer, and equipment management. Centralizing these services also standardizes how they are implemented, thereby reducing the costs incurred by using various methods on different projects.

Scales of economy with common resources across projects enable an organization to be in a better position to negotiate. Based on a business plan and gap with availability, the PMO can plan the resource for the fiscal year well in advance to fill the gap. This helps to minimize the resource conflict when using limited resources.

The PMO often manages long-term project resources (staff and equipment) and project resources that are shared across projects. It may also maintain searchable resource databases containing information such as skills, experience, and training imparted either formally or through project work.

By establishing a resource management model and tracking utilization, the PMO can make better decisions for resource utilization. The key to an effective resource management model is the quality and reliability of the underlying data. The PMO manages the data collection and reporting process.

Acquisition

Resources are acquired to meet the projected demand from projects with appropriate timelines. Considering long-term objectives, equipment is taken on lease or purchased. (It is good to procure equipment rather than leasing it if the lease amount for all projects together—in sequence—is around the cost of equipment.) Similarly, employees are hired or services are secured on a contractual basis.

Deployment and Redeployment

Resource deployment and redeployment, particularly for primary resources, is one of the main responsibilities of the PMO. Based on the business plan and resource requests from projects, priorities are set by management, shared or key resources are allocated, and, upon release, resources are redeployed if there is any other requirement.

Training

The PMO arranges appropriate training that covers technical, functional, management, and soft skills, keeping resources ready to meet the immediate and future project requirements. This training should focus on:

- Ensuring project success by knowing the PMO's role and responsibility
- Understanding the impact of project management on the organization's continued success
- Ensuring the strategic alignment of all projects
- Creating a culture that supports a project management environment
- Implementing best practices for strategic project management
- Creating a strategic project measurement system

Mentoring

With a PMO in place, it now has the responsibility to help develop organizational capacity around project management disciplines. Mentoring and knowledge transfer within the PMO, via peer-to-peer training of the junior project managers by senior subject-matter experts, helps to further develop this organizational capacity.

Effective project managers not only promote the project management practices within the organization, but are able also to coach, mentor, and develop the project managers' skill sets. Effective PMOs are staffed with resources that can deliver projects and successfully share knowledge with junior project managers. Organizations have different levels of project management capability, and project managers help to improve the capability by promoting and sharing project management best practices. Successful candidates should be able to cite past experiences, share lessons learned, provide best practices, or impart methodology knowledge to other project managers. A key function of an effective PMO is training and consulting other project managers on project and program management techniques. It coaches project managers to prevent projects from getting into trouble and assists with at-risk projects to mitigate further issues and risks. The office facilitates improved project team communication by having common processes, deliverables, and terminology.

Appraisal and Release

Timely appraisals are important in that they provide feedback and work to improve and strengthen the positive. With the help of respective managers, the PMO arranges midterm and end-of-project appraisals that are communicated to staff and vendors for contractors. It ensures the timely release of resources at the end of the project and redeployment or release, according to the terms of engagement, to return to the parent department or the vendor.

Similarly, equipment (leased or owned) is appraised for its usefulness in the future. The PMO coordinates with the appropriate respective agency to ensure that equipment is appraised and ready to use. For leased equipment that is no longer required, equipment is released and returned to the vendor according to the terms of engagement. Owned equipment is also disposed of per the organization's disposal policy after the completion of a useful life. New equipment is then procured as needed for future use.

Risk Management

Although managing project risks lies within the respective project manager's domain, the PMO supports individual projects by identifying and evaluating risk, issues, and response plans. It consolidates common risk scenarios with a potential impact and handling plan. Inter-project dependency risks are coordinated by the PMO with the respective project managers to insure they are managed. Like risks, issues are also managed. The PMO helps to resolve escalated risks and forward issues to higher management.

The PMO manages specific reviews and documents key decisions. Projects are organized within a program due to synergies gained from working as an integrated set of activities. Coordinated efforts to manage risks increase the probability of success. From past project experience, the PMO prepares the list of generic project risks to assist projects in identifying them.

Project Review

The PMO is involved in the project's checkpoint review process as an effective approach to communicate the status on a regular basis. In some organizations, it manages the checkpoint review for the project manager, proactively monitors approaching checkpoints, and helps the project manager facilitate the approval process. Engaging the PMO in a checkpoint review will also provide an objective assessment of the project and provide additional insight into issues and risks not perceived by the project manager. Since it is engaged in multiple projects, similar issues and lessons learned can be shared.

There are also additional roles that a PMO can take on while projects are running, such as project tracking. Traditionally, projects are tracked by the departments or project teams that are responsible for their execution, but there are advantages to having the PMO involved. It can provide a centralized view of project activity throughout the organization. It may also liaise to ensure that projects are deployed to meet project objectives; all knowledge is provided by the project team and necessary support is provided during transition.

Project Health Check

The overall purpose of the project health check is to create and maintain quality in projects through a systematic process that ensures:

- The stated and implied needs of customers are understood and met.
- Interested stakeholders' needs are understood and evaluated.
- The organization's quality policy is incorporated into project management.
- The setup of a review process is initiated, whereby the peer project managers conduct a project audit. The peer project manager is happy to guide fellow project managers.

Project documentation ensures:

- Each managed project is clear and well documented.
- The creation and maintenance of the team is documented.
- Changes to the project are apparent and documented.
- Risk management is continuous, documented, and followed.
- Task completion is reviewed, documented, and followed.
- Budget reviews are documented and followed.
- The closing and evaluation of the project is documented and followed.

Management Reporting

The PMO will update plans and produce status reports for projects, programs, and portfolios. Depending on the knowledge base's level of sophistication, this may be either a manual activity or a thoroughly automated function.

The performance management function integrates project-level status reporting and generates the program-level status for executive reviews. The PMO investigates specific performance issues and communicates early warning signs of troubled projects. It also enforces consistent performance-reporting guidelines so that each project consistently reports project performance.

The PMO aims to support the ongoing measurement of the project portfolio so that each project can be monitored for its relative contribution to business goals. If a project is either performing below expectations (cost overruns or benefit erosion, for example) or is no longer highly aligned to business objectives (which change with natural market and statutory evolution), management can choose to cancel a project and redirect its resources. Done periodically, this analysis will refresh the portfolio to better align with current states and needs.

One trait that most PMOs have in common is the need to report to management and stakeholders on the progress of projects. Project managers will complete their status reports and provide that information to the PMO—usually on a weekly basis. The PMO will then need to create its own report that consolidates the individual project reports into a summary, or dashboard.

PMO reporting includes a periodic dashboard that provides the status of ongoing projects as well as plans for the future, including specific recommendations to continue or terminate the project when it appears likely that the project will miss the objective or that the product of the project will not be viable. It also provides an independent assessment of key projects.

One essential responsibility is tracking the incremental benefit delivery of completed projects as well as tracking benefits against projections. Completed projects are delivered to the customer or moved to production.

Management reporting is probably one of the most visible functions by which a PMO can show value. The reports are sent to management and decisions are made based on that data. By providing accurate and timely information in those reports, the PMO ensures that the foundations of corporate decision making are solid and built on the best information available.

There are several types of reports for which the PMO may be responsible, including department, project, portfolio, and PMO reporting.

Let's take a quick look:

- *Department reporting* takes several forms; one common form is resource management and projections. The focus of these reports is to give information on a department or group.
- *Project reporting* is probably the most familiar. This can take the form of your red/green/amber status reports, buffer reports, or earned value reports. These reports give information on a project or projects.
- *Portfolio reporting* provides information about a collection of projects. Some common reports are the pipeline reports that show where each project is as it moves through the project lifecycle. Other reports include a project priority list, resource and cost projections, and other, possibly

more sophisticated, sets of information. While project reports are more tactical in nature, portfolio reports are used more for strategic decision making.

- *PMO reporting* provides information about how the PMO is doing. Some examples are budget reports, balanced scorecards, and staffing.

Author Biography

Shyamprakash (Shyam) Agrawal, PMP, holds a masters degree in physics with over 26 years experience in directing project and program managers, as well as designing applications. For the past three years, he has worked exclusively for the PMO managing programs and projects with project teams of up to 100 members and annual budgets of more than 30 million dollars with average budget increases up to 25 percent annually.

Shyam has managed projects in different time zones, geographies, and cultures by ensuring quality deliverables as per agreed timelines. He has effectively used different models for implementation to take advantage of cost benefits, including onshore, offshore, and offsite development.

He has been involved in business applications for financial systems, banking (retail and wholesale), telecom billing, insurance, railways, payroll systems, personnel management systems, energy management systems, IT infrastructure, and IT security. He was instrumental in defining minimum governing standards for an enterprise-level PMO, establishing a link with the strategy and vision of his organization.

References

Allprojectmanager website, http://www.allpm.com.

Gantthead website, http://www.gantthead.com.

Project Management Institute, *A Guide to the Project Management Body of Knowledge (PMBOK® Guide)*, 4th edition, Newtown Square, PA, PMI®, 2008.

Project Management Institute, *Organizational Project Management Maturity Model (OPM3®)*, 2nd edition, Newtown Square, PA, PMI®, 2008.

Project Management Institute, *The Standard for Program Management*, 2nd edition, Newtown Square, PA, PMI®, 2008.

Projects@work website, http://www.projectsatwork.com.

2

Program Types:
Categorization and
Its Benefits

Sherry Remington, PMP, SCPM

Introduction

This chapter seeks to define key components of program categorization and provides an overview of the benefits that can be achieved by implementing program categorization. Before programs can be categorized, an understanding of what programs are is in order. According to the Merriam-Webster dictionary, the term *program* can be a noun or a verb. As a noun, program speaks to printed documents, a sequence or order to be followed, or a theatrical performance. It could also refer to goals for a plan or system such as computer programming. As a verb, program means the act of working out a sequence of operations to be performed or the act of inserting a particular action to control. It may also refer to the act of predetermining the thought, behavior, or operations of something.

So, what is a program? In the realm of business and management, programs are made up of similar groups of work products, whether the products are projects, processes, systems, data, or organizations. Programs have common strategies, prioritization, and goals. Programs can be time bound like a group of projects or can follow a lifecycle with no specific end time. Why does it matter? Because understanding what program type is being addressed will help categorize, monitor, and track it more effectively.

In *Project Management Terms: A Working Glossary* by J. LeRoy Ward, he defines program management as "management of a related series of projects over a period of time to accomplish broad goals to which the individual projects contribute" (Ward, 2000).

Since we are clearing up the questions of definition, let us also take a look at the hierarchy and definitions of the related ideas of projects and portfolios. The *PMBOK® Guide—Fourth Edition*, defines a project, program, and portfolio as:

> *Project*—A temporary endeavor undertaken to create a unique product, service, or result.
>
> *Program*—A group of related projects managed in a coordinated way to obtain benefits and control that are otherwise unavailable when managed individually. Programs may include elements of related work outside the scope of the discrete projects in the program.
>
> *Portfolio*—A collection of projects or programs and other work grouped together to facilitate effective management of that work to meet strategic business objectives. The projects or programs of the portfolio may not necessarily be interdependent or directly related.

These three terms work together. Projects can stand alone. One project can start and end on its own without being related to or a part of the other entities. Programs can include one or more projects and also have operational work that is not project related. Portfolios can have the entire group mentioned, including individual projects, projects within a program, or programs that include operational work. So then, what is the value of a program? A program helps to coordinate the work in ways that are observable and provides information to manage the business benefit to the company better. Figure 2.1 is an example of how each process aligns to different sections of an enterprise vision, strategy, and execution plan.

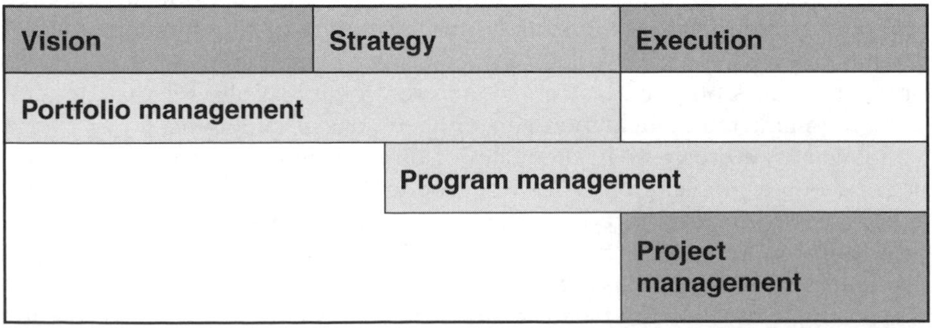

Vision	Strategy	Execution
Portfolio management		
	Program management	
		Project management

Figure 2.1   Process alignment.

Portfolio management best aligns with vision and strategy as it governs what goes into an enterprise portfolio. Programs and projects are selected based on the criteria that best aligns them to the vision and strategy of the company.

Program management aligns to strategy and execution as it guides organizations to execute against the enterprise strategy via projects and operational teams that are performing against the corporate processes. Project management aligns to execution, as that is what it is designed to do; to bring vision and strategy to reality. It deliver the results.

Why Categorize?

Categorization of programs should be completed to manage outcomes better. All programs are not equal or similar and should not be treated as such. It can be said that there are repeatable processes and best practices that cross all types of programs, and this is true. The management and style of the differences will determine the success of the programs. Let us consider the types of programs and explore the commonalities and differences.

Strategic Programs

A strategic program executes projects or operational work to align with the strategy of the organization.

Projects: The types of projects in these programs are typically short term, so the benefit and value of the vision and strategy can be realized early on. This helps to gauge the correctness of the vision and strategy.

Operations: Operational work in a strategic program serves primarily to support a project in driving the process, system, and data changes within an operational group. This work may be outside the normal realms of an established operations team. Its purpose is to validate the strategy and make it operational.

Organizational: A strategically aligned program is most often aligned with the executive team or thought leaders of the organization. The executives are the keepers of the vision. Therefore, they need a close connection with the validation of the vision which comes from strategic program execution.

How Are They Funded?

Funding for these programs can be from several places. It is appropriate to fund these programs from a pool of investment funds; at the top of an organization or at the top of a function or business unit. Funding is typically initiated from the top down due to the strategic nature of the program, and also because the benefit horizon may be longer term.

What Do They Provide?

1. *A new process or standard of doing business*—If a strategic program is being introduced by a company, it is for the purpose of changing, adding, or deleting the current state of being. A strategic program provides the venue to encourage the change to occur.
2. *New best practices, processes, standards, and a new way to work*—The strategic program may be introducing a variety of new solutions that can be very different from the current norm. The strategic program will identify, organize, communicate, and implement the new or different practices.
3. *Resourcing for strategic programs may be quite different from resourcing within the current resource pool*—For instance, if you are creating a new business model or technology that has no space in the marketplace, who will shepherd it and introduce it to the market? New skills are needed and a strategic program will identify and cultivate those new skills to make the strategic program a success.
4. *Governance for strategic programs may not follow the same process, approvals, or lifecycle that other programs utilize*—Because strategic programs are all about newness and change, these programs may not fit into a more formalized governance structure. All programs, including the strategic programs, need leadership and project managers to lead projects. Strategic programs also need execution measurements, but this may be where the difference lies. Execution measurements are typically in the red zone, because when dealing with new strategic solutions, the amount of funding, timeframes, and deliverables are all subject to variance due to the nature of the program often involving working for the first time on executing a particular, unique deliverable.

What Are the Benefits of Strategic Programs?

- New business models to increase revenues or profits
- Prioritization to align to the enterprise vision and strategy
- Productivity of work continuation in the form of pipeline management
- Validation of strategic direction

Operational Programs

An operational program is one that executes projects or operational work to support the ongoing business of the organization. Operational programs drive productivity and efficiency.

Projects: The types of projects in these programs can be brief in duration to improve systems, data, or processes of the current work. They can also be longer term to add new capabilities or functionality that may take longer to implement. This helps to improve productivity and stay in alignment with strategy.

Operations: Operational work in an operational program is primarily to support the current business systems, processes, and data for a functional group. This work may include the normal day-to-day operations of a function or team. Its purpose is to be efficient and cost effective. Six Sigma and Lean processes are commonly used tools in these types of programs.

Organizational: An operationally aligned program is most often found within a functional unit or support organization of the enterprise. The functions are responsible for the execution of the day-to-day work and, therefore, have the need for a close connection to the customer-facing teams, such as sales or support teams. Some examples of operational programs could reside in functions like sales operations, manufacturing, and customer support.

How Are They Funded?

Funding for these programs are usually in alignment with the function they support. Funding is typically initiated from the function or business unit to support the changing needs of the function they serve. These types of programs may be viewed as overhead so they are tracked tightly to productivity metrics. The benefit of the operational program spans the horizon from short term to long term, depending on the program's change model. Programs can follow a release model where capabilities and functionality are implemented on a standard periodic basis, or they can follow a project model in which the programs are driven via projects as a result of a perceived business need or value.

What Do They Provide?

1. *Stability and predictability*—Operational programs take the current processes and track, monitor, and control them in a way that ensures predictability in enterprise success.
2. *Improved processes, best practices, and standards to improve the current work methods*—The operational program provides insight to the metrics-driven execution of a system, process, or data, allowing the effectiveness to be maximized.
3. *Resourcing for operational programs consist of business analysts, operation managers, resources skilled in customer service, and subject-matter experts*—Their skills are specific to the operational process for which they are responsible, thus resources in operational programs tend to be experts due to the repetitive nature of the work or the myopic focus on a specific work process, system, or data.
4. *Governance for operational programs follows the standard lifecycle methodologies that are promoted by PMI® and other standards bodies*—Because operational programs are about stability and predictability, more formalized

governance structures are utilized. Execution measurements are detailed and specific, and many of the projects and operations in an operational program are managed more effectively to a successful end because of the usage of standard and specific metrics.

What Are the Benefits of Operational Programs?

- *Quality*—As a result of monitoring and controlling repeatable processes systems and data, operational programs tend to produce higher quality.
- *Productivity and efficiency*—These are natural byproducts of an operational program due to the scrutiny of the processes, systems, and data.
- *Development of subject-matter experts*—Because of the myopic focus on process, systems, and data, development of subject matter experts are also a result of operational programs.

Product Programs

A product program aligns to a specific product for the lifecycle of the product. This equates to the initial development of the product, the marketing plans, the growth plans, and to the end-of-life plans.

Projects: The types of projects in product programs are aligned to the product lifecycle. They can be short or long term, depending on the phase they cover and the timeline to implement. They may involve creating new capabilities for or revisions to the product. Product programs help to improve company position in the marketplace and increase alignment with branding and strategy.

Operations: Operational work in a product program serves primarily to support the product in marketing, growth, and end-of-life processes. This work may include the normal (day-to-day) operations of a function or team. Its purpose is to support the product in marketing, branding, efficient and cost effective product updates, and to improve sales cycles.

Organizational: A product program is most often aligned with a product or technology business unit of the enterprise. The product programs are responsible for the end-to-end execution of the product and, therefore, need to be closely connected to marketing, manufacturing, and customer support. Some examples of product programs could reside in functions such as technology, manufacturing, or within a particular department.

How Are They Funded?

Funding for product programs are usually aligned with the development organization. Funding is typically initiated from an enterprise level to support the development, marketing, manufacturing, and support that span across an enterprise. The benefit of the product program spans the horizon from short to long term, depending on the lifecycle phase of the product. The scope of the benefit may also depend on the adoption of the product in the marketplace.

What Do They Provide?

1. *Best practices, Six Sigma, and Lean Manufacturing*—Most product programs are highly visible to the enterprise executives. They follow rigorous quality processes utilizing best practices and quality measurement techniques to ensure a successful launch.
2. *Governance*—Product programs follow a release model in which the initial capability is released and subsequent capabilities and functionality are implemented on a standard periodic basis. The methods used to govern product programs can be varied, including Waterfall, Agile, and Scrum, among others, all with the intent to get the product to market as quickly as possible with the needed element of quality to satisfy the stakeholders.

What Are the Benefits of Product Programs?

- *Best-in-class products*—Both executive visibility and enterprise revenue pressure the product management team to provide a best-in-class product.
- *Quality control and release management*—The level of rigor for product programs is typically high and results in a more standard method of production with predictable outcomes.
- *Budget controls*—As a result of following standards, quality best practices, and innovative governance models, these programs have better control of their spend patterns.

Functional Programs

A functional program is a program that aligns to a specific organization or function of the enterprise, such as regulatory, service delivery, information technology, or sales. These programs are focused on excellence and value.

Projects: The types of projects in functional programs are aligned to the functional processes or the need to change a process. They can be short or long term, depending on the needs of the function. They may involve creating new capabilities or driving change and adoption in the organization. Functional projects are specifically designed to improve the function and its value to the enterprise. Many times operational programs fall under the purview and governance of functional program management offices.

Operations: Operational work in a functional program serves primarily to support the function. This work may include the normal operations of a function or team. Its purpose is to drive value and improvement in the function.

Organizational: A functional program is most aligned with the function it supports. The functional programs are responsible for operations and the business value of the function to the enterprise.

How Are They Funded?

Funding for functional programs is derived from the function itself. Functional programs are considered overhead and must run as efficiently and productively as possible. The benefit of the functional program is displayed in the ability of the function to make new projects and processes operational as quickly as possible, thereby reducing adoption and management costs and, thus, increasing value.

What Do They Provide?

1. *Functional expertise*—Resources engaged in a functional program will become experts in the processes, systems, and data of the function.
2. *Functional oversight*—Functional programs provide oversight to the function on success metrics and add value to the enterprise.

What Are the Benefits of Functional Programs?

- *Achievement of functional goals*—Because functional programs are specific to an organizational group, they execute against the functional and organizational goals.
- *Knowledge advancement*—Subject-matter experts are generated from these programs due to the functional focus. Functional programs serve as learning grounds for employees.
- *Budget controls*—Similar to the product program, functional programs follow quality best practices and innovative governance models. The functional programs also have better control of their spend patterns.

Enterprise Programs

Enterprise programs span across multiple and cross-functional groups of the enterprise. These programs are large, complex, and present risk to the business.

Projects: Projects in enterprise programs are aligned to the strategy of the enterprise and cause significant changes to multiple functions within the enterprise. Enterprise programs are typically longer term and have higher expenditures than other program types. They may involve creating new business models or driving change and adoption across functions. Enterprise projects are about overall change and the positive impact they can have on the enterprise.

Operations: Operational work is virtually nonexistent in enterprise programs. Once the programs and projects have been completed, most of the ongoing work is released into the functions for maintenance and operations.

Organizational: An enterprise program is cross functional. The strategic, operations, product, and functional teams participate in the program at the level agreed to by the enterprise program team and the individual programs teams.

How Are They Funded?

Funding for enterprise programs is typically from a conglomerate pool of all of the teams and functions participating in the enterprise program. The teams participate in funding an enterprise program based on the benefit and value to the overall enterprise.

What Do They Provide?

1. *Change in direction*—These programs typically take the enterprise in a new direction and engage the functions and teams to adapt to the new direction and vision.
2. *New opportunities for growth*—The goal of this benefit is to gain market share or grow the enterprise to meet current or new market demands.

What Are the Benefits of Enterprise Programs?

- *Achievement of enterprise goals*—Enterprise programs are broad sweeping engagements made in an effort to achieve enterprise short- and long-range goals.
- *Leadership development*—Leaders emerge from these large cross functional programs. A strong leader sharpens his skills as he guides teams through these large, complex enterprise programs.

Enterprise Program Management Office

Several types of programs have been discussed, each having its own program management office to manage the breadth of scope within the program. There are often no straight lines of authority or formal organization structures; only program management offices partnering among themselves and governing their areas of responsibility and accountability.

We reflect briefly on the need of an overarching program management office and why it would be beneficial to all of the other PMOs to have an enterprise program management office (EPMO).

First, an EPMO is beneficial in taxonomy and nomenclature. Once teams begin to speak the same language, a common understanding develops. Also, having the same taxonomy and nomenclature eliminates redundancy and adds clarity to standards and best practices. For example, stop light indicators have various meanings to different groups unless there is a stated meaning by an authority. So if the EPMO says that a red schedule indicator means the program is two weeks behind schedule, there will be a common understanding among functions, teams, groups, and other PMOs that the red schedule means the program is two weeks behind.

Second, processes, templates, and documentation add productivity and reduce redundancy for project and program managers. How many times have e-mail requests been sent out to a broad audience requesting a standard template and seven to ten responses were provided, all with the same content but different formatting and guidelines? Having an EPMO that provides standard processes, templates, documentation, and guidelines improves communication and the review proces while decreasing the risk of missing valuable data.

The third benefit is that the knowledge base and training is reduced and simplified. When standard templates and processes are in place, educating the workforce is streamlined. The burden to other PMOs is lightened when training is removed from their responsibilities. Additionally, all resources are trained to the same standard, improving consistency of knowledge across the enterprise.

The last benefit is the mentoring aspect. An EPMO can track the expertise of individuals in the program and project management profession. Career paths as well as job opportunities can be administrated through an EPMO, again centralizing and eliminating redundant work for the other PMOs.

Which One?

Now, the questions are: *Which one should I use? Which one is better for my business?* How do you determine which is better for your needs? I would suggest that they all are equally effective and provide benefits to an enterprise. The real question is: *Which one does the enterprise need based on apparent deficiencies?* If the enterprise is in a place where it needs to make serious changes to survive, then perhaps a strategic program might be in order. If the enterprise needs to update, improve, or add new technology to the marketplace for growth, then perhaps a product program would be where to start. If the enterprise needs to cut costs and improve customer satisfaction, then an operational or functional program might be the fit.

If a clean sheet of paper is the starting point, then the first step is to understand what is needed, where it is needed, how much of it is needed, and then to fulfill those needs by implementing the programs described. Because each enterprise is so unique, one size does not fit all, but there is a size and fit for everyone.

In the organizational structure of an enterprise, as shown in Figure 2.2, all types of programs should be present to maximize productivity, increase growth, and improve market positioning. Now, what enterprise would not want to do that?

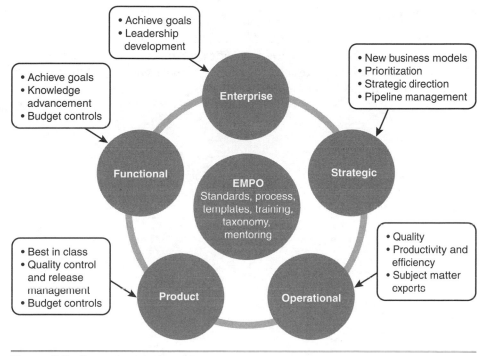

Figure 2.2   Program types.

Author Biography

Sherry S. Remington, PMP, is currently a program manager for a high-tech company in the Silicon Valley. She works in a strategic portfolio management office and currently holds a business degree from the University of Southern Mississippi, a Stanford Certified Program Manager (SCPM) Certificate from Stanford University, and a masters certificate from George Washington University. Sherry's areas of expertise are in projects, programs, process and operations, financials, and Web 2.0 content management. She also specializes in forums and leads PMI® PMO breakfast meetings.

In her free time, Sherry volunteers for many nonprofit organizations that benefit the local community as well as state and national disaster relief organizations. She also enjoys boating, bicycling, reading, and spending time with her friends, families, and pet.

References

Project Management Institute, *A Guide to the Project Management Body of Knowledge (PMBOK® Guide)*, 4th edition, Newtown Square, PA, PMI®, 2008.

Ward, J. LeRoy. *Project Management Terms: A Working Glossary.* Arlington, VA, ESI International, 2000.

3

The PMO as an Enabler for Large-Scale, Global Program Success

---

Steven Weber, MBA, PMP

This chapter outlines real-life program management office (PMO) challenges encountered in large-scale programs. The underlying basis for this case study was my experience gathered over more than two years of PMO management while conducting a large-scale business transformation program involving the implementation of an enterprise resource planning (ERP) system.

Case Study

Multiple international locations were involved in this ERP implementation program with more than 250 project members, 30 percent of which were provided by external suppliers. The remaining 70 percent were internal resources that originally were based all over the world and came together to form the central team at the program headquarters in Switzerland. Around 60 percent of the internal resources were specialists from various business departments. The rest of the team was from various IT departments. The program objective was to define, develop, and rollout the ERP solution in more than 40 countries (as individual projects) within four years.

The ERP program was divided into three main phases:

1. Requirements management, process definitions, and creating the program business blueprint
2. The build phase that included specification of functionality, development, and system configuration

3. The deployment phase that began one year after the build phase and included the implementation of new processes and new systems

PMO Tasks

Within the program, a dedicated PMO was created consisting of internal and external people centrally based in Switzerland with an average team size of 10 full-time employees covering a wide variety of tasks and activities. Only a subset of these tasks and activities are discussed:

- The main responsibility of the PMO was program governance. This involved providing the methodology, including the rules, guidelines, templates, and standards used to conduct the projects from the initiation phase through closure.
- All human resource-related aspects (new hires, on- and off-boarding planning, releases, and training) for the program were under the jurisdiction of the PMO.
- A strong focus was placed on program monitoring, controlling, and reporting. Additional deliverables included creating the program business case and preparing decision papers for management.
- Communication was essential in such a large program. As the central support organization, the PMO also had to define and develop a communication plan and maintain communication flow.
- The ownership for all program tools was within the PMO with the exception of the main ERP system.
- Proper program tools for time tracking, planning, document management, risk management, and change management processes were developed.
- Additional activities required removing obstacles and supporting the program director and individual project managers.

The selected tasks faced numerous challenges during the course of this program.

Challenges Encountered

There were a number of challenges faced during the course of the program that were of different natures and had varying impacts on the overall success of the effort.

PMO Perception

"We give you all this information! What do you give us in return? What kind of value does the PMO provide other than incurring overhead costs?" Many program members did not know what a PMO was or the function of a PMO. If its tasks and

values are not clearly understood, which is highly likely, the PMO can slip into a purely administrative support function. Remedying this issue often involves educating the organization and program stakeholders regarding the role of the PMO and seeking to understand specific needs of certain programs so that it can staff itself appropriately to address those needs.

Politics

Dealing with internal and international politics is a challenge that plagues all large programs. The question is how to ensure project success. Differentiating politics between the program itself and the program goals is a must.

Political challenges to the program itself surfaced among various individual stakeholders in both the reporting line and the special reporting needs area during program execution. Different countries had varying needs and wishes. Among them were nondisclosure of financial figures, such as total project cost that included country internal costs.

Another issue involved requests to answer questions from one particular group regarding its internal resources that included the program team. These questions were not uncommon: *What are these resources actually doing? How are they committed to the program? What is the running and estimated cost of their involvement? How long will they be required?*

Fortunately, the cost/benefit question was not asked directly because this would have been difficult to answer since the benefit calculations did not include a detailed breakdown on the individual resource level, and even group-level details were not available.

Due to the nature of the program goals (new processes, possible restructuring, new roles and responsibilities), each country involved had potential reservations about the upcoming changes. For example, due to the future centralization of all ERP support personnel, a large internal local IT department in charge of their old ERP system would no longer be needed for this task. So, either a different position had to be found or these resources had to be released.

Program Human Resources

Program staffing is always challenging, especially when introducing a program with a large, new scope that requires many different resources with technical skills and business process knowledge that need to be found, managed, and also properly released. On this program it was challenging to get the right people when the need was always for an urgent, top-priority task. Many resources were recruited from around the world with the central team located in Switzerland.

The quick ramp-up of the program resource expansion was challenging, and one minor issue was office space availability. There were so many new arrivals, that people had to sit in corridors or share desks. Infrastructure growth could not keep up with resource growth with regard to meeting rooms, phones, desks, chairs, and electrical outlets.

A more delicate issue involved the recruitment of certain qualified resources. One example was inadequately skilled internal resources who were provided by the businesses in error due to a misunderstanding. Another issue arose when the businesses parked available resources elsewhere. Instead of sending specialists for the manufacturing processes, quality managers were sent. External parties also tried to introduce junior consultants as experts. There was quite a high variance in the experience levels of the project team members, which can affect training requirements and necessitate on-the-job training.

In the instances where highly qualified resources were provided, there was sometimes a mismatch regarding the requested capacity (i.e., 50 percent compared to the actual requirements of 100 percent for three months and then decreasing for the remaining six months).

Another personnel-related challenge was the high turnover of resources that occurred due to incorrect resources being replaced, assignment time lapsing, different or new assignments, and burnout.

If the approval process for new program resources is unknown or not enforced, a new challenge may surface as invoices from new hires (both internal and external) arrive even before the PMO's official resource acceptance review/approval process is conducted and the resources are officially approved for use in the program. For this program, it usually occurred when firefighting situations surfaced and an immediate reaction was required. Going through the predefined procedure could take some time. Bypassing it meant having somebody working on the problem immediately. Unfortunately, allowing individual judgment of severance actions required the PMO to sort out the situation.

As more than 80 percent of all program resources were not initially located in Switzerland, special permits were required for them to be able to work there. The necessary approval process took a significant amount of time, depending on work duration and on the special requirements that needed to be considered. The resources should have been available at the right time and not two months later.

For EU citizens, the approval process was fairly quick. For all other countries, the process took up to four months. Satisfying work permit requirements was a significant challenge and required substantial effort.

Monitoring

Monitoring individual project progress and performance was difficult, and data consolidating was tedious due to the program size and the multiple parallel projects conducted in different countries. One of the main challenges was that internal project resources often did not record their work times devoted to the program on a weekly basis because they either had to record their time for the business already using processes outside of the program, or they did not need to report their effort to the business middle managers or higher level supervisors. Therefore, they failed to record the time dedicated to the program because the process was not something that they were typically required to complete. Because of these issues, the individual hours worked on the program were not tracked. The consequence was that nonconformance lists were created and time was wasted consolidating and correcting errors so that valid weekly reports could be generated.

Information Flow

The larger the project the more difficult it is to ensure that all project members have the right information at the correct time. The project team members are not the only people who need to be informed. The future rollout-site business customers and senior management must be informed as well. Therefore, information management must provide the proper tools to assure effective information flow. E-mails alone are an ineffective communication tool.

Over the course of the program, senior management was confronted with many proposals and change requests, including decisions about the modification of processes for individual countries and staffing requests. All these decisions required an appropriate amount of information that was not always available on time. Also, the impact of decisions must be known, or at least somewhat understood, which was not always the case.

Knowledge Management for the Program

Two main aspects were taken into consideration. The first was collecting the *how* and *why* of solution configuration, which is a special task that needed extra attention. To ensure knowledge retention and a more easily changeable system, this information was vital. The following questions needed to be answered: *What is the reasoning behind this setting? Why does this function deviate from the standard? Who released the requirement? Is there an alignment to the defined processes? Is this special setting or function also used elsewhere?* Good examples for this were needed as they impacted the key design decisions for the requirements phase in the project. If they were not configured according to the requirements, the reasons why would not have otherwise been recorded. In later steps it would have been nearly impossible to change the setting as there would be conflicting information: requirements say "yes", but it was originally configured with "no."

The second aspect was collecting feedback and lessons learned from previous rollout projects to avoid making the same mistakes. Capturing this was important because of the personnel challenges discussed. For example, external key resources might not be available for the next rollout in another country and this information is crucial for proper staffing.

Using the Right Tools Due to Size and Internationality

Providing the right tools will support a program, whereas insufficient ones can limit and weaken it. The tools must cope with the size and the internationality of a program. Challenges encountered in this program included:

- Incompatible program versions (e.g., the old vs. new version of MS Excel).
- Slow network connections that were inefficient for large file transfers.
- Availability and access to specific items (process modeling software such as process maps, e-mail, and documents) were not available or took too long to acquire.
- Data replication issues, resulting in too much data for too many locations.
- The lack of user friendliness and functionality of applications that impacted timeline and resources. If an application was difficult to use, more training was required or the application was not used. If a function was not available (e.g., a full-text search without content analysis), more time was wasted in the search and retrieval process.

An example of an improper tool was found when rollout countries needed to access central basis information about the new ERP solution that was to be deployed after localization. The main information on processes and functionality must be provided, documented, and distributed. Local document management tools were no longer sufficient and a new web-based solution had to be introduced.

A second example of an improper tool was the necessary replacement of the enterprise project management suite consisting of a time-tracking module, risk and issue logs, change request, and a test-tracking module provided by the implementation partner. Due to technology changes resulting in new version incompatibilities and the end of support for the existing suite, all project management tools had to be replaced. This caused additional effort as development, configuration, migration, introduction, and new-tool training had to be conducted in a limited amount of time (project within the project).

Confronted with all these challenges, what can a PMO do to minimize impact? The next section will highlight how the PMO supported the program.

The Role of the PMO

A properly managed PMO can tackle these challenges, at least to a certain extent. Politics, which come in so many colors and flavors, may not be able to be completely remedied but its effects should be dampened.

A PMO can overcome these issues by serving the specific roles illustrated in Figure 3.1.

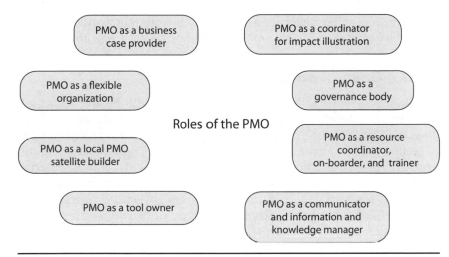

Figure 3.1   Roles of the PMO in the business.

PMO as a Business Case Provider

The PMO was tasked with preparing a business case to support the ERP program, providing input to the individual rollout countries and convincing program stakeholders. This was to improve the delivery success rate of the overall program and benefits both the value of the program and the business objectives. The distribution of the complete business case was limited to executive management and senior program management. Limited business case details were available for general review, resulting in two versions of the business case. Two versions were required because some of the benefit assumptions involved a heavy reorganization in major departments of the business. The reorganization required careful preparation before involving all affected parties. In this case, the PMO supported business politics by reasoning, justifying, and selling the program and, therefore, helping to ensure the success of the program.

PMO as a Coordinator for Impact Illustration

In a coordination function, a PMO can take the lead to ensure that the different impacts regarding decisions become known and understood. An important factor is that a PMO works together with all the involved projects, subprojects, and teams in all specialties areas (manufacturing, sales, project management, finance, and supply chain management).

If decisions are required, for example in the manufacturing domain, a PMO can organize specialist meetings to collect and prepare the required information and have the specialist work out possible impacts. It can then ensure that the correct communication channels are applied to disseminate the information, which was essential on this program and would be on most any program.

PMO as a Governance Body

A PMO that provides standards and guidelines must still be able to act on and react to changing requirements within a program. Initial work on this program involved defining reporting requirements and the project management methodology, setting up documentation structures, and providing templates and process descriptions (e.g., on-boarding approval process). Later, it became important to adjust the templates and rules to the new phases, and to ensure that everyone was adhering to the guidelines. Ensuring program governance required training on the predefined project management practices, guidelines, and accompanying tools. Special emphasis was given to tools that support governance. As the governance body, the challenges of resource management, monitoring, information flow, tools, and knowledge management can be addressed by the PMO.

PMO as a Flexible Organization

Flexibility is crucial for a PMO to be able to react to a particular issue or challenge, but more importantly to be able to take any necessary steps proactively before a problem arises. To address new PMO requirements, political climate changes, reporting requirements, and resolution of central and local issues, flexibility and farsightedness within the PMO was essential to this program. Successfully meeting these challenges required having high-quality resources available within the PMO. A thorough knowledge of the challenges faced by previous ERP projects was helpful in planning future required adjustments.

One approach to developing a flexible PMO can be to have interchangeable team members where individual resources can cover more than one role and help by doubling the available staff. For example, increased reporting needs in one country can be supported by an additional central PMO resource, or a health check conducted for the program may require short-term support by a team member who could temporarily be replaced by a colleague to complete his normal planning tasks.

Another approach is to work with third-party suppliers as they can help to cope with workload peaks, provide specific skills for special activities, and work in areas where the internal skills are not strong. Additionally, internal novice PMO members can gain knowledge and training on the job with external experts.

If external resources are mainly provided by one supplier, you should keep the possible dependency risk in mind. Sometimes, an alternate supplier may be a good option if they can provide more senior resources and a higher value.

Including a resource from the main external implementation partner into the PMO team can be a good solution as well. This allows for a better understanding of the delivery method and better insights into the project execution from the viewpoint of the main partner. A possible drawback to this approach is that the controlling function of the PMO team regarding all external resources with a focus on the implementation partner might become slightly biased, and special strategies and internal information would become available to the external partner. PMO neutrality as it pertains to governance becomes trickier when you have this kind of a PMO team setup. This problem can be circumvented by having special meetings and side agendas. However, the distrust that sometimes develops from having side agendas, where specific people are excluded, is not helpful in developing a cohesive team that works well together. It should be analyzed properly and the decision should fit within the overall strategy and the program director's plan.

In this program it was decided to have a part-time (20 to 40 percent allocated) resource in the PMO. This led to an increased knowledge level in the team, and still left enough room to ensure the required neutrality. Information was passed on to external parties on a need-to-know basis, but in an open and direct way. The PMO with a flexible organization can help address challenges in resource management, monitoring, tools, information, and knowledge management.

Central PMO as a Local PMO Satellite Builder

On this program the PMO included a central program management office (central PMO) that included several PMO satellites located in dedicated rollout countries to help them conform to project rules. Satellite PMO ramp up started in program Phase 2 as preparation for the third phase began. The dedicated PMOs in each country were essentially extended arms of the central PMO. The role of the local satellite PMO was that of a manager with limited scope (country specific), having backup from the central team. A certain degree of independence was given to the satellite PMOs so that they could react to country-specific requirements while still adhering to program guidelines.

In the first pilot project, the local team included a PMO team member from the next country to receive the new solution and a member from the central PMO to speed up the process and ensure all went well with future satellite PMOs. The pilot satellite provided valuable insights into how to setup a local PMO, including local language skills needed, unique planning and reporting needs, and how to conduct successful training sessions. Making an employee of the rollout country a member of the local project team led to a higher acceptance and adherence to program rules, and feedback was directly captured by the local satellite team itself without involving any intermediate people.

Important success factors for the PMO satellites were that each one was set up before the start of the local rollout project with clearly defined accountabilities and governance communicated up front. This ensured buy-in and acceptance to the reporting. They worked together as partners with the local project management team and the local business and followed the PMO guidelines and procedures defined centrally, as well as adapted the tools to local context requirements (e.g., translation of training material and special data privacy protection laws). The local PMO setup concept was also important for success. It started with the central team training the local team, then conducting onsite setup in the local rollout country. One central team member was used as the single point of contact for the local PMO and provided onsite support and guidance for the first two or three weeks. Afterwards, remote and ad hoc support was implemented by the central team. With a local PMO satellite, the challenges of governance enforcement, local resource management, time monitoring, use of standardized tool sets, and information and knowledge management were addressed directly.

PMO as a Resource Coordinator, On-Boarder, and Trainer

As a resource coordinator, the PMO on this program defined a strict on-boarding policy, ensuring that only new resources were added to the program when the defined process was followed and all approvals had been given. Controlling the on-boarding situation is a challenge even with the aid of a resource coordinator when working with multiple teams in a central program setup. With the start of the rollouts, this became a very complex task. The local PMO was an extension of the central PMO and key to ensuring that for the local projects, the process was understood and followed. With a new approval process now enforced for all entities (the central team and each individual rollout country), it was always clear who was on the program, who was leaving, who was on the on-boarding list (awaiting approval), etc. With a special focus on all external consultants and support personnel, the human resource impacts on the program were better controlled and planned.

Time tracking issues must be resolved by a PMO to improve monitoring and increase reporting accuracy. Missing and incorrect time entries distort tasks assigned to program team members. The right level must be identified to ensure data is entered correctly. As for external team members, billing was directly linked to times recorded in program time-tracking applications, making it easier and more straightforward; no separate information, spreadsheets, or other methods of reporting time were tolerated and invoices were not released unless correct booking was done using the established time-tracking processes for the program. Dealing with noncompliant internal resources is more difficult. In this case study, bonus payments for participating in the program were directly linked to accurate time recording.

In addition, on-board training strengthened the commitment and buy-in from all participants. In a two- to three-day training period, three main lectures were given. The first lecture included an introduction to the program, its organization, the deployment methodology, and an illustration of how the program was aligned to business strategy. The second session covered the functional overview and the business processes addressed by the new ERP solution. In the third session, special emphasis was given to project management and PMO topics, illustrating the detailed requirements for each team member (reporting, time-tracking, rules, guidelines, and standards). The PMO was presented with its tasks and roles in the program, which is essential for recognition.

For the local rollout projects, special training on effective project management methodology and PMO processes used in the program were conducted for the local project manager and the local PMO, thus helping the local business project managers and local PMOs to better understand their respective roles and relationship to the central team.

PMO as a Tool Owner

The PMO has the ownership and provides all support for the complete set of applications used in a program. At the beginning of this program, the PMO was tasked with evaluating and selecting the program tools.

Selecting the tools for managing a program is vital to ensure that they provide a good solution. Manual work and rework to cope with application insufficiencies should not be tolerated. When selecting a tool provider, software-as-a-service, or hosting solution, it is essential to ensure long-lasting stability and availability without any interruptions. A long-term relationship must be the goal.

One option is to use internal company software, which requires very little training as most internal users are familiar with it. Training only needs to be based on the specific use of the applications in the context of the program. There is almost no need to train members on the general usage of the systems themselves.

For the external consultants, most of the applications are usually already well known as they have come into contact with a variety of them during their assignments, and their adaptation is usually much faster. The other option is to introduce new applications. This might lead to increased training efforts as the usage and handling of the tools needs to be learned, but a new solution might be necessary. For example, at the beginning of the program in this case study, the document-management solution was sufficient for the first rollout in Europe, but unusable for multiple rollouts in countries outside Europe. For this reason a new application had to be found. When providing new tools to the program team, it was vital to get them up and running as soon as possible.

Special support was also required from internal IT departments and the IT support organization to gain delivery commitments and to help get things done. Taking over the coordination and controlling function to support PMO tools was a success factor for the PMO.

In the beginning the staffing database was used to classify the work permit requirements for all personnel. Later during the course of the program, it was extended to manage all resource issues such as skills, capacity, availability, and current location of the resource so key resources could jump from one project to the other. This helps a program team and PMO better plan resource availabilities and deal with all resource related issues.

An enterprise project management suite enables time tracking based on assigned tasks, program planning and project-plan consolidation, budget control, and progress tracking. Additional modules are used for managing risks, issues, and change requests.

Creation of an information portal on the program in this case study was vital for communications, information flow, and knowledge management. The new document management system was a solution for organizing and facilitating collaborative creation of documents and other types of content, enabling the monitoring of content, tracking changes to content, and controlling user access. Sharing content with others, providing the right level of security, versioning rules, and approving workflows with worldwide access was possible and no client software installation was necessary.

This program document-management solution provided the main storage location, including structures for all program related documents (reports, minutes of meetings, specifications, budgets, and communication material). System access was also made possible via an intranet portal that included links to the process mapping solution and other business guidelines. This portal was project specific, making all project news, relevant links, and organizational information available. The program document information that could be found on the intranet portal also had full-text search capabilities.

If the right tools are in place, which is the task of a PMO as tool owner, the tools can provide guidance and enforce proper program execution. A major success factor is the tool set used for a program. Incorrect tools will hinder program success and progress instead of providing support.

PMO as a Communicator and Information and Knowledge Manager

Providing and communicating the correct information at the right time is essential. A PMO should be the extended arm of management and its main communication channel. The idea is to control the information flow to everyone involved and all interested parties. One step is to define a communication plan that identifies the *who, what, when*, and *how* information will be delivered and how the communication needs will be fulfilled. When developing a communication plan it should include the creation of a short *elevator speech* that can be communicated to an interested person in about the amount of time it takes for a brief ride in an elevator and it should concisely answer the following questions:

- What is the program all about?
- Why is it being conducted?

- What are the objectives?
- What will the new system and processes look like?

Knowledge management is important for the success of a program and a PMO is in the driver seat. Types of information to be included in the knowledge base are lessons learned, FAQs, issues, and resolution to those issues. All information should be stored in a clear and structured way and be accessible via the web. People should be able to find a solution or an answer to an already solved problem when they encounter one. This helps avoid solving problems more than once, thus saving the related costs and time. What the problem was, where it occurred, who reported it, and who solved the problem, along with a detailed description on how to avoid or resolve the problem should be included. A FAQ section should not only deal with problems, but also target implementation.

In this program, the management of business (processes) and technical knowledge, and the management of projects knowledge (rollout) were distinguished. For the management of business and technical knowledge, a tool or module called a solution manager was used. Its main functionality can be described as follows: it centralized the implementation, operation, support, and upgrade of ERP solutions, and provided functions and content to increase efficiency and reliability throughout the ERP program lifecycle. The key functional implementation aspects such as the blueprint, configuration, development, testing, and rollout activities were managed with a business process focus. In operations it was used to identify errors, support change request analyses, as well as to provide a live overview of all implemented functionality for all deployed countries and solution variants or adaptations. Knowledge management was conducted by mapping the business processes with the related ERP system configurations and all ERP project documentation (requirements, solution configuration documents, test scripts, and even training material when desired) in one place. The result was a central documentation of the ERP system landscape and core business processes transferred from the process modeling tool. It allowed a real-time monitoring of ERP system components and business processes, therefore advancing message handling for fast problem analysis and resolution. This enabled a direct connection to the application support back office.

Capturing knowledge is required so that team members can learn from one another and plan for resource turnover. In this way the program momentum is not lost and continuous improvement is enabled. Additionally, the startup time for replacement resources is minimized. Knowledge management of the projects in the various rollout countries in this program was accomplished through organizing lessons-learned meetings, providing surveys, and storing this information for later use.

In addition, the use of an intranet portal that contained all relevant information regarding the program for distribution to future roll out countries was helpful. This was used for on-boarding training and for informing interested stakeholders and management.

PMO Success Factors

To be an enabler for large-scale program success, a PMO must be perceived as offering high value. Its tasks and roles in the program must be known and understood. On-boarding training provided by a PMO can ensure this understanding of its roles, responsibilities and support functions throughout a program. In other words, a PMO needs to actively promote its offered services.

One way to evaluate the perceived value from a PMO is to conduct surveys that capture its overall quality, as well as what it should be doing from the clients' perspective. Keep the number of pure PMO surveys to a minimum as the program team has other daily problems to struggle with and will not have the time to constantly answer questions. Some surveys have been known to come back with questions relating to whether it exists purely to create and analyze its own surveys.

If the project teams do not approach a PMO, it should reach out and offer its services to the team. In many cases, the time factor inhibits project teams from contacting a PMO for inquiries. Just knowing it exists does not automatically help sell the value of the additional nonreporting-oriented services; a PMO is still required to reach out to the project teams to make them aware of the benefits it can provide.

Key stakeholders should be asked about the PMO's perceived value. Criticism must be taken seriously and alternative strategies should be adopted to create more value.

In general a PMO should be actively present. The aforementioned networking strategy is intended to minimize political impact and increase the time available to react to issues before they really surface. Having such an early warning system in place allows interested parties to know what is going on behind the scenes. Without support from top management it could be difficult (if not impossible) to establish and operate a PMO that can provide sustainable program support. The PMO head should seek to become a trusted advisor.

Having all inquiries regarding a program directed to a PMO enables it to serve as an information hub dealing with all channels—both formal and informal. It can be a living knowledge base with access to all relevant information and documentation.

Being empowered as an information hub can be a success factor to ensure a PMO gets things done. It can act as a supervisor by actively communicating via different channels, and interacting and pursuing tasks so they get taken care of in a defined way, thus observing its governance role. Clearly communicating and regularly monitoring governance, provided it is aligned to the program strategy, ensures better program results.

Providing the right tools secures a program's controllability and manageability. These tools help to ensure that the defined processes are followed. Interpretation of processes is minimized as the tools guide the users through them, providing boundaries.

In this case example, proper governance was observed. PMO satellites were set up in the different rollout countries as an extended arm of the central PMO. This ensured that the right set of tools was implemented and used, and that there was consistent reporting for all projects. Management was able to assess trends and make informed decisions due to consolidated data. Local satellites have proven to help make certain that a global program can be managed more efficiently and successfully.

What would this large-scale program have done without a PMO? They most likely would have managed—somehow—but efforts would have surely been more chaotic and misdirected. Controlling and monitoring the program would have been a nightmare. Budgets would have been exceeded and schedules would have drifted. If push came to shove, the program might have been abandoned. A well-managed PMO that plays the roles described can help ensure program success.

Author Biography

Steven Weber, PMP, lives near Zurich, Switzerland. He is the managing director of Resultaire Corporation that provides consulting services for various industries on PMO management, project management, and enterprise content management (document lifecycle management). He has held various business improvement and IT management positions with the main focus of his experience in plant engineering, pharmaceuticals, medical devices, and automotive suppliers.

Mr. Weber received his MBA from the graduate school of Business Administration in Zurich, Switzerland, and from the University at Albany, New York. He also holds a degree in business information systems.

4

Stakeholder Relationship Management: Enhancing PMO Services Through Effective Engagement and Communication

Dr. Lynda Bourne

Introduction

Many technically competent project management offices fail to realize their full value because they are focused on technology and process compliance. This type of PMO is often seen as administrative overhead. It is possible to transform the perception of the value of such an office from being seen simply as overhead, or even ineffective or irrelevant, into a valuable and essential organizational resource. This transformation is made possible through communication and engagement strategies that provide effective and appropriate information and support to the organization at all levels. Unfortunately, the same perception of irrelevance can also be detected in organizations where the PMO has been staffed with competent practitioners who are skilled in the techniques of project management and project controls. In this case, the perception of irrelevance is connected to the staff's failure to understand and manage relationships with their stakeholders and to communicate effectively.

A relationship-focused PMO understands the need to communicate effectively with all stakeholders. The relationship-focused PMO is trusted by the project and program community and has credibility with senior management. By understanding its stakeholders and customizing its communication strategy to meet the differing requirements of all stakeholders, the PMO can become a valuable resource and partner to everyone, delivering supersized performance.

The PMO is most effective when its structure has been designed by management to align with the maturity of the organization. Maturity in this sense is the organization's ability to translate from business strategy to business benefit and competitive advantage through the successful delivery of programs and projects. For its part, the office must recognize that project and program teams have different perceptions, expectations, and measures of success from those of senior management, and therefore, it must customize its communication strategy to meet the different requirements of different types of stakeholders. By using appropriate management and communication strategies, the PMO builds credibility and robust relationships through ensuring that its services meet the needs of the communities it serves. The relationship-focused PMO will be perceived to be strategically significant to the success of the organization.

The main theme of this chapter will be the importance of stakeholder engagement and effective communication—the chief enablers of delivering PMO value. Value is delivered through building and maintaining robust, dynamic, and mutually beneficial relationships between the PMOs and their stakeholder community. This value is delivered to the organization when the PMO takes a leadership role in stakeholder relationship management, in the tactical realm as well as the strategic. The first section of this chapter discusses the definition of a PMO. The second section defines stakeholders and describes a structured yet flexible methodology to assist in the identification of their important stakeholders and then engage these stakeholders through a monitored program of targeted, purposeful communication. This is followed by a discussion on specific types of stakeholders and describes ways to manage that engagement.

What Is a PMO, Really?

Within many organizations, the three layers of project, program, and portfolio exist independently as well as interdependently. Delivery of strategic business objectives through this layered structure is illustrated in Figure 4.1. The organization develops a vision, which is articulated as a series of strategic goals, which in turn become portfolios. Programs are established to achieve these goals; projects are authorized in line with these goals and generally organized within programs.

A PMO will have various roles and responsibilities according to whether the service (or support) is focused at the project, program, or portfolio level. The project management office (PjMO)* provides centralized and coordinated man-

---

*To avoid confusion, the different versions of PMO will have different titles. Project management office will be PjMO, program management office will be PgMO and portfolio management office will be PtMO.

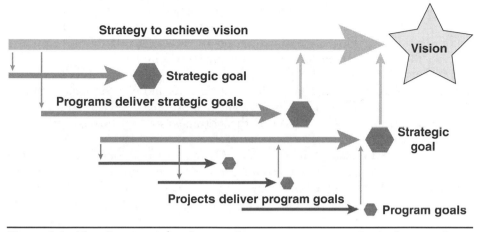

Figure 4.1   The alignment of projects and programs to an organization's strategic goals.

agement of those projects for which it is responsible, while the program management office (PgMO) provides strategic and centralized support and management of shared resources, methodologies, tools, and techniques (Project Management Institute, 2008). The portfolio management office (PtMO) will provide support at a strategic level within the governance and strategic project selection and management domain. PMOs have been defined in terms of a continuum of maturity from project office to center of excellence with functions that include support at various levels of inclusion and competency:

- Strategic planning
- Benchmarking and continuous improvement
- Training and mentorship for project managers
- Knowledge management in the form of lessons learned, estimating databases, and project management experience (Kerzner, 2005)

Elsewhere, the role of a PMO has been described as, "assisting both the project manager and the relevant organization with the application of professional project management practices and the adaptation and integration of business interests into the management and successful delivery of projects and programs" (Hill, 2004).

However PMOs are described, there is an underlying concept that there is a common structure and a common set of roles, the only difference being whether it supports the organization at the project, program, or portfolio level. The underlying assertion of this chapter is that *there is no such thing as a standard PMO structure*.

If the vision of an organization and its subsequent strategic goals define the framework for the structure of projects, programs, and portfolio to deliver the specific business strategy of the organization, how can a standard PMO structure support the unique framework of the organization? The PMO's structure, roles, and responsibilities will be unique to, and defined by, the organization's selection and governance process as well as the requirements and expectations of the organization's management. Therefore, the most appropriate description for a body that assists organizations in delivering their business strategy through projects is the term *PMO presence* (Dai and Wells, 2004).

This chapter proposes a model of PMO presence developed on two foundations. The first is the three-layered structure for delivering business strategy through projects as outlined in Figure 4.1. The second is based on the foundation functions of a PMO (whether supporting a project, program, or portfolio): monitoring, methodology, and mentoring. These three categories of support are in accord with the early stages of the five levels of PMO maturity developed by Kerzner (2005) and Hill (2004). A matrix of functions and areas of organizational support are shown in Figure 4.2. *R* indicates some level of functional responsibility, and *A* denotes the need for awareness without functional responsibility.

In this model, a PMO, whether it is a PjMO, PgMO, or PtMO, will deliver support within three major and common function sets: monitoring (and control); methodology (infrastructure support and resource management); and mentoring (PM training and career development). Additional functions should be included when addressing portfolio support (always) and program support (sometimes). These additional services support improved corporate governance by strategically aligning projects to corporate strategy as well as deliver value through benefits realization (KPMG, 2005). There is a sixth function essential for PMO success which is common to all types of PMOs. That additional function is concerned with engaging PMO stakeholders through monitored, targeted, and purposeful communication, thus ensuring that the services it provides meet the organization's current needs and that it is perceived to meet the organization's needs (Bourne, 2006). This is the main factor that determines the success of the PMO and the project, program, or portfolio that it supports.

Measures of Success (and Failure)

When projects or programs fail, the performing organization is affected because some aspect of its strategic objectives will not be delivered as planned, scarce resources will be wasted, and individuals and groups (stakeholders) who had expected some benefit from the outcome of the project will be negatively impacted. A survey conducted by KPMG (2005) reported that in the twelve months prior:

- Forty-nine percent of participants had experienced at least one project failure.

	1	2	3	4	5	6
	Monitor and control	Methodology and resourcing support	Mentoring and PM career support	Governance support and strategy alignment	Value delivery and benefits realization	Manage relation-ships
Project-PjMO	R	R	A? / R?	A	A	R
Program-PgMO	R	R	R	A? / R?	R	R
Portfolio-PtMO	R	R	R	R	R	R

Figure 4.2 A three-layered model of PMO responsibility.

- Only 2 percent achieved targeted benefits all the time.
- Eighty-six percent of organizations lost up to 25 percent of target benefits across their entire portfolio.

Research conducted over the last 13 years (Canadian Management Accounting Society, 1998; Jiang and Klein, 1999; James, 1997; Glass, 1998; Lemon, et al., 2002; Bourne and Walker, 2003; KPMG, 2005; Bourne and Walker, 2005) has shown that project, program and portfolio success is influenced by:

- The level of knowledge, skills, and experience of the project or program manager and team
- Appropriate and consistent use of project management tools, processes, and methodologies
- Alignment of the outcomes of the project, program, or portfolio to the organization strategy
- Managing the expectations of stakeholders
- Appropriate, timely, and consistent involvement by users and managers
- Timely management of risk

Successful project, program, or PMO management depends on balancing the conflicting requirements of managing within the constraints of time, cost, and scope to deliver the defined strategic benefits to the performing organization through a temporary organizational structure (*value delivery*). At the same time, the needs and expectations of the project's stakeholders must be managed (*relationship management*) within an environment of uncertainty and ambiguity (*risk management*) (Bourne, 2009).

Figure 4.3 describes the interrelatedness of these elements of project (or PMO) success and the importance of stakeholders to the achievement of this success. Each of the elements is essential for a project, program, portfolio, or PMO to be perceived as successful by its stakeholders, but none of them can be clearly defined in isolation to the others, nor can one stand alone as more important than any other. Delivering value through managing the schedule, budget, scope or quality, and the realization of business and organizational benefits is not just about conformance to the project or program plan. Delivering value requires managing relationships and managing risks by ensuring that the expectations of all stakeholders are met with regard to *what* is delivered as well as *when* and *how*. It is important for the PMO manager and team to understand how stakeholders perceive value and then to align management of the project or program and the performance metrics to the expectations generated from these perceptions, or to negotiate within the relationships to align expectations with feasible outcomes. These are areas where a PMO can add value. The concept of balancing all aspects without dominance of any one aspect is the starting point to an understanding of how PMOs can add value to an organization.

The basic role of the PMO is always defined by the performing organization it supports, and it must operate effectively within that organization's unique

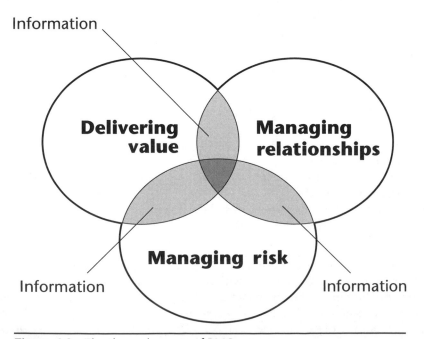

Figure 4.3   The three elements of PMO success.

culture. These constraints make it impossible to design a *one-size-fits-all* PMO. However, every PMO can supersize the value it delivers and make a significant contribution to its host organization's bottom line by including an appropriate focus on relationship management within its way of working. Competence in monitoring, methodology support, and mentoring is still a vital requirement. If this is missing, there is no point in communicating. Once competency issues are conquered, the difference between average and exceptional performance is found in the capability of the office leadership and staff to effectively relate and communicate throughout the organization. To achieve *supersized performance,** the PMO must recognize that project teams and senior management have different perceptions, expectations, and measures of success. By understanding its stakeholders and customizing its communication strategy to meet the different requirements, the PMO transforms their perceptions from being seen as an administrative overhead into a valuable resource.

The *Stakeholder Circle®* is a relationship management methodology and tool that can be used by PMO management to facilitate the transition to a relationship-focused organization delivering supersized value. Its value to the PMO and host organization as well as to management and practitioners within it lies in providing guidance on understanding the stakeholder community and through this understanding, the best way to engage stakeholders and deliver their requirements and expectations.

The *Stakeholder Circle®* is a flexible model that can be adjusted to cater for changes in stakeholder community membership and stakeholder influence throughout the life of the activity. There are five steps to the methodology:

- **Step 1:** Identification of all stakeholders
- **Step 2:** Prioritization to determine who is important
- **Step 3:** Visualization to understand the overall stakeholder community
- **Step 4:** Engagement through effective communications
- **Step 5:** Monitoring the effect of the engagement

Software can support an organization's management of its stakeholder relationships through the ability to maintain a history of stakeholder relationship management, to simplify information gathering about stakeholders and their attitudes to the work of the organization, to enable more effective monitoring and measurement of communication effectiveness, and finally to gather data to support predictive risk and stakeholder analysis.**

**Supersized performance* refers to the delivery of services and support to an organization and its projects and programs through engaging the PMO's important stakeholders, building and maintaining robust relationships, and delivering stakeholder requirements and expectations.

**For more information about the use of software, see www.stakeholder-management.com. It is important to note that while software improves recordkeeping for organizations using stakeholder relationship management practices, it is not essential to the successful engagement of stakeholders.

Understanding Stakeholders

Stakeholders are groups or individuals who supply critical resources, or who place something of value at risk through their investment of funds, career, or time in pursuit of the organization's business strategies or goals. Alternatively, stakeholders may be groups or individuals who are opposed to the organization or some aspect of its activities. Stakeholders are defined as:

> *Individuals or groups who will be impacted by, or can influence the success or failure of an organization's activities (Walker, Bourne, and Rowlinson, 2008).*

What Is at Stake?

By definition a stakeholder has a stake in the activity. This stake may be:

- An interest
- Rights (legal or moral)
- Ownership
- Contribution in the form of knowledge or support

It is important to consider the nature of a stakeholder's investment when defining a stakeholder's needs, requirements, or how the individual or group can impact the organization's activities.

- *Interest*—A circumstance in which a person or group will be affected by a decision, action, or outcome. An example of interest is to consider a public event (e.g., a major sporting contest) being conducted in a residential area. During the event the residents will have an interest in that event, even if they are not interested in that particular sport.
- *Rights*—Either legal or moral rights:
  - ○ Legal rights cover the legal claim of a group or individual to be treated in a certain way or to have a particular right protected. Legal rights are usually enshrined in a country's legislation. Examples include privacy laws and occupational health and safety.
  - ○ Moral rights cover moral issues that may affect large groups of people or natural phenomena, such as environmental, heritage, or social issues. Moral rights are usually not covered by legislation. Moral rights, such as the rights described here, are what organizations may address in corporate social responsibility activities.
- *Ownership*—Many individuals will also have a stake of ownership, such as:
  - ○ A worker's right to earn their living from his or her knowledge
  - ○ Shareholders' ownership of a portion of an organization's assets
  - ○ Intellectual property resulting from the exploitation of an idea
  - ○ Legal title to an asset or a property

- Knowledge—A team member or employee who applies experience or knowledge to the production of an asset for an organization will be making a contribution to the organization's activity.
- Contribution—The contribution that a stakeholder may make to the activity falls into the following categories:
    - Allocation of resources whether people or materials
    - Provision of funds, either the initial approval or ongoing assurance of continued funding
    - Knowledge or experience essential for successful achievement of the objectives of the activity

The Right Stakeholders

Identification of stakeholders is the first stage of a continuous process to collect the information needed to build a profile of each stakeholder for the purpose of effective communication. Every step of the *Stakeholder Circle*® methodology focuses on gathering, confirming, or modifying this key information about stakeholders.

Step 1: Identify

The essential first step in managing stakeholder relationships is to know who the stakeholders are. It provides a course of action for:

- Knowing who stakeholders are for a particular time, such as *time now*
- Gathering information about each individual or group identified as stakeholders, in anticipation of planning targeted communication

Step 1 consists of three activities:

1. Developing a list of stakeholders
2. Identifying mutuality:
    - How each stakeholder is important to the work
    - What each stakeholder expects from success (or failure) of the work
3. Categorize by documenting each stakeholder's:
    - *Directions of influence*: these are *upward, downward, outward,* and *sidewar*
    - Relationship to the organization: *internal* or *external*

Mutuality defines the nature of the relationship between the PMO and each stakeholder or stakeholder group. It clarifies both the expectations and the importance of the stakeholder to the success of the PMO.

Directions of Influence

There are two sets of influence (on the manager and team) to consider:

1. Is the *direction of influence* of the stakeholder *upward, downward, outward,* or *sideward?* These influences are shown in Figure 4.4.

Upward defines the influence that senior management, especially the sponsor, exerts over the activity. *Downward* denotes team members, whether full-time staff, consultants, contractors, or specialists who work with the manager to achieve the objectives or outcomes of the activity. *Outward* stakeholders are those outside the entity who do the work and include individuals and groups such as end users, government, regulators, the public, shareholders, and lobby groups. S*ideward* stakeholders are peers of the manager, industry groups, and managers within the organization who are considered to be at the same level professionally.

2. Is the stakeholder part of the organization or outside it? Is the stakeholder *internal* to the organization or *external* to the organization?

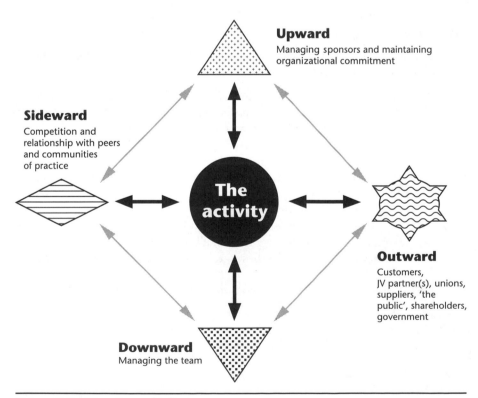

Figure 4.4   Directions of influence.

Categorizations for internal and external are primarily directed to understanding the potential communication channels. Direct access in some form should be available to internal stakeholders, whereas external stakeholders may be more difficult to contact.

Stakeholder identification is best conducted through workshops with PMO team members and individuals from the organization who are familiar with the PMO's responsibilities, functions, and constraints, and with the organization's structure and politics. The information collected in this workshop is put into a database for the next step—prioritization of the identified stakeholders.

Step 2: Prioritize

The assessment of each stakeholder based on ratings from the PMO team members of their perceived *power, proximity,* and *urgency** produces an *index* for each stakeholder. Sorting the index numbers thus obtained will result in a ranked list of stakeholders with the highest number being applied to the stakeholder considered most important. This list, with its associated data on each stakeholder, supports the development of an engagement strategy for ensuring that the expectations of these key stakeholders are understood, acknowledged, and managed.

Step 3: Visualize

Once the stakeholders have been listed by priority, it is important to map them in such a way that everyone (including the stakeholders) will know who has been identified as the most important stakeholders for this particular time—*time now*. This can be achieved in a number of ways with a simple list in ranked order, or a 2×2 matrix with power on one axis and influence on the other. A more sophisticated mapping process is shown in Figure 4.5, which provides a multidimensional view of the top 15 stakeholders, also incorporating other information that has been gathered such as power, urgency, and influence. Figure 4.6 provides a key to interpret the Stakeholder Circle® map of the stakeholder community.

Step 4: Engage

The information that has been assembled about the stakeholder community is now the starting point and foundation for building and maintaining the relationships necessary for the success of the PMO. Understanding the *mutuality* within

---

*Power is rated from 1–4, where 4 is very high and refers to the stakeholder's ability to kill the project. *Proximity* is also rated from 1–4, where 4 refers to a full-time team member and 1 refers to a stakeholder who is 'remote' from the work of the PMO, such as the CEO. *Urgency* is rated in two stages—*value* (the stake the stakeholder has in the outcomes) and *action* (the likelihood the stakeholder will act to achieve a desired outcome): both are rated 1–5 where 5 is very high.

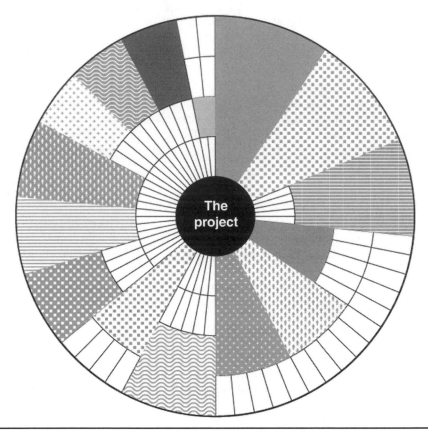

Figure 4.5   An example of the Stakeholder Circle® map of a stakeholder community.

the relationship* and directions of influence** the PMO team can develop and implement monitored, targeted, and purposeful communication. Defining appropriate responses requires an understanding of the purpose of the message. Which stakeholders need to be involved in the day-to-day workings of the PMO? Who needs more information to minimize opposition? Who are the important stakeholders? The *who, what, when, and how* strategy of delivering the tailored messages defined for the stakeholders must be converted into action. The communication plan should be part of the PMO's work plan and reported on through team meetings and regular reports to management.

---

*Information previously gathered about why this individual or group is important to the PMO and also what their requirements or *expectations* are.

**Upward, downward, outward, or sideward,* as well as *internal* and *external:* the format and the content of any communication will reflect the influence of each stakeholder on the PMO.

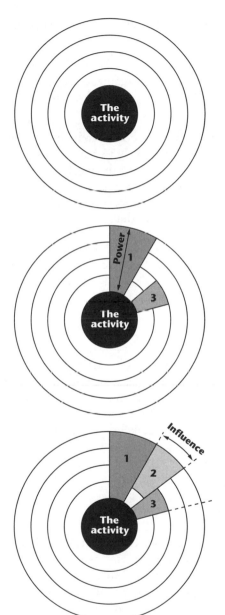

The Stakeholder Circle® represents the work of the activity surrounded by its stakeholder community.

The activity leader or project manager represents the work, and all dimensions of the stakeholder analysis are relative to this person; e.g., *downward* represents the team members working for the leader.

Four concentric circles represent the *proximity* of the stakeholders to the work and their *power*. The closer a stakeholder is to the work, the nearer it will be drawn to the center of the circle.

Stakeholders are represented by segments of the circle.

The *power* of the stakeholder is represented by the radial depth of the segment.

Stakeholder 1 has a *power* of 4 and can 'kill' the project; it 'cuts the circle'. This person is a key stakeholder.

Stakeholder 3 has a *power* rating of 2, a significant informal capacity to cause change. This stakeholder is also close to the work, possibly a team member.

The importance of each stakeholder and his or her degree of influence is indicated by the relative size of each segment measured on the outer circumference of the circle. The larger the segment, the more influential the stakeholder.

The most important stakeholder (with the highest level of influence) is plotted at position 1, starting at 12:00 o'clock, the second most important is next, through to the 15th most important.*

Finally, shadings indicate the direction of influence of the stakeholder and whether the stakeholder is internal or external to the organization.

*Note: The design constraint in the Stakeholder Circle® to plot the top 15 stakeholders does not mean these are the only important stakeholders or that every activity should always manage all 15. The number of important stakeholders who need active management is entirely dependent on the nature of the activity. The choice of 15 stakeholders for the Stakeholder Circle® display was based on empirical observation of 'who mattered' during the development of the tool.

Figure 4.6   Reading a Stakeholder Circle® map.

A stakeholder's *attitude* toward a PMO or any of its activities can be driven by many factors including:

- Whether involvement is voluntary or involuntary
- Whether involvement is beneficial personally or organizationally
- The level of a stakeholder's investment in the activity, either financially or emotionally

If the stake in the PMO of the individual or group is perceived to be beneficial or potentially beneficial to them, stakeholders are more likely to have a positive attitude toward the activity and be prepared to contribute to the work to deliver it. If, on the other hand, they see themselves as victims or losers, they will be more likely to have a negative attitude toward that activity. Part of the assessment of the stakeholder's attitude will be a review of the stake that the stakeholder has, and his or her expectations and requirements for success or failure of the activity. The assessment will need to take into account the elements that shape attitude such as culture, whether the stakeholder identifies with or has a stake in the work or outcomes of the PMO, or the stakeholder's perception of the importance of the PMO.

How to Gauge Attitude

The steps in the process are to rate the current level of *support* of the stakeholder(s),* and the current level of *receptiveness* of each stakeholder to information from (or about) the PMO. The rating process is then repeated, but including viewing the level of support and receptiveness that needed to be achieved to meet the needs of the work of the PMO and the stakeholder. If an important stakeholder is rated as very low in support and receptiveness, the PMO team will need to apply a different engagement approach from stakeholders who are rated as highly supportive and highly receptive.

Examples of Engagement Profiles

Figure 4.7 shows some examples of engagement profile assessments. Stakeholder 1 has been assessed as being neutral about the PMO (3), and as not really being interested in receiving any information about or from the PMO (2). These results are designated by the X in the appropriate boxes in the matrix. However, the team has decided that the target attitude should be *neutral* in both attitudes of support (3) and receptiveness (3). This is shown with a bold circle. In this assessment, there is only a small gap between the stakeholder's current attitude and

---

Support is rated from 1–5 where 1 is very low and 5 is very high. *Receptiveness* is also rated in the same way from 1–5.

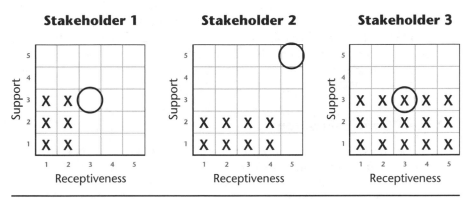

Figure 4.7   Results of Step 4: engage.

the attitude that the team has agreed is essential for the success of the activity; the engagement profile is shown as being close to optimal.*

Stakeholder 2 has been assessed as (2) for support and (4) for receptiveness. The engagement profile should be (5) for support and (5) for receptiveness. In this case, the gap between the current engagement profile and the optimal profile indicates that a high level of effort will be required to develop good communication strategies for this stakeholder, to encourage his or her support and interest in information about the activity. Generally, this level of support is only needed from key stakeholders such as the sponsor, steering committee, or a member of the steering committee.

Stakeholder 3 has been assessed as (3) for support, but (5) for receptiveness. The team has assessed that this stakeholder should be at a level (3) for receptiveness. This is a situation where the current profile is quite different from the optimal profile, requiring careful handling from the team to avoid alienating the stakeholder.

Analysis of Stakeholder 3 Example

The options for closing the gaps between the current and target attitude for Stakeholders 1 and 2 are not complex. On the other hand, there could be a number of paths to resolve the Stakeholder 3 example, such as:

• The stakeholder is a manager, not necessarily important to the success of the PMO, but one who regularly requires much information. It may be necessary to interview this stakeholder to offer him more targeted information.

---

*It is not essential that all stakeholders have a high level of support and receptiveness toward the activity. Part of the key decision the team has to make is whether the stakeholder in question is important enough to warrant the work that is necessary to achieve this high level of support. This information has been gathered through the analysis in Steps 1–3.

- He or she doesn't know what information about the activities of the PMO is needed, and therefore requires as much data as is available. In this case, it may be necessary to meet with the stakeholder and reaffirm expectations and requirements. If the stakeholder is searching for more specific information, the PMO can provide a valuable service.

Targeted Communication

Based on the overall level of engagement and the mutuality factors identified in Step 1, a targeted communications plan can be developed, focusing first on the most important stakeholders and those stakeholders who are important but have a significant gap between their current attitude and the target attitude, such as Stakeholder 2. Communication strategies will need to be developed for other identified stakeholders, but often existing communication such as reports and regular meetings will be sufficient.

Why Target Communication?

To manage within the constraints of time and resource availability, the PMO team will need to consider how best to manage its communication activities for maximum efficiency and effectiveness. A strategy to help the team target those stakeholders whose support is essential or who are important but not supportive will ensure that the team can identify where to focus its scarce resources most effectively.

However, there are other more strategic reasons for a targeted approach to communication. Stakeholders who have been identified as essential to the success of the activity may be equally essential to other activities. Focused and relevant communication will have a better chance of receiving the desired response than communication that is less relevant to the stakeholder.

Communication Planning

The basis for an effective communication plan is defining for each stakeholder, particularly those identified as essential to the success of the PMO:

- The most appropriate information, or a purposeful message
- The most effective message format
- The most efficient methods and frequency of transmission or delivery

The Most Appropriate Information

Directions of influence (from Step 1: Identify) will help define the format and content of the message (this is detailed later in the chapter):

- Upward
- Downward

- Sideward
- Outward
- Internal (to the organization) or external (to the organization)

The Most Effective Message

Mutuality (from Step 1: Identify) will define the focus of the message based on:

- Why this individual or group has been selected as a stakeholder; why they are important to the success of the activity
- What the stakeholder requires from success or failure of the activity, or a stakeholder's expectations or requirements

If the message is crafted to give the stakeholder information that shows his requirements are known and being considered, this will sustain a perception that the activity is well-managed.

The Most Efficient Methods

One of the most important aspects to consider is efficient delivery of the necessary information. The following guidelines provide the team with an understanding of where to focus their communication efforts. It is based on the analysis of engagement profiles described earlier in this chapter (Step 4: Engage), and by defining different levels of communication activities depending on whether the current engagement position:

- Is *equal to* the optimal position
- Is *less than* the optimal position (see Stakeholder 2, Figure 4.7)
- Is *greater than* the optimal position (see Stakeholder 3, Figure 4.7)

In the first instance where the current engagement position is equal to the optimal position, communication can be maintained at its current level. The defined level and frequency of regular reports, meetings, and presentations can be safely maintained. This might be flagged as green in an organization's reporting schema as needs are being met. For the situation where the current engagement position is greater than the optimal position, two possible approaches need to be considered, depending on the results of the engagement matrix. Stakeholder 3 is rated as being well above the level of receptiveness to messages necessary for success of the activity, but at the appropriate level of support of the activity to ensure success of support. The decision the team has to make regarding Stakeholder 3 is whether to reduce the level of information flowing to this stakeholder (and risk a reduction in support from this stakeholder) or to maintain the current level of communication. The decision can only be made in the light of the knowledge that the team has gained during the preceding steps of the stakeholder analysis.

In the third category, the current engagement position is less than the optimal position. If the stakeholder is important, the team needs to focus their efforts on *heroic* communication (discussed later); Stakeholders 1 and 2 are in this category. This type of communication is generally needed for only a small percentage of stakeholders, but any effort expended on increasing the levels of support and receptiveness to the optimal position will significantly benefit the activity. Generally, in this case, a number of different communication approaches need to be used for the regular reports and meetings through special presentations and possibly even using the influence of other important but supportive stakeholders to deliver the activity information. Multiple complex communication activities must be coordinated by a relationship manager who could be the manager responsible for the activity, a functional manager, or a supportive senior stakeholder.

The Communication Plan

Based on each stakeholder's engagement strategy, a communication plan can be developed. The communication plan should contain:

- Stakeholder name and role
- Mutuality:
  - How the stakeholder is important to the activity
  - The stakeholder's stake
  - The stakeholder's expectations
- Categorization of influence (upward, downward, outward, sideward, internal or external)
- Engagement profile preferably in graphical form (see Figure 4.7):
  - Level of support for the activity
  - Level of receptiveness to information about the activity
  - Target engagement: target levels of support and receptiveness
- Strategies for delivering the message:
  - Who will deliver the message
  - What the message will be, including regular activity reports or special messages
  - How it will be delivered, be it formal or informal, written or oral, the type of technology used (e-mails, written memos, meetings)
  - When, including how frequently it will be delivered and over what timeframe (where applicable)
  - Why, including the purpose for the communication (this is a function of mutuality; why the stakeholder is important for activity success and what the stakeholder requires from the activity)
  - Communication item, or the information that will be distributed (the content of the report or message)

Effective Communication

Communication is the primary tool for stakeholder engagement. The effectiveness of the communication is influenced by many factors including:

- The relationship between sender and receiver
- Other barriers to effective communication

Relationship Between Sender and Receiver

Irrespective of how well the communication strategy and plan are crafted, other factors must be considered in preparing the communication plan. These factors include:

- The different levels of power or influence between the team and the stakeholder. It may be considered inappropriate for an individual from the team to communicate with a stakeholder at a higher level in the organization or the community outside the organization:
  - In general, the more powerful the stakeholder, the less detail and more focused the report or message should be.
  - It is helpful to know a stakeholder's preferences. Does the powerful stakeholder prefer graphical representation, spreadsheets, or words?
- The role of the stakeholder:
  - Sponsors or other political activity supporters may require exception reports, briefing data sufficient to be able to defend the activity, and *no surprises*.
  - Middle managers who supply activity resources need more comprehensive information such as timeframes, resource data, and reports on adherence to resource plans and effectiveness of resources provided.
  - Staff working on the activity and other activity team members need detailed but focused information that will enable them to perform their activity roles effectively.
  - Other staff need updates on the progress of activity, particularly information on how it will affect their own work roles.
  - External stakeholders will also require regular planned and managed updates on the activity, its deliverables, impact, and progress.
- Credibility of the messenger and the message. The more the team has worked to build trust and a perception of trustworthiness and competence, the more readily a stakeholder will receive and act on information. Credibility of this nature takes time to develop and is often the result of previous positive experiences, a reputation for being trustworthy and timely information deliverers.
- The relevance of the information to the recipient. The team must ensure that information is of interest to the stakeholder and is delivered in a manner that is most easily read and absorbed.

- The format and content of the message. The most appropriate level of detail and presentation style will also assist in ensuring that information is received and responded to in the most suitable way.

Communicating with Unsupportive Stakeholders

A stakeholder who has been identified as being supportive should not be ignored or taken for granted, but should be given the appropriate information in the manner that best suits that stakeholder's requirements. Every PMO will encounter situations in which stakeholders previously identified as important to the success of the PMO are unsupportive. One approach requires an analysis of the reason or reasons for the lack of support or receptiveness. This information should already have been documented in the stakeholder identification and prioritization exercises:

- If the stakeholder is unsupportive of this activity because he or she is supportive of another competing activity, negotiation needs to occur to resolve the competition. If the stakeholder will not negotiate, the PMO manager should work with peers (sideward stakeholders) to resolve the issue.
- If the stakeholder is too busy to receive information about the PMO's activities and therefore will not read e-mails or attend meetings, a number of options can be considered. This may include informal meetings over coffee or including short reports in the meetings that this stakeholder does attend.
- A supportive stakeholder may be prepared to act as a conduit to other less supportive stakeholders.

Special Groups, Broadcast, or General Messages

In describing the actions necessary to develop a communication plan for appropriate communication to stakeholders, the focus has been on assuming that PMO team members have access to their stakeholders. However, activities that an organization initiates may impact large groups of stakeholders who:

- Are globally dispersed
- Require specialized information or specialized management
- Are external organizations with contractual arrangements
- Are potentially disadvantaged by the work of the PMO or its outcome

In such cases, a corporate communications group must be briefed to prepare, manage, and disseminate the messages on behalf of the team.

The discussions on the preparation of messages to stakeholders have centered primarily on groups and individuals who have been prioritized as being relatively important to the success of the activity. It is essential to ensure that the stakeholders who are not considered as being in the relatively important category are not ignored. Such stakeholders will often merit broadcast or general messages.

Implementing Communication Plans

The contents of the communication plan should be:

- Available to all interested parties, especially activity stakeholders
- Able to be amended when activity conditions change
- Able to be monitored and measured

The communication plan should state clearly who will deliver the message to all identified stakeholders, what the message will be, when it will be delivered, and under what circumstance the message will be delivered. The key communication points for each stakeholder and each messenger should be included in the activity schedule and reported in activity team meetings.

Changes to the Communication Plan

When conditions change to the extent that the stakeholder community changes, it will be necessary to review and perhaps amend the communication plan to reflect any changes to the stakeholder community. The trigger points for making these changes will generally be occasions when stakeholders change roles and no longer have a stake in the work of the PMO, and new people join the organization who have no knowledge of, or interest in, the work of the PMO.

Monitoring the Engagement

The guidelines for building a communication plan provide a framework for building a targeted purposeful communication plan to meet the unique needs of the PMO and its stakeholders. This plan is the starting point for engaging key stakeholders in the most appropriate way. To achieve an effective engagement of key stakeholders for the benefit of the organization, the plan must be implemented and the effectiveness of the communication must be measured and monitored. These activities are the essential parts of an effective Step 5: Monitor.

Monitoring the Effectiveness of the Communication Plan

The process of monitoring the effectiveness of communication has three parts:

1. Ensuring that the communication plan is implemented
2. Review of the stakeholder community to ensure that the membership is current (the right stakeholders for the current phase or time)
3. Review of the stakeholder engagement profile

The who, what, when, and how strategy for delivering the tailored messages to important stakeholders must be converted into action.

The work of Step 5: Monitor includes implementing the planned communication action, and then monitoring and evaluating the results to understand the effects of the implementation and derive learnings. Once the communication plan has been developed and team communication responsibilities have been allocated, the principal communication points must be included in the schedule and reported through the PMO's monthly report and sponsor update.

Continuous Review of the Stakeholder Community

Part of the practice of continuous improvement and also the foundation of the Stakeholder Circle® methodology is understanding that successful implementation of an organization's activities is through stakeholder relationship management. The key to managing these relationships is understanding that the stakeholder community is a network of people. It is impossible to develop relationships that will never change, just as it is impossible to make objective decisions about people. At best, a methodology should aim to reduce the subjectivity that is inherent in people who make decisions about how to develop and maintain robust relationships with other people.

Because relationships are not fixed, it is necessary to review the membership of the stakeholder community regularly and continuously. This will ensure that throughout the implementation of any activity, the team has the most current information to manage the right stakeholders at that particular time. Regular reviews should be programmed:

- When the work of the activity moves from one stage of its implementation to the next (e.g., from planning to build, or from build to implement)
- At regular intervals within a particular phase, if that phase is intended to go for a long time (typically three months)

The team also needs to continuously scan their stakeholder community for unplanned occurrences that may trigger a review when:

- The activity moves from one stage of its implementation to the next (e.g., from planning the work to doing the work, or from doing the work to managing its implementation, then to closing or completion)
- New personnel join the team

Each time the dynamics of the stakeholder community change, membership of the community must be reassessed.

Review of the Stakeholder Engagement Profile

Each time the stakeholder community is reassessed, the corresponding engagement profile should also be reviewed, and any movement in the gap between the stakeholder's current attitude and the optimal attitude must be considered. This movement will provide an indicator of the effectiveness of the communication. Additional ad hoc reviews are triggered when the team observes an unexpected change in the attitude of a key stakeholder.

Regular (Planned) Reviews

When the team meets for regular progress meetings, the communication schedule must be updated to reflect actual communication activity. The schedule should also include milestones to initiate a review of the engagement profiles of the key stakeholders. The process of review is a reassessment of the ratings for attitude, which includes assessing the current level of:

- Support
- Receptiveness

The current ratings are compared to the defined target attitude and any previous assessment to measure any changes in the gaps between the current assessment and the target assessment and between the current and previous assessment. It may also be necessary to re-evaluate these targets; if there has been a change in the importance of a stakeholder, the target attitude may need to be increased or decreased to reflect changes in that stakeholder's relative importance.

Some Examples of Results of Reviews

Stakeholder 1 has been rated as the most important member of the community at this particular time. This stakeholder fits the profile of a government agency that is significant to the activity through its power to provide approvals. Like most government bodies, it is neutral in support but requires more information (regular reports and other regulatory requirements). The first assessment of Stakeholder 1 (see Figure 4.8) showed that there was not a large gap between the current attitude and the target attitude.* To maintain this relationship, the team must provide any and all information necessary to meet the government's requirements and the team's need for the approvals. On the next scheduled review, the attitude of Stakeholder 1 has reached the target. No new action will be necessary as a result of this review. A subsequent review, the 3rd assessment, shows that the engagement profile is still at the optimal level, and this stakeholder is at the same level of importance—Number 1. No additional communication effort is necessary under the current conditions.

Stakeholder 2 fits the profile of a senior manager in the organization, perhaps the sponsor or a group such as the senior leadership team. It may also describe a

---

*Attitude is the combination of ratings for support and receptiveness. The current attitude is shown by X and the target attitude is shown with a bold circle. The engagement profile is the combination of current and target attitudes depicted in the 5×5 matrix.

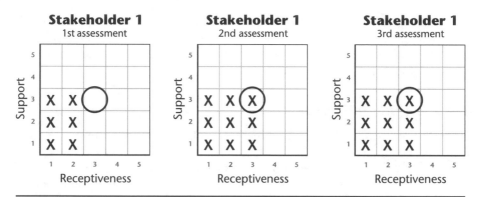

Figure 4.8   Results of reviews of the attitude of Stakeholder 1 over time.

stakeholder outside the organization, such as a government minister or power-ful lobby group. For Stakeholder 2 (shown in Figure 4.9), the first assessment shows that *heroic** communication efforts are required to close the gap between the current and target attitudes. In this case, the intention of any communication must be to increase the stakeholder's level of support and receptiveness to in-formation about the activity, its progress, and its issues. The second assessment reveals that some progress had been made, but more work is necessary to achieve the desired level of engagement. The decision the team needs to make at this point is whether to continue at the same level of communication (expecting a steady growth in this stakeholder's attitude) or to include additional techniques and messages to raise the levels of support and receptiveness to the desired level.

In the case of Stakeholder 2, whatever the team decided to do, their efforts were moderately successful: the stakeholder was rated as (4), and the target had been defined as (5). The decision the team must make at this stage is whether to aim for the highest level of support or be satisfied with the result achieved to date. This decision must be made in the context of the needs of the activity, the amount of available time and personnel that can be devoted to this task, and whether the team can actually gain any more of the stakeholder's time and atten-tion. The team may need to:

- Seek advice from other stakeholders who have more knowledge and ex-perience of the politics of the organization and the expectations of the stakeholder under consideration
- Draw on the combined knowledge and experience of its members to sup-port decisions about whether to continue as planned or to modify the communication plan or target attitude

---

*Heroic communication is the highest level of communication activity required when there is a large gap between the current attitude and the target attitude of a key stakeholder.

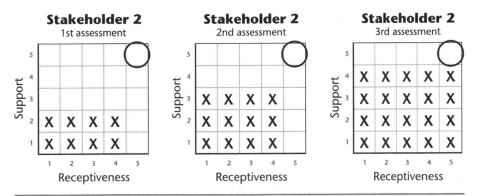

Figure 4.9 Results of reviews of the attitude of Stakeholder 2 over time.

Monitoring Trends

It is impossible to objectively measure the relationships between a PMO and its stakeholders. The process of this methodology depends on one group of people making decisions about the needs, requirements, and attitudes of other people. There are two issues that reduce the possibility of objective or fixed measures of peoples' attitudes towards a PMO. The first is the observation that peoples' needs, requirements, and attitudes do not remain fixed. The second is that we cannot read the hearts and minds of others, no matter how empathetic we believe we are, or how close our relationship is with them.

Rather than attempt to measure absolutes, trend reporting is commonly used for measuring intangible or immeasurable data. This is achieved by measuring progress such as actual against planned or other changes usually assessed against the first record—the baseline. By comparing each new set of data against the baseline or previous sets of data, the changes or differences will provide an indication of the success of whatever is being measured. This is a standard method for measuring and reporting progress in organizations.

The data collected through Step 5: Monitor provides the way to measure changes over time against a baseline. In the examples shown in this chapter, the baseline is the first engagement profile. Subsequent measures of the engagement profile, always rated from the same set of statements, can be compared to the baseline. Progress—or lack of progress—in building that relationship can be understood through the changes from the baseline data. This can be seen at the individual level using the engagement profile matrix used in Figures 4.8 and 4.9. The Stakeholder Circle® database provides an aggregate report for the activity, showing the changes of each stakeholder but within the total environment of the activity.

Considerations for Stakeholder Relationship Management

The foregoing sections have provided sufficient detail of the steps of the Stakeholder Circle® methodology to allow PMO team members and managers to use all, or parts, of the structure of the methodology to manage particular aspects of building and maintaining robust relationships between the PMO and its stakeholders. However, application of the personal leadership characteristics necessary to communicate to stakeholders is an essential second step.

Managing the PMO's Stakeholders

Understanding the power environment within the organization and the position of those within it for particular issues is critical. It requires knowledge of the environment and all the stakeholders in this process and what their needs and wants are. Without formal power, the manager must to be able to influence people and outcomes. The political tools that a manager should be capable and willing to use to ensure success include:

- Gaining and maintaining support such as the sponsorship of a powerful champion
- Building alliances
- Controlling a critical resource, decision process, or committee process through the agenda, membership, or minutes
- Use of positional authority such as rewards, coercion, training, information, or favors

These tools are essential components for success. The theme of stakeholder relationship management is that communication is the key to successful distribution of information and wielding of influence. Part of this communication is development of accurate routine reports that form an essential part of the information needed to maintain stakeholder relationships. With important stakeholders, however, it is essential to take the time to ensure that their particular information needs are met and that rapport is built to strengthen and sustain the relationships.

Not Just the PMO's Stakeholders

It is also important to recognize that part of the range of services that the PMO can provide is support for their clients and to manage the clients' stakeholders in the form of facilitation, record keeping, training, consultancy, and maintenance of data about the stakeholder community. This service would be in the form of a *center of excellence* for the stakeholder relationship management tools and methodologies, thus supporting increasing maturity of the organization in stakeholder relationship management.

Successful and effective communication can only be achieved through the sustained efforts of individuals who understand the power environment within the organization, understand how to engage stakeholders appropriately, and are willing to operate within that environment. Managing upward successfully to gain credibility with senior stakeholders for the longer term success of the PMO requires a mature, long-term effort. Motivating the team to work together to deliver the PMO services must be considered part of the role of stakeholder management. Working with others in the organization to provide appropriate services and to assist other parts of the organization in using the methodology for a consistent set of processes and practices should also be considered part of the role and responsibility of the fully-functioning mature PMO.

Conclusion

Research has shown that organizations that use project and program management processes and practices are more successful when those processes and practices are supported by a PMO. Whether the PMO organization operates in the project, program, or portfolio domain, a common concern and focus must be on understanding the community of stakeholders that impact the work of the PMO or are impacted by that work, whether positively or negatively. Building and maintaining robust and mutually rewarding relationships between the PMO and its stakeholder community means that the right stakeholders are identified, and appropriate, targeted, and purposeful communication strategies can be developed and implemented to ensure that the PMO continues to be relevant to the organization and is also perceived as such.

Author Biography

Dr. Lynda Bourne is the CEO and founder of Stakeholder Management Pty, responsible for the overall development and marketing of the *Stakeholder Circle®* methodology and tools, and the SRMM® maturity model for assessing organizational readiness to implement stakeholder relationship management. She is a Fellow of the Australian Institute of Management and a recognized international consultant, seminar leader, speaker, and author specializing in stakeholder relationship management and related topics.

Within the Project Management Institute, Lynda is the 2010 president of the Melbourne, Australia, chapter and a certified OPM3® product suite assessor and consultant. She has contributed to a number of PMI® standard development teams and was chair of the OPM3® ProductSuite Examination Committee from 2006 to 2008.

Dr. Bourne graduated from RMIT University, Melbourne, as the first professional doctorate of project management in 2005. Her research on defining and managing stakeholder relationships has lead to the development of the *Stake-*

holder Circle®. Prior to this, she had gained extensive experience as a senior project manager and project director specializing in delivery of IT and other business-related projects.

References

Bourne, L. 2009. *Stakeholder Relationship Management: A maturity model for organisaitonal implementation*. Farnham, Surrey, UK: Gower.

Bourne, L. 2006. *Supersizing PMO Performance*. Presented at *PMI*® *Global Congress—Asia Pacific*: Bangkok.

Bourne, L., and Walker, D. 2005. The Paradox of Project Control. *Team Performance Management Journal* (Summer 2005).

Bourne, L., and Walker, D. H. T. 2003. *Tapping into the Power Lines-A 3rd dimension of project management beyond leading and managing*. Presented at *17th World Congress on Project Management*. Moscow, Russia.

Canadian Management Accounting Society. 1998. *IT failures costing billions*. *CMA Management* 72:37–38.

Dai, C. X. and Wells, W. G. 2004. An exploration of project management office features and their relationship to project performance. *International Journal of Project Management* 22:523–532.

Glass, R. 1998. Short-Term and Long-Term Remedies for Runaway Projects. *Communications of the ACM* 41(7): 7.

Hill, G. M. 2004. *Evolving the project management office: a competency continuum*. IS Governance (Fall, 2004): 45–51.

James, G. 1997. *IT fiascos and how to avoid them. Datamation* 43(11): 84–88.

Jiang, J., and Klein, G. 1999. Risks to different aspects of system success. *Information and Management* 36(5): 263–271.

Kerzner, H. 2005. *Using the Project Management Maturity Model: Strategic Planning for Project Management*. 2nd ed. Hoboken, NJ: John Wiley & Sons.

KPMG. 2005. *Global IT Project Management Survey: How committed are you?* KPMG International.

Lemon, W. F., et al., 2002. Information systems project failure: a comparative study of two countries. *Journal of Global Information Management*. April-June 2002: 28–28.

Project Management Institute, *A Guide to the Project Management Body of Knowledge (PMBOK*® *Guide)*, 4th edition, Newtown Square, PA, PMI®, 2008.

Walker, D. H. T., Bourne, L., and Rowlinson, S. 2008. Stakeholders and the Supply Chain: from *Procurement Systems: a cross-industry project management perspective*, D. H. T. Walker and S. Rowlinson, Editors. London: Taylor & Francis.

5

The PMO: Strategy Execution Office

J. Kent Crawford

Introduction

Strategy provides a framework for managerial decisions. Without such a framework, it is easy for an organization—even a small one—to spin toward chaos. A business is presented with new opportunities and challenges each day; without some guiding point of reference to anchor present decision making to the future, the various functions in the organization can wind up working at cross-purposes to each other.

A strategy reflects an organization's understanding of how, when, and where it should compete; against whom; and for what purposes. Strategy integrates the vision and direction of the organization with the projects and programs by which it communicates and implements that vision and direction. Strategy answers the question: how will our company position itself against competition in the market over the long run to secure a sustainable competitive advantage?

Strategy has, alas, become something of a buzzword. Many companies claim to have strategies that have, in fact, nothing but a wish list of outcomes or a shopping list of tactics. Often, companies fail to distinguish between *operational effectiveness* and *strategy*. Targets for productivity, quality, sales, efficiency, or speed masquerade as strategies. These targets, while essential to superior performance, do not move an organization towards a strategic position in the marketplace. As an article in the *Harvard Business Review* stated, "Operational effectiveness means performing similar activities *better* than rivals perform them. . . . In contrast, strategic positioning means performing *different* activities from rivals' or performing similar activities in *different* ways" (Matheson and Matheson, 1998).

Vague strategies cannot easily be translated into measurable objectives, which is vital to achieving stretch goals. Unclear corporate and business plans inhibit integration of objectives, activities, and strategies between the corporate and business levels. Simply put, poor strategies result in poor execution.

This may seem obvious on paper, and yet we are all familiar with organizations in which the left hand doesn't know what the right hand is doing. Such clichés have entered our lexicon simply because they express common truths. In the absence of structured strategy management processes, entropy will set in and departments—even people within departments—will be working on conflicting objectives.

Processes that Support Strategic Execution

Recent research on strategy has zeroed in on the problem of nonexecution of strategies. Anyone familiar with project management processes will immediately recognize the components in this list of recommended processes:

Communication—The operational components of strategy and the method of measuring execution results is not clearly communicated to all stakeholders in the organization. Such communication brings its own rewards in terms of increased employee engagement, which yields bottom-line results (Gibbons, 2006).

Monitoring or control—Systems for linking strategies to departmental and personal goal achievement, metrics to record progress toward goal achievement, and a compliance structure to make sure the identified strategic processes are being used.

Strategy improvement—An iterative process whereby the strategic initiatives that support the goals and objectives are periodically reviewed for progress and adjustment, and a related process for revising and updating the strategies themselves (Grant, 2007).

The office of strategy management—Writing in *The Harvard Business Review*, Balanced Scorecard creators Kaplan and Norton called for a new organizational entity to oversee the execution of strategy. They argued that under "The Old Strategy Calendar," with its periodic activities related to strategy that are carried out at various times in various silos, most activities take place largely in isolation and without guidance from the enterprise strategy. This widens the gulf between an organization's strategy and its processes, systems, and people. The authors note that surveys revealed, "HR and IT departmental plans rarely support corporate or business-unit strategic initiatives. Budgeting is similarly disconnected: some 60% of organizations do not link their financial budgets to strategic priorities. Incentives aren't aligned, either: the compensation packages of 70% of middle managers and more than 90% of frontline employees have no link to the success or failure of strategy implementation. Periodic management meetings, corporate communication, and knowledge management are similarly not focused on strategy execution" (Kaplan and Norton, 2001).

The answer, they propose, is an office of strategy management. Such an office would:

- Provide an organizational lens for focusing a strategic lens on each and every initiative.
- Provide a process for executing the strategic choices by means of budgeted resource allocations.
- Focus on getting the work of the business done efficiently and effectively.
- Monitor and control via a process for tracking a strategy as it is executed, detecting problems or changes in its underlying premises, and reporting to appropriate management levels.
- Provide a process for strategy improvement; a way of making necessary adjustments based on monitoring and control information and strategy performance review.
- Oversee the *planning integration* for strategy. Strategy management planning includes developing annual objectives and specific initiative plans that are logically linked to the results of strategy analysis.
- Oversee the *monitoring* or *control integration*, tracking the performance of a strategy as it is executed.

Fortunately, many organizations already have such an office, *although they may not yet realize it!* Any organization with an enterprise-level project management office has the capability to oversee the execution of strategy at their fingertips. Smart organizations will leverage this already-existing structure and process to move organizations from vision to execution.

Performance reporting from portfolios, programs, and projects are necessary to understand how well the organization's strategy is working. This information may reveal problems in the strategy or in its underlying premises, or it may reveal errors in strategy formulation, where organizational capability and environmental analysis informed the strategy selection process.

To ensure effective strategy execution, strategy must be communicated clearly to those developing portfolio and program or project plans, to ensure that those initiatives support the organization's strategy. At the same time, portfolio analysis and program or project initiation processes must be integrated with the strategy management planning processes to provide the information needed for effective strategic planning.

The key processes for execution, project and program processes, portfolio processes, and performance management processes need one more thing to bring order to the strategic execution project: an organizational structure that supports their effective use.

The Evolution of an Effective Organizational Structure for Project Execution

Organizational structure—the grouping of people and reporting relationships, the rules and procedures that determine what various groups do, and the patterns of interaction that result—determines the speed of adaptability to the changing business environment. Structures take on many forms, all of which have different effects on the speed at which change can be brought about. Research and experience tells us that to execute a strategy quickly, one must be capable of adjusting to changing markets and focused on the actions that will move the enterprise forward toward long-term goals. The best organizations are structured for goal achievement; bureaucracy is minimized and information flows freely.

Yet this does not describe the majority of organizations. Often, the ideas people have about how work could best be accomplished are far ahead of how companies actually operate. The present organizational structures—functional silos locked in a pyramid of bureaucracy—were bequeathed to us by the Industrial Age, and like a giant battleship, are hard to turn around.

Corporate strategy affects the choice of organizational structure. At the same time, organizational structure can either impede or facilitate the execution of corporate strategy. To execute strategy effectively, managers must make sound decisions about structure and develop methods or processes to achieve the integration of structural units. Over the past decade, the enterprise-level project or program management office has increasingly taken a leading role in helping the enterprise to integrate activities with strategy, erase communication barriers within the organization, and flatten the reporting structure.

The Legacy of the Functional Organization

Dr. Frank Toney, founder of the Project Management Benchmarking Forum, has done extensive research into the effects of organizational structure on project and program success. Using both meta-analysis of the literature and action research methods in the Forums, Toney identified a host of dilemmas resulting primarily from a functional structure as well as from organization size (Toney, 2001).

As organizations become larger, functional units become increasingly independent; fewer opportunities naturally arise for cooperation and integration of processes. Functional managers may be reluctant to share projects with other areas or relinquish control when project-related activities leave their area. At the same time, leadership becomes progressively distanced from the working groups. The addition of each layer of management makes it more difficult for the leader of the company to communicate the organizational vision and goals to management and workers within functional areas. Communications between functional areas become strained as each increment of organizational growth results in additional layers of management filters and information barriers. The formal communications pipeline becomes longer. Under these conditions, it is not surprising that few corporate strategies are understood or enacted at the project and operations levels of the organization.

The Addition of Projects to the Organization

The concept of the project as an organizing principle and a management specialty—with its own techniques, tools, and vocabulary—had its beginnings in the 20th-century military. These military origins help to explain why the initial focus in projects was on planning and controlling. In fact, control might be considered the *raison d'etre* for project management: control of schedules, costs, and scope on endeavors that otherwise might career over budget, over time, or fail to meet specifications.

At the same time, in spite of the focus on control, projects have a tendency to feel out-of-control and frequently run amok in reality as well as in perception. This out-of-control feel stems from the way projects were superimposed on existing bureaucratic structures with their bulky communications mechanisms. Obeying the strictures inherent in the hierarchy, while at the same time acting for the best interest of the project, has been difficult at best—and often downright impossible. When projects are conducted within functional departments, they often have limited access to resources and face numerous challenges when working with other functional and geographic groups. To further complicate matters, most employees in functionally structured organizations already have a full-time job. When a project is initiated, the time required to participate is often committed at the sacrifice of the day-to-day job accomplishment. It is rare in such an organization to find professional, trained project managers; thus, projects are executed in an ad hoc manner by whoever is available. Project performance is difficult to evaluate as there are few measurement metrics. The functional organization structure tends to undermine the authority and decision-making capability of project managers, making project success more difficult.

The Matrix Organization...Better, But Not Ideal

The earliest uses of project management—in capital construction, civil engineering, and research and development—imposed the idea of the project schedule, project objectives, and project team on an existing organizational structure that was very rigid. Without a departmental home or a functional silo of its own, a project was the organizational stepchild. As a way to overcome this hurdle, project managers developed the concept of the *matrix organization*—a stopgap way of defining how projects were supposed to get done within an organizational structure unsuitable to project work. It was a *patch*, to use a software development term—not a new version of the organization.

The matrix project organization structure is based on appointing a project manager from within a functional area. Usually, the project manager still has a full-time job and is reporting to a functional manager. Team members and financial resources are borrowed from other departments. Team members have two bosses, the project manager and their functional unit managers. The governance of such a structure depends largely on the project manager's finesse and persuasion. In essence, team members only follow the project manager because of his or her leadership skills rather than his or her formal authority.

The theoretical benefits of the matrix organization appeared so inviting that it was applied by organizations to the management of nearly all large multifunctional projects. Companies embraced the concept, hoping to get something for nothing, as a way to use existing people and resources to execute projects within the cultural confines and constraints of traditional functionally organized enterprises. However, these desired results rarely materialized. Organizations found that executing large multifunctional projects with a matrix-structured project team within functional departments often resulted in an imposition on employees who were already performing a full-time job. The borrowed resources element of the matrix equation also proved difficult; particularly, when the resources that the project team was trying to borrow were scarce funds and people.

In his book, *Project Management: Strategic Design and Implementation*, David Cleland reviews the research and literature associated with matrix project organizations. He quotes Texas Instruments as announcing that their attempt at matrix management was a key reason for their economic decline. Xerox said that matrix management proved to be a deterrent to product development. Other cases cited concluded that the matrix style of project organization was more cumbersome and costly than an independent project organization. Further results from the PM Benchmarking Forums have shown that using matrix organizations to execute large multifunctional projects are consistently less successful than utilizing full-time project managers and team members.

Many of the problems associated with the matrix design have to do with upper management's inability to work out the required power sharing; imbalance of power between departments and projects inevitably causes conflicts to arise on the projects. The matrix structure contains no inherent methods for conflict resolution, so without proper power sharing among upper managers, project managers are left to fend for themselves. A study of matrix organizations cited by Jeffrey Pinto found that the three most intense areas of conflict (schedules, priorities, and personnel resources) result from the split-authority problem between project managers and functional departments.

The Strategic PMO Today

In recent years, as organizations have noticed that the rise in cross-departmental work has created problems in quality, customer service, and cycle time reduction, a new *superfunction* has been born: one that exists to work and to provide value and cross-functionality. Variously called the enterprise project management office, the strategic project office, or even—and probably most accurately—the office of strategy management, this addition to organizational structure seeks to maximize business results by having the project management function report to an executive or executive committee whose authority extends across multifunctional business units. The discipline that delivers results had an organizational home, at last.

Key roles of this organizational structure include:

- Developer and custodian of the standards, processes, and methodologies that improve strategy execution performance organization-wide
- Consultant and mentoring to ensure alignment with strategy at all levels (organizational and individual)
- Designer of and reporter on strategy performance measures
- Manager of the strategy performance process via oversight of the project portfolio
- Creator of a comprehensive communication and education process focused on strategy execution
- Facilitator with senior executives to shape the agenda for strategy review and learning
- Center for the management of strategic initiatives (portfolios, programs, and projects)
- Facilitator of processes to identify and share best practices
- Knowledge center, where information on objectives, budgets, progress, and history are stored
- Facilitator of strategy execution processes

Whatever you name it, a home base for project managers and project management is a must for organizations to move from doing a less-than-adequate job of managing projects on an individual basis to creating the organizational synergy around projects that adds value—dependably and repeatedly—to the entire portfolio. The only way to maintain a global sense of how a company's strategic projects are doing is to have this sort of project focus point.

The PMO's Rising Influence

In 2000, the Gartner Group proposed as a "Strategic Planning Assumption" for companies, that organizations that established *enterprise* standards for project management, *including a project office with suitable governance* (italics ours), would experience half as many major project cost overruns, delays, and cancellations as those that failed to do so. Many organizations jumped onto the project management office (PMO) bandwagon, with mixed results. PMOs were sometimes put in place without being fully thought through or properly staffed. In our 2001 book, we offered a blueprint for implementing a PMO; since then, the project office we envisioned has taken hold in organizations: 2007 research, updated in

2010, on the *State of the PMO* found that enterprise-level, strategic PMOs are becoming the most common organizational structure for executing strategic projects and programs. These strategic PMOs sit at a high level in their organizations, typically reporting to a C-level executive—sometimes the CEO. In fact, in an update to that study completed in April 2010, it was found that PMO directors themselves are moving toward the C-level, with 15 percent of the respondents holding a title at the vice-president or director level (PM Solutions Research, 2010).

The strategic PMO thus addresses both ends of the corporate dilemma: the reasons for project failures as well as the reasons for strategy failures. In the strategic PMO, strategy and projects meet and work together seamlessly for the good of the entire organization.

A study published in the *Project Management Journal* (Sauer, et al., 1999) focused on the ways that project-centered companies build their organizational capability to manage the project portfolio. They found that organizations with the ability to leverage projects for competitive success display the following organizational features:

1. They "reframe the management task" so that the enterprise's objective is to improve the way the organization manages its project managers and its project management processes. Improved performance on individual projects then follows as an outcome of the redesigned management structure and processes. This systemic approach contrasts with many organizations' habit of focusing on and intervening in individual projects on a case-by-case (often, crisis-by-crisis) basis.

2. They have a flat organizational structure. No more than two levels separate project managers from the C-level, ensuring ready access to powerful decision makers. Functional departments are relatively small, and therefore act as support units rather than empires that compete with projects. This structure clearly signals the importance of projects to the business. The result is that projects can be managed with minimal internal tensions and conflict.

3. They streamline reporting processes. The flat structure's short lines of authority combine well with tight and frequent reporting and control processes to ensure that the organization concentrates on project performance. Informal reporting keeps the project director informed about progress and difficulties, sometimes several times per day. This eradicates the long-lamented disconnect between project management and executive management—and thus between projects and strategy.

When we initiated our own broad survey of the status of PMOs in 2007, the burning question was not, *What is a PMO?* or *Why do we need one?* The question was, *What kind of PMO do we need, and how can we objectively measure the value it brings to the organization?* The results were astonishing: For example, in our 2000 *Value of Project*

Management study, only 47 percent of the respondents had implemented a project office of any type. By 2006, 77 percent of the respondents to our *Project Management: The State of the Industry* survey had implemented PMOs; of those, 35 percent had an enterprise-level (or strategic) PMO. In 2007, 54 percent of the respondents reported having an enterprise-level PMO in place. In 2010, the figure was 84 percent. Of those who did not have a PMO, half were planning to implement one within the coming year. Even factoring in the differing research objectives of these studies, the upward trend is unmistakable, both in the sheer numbers of PMOs and in the rising organizational clout (Pennypacker, 2000, 2006, 2008).

But, most important, those strategic PMOs that had been in place for four years or longer seemed to be making a definite difference in organizational performance. The results suggested that merely implementing a PMO is not a panacea. Instead, it is *maturity* that makes a difference to the organization. As they become more mature, our data suggests, organizational success metrics improve. In addition, the mature PMO takes on more roles—in portfolio management, in people management, and in performance management, further elevating its value to the organization.

In 2008 and 2009, the strategic PMO faced unprecedented stresses: a global economic downturn left many companies reeling and scrambling for ways to cut costs. Yet our best-in-class PMOs continue to thrive, because they allow companies to make the most of slim resources; streamlining the portfolio, accurately forecasting resource availability, and allowing changes in strategic focus necessitated by economic factors to be seamlessly carried out, because the project portfolio management processes add nimbleness to the organization. And, the PMO received an unexpected boost from an unlikely quarter in 2009, when the U.S. Federal Government implemented The American Recovery and Reinvestment Act, along with an unprecedented focus on excellent program management and transparency of results. Suddenly, federal agencies from NOAA to the USDA wanted strategic PMOs! How this will play out over the long term is uncertain at this writing, but it is a positive note both for the status of project management and for the beleaguered taxpayer.

The Impact of the Mature Strategic PMO

There is a strong correlation between organizational performance and the maturity of PMOs. Mature PMOs show significant improvement in organizational performance, as can be seen from Figure 5.1.

Best of all, organizations with PMOs showed significant improvement *at each level* of maturity; that is, for each incremental improvement in process maturity, there was a corresponding impact on organizational performance measures, including financial performance and customer satisfaction:

- Overall performance improvement of 6.2 percent from PMO Level 1 to Level 2

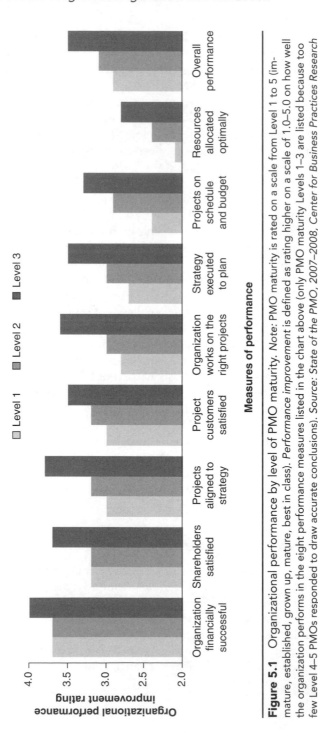

Figure 5.1 Organizational performance by level of PMO maturity. *Note:* PMO maturity is rated on a scale from Level 1 to 5 (immature, established, grown up, mature, best in class). *Performance improvement* is defined as rating higher on a scale of 1.0–5.0 on how well the organization performs in the eight performance measures listed in the chart above (only PMO maturity Levels 1–3 are listed because too few Level 4–5 PMOs responded to draw accurate conclusions). *Source: State of the PMO, 2007–2008, Center for Business Practices Research Study.*

- Overall performance improvement of 14.6 percent from PMO Level 2 to Level 3
- Overall performance improvement of 10.5 percent from PMO Level 3 to Level 4
- Organizations with PMOs at Level 3 maturity and higher showed a 16 percent budget or schedule performance improvement compared to those organizations without.

As PMOs mature, they are significantly better at meeting critical success factors, including having effective sponsorship, accountability, competent staff, quality leadership, and demonstrated value. They have significantly fewer challenges, including stakeholder acceptance, appropriate funding, demonstration of value, role clarification, conflicting authority, and consistent application of processes.

And—gratifying since we advocated this in our 2005 book on the HR aspects of managing by projects (Crawford and Cabanis-Brewin, 2009)—as PMOs mature, they are more likely to staff professional planners, schedulers, and controllers:

- Level 2 PMOs have 14 percent more planners, schedulers, and controllers than do Level 1.
- Level 3 PMOs have 24 percent more planners, schedulers, and controllers than do Level 2.
- Level 4 PMOs have 70 percent more planners, schedulers, and controllers than do Level 3.

Across the board, this study showed that high-performing organizations are more likely to have an enterprise PMO (65.8 percent of high-performing organizations have EPMOs compared to only 48.6 percent of low-performing organizations). The PMOs in high-performing organizations have been in place 29 percent longer (4.5 years) than in low-performing organizations (3.5 years); and high-performing companies have PMOs that perform a wider variety of functions, including strategy formulation, portfolio risk management, benefits realization analysis, contract preparation, outsourcing, project opportunity process development, resource assignment process development, management of a staff of project planners or controllers and business relationship managers, and resource identification and optimization (Pennypacker, 2008).

Ending the Failures of Strategic Projects

Some reasons for project failure on which establishing a strategic PMO can have a direct impact include:

- Project managers who lack enterprise-wide multiproject planning and control skills and tools often find it impossible to comprehend the big picture.

Thus, projects get worked on individually, but overall company priorities are not necessarily supported.

- Projects are not actively and realistically tracked and managed throughout execution. For this reason, change, kill, or recover decisions are not made early enough.
- Most organizations promote proficient technicians instead of developing needed project management skills. Many organizations have raised a crop of project managers who are administrative in outlook—reactive managers who merely report trouble after it has occurred, rather than being able to take responsibility for outcomes and act to resolve problems.
- Executive support for projects and understanding of projects is lacking in many organizations, and there is a high correlation between lack of clear project sponsorship and failure.

Many of the best practices for preventing failures are directly related to a strategic PMO (SPMO):

- A repository for best practices in planning, estimating, risk assessment, scope containment, skills tracking, time and project reporting, the SPMO maintains and supports best practices for the project manager, providing the organization consistency in project performance.
- Project managers must be competent. They must be able to define requirements, estimate resources and schedule their delivery, budget and manage costs, motivate teams, resolve conflicts, negotiate external resources, manage contracts, assess and reduce risks, and adhere to standard methodology and quality processes. Such project managers are grown in an environment that trains, mentors, and rewards them based on performance in projects—an environment best created under the oversight of the SPMO.
- Project metrics and milestones must be defined, measured, and reported in a consistent manner. Setting up such processes is a core activity of the SPMO.
- Critical dates must be monitored via enterprise time-tracking software—usually web-based for ease of use. This is a necessity for larger projects, multiproject environments, and dispersed project teams. Enterprise-wide software implementation and multiproject oversight cannot be well managed except by a PMO.
- Projects must be carried out in a standard, published way, with a project methodology that sets planning and control standards, review points, the nature and frequency of project management meetings, and change control procedures.
- Enterprises should harvest best practices and lessons learned, and identify reuse opportunities in order to lay the groundwork for future success.

- Project portfolio management—the systematic selection, prioritization, and evaluation of projects across the enterprise—cannot be effectively engaged in without an SPMO.

Most organizations have approached bringing project management into their organization by implementing enterprise project management software tools or launching a training program. The frequent failure of these one-dimensional approaches has shown that implementing project management is a multifaceted initiative that involves a combination of processes, skills building, enabling tools, as well as organizational and change agents. To succeed, these types of initiatives require the organization, coordination, and sponsorship of an enterprise-level PMO.

"Project sponsors and managers need 'islands of stability' to guide teams and to ensure the integration of project deliverables into the organization," write Comninos and Verwey in the *Management Services* journal. "Without this stability, project results will not align with organization strategy and stakeholder expectations. Project participants and stakeholders will have difficulty comprehending the project's contribution to the organization's vision, resulting in unproductive activity and high levels of de-motivation and frustration" (Comninos and Verwey, 2002).

The elements of stability—a sustainable corporate strategy, a project management culture, capable and adequate human capital to deliver results, and a clear link between project activities and strategy—is achievable. However, it won't be achievable by a fragmented organization in which projects are one problem, strategy another, and human resources something separate. The strategic project office offers the hope of creating the island of stability in today's chaotic organizational life. However, all the organizational-improvement potential of the SPMO that we have discussed in this chapter is dependent on the knowledge and skills of project managers, team members, and other project personnel. Therefore, resource management within the strategic PMO is the keystone to realizing the business potential of project management.

Functions and Roles of the Strategic Project Office

There are seven primary components to any PMO, which grow in capability and complexity as the PMO takes on more strategic responsibilities and morphs into an SPMO, as described in our 2007 book, *Seven Steps to Strategy Execution*:

1. *Processes, standards, and methodologies*: A primary role is as developer and maintainer of the processes and methodologies pertaining to the management of projects as well as the management of strategy. It serves as a central library for these standards, and the expert on their deployment. The SPMO also incorporates lessons learned on projects nearing completion into the project

management methodology. As the keeper of these standards, the PMO also maintains the templates, forms, and checklists developed to ease the paper-work burden on project managers, teams, and executives.

The methods and standards function may also serve as a quality audit and continuous improvement function for project management. Methodologists understand what should be done in terms of methodology and process and can audit whether or not it is being done and, if so, whether or not it is showing value and productivity.

2. Project managers and project support staff: The SPMO takes charge of the development of professional, proactive managers. Initially, the SPMO must aggressively follow a three-point strategy for getting top-flight project manag-ers in place: new project managers may be hired or contracted, and personnel with promise may be developed within the organization. Coordinating both the efforts and the development of project managers from diverse sources is a critical role.

In the fully deployed SPMO, project managers actually report to the SPMO and are deployed to projects either as full-time managers or on a part-time basis. The SPMO maintains a database of project managers, their skill sets, capabilities, specialties, experience, and technical skills. New projects can be staffed from this database, while project managers between full-time assign-ments work on special projects such as developing new processes, method-ologies, techniques, templates, and capabilities. A highly competent project manager is too valuable to be idle just because he or she is between projects. This infrastructure development aspect of the SPO allows the organization to derive full value from a project manager's expertise and experience as well as avoid the high cost of turnover.

In the recent past, it was rare for SPMOs to maintain and manage their own project management staff. However, the past few years have seen a significant trend in this direction. It is only logical that as organizations move further and further away from the functional organization and ad hoc projects, project expertise becomes more centralized. Today, the most successful organizations are those with enterprise SPOs that manage a staff of project managers and project support roles. In fact, organizations identified as high performers by the *State of the PMO 2007* study have larger PMOs (30 percent more staff) and rely on more specialized roles (i.e., they have more staff performing those roles), including mentors (a 136 percent increase over low-performing organi-zations), team leads (467 percent increase), planners (147 percent increase), controllers (116 percent increase) and relationship managers (698 percent in-crease). And, the more mature the PMO, the more planners, schedulers, and controllers they employ: at Level 4 maturity (utilizing PM Solutions' Project Management Maturity Model), they have 70 percent more of these positions than do Level 3 maturity PMOs. This inference is underscored by the fact that the most mature ones in the study showed the greatest improvements in performance metrics. PMOs at Level 3 maturity showed a 16 percent budget or schedule performance improvement compared to those without a PMO, and an 8 percent improvement over those assessed at Level 2 maturity.

3. *Training and professional development*: One of the biggest challenges in most organizations is that they have subject matter experts (technology gurus in IT organizations; clinical experts in pharmaceutical research and development organizations), but few professional project managers who are skilled in the disciplines of project management (planning, scheduling, communicating to uncover problems, resolving and removing problems, reworking the project, and communicating with stakeholders to meet objectives). The SPMO is the center of focus for project manager and team training and development. It identifies competencies needed by high-performance project managers and for executive awareness and team member participation. The SPMO participates with a specialized project management training vendor, typically in tailoring standardized courses around the culture and methodologies that apply specifically to the organization. Just as important as contracting for training is the development of promising project managers into high-performance project managers. Such professional development includes training, but begins with identifying project manager competencies, and then hiring for or identifying those competencies in-house, creating performance metrics that reward project managers for the right behaviors, and so on.

4. *Project support*: With an appropriate level of technical support, project managers can focus on the things on which they can have a greater impact. In a fully staffed SPMO, the project support group performs the science of project management as opposed to the art. They are responsible for estimating and budgeting, including cost estimating and capital estimating. They develop plans and schedules and provide status updates, pulling data from time collection, timesheets, and the financial system to update the status against the plan. They perform variance analysis, and are also critical to change control.

Project support also entails keeping a project repository, which may be as simple as a book or as complex as a knowledge management system. Project support also maintains issues tracking and handles progress reports. Therefore, the project support organization is responsible for the executive dashboard. Project support acts as a resource broker with functional heads to ensure that the right resources are working on the right projects at the right time.

If the organization does not have direct access to cost information at the project level (through integrated enterprise-wide software), a lot of legwork is required to provide project managers with current, accurate, and complete cost information. Members of the project support team within the SPMO literally mine the cost-tracking information they need from available data sources.

These metric-tracking responsibilities reflect the performance management role of the SPMO—tracking and evaluating not only project performance, but also portfolio performance.

Finally, project support handles all issues surrounding the project management software support—a category of responsibility so large we have also named it one of the central components of the SPMO.

5. *Software tools:* The SPMO centralizes the establishment and maintenance of project-related software tools, maintains project management software standards, and acquires project management software and supporting software (time-collection software, time-reporting software, configuration control software, documentation software, knowledge management software, database software, spreadsheets, and other applications). The project support group identifies software, facilitates or performs the integration and use of software, and maintains and monitors its performance. Where other enterprise applications are in use to the extent that their functionalities play a role in strategy deployment, the SPMO may also have an IT oversight role.

6. *Mentoring and coaching:* When another department in the enterprise wants to manage a project themselves, the SPMO can provide expert assistance in the form of mentoring and coaching for the staff involved. This also provides an audit function for existing projects to determine how effectively the project management process is being utilized within the organization.

The entire organization should view the SPMO as a source of experts with focused ability in project management. When a project needs additional oversight and guidance to achieve project recovery, the mentor can help develop workaround plans, new estimates of cost, resource reallocations, and replanning. Finally, mentors and coaches from the SPMO are the logical personnel to do project assessments or audits.

In sum, the role of project mentors and coaches is to transfer the knowledge they have developed to project managers and project teams to enable them to better perform on current and future projects. Knowledge transfer is the key, since mentors are not provided on a continual basis.

7. *Portfolio management:* As a central clearinghouse for project information, the PMO is the owner of the portfolio management process, coordinating between project level and portfolio level to make sure that decision makers have the best information in the most accessible format. The investment decisions reflected in the portfolio form the blueprint for the work carried out by the project managers and teams within (or mentored by) the PMO.

Project portfolio management (PPM) provides a consistent way to evaluate, select, prioritize, budget for, and plan for the right projects—those that offer the greatest value and contribution to the strategic interests of the organization (Dye and Pennypacker, 1999). Doing the right thing starts with developing a strategic focus and ends with project selection; that is PPM. Doing the right things *right* (and quickly) is project management.

But you can't manage what you can't measure, as the old saying goes, and unless all the projects on the table can be held up to the light and compared to each other, a company has no way of managing them strategically, no way of making intelligent resource allocation decisions, and no way of knowing what to delete and what to add. Project portfolio management brings order to this situation in two important ways:

1. It brings realism to an organization's planning processes by aligning what an organization *wants* to do with the resources—the money, hours, people, time, and equipment—with what is required to *get it done*.
2. It brings rationality to the allocation of resources, both human and financial.

While most decision making on the project level is concerned with tactical issues (*how can we do this thing right?*), decision making on the portfolio level is concerned with strategic issues (*how can we be sure we are doing the right things?*) Today's emphasis on PPM is part of a general trend toward systems thinking in organizational life. Instead of tweaking the parts (individual projects, departments, or processes), systems theory encourages us to look first at the whole: the enterprise. PPM provides a solution to many of the problems that commonly plague projects and the companies that depend on them:

> *Project failure*—Applying PPM to projects helps to resolve some of the key issues that lead to project failure. Of the top ten factors leading to project failure, five—incomplete requirements; lack of user involvement; lack of resources; unrealistic expectations; and lack of executive support—are addressed by the implementation of a system that engages corporate leadership in a structured process of selecting and prioritizing projects.
>
> One immediate benefit of PPM is the ability to choose and prioritize projects in such a way that responsible decisions can be made regarding which projects to kill and when. Jim Johnson, chairman of the Standish Group, has identified portfolio management as *the* process that can make the difference in project success. Said Johnson, "Companies need a process for taking a regular look at their portfolio of projects and deciding, again and again, if the investment is going to pay off. As it stands now, for most companies, projects can take on a life of their own" (Johnson, 1999).
>
> Johnson stressed that continuous self-assessment should be built in, allowing earlier kill decisions on failing projects, with the associated cost savings. This frees up money and personnel for dedication to projects that are worth pursuing. Killing a project, said Johnson, should be seen as "successful resource management, not as an admission of failure" (Cooper, Edgett, and Kleinschmid, 1998).

Financial performance—Proper portfolio management results in bottom-line yields—another reason why it is important for the executive level to champion this process. And project portfolio management should be an easy sell: Research by Cooper, Edgett, and Klienschmidt reveals that for research and development portfolios, the top 20 percent of companies had an explicit, established method of portfolio management, consistently applied across the organization. The same research showed that even rudimentary portfolio management processes created a spike of benefits almost immediately. Of those in the top 20 percent, about 70 percent had used the portfolio management method for more than two years. So, even businesses that are relatively new to portfolio management begin to see positive results quickly.

Time to market—Toney and Powers found that in large functional organizations that implement a project management group and its corollary practices (including portfolio management), lead times to market have been reduced by as much as 60 percent, development costs have declined, quality has improved, and forecasting accuracy has increased (Toney, 2001).

Risk management—In addition, assessing and managing risk becomes easier within the context of a project portfolio, according to research by E. L Jarrett (Jarrett, 2000). To deal with any significant risk, there must be diversification, along with other kinds of balance to ensure enterprise continuity and health, such as investing in lower-risk projects that provide a near-certain return, or investing in higher-risk projects, the path to extraordinary returns.

Apolitical decision making—Jim Johnson has observed: "All failures are political. When projects are selected and planned in an ad hoc, chaotic environment, objectivity about value goes out the window." Johnson stressed that having a standard methodology helps to take the politics out of decision making. "Instead of opinion, we have process" (Johnson, 1999). A *Research Technology Management* article listed the factors that can delay—or conceal—the need to terminate projects. First on the list was "personal pride" (Jarrett, 2000). PPM methodology cleans up the project selection process by offering a checklist of criteria for project approval.

Chunking for success—Big projects, simply, are more prone to failure. Jim Johnson credited the rising project success rate to "very small projects that get going very quickly . . . you get to the important milestones very quickly . . . if you are failing you can tell quickly if you need to kill it. You can act to save time, money and resources." A *CIO Magazine* article described the process necessary to reorganize around small projects: reframing big initiatives as a series of smaller, $1 million to $2 million initiatives, but warned that this cannot happen in the absence of a PPM methodology (Cramm, 2002).

Better asset management—PPM is simply managing your assets. In a way, the project management language (or angle) on portfolio management is a distraction; portfolio management has less to do with project management skills and more to do with strategic planning. Of course, in order to make sound decisions on a portfolio level, decision makers must have sound information on the project and program level.

Better resource management—Even if your company has not been downsizing in search of short-term profits, top-performing subject matter experts are not exactly a dime a dozen. How can you make sure your smartest people are working on your top-priority activities? This is a two-sided issue: one side impacts corporate profitability and the other impacts employee morale (which, by the way, impacts corporate profitability, according to RHI's Human Capital Index) (Watson Wyatt, 2010).

Achieving strategic goals—Ideally, an organization would conceive of, fund, plan, and monitor its projects through a strategic lens. Without such a holistic view, it is easy to have lots of activity going on without much of it being of real value. (Value is not necessarily profit, but can include the development of intellectual capital, the improvement of public image, or movement toward a long-term evolution into a new kind of business.) Mistakes, innovations, even losses can all come into focus through this lens. For project-oriented companies, that lens is PPM.

Although PPM has long languished within IT departments among "those project management types," there is simply no way for top-level corporate leadership to hand off leadership on the project portfolio management issue. That's because choosing the groups of activities that create value is inherently a strategic activity. And, the basic issues that arise when developing a portfolio management system (not a software system, but a collection of processes—a PPM methodology) are issues that touch on organizational development. Jim and David Matheson identified some of the issues as:

- How can we aggregate our opportunities into manageable strategic projects?
- Who is the overall process owner? Who will facilitate the analytical process?

- How do we get top management and project leadership to buy in to the results?
- How will business and marketing units interact in the process? Should we use one cross-functional decision team for the whole portfolio, divide responsibilities by business or technical areas, or use a multilevel review structure (Matheson and Matheson, 2008)?

These are not project management questions. The management of the corporate portfolio of projects is a strategic management issue. In summary, project portfolio management provides a consistent way to evaluate, prioritize, select, budget for, and plan the right projects—those that offer the greatest value and contribution to the strategic interests of the organization. When used effectively, portfolio management ensures that projects are aligned with corporate strategies and priorities, that the portfolio contains the right mix of projects, and that resource allocation is optimized. It is the practice that bridges the gap between the executive decision process and project execution.

In high-performing organizations, the SPMO owns the PPM process (Pennypacker, 2008). It ensures that an organization's projects are linked to strategic plans. It may be involved in facilitating the prioritization and project selection processes, and typically is intimately involved in resource allocation decisions. The SPMO also coordinates tracking of the current portfolio, analyzes portfolio performance, and is instrumental in administering the stage-gate process for all projects. As of 2010, well over half of all PMOs are now involved in all phases of portfolio management, from facilitating executive involvement to tracking portfolio results (PM Solutions Research, 2010).

Portfolio management begins with the selection of the portfolio. Just as it is beyond the scope and charter of individual project managers to manage a portfolio of projects, it is beyond the scope of a divisional project office to manage a corporate-wide portfolio. That leads to the need for a strategic PMO and is, in fact, one of the primary reasons for the existence of the SPMO. The SPMO is the voice of the projects on the executive-level steering committee that must decide which of the many opportunities to pursue with the limited amount of resources. The decision of which projects to authorize is complex and depends on a number of factors, such as return on investment, fit with the current portfolio, desire to introduce a new product line, availability of resources, and many others. This is a classic executive decision involving many decision criteria and alternatives. The first task for the committee is to select a decision support tool to help organize and simplify the decision process. This can be done via a proprietary tool or with commercially available software decision tools. The important thing is not the method, but the organizational will to organize around strategy execution.

The SPMO is the optimum organizational solution for aligning projects to strategy and tracking project and portfolios to ensure they continue to meet the needs of the business, even as these needs continue to change over time. It serves as the critical link between business strategy and execution of tactical plans.

The literature on project portfolio management—while vast compared to what was out there even three years ago—is still new enough to be confusing, and in many cases, full of untried optimism and untested theories. Writers stumble over each other to offer the three elements, four phases, five steps, and so on. From the executive leadership point of view, all these checklists miss the point. The question that must be addressed when an organization commits to PPM is not merely which tools to buy or which mental model to use. It is a question of maturity: only organizations mature enough in project management practice to implement a PMO can succeed at portfolio management; and only mature strategic PMOs fully realize the strategy-execution promise of PPM.

Best Practices in Organizational Structure

The *Strategy & Projects* study carried out by PM Solutions' research arm found that there were two practices related to organizational structure that set high-performing companies apart from the rest:

- The enterprise project office allows the organization to manage its entire collection of projects as one or more interrelated portfolios
- The company has an organizational structure (strategic project office, office of strategy management, strategic steering committee, etc.) that is responsible for managing strategy execution

Other identified best practices for organizational structure were:

- A strategic (enterprise) project office plays a role in linking the organization's projects to its strategic plans.
- The organizational structure is flexible and adaptable to today's dynamic, rapidly changing business environments.
- Project management is clearly established and embedded within the organization's business management structure.
- Information about strategy and projects flows freely between business units facilitating strategy execution.

The most often used practice by high-performing organizations is having project management clearly established and embedded within the organization's business management structure.

Organizations that have put a strategic PMO in place can congratulate themselves, but, as James P. Lewis noted in *The Project Manager's Desk Reference,* "To expect that the design of an organization is finished 'once-and-for-all' is to limit ourselves to new possibilities and also to freeze our response capability in the face of changes that make the old design obsolete. It is better to regard design work as a part of regular operations and not a separate front-end activity."

Lewis recommends setting goals for people development so that appropriate skills and flexibility are generated to respond to the changing environment. If project office staff keeps up with the latest developments of project management practice by monitoring project management and industry literature and keeping training fresh, the SPMO will exhibit an execution excellence culture and model it for the rest of the organization.

Author Biography

J. Kent Crawford, PMP, is founder and CEO of Project Management Solutions (PM Solutions), a project management firm helping organizations execute, govern, and measure their portfolios to improve business performance. The company specializes in applying project and portfolio management processes and practices to drive operational efficiency for its clients. Prior to establishing PM Solutions, Mr. Crawford served as a president and chairman of the Project Management Institute (PMI®). Mr. Crawford is a recipient of the PMI® Fellow Award and the award-winning author of *The Strategic Project Office: A Guide to Improving Organizational Performance* (for which he won the 2002 David I. Cleland Project Management Literature Award from PMI), *Project Management Maturity Model: Providing a Proven Path to Project Management Excellence, Second Edition*, and *Optimizing Human Capital with a Strategic Project Office*. His latest book, *Seven Steps to Strategy Execution*, provides the framework for organizations to execute and deliver corporate strategy through the use of strategy performance management. A prolific speaker, Mr. Crawford has served as a presenter and keynote at events such as the PMI® Global Congress, ProjectWorld, Strategy & Projects Summit, and the PMO Symposium. He also leads the *Ultimate PMO* course as part of PMI's popular SeminarsWorld program.

References

Comninos, D., and Verwey, A. 2002. Business-focused project management, *Management Services* (January).

Cooper, R. G., Edgett, S. J., and Kleinschmidt, E. J. 1998. *Portfolio Management for New Products.* Reading, MA: Perseus Books.

Cramm, S. 2002. Organizational physics, *CIO* (August).

Crawford, J. K., and Cabanis-Brewin, J. 2005. *Optimizing Human Capital with a Strategic Project Office*, Auerbach Books.

Dye, L. D., and Pennypacker, J. S. 1999. *Project Portfolio Management: Selecting and prioritizing projects for competitive advantage.* West Chester, PA: Center for

Business Practices. (Note: The Center for Business Practices is now known as PM Solutions' Research.)

Gibbons, J. 2006. Employee Engagement: A review of current research and its implications. *The Conference Board of Canada* (November).

Grant, R. M. 2007. *Contemporary Strategy Analysis*. Malden, MA: Blackwell Publishing.

Jarrett, E. L. 2000. The role of risk in business decision-making, or how to stop worrying and love the bombs, *Research Technology Management* (November).

Johnson, J. 1999. Turning CHAOS into SUCCESS. *Software* (December).

Kaplan, R. S., and Norton, D. P. 2001. *The Strategy-Focused Organization*. Harvard Business School Press.

Matheson, J., and Matheson, D. 1998.*The Smart Organization: Creating value through strategic R&D*. Harvard Business School Press.

Pennypacker, J. S. 2000. *The Value of Project Management*. Center for Business Practices.

Pennypacker, J. S. 2006. *Project Management: The State of the Industry*. Center for Business Practices.

Pennypacker, J. S. 2008. *The State of the PMO, 2007 - 2008*, Center for Business Practices.

PM Solutions Research. 2010. *The State of the PMO 2010*. Glen Mills, PA: PM Solutions.

Sauer, C., et al.1999. Where Project Managers are Kings, *Project Management Journal* (December).

Toney, F. 2001. *The Superior Project Organization: Global competency standards and best practices*. New York: Marcel Dekker and the Center for Business Practices.

Watson Wyatt. The Human Capital Index. http://www.watsonwyatt.com/research/resrender.asp?id=w-488&page=1 (accessed Feb. 2010).

6

Partnership, Persuasion, and Politics

Paul Risk, PMP

Introduction

The road to partnership is like the road to hell—paved with good intentions and littered with careers. To be effective, a project management professional must position himself or herself between information technology (IT) and the business and foster partnership—without getting in the way.

Partnership is vital to aligning the strategic goals and direction of the business units, IT, the project management office (PMO), and the enterprise as a whole, and is essential to long-term success. Without partnership, the PMO and the business can find themselves in disagreement, or worse, see each other as adversaries. True partnership can take a long and often tortuous path, and cannot be achieved in a single step. It cannot be directed and is not as simple as saying, "Let's be best friends." It cannot even be forged over happy hour.

As project management professionals, we often focus on the tangible—demonstrating value, having cutting-edge tools, using the best methodologies, and delivering outstanding results. Yet these factors do not always ensure success. Long-term, repeatable success depends on having true and stable partnerships in place with key stakeholders and business units throughout the organization. It sounds simple enough, yet can be agonizingly elusive.

To truly shape partnership, one also needs to learn and master the other two Ps—*persuasion* and *politics*. Establishing effective partnership is not possible without understanding—and mastering—the roles persuasion and politics play. Through a simple roadmap for establishing partnership, you will learn how the PMO and the project manager (PM) can engage the business and IT, tactically and strategically, to forge an effective and enduring partnership. We will discuss common obstacles from the political to the emotional, and how to overcome them.

How Partnership is Traditionally Established

How does one go about establishing partnership? There are several common techniques. One is the *vendor approach*. Invariably, when meeting with a vendor, contractor, or other person or company attempting to sell you some kind of service or product, the vendor will mention how much he or she looks forward to "a long partnership" with your organization. Compare this corporate approach to a personal one: you are in a social setting and a stranger (or someone you barely know) walks up to you and, after a few minutes of chatting, asks you to be his or her partner. Your initial reaction will almost always be negative. Yet we put up with this sort of behavior from vendors, almost without question, and often without enough skepticism.

Another technique is called the *contractual approach*. In this approach, teams of lawyers write up a contract detailed enough to attempt to foresee and premediate every possible conflict or dispute. Invariably, the one dispute that comes up is something that neither team's lawyers had thought of. Compare this approach to a personal one: no one likes to prenegotiate a relationship; it doesn't feel right and seldom works. Interestingly many corporate relationships in the United States use this approach in varying degrees. The contract comes first, and the relationship follows—or so they hope. Contrast this approach to Japan, where a contract is rarely entered into unless a substantial relationship has already been established. The contract simply spells out what both parties already know.

And, finally, there is the *natural approach*—building a relationship one step at a time. Successful sales people use this approach. They spend time with their clients and prospects even when no sale is on the horizon. The relationship is built up over many meetings and lunches, one block at a time. It is this approach that one must use to forge successful partnerships between the PMO and the business areas.

The Role of Partnership

Partnership is the glue that holds business relationships together. Without it, long-term cooperation between the business and PMO is virtually impossible. Since nature abhors a vacuum, some kind of relationship must fill the void. If the PMO and the business are not partners, then what are they—friends or adversaries? Most often, the absence of partnership produces an environment conducive to less-than-ideal relationships. In the best scenario, an uneasy truce emerges, with neither side trusting the other. In the worst case, the PMO (or IT) and the business actively compete and see each other as enemies. This type of relationship is not really tenable in the long term, and is not conducive to any sort of good business practice. Projects suffer, morale declines, finger-pointing ensues, and nobody wins.

How to Build the Partnership Pyramid

In the corporate world, partnership is built on two key building blocks—*trust* and *respect*. It is impossible to have a partnership without both of these elements. Think back to your personal relationships. If you were asked to identify two key words to describe your relationship with your significant other, trust and respect would be at the top of the list (love would also likely be there, but in corporate America, it is not necessary to love your business partner). The two go hand in hand; it is hard to trust someone you do not respect, and you cannot really respect someone you do not trust.

While it is easy to say that trust and respect are key to partnership, how does one go about building trust and earning respect? Again, thinking back to your own relationships, the keys are communication, visibility (or transparency), and execution. You expect your significant other to communicate openly with you, to not keep secrets, and to be a good, reliable partner. Similarly, a successful PMO communicates clearly (and often), is transparent in its dealings and operations, and executes well.

So, how do we communicate, execute, and stay transparent? We do the things that PMOs do. We educate, govern, provide oversight, establish methodologies, measure performance, and a whole host of other things. But instead of doing each of these in a vacuum, we do them together, knitted in a tight fabric, with an eye toward influencing people's opinions and establishing partnership, rather than just performing singular tasks or projects.

Foundation

In the physical world, pyramids are built from the ground up, not from the top down. In the project management world, to reach the pinnacle of true partnership, we must start by laying a foundation as illustrated in Figure 6.1. In most organizations, the PMO or IT already does most of the activities described. However, most are done individually, with no central focus or greater goal envisioned. For example, the PMO provides project oversight because that is just what a PMO does; it is our job. However, the thinking and rationale should extend beyond the mere task of providing oversight and excellent project results. The thinking should go something like, "If we provide consistent project oversight, it will lead to better execution. The business will respect us because we deliver results. They will trust us because we deliver them consistently. If they trust and respect us, they will partner with us."

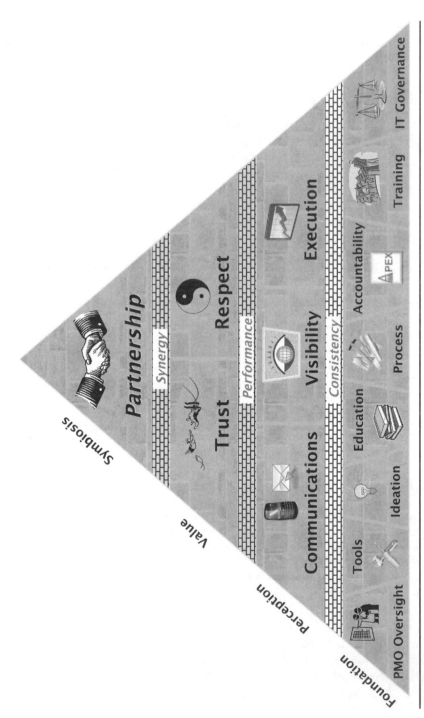

Figure 6.1   Partnership pyramid.

One item to note is that the building blocks do not all aim influence in the same direction. Some are directed at the PMO and IT. Some are aimed at the business. Some are aimed at both, and some seek influence from the business, as illustrated in Figure 6.2.

Oversight

The pyramid foundation in Figure 6.2 illustrates eight foundation building blocks. The two cornerstones are *oversight* and *governance*. Let us start with oversight. If there is one thing that most PMOs do well instinctively, it is manage projects. And while successful project execution—and all that goes with it—is the primary goal of many, there is a key secondary goal that is often of much interest to the business: consistency. Business areas like stability from their support organizations. By providing consistency in the project management process and outputs—consistency in areas such as communications, project management style, issues and risk management and reporting, to name but a few—the business learns to trust the quality of the PMO's product. Naturally, there will be some level of variance in the skill level of the project managers. However the PMO should do certain things to smooth out the variances, and to all outward appearances, have a fairly consistent group of project managers. Most of what is described here is the PMO's bread and butter, but it bears repeating.

Be leaders—Project managers are leaders by definition. However, the PMO should strive to take a leadership role in the organization, not just in IT but in the enterprise, and take a big-picture approach. This means taking some political risks, which we will detail later in this chapter.

Meet with PMs regularly—This should go without saying, but it is important to meet with the project managers as a group for several reasons.

1. To see what is going on
2. So the project managers know what is going on in other projects, even though it may not have a direct impact on their projects
3. To encourage coherence among the project managers

Meet with the business units regularly—It is informative to meet with the business areas regularly, even when there is not a big project going on, to get their pulse on the PMO and the project managers in general. Meeting with business units regularly enables them to:

- Establish regular checkpoints along the way to monitor project health and team performance
- Regularly monitor project collaboration sites
- Supply methods, techniques, and advice
- Enforce consistency across projects
- Be an objective party that both IT and business can come to with suggestions, compliments, and concerns

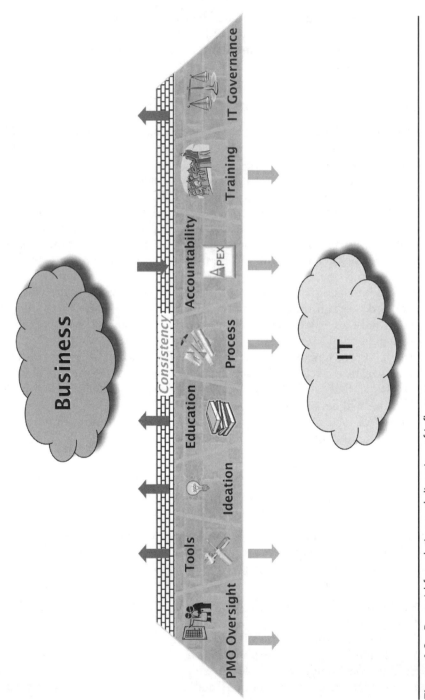

Figure 6.2　Pyramid foundation and direction of influence.

Tools

Whether your PMO has a state-of-the-art project and portfolio management (PPM) system or still manages resources using a whiteboard, some level of automation and technology is necessary. If you already have a PPM tool, refamiliarize yourself with it. Ask yourself a few basic questions:

- Is use of the tool aligned with the goals and functions of the PMO, and with the business as a whole?
- Does reporting from the tool give meaningful, insightful, and actionable information?
- Is it properly scaled to meet the demands of the organization?
- Does the tool support the PMO, or is the PMO supporting the tool?

If your organization does not have a tool, or uses the X:\ drive, the PM's laptop, or a shared flash drive as a makeshift collaboration site, the PMO should embark on getting some kind of automation. The tool should be scaled to fit the organization, and reflect an incremental step forward from the current status quo. It should be evolutionary, not revolutionary. The reason for this is that while an IT group might be willing to try something new and flashy, most business users will not. A tool can introduce a host of new processes, which take users time to adapt to. Culturally, the organization may not accept such a drastic change in a short period. Make sure the change of pace that a new tool introduces is not much faster than the pace at which the organization normally operates.

There are many vendors available who offer PPM tools. When embarking on a PPM selection project, follow these rules of thumb:

- Start small and work your way up
- Leverage what you already have
- Take incremental steps forward
- Encourage everyone on the project (IT, business, and vendor) to use the tool and contribute
- Do not get bogged down in a big PPM project that distracts from the goal of partnership
- Get IT and the PMO behind it first, or the business will never go along
- Remember that a key goal is to provide consistency and transparency

At a minimum, the right tools must do a few things:

- Allow you to manage project objects (issues, risks, deliverables, change requests, etc.)
- Handle resource management
- Manage finances and time tracking
- Facilitate reporting on each project and across projects—up, down, and across the organization

- Be a central repository to store project stuff
- Embrace simple tools like SharePoint or robust tools like a full-blown PPM tool
- Do not limit your tools to using an "X:\ drive", the PM's laptop, or a shared flash drive
- Do not forget integration; your tools can also be leveraged for communications, calendaring, and collaboration

Consider the tools from multiple perspectives:

- Project manager
- IT management
- Business users
- Business unit management
- PMO
- Being able to demonstrate value and report on data
- Being able to manage key performance indicators

Ideation

Unfortunately, in too many organizations, the PMO acts as a glorified order-taker. The business decides it wants a new system (accounting, sales, retail, etc.), perhaps does some research, maybe even signs a contract with a vendor, and then asks the PMO to install it. Conversely, some business units take a minimalist approach—simply asking the PMO or IT to deliver a new system and leaving it to the PMO to decide what is needed.

Neither approach is very good. The process shown in Figure 6.3 represents a common approach. The entire initiation phase of the project is handled by the business, without input from IT. As a result, it is less likely to be a comprehensive solution, and will likely be more expensive than anticipated by the business since IT costs will not have been thoroughly analyzed.

A better approach is represented as shown in Figure 6.4. IT and the business work together at the very inception of the project to refine the idea and integrate technology upfront. The result is almost always a better solution for the business. Surprises and risks are reduced, weak ideas are killed off early, and approved projects have a better likelihood of success.

It is important to note that of the eight foundational building blocks in the partnership pyramid, ideation is the only one that directly seeks partnership as a goal. It is a direct appeal to the business units to work with the PMO. Be sure to line up high-level support before publicizing an ideation process.

Having gone through this exercise with the business, it is important to note that just because an idea has been vetted doesn't mean it will (or should) become a project. Projects compete for resources, and it is incumbent on the PMO to have a way to objectively prioritize competing projects, even if it is unofficial.

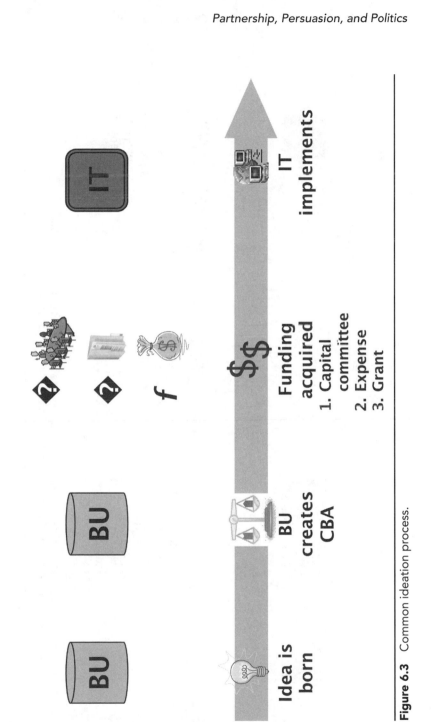

Figure 6.3   Common ideation process.

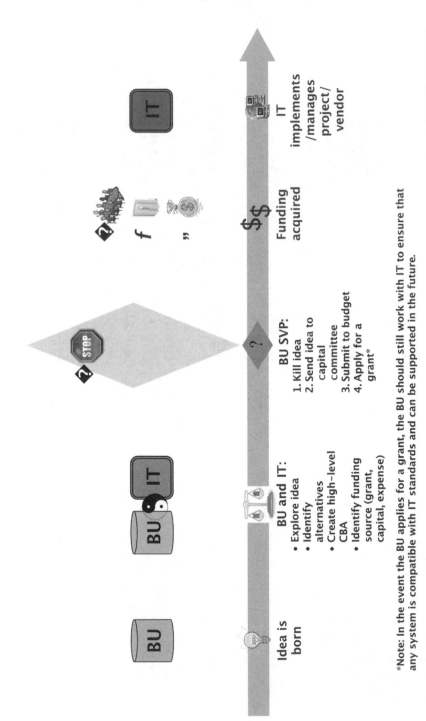

Figure 6.4   Preferred ideation process.

*Note: In the event the BU applies for a grant, the BU should still work with IT to ensure that any system is compatible with IT standards and can be supported in the future.

A common method is to build a project comparison model. Use of a model helps depoliticize the project selection process. There are many such scoring models commercially and publicly available. Whichever one you choose, follow a few simple rules:

- It must be able to objectively compare projects
- It should score projects based on the benefit to the enterprise as a whole, using metrics that are easily recognizable to all parts of the organization
- Keep it simple

One model, as an example, scores projects on two axes, risk versus impact, each scaled from 0 to 100. The *impact* questions revolve mostly around the benefit to the business, such as justification, number of affected end-users, customers, or business areas, and estimated time. It also asks and scores normally subjective questions, such as public relations impact, political interest by high-ranking executives, etc. The *risk* questions focus on project implementation—cost, number of resources, number of interfaces, data conversion or migration, etc. The subjective questions focus on ongoing maintenance, skill sets, third-party support, etc.

The results are displayed in a four-quadrant graph as illustrated in Figure 6.5 and are displayed in a simple form that is familiar to most people. The model also computes an impact-to-risk ratio, so the whole model can be boiled down to a single number, which is also easy to understand and compare across projects.

If the PMO can encourage the use of a scoring model within the business areas to assist with project prioritization, so much the better. Even if it cannot, such a model is useful within the PMO so that it can have an objective idea of the value of projects and their relative worth to the enterprise as a whole.

Education

One of the issues IT and the PMO often face is a fundamental lack of understanding among business users of what, exactly, IT does. IT is often a mystery to the business. We speak our own language and tend to think in terms of technology. In all fairness, some people in technology like maintaining an aura of mystery. However, in order to effectively communicate with the business area, IT has to be able to speak in layman's terms at the very least, and preferably the business's own language.

To this end, create an *IT Road Show*, which is essentially a presentation describing what IT does, how it does it, and most importantly, why that information is important to the business. Make the road show relevant to the business unit. Help business units become better consumers of IT services, so that they will get more satisfaction. The key objective in any road show is to demystify IT—make it relevant to the business needs (revenue, speed, productivity). Start by educating key individuals, then departments. This is a vital component to setting expectations. Keep the language simple and avoid technical jargon.

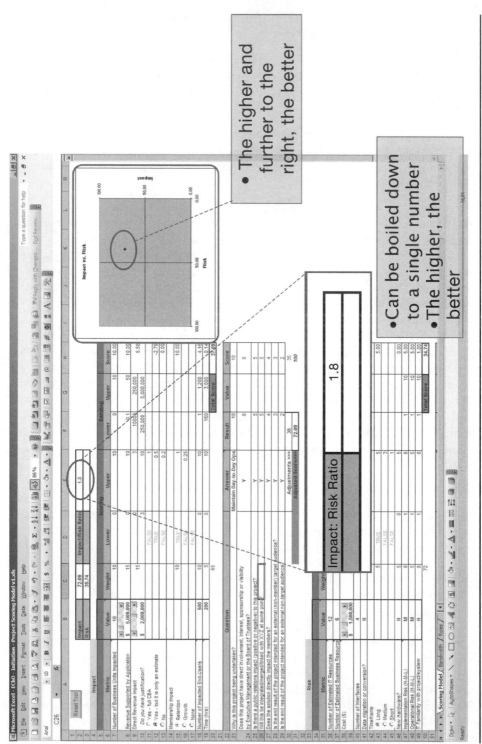

Figure 6.5 Project scoring model.

Key questions the road show must address:

- What should a business unit expect from IT?
- What should the business expect from the IT project manager?
- What should IT expect from a business area?
- How can the business become a better customer of IT services?
- What does the IT account manager (AM) or liaison do?
- How can a business unit work effectively with the AM and share a success story?

Process

Every PMO uses (or should use) some kind of methodology—scaled, sized, and adapted to fit the organization. It can be as large as major commercial methodologies or as small as a home-grown process. It can be as rigid as waterfall or as flexible as Extreme Programming. Size does not matter by itself, as long as it suits the kind of projects it is used on.

We tend to think of methodologies as processes a PM must follow to achieve a desired result. However, it is better to think of a methodology as a set of guardrails, intended to keep the project headed in the right direction and from veering off the road. With that analogy in mind, the methodology can be as wide as a six-lane highway (very flexible and lots of room to maneuver) or as narrow as a one-lane road (rigid and unforgiving). It is up to the PMO to decide which is right for the organization, project, and PM. Give your project managers enough rope to tangle themselves, but not enough to hang themselves.

Process-based methodologies:

- Improve project execution
- Reduce red tape and paperwork
- Streamline project management
- Provide for better project control
- Are tailored for use at your company

Accountability

Incorporate methodologies into project managers' annual goals by:

- Tying project performance directly to annual results
- Including a customer satisfaction survey on all post-project reviews; it should be part of the evaluation process filled out by the sponsors
- Closing the loop that began with the project charter—the sponsor gave the PM authority to execute the project; now the sponsor evaluates how well the PM performed

Area	Very dissatisfied			Very satisfied
How satisfied are you with:				
Project planning					X
General project management				X	
Communications				X	
Issue and risk management				X	
Resource management				X	
Cost management				X	
Vendor management				X	
Time management				X	
Change management			X		
Overall product quality				X	
Final score: 4.00					

Figure 6.6   Satisfaction survey.

The sample survey shown in Figure 6.6 may look somewhat familiar. In this particular case, the format and scoring was borrowed from a survey that the help desk uses, thus it was familiar to users as just another version of a survey they already use.

Training

Technology changes quickly. It is important to keep the IT and PMO staff at the forefront of technology, so that they can make informed business decisions regarding which technology to use for solving business challenges. While some training (particularly certain technical courses or certifications) can be expensive, there are also low- or no-cost alternatives. In any case, and regardless of your budget, follow a few simple rules in regards to training the IT and PMO staff:

- Commit to educating the PMs
- Encourage (or require) PMs to sit for the PMP® Exam
- Conduct periodic training sessions for all PMs
- Share best practices
- Encourage peer presentations on projects, issues, risks, etc.

- Encourage PMs to move outside their comfort zone
- Try to foster cohesion among the PMs

Governance and Compliance

An IT department without good policies and governance is an IT department which will get steamrolled by the business every time. Borrow a page from human resources (HR) and finance, and set out a clear list of policies and procedures for IT and the PMO. IT policies should clearly outline its principles, positions, and direction on all matters relating to technology and projects. They provide guidelines to the acquisition, implementation, and use of technology at the company, and act as a roadmap and strategy for the IT department and technology in general.

Understand that you will be asserting authority and control over other parts of the enterprise. Approximately 80 percent of the policies will be clearly within the purview of the IT department. The remaining 20 percent will cross a boundary into other areas, and will require some high-level negotiating in order to implement.

The PMO is an ideal starting point because it has visibility into all of IT as well as the business. Implementing sound policies and a governance plan has significant benefits to IT and the PMO, such as:

- Establishing governance and compliance within IT
- Enforcing understanding of strategy and priorities
- Positioning IT and PMO as contributors to corporate governance
- Enabling IT and PMO to act as vanguards, establishing both infrastructure and methods of control
- Guiding discussions of IT's strategic role
- Serving as structure to understand IT and PMO contributions to corporate priorities
- Demonstrating acceptance of shared responsibility for corporate oversight

Policies can be grouped into the following six logical areas:

- IT management and leadership
- Application and business support
- Project management
- User education and support
- Architecture and infrastructure
- Systems security, integrity, and continuity

From there, policies and procedures can be further defined. One can leverage or reuse existing policies, and some policies will already exist, either in IT or in other areas (HR, legal, finance, etc.).

A good approach is to get IT leaders together in a room to define areas of responsibility and policy topics. It is critical to work closely with other areas that set policies—HR, legal, finance, etc.—and look at IT policies through their eyes. They will appreciate being involved, and can provide useful guidance on how to implement policies. Be sure to confirm the mandate and corporate characteristics with executives (general strategy, responsibilities, organization, and culture). Implementing policies is a top-down exercise, so be sure to get the people at the top involved early; they are your sponsors.

Mortar and Bricks

In the preceding section we discussed the building blocks—the bricks—of the partnership pyramid as illustrated in Figure 6.7. To take the analogy a step further, bricks requires mortar to hold them together. Pay attention to the mortar holding the blocks together.

The foundation layer has, as its mortar, *consistency*. The key goal of the foundational building blocks is to provide a level of consistency to all that IT and the PMO do. For the perception layer, *performance* is the key. Good communications, visibility, and project execution create a perception of high performance—that IT and the PMO consistently perform well. And, finally, for the value layer we have *synergy*. Business units like to work with partners who perform well and consistently. Business leaders feel that teaming with these kinds of partners leads to greater success.

Perception

Perception is often more important than reality. It is important for the PMO to accurately gage several pieces of perception and reality. In any organization, not everyone is going to get along. Individuals—and even departments—will have both friends and enemies. Opinions of IT will rarely be uniform throughout the organization. You must work to identify where your organization falls in the pro-IT versus anti-IT continuum, by department and by key individual. Who likes IT, who dislikes IT, and who merely puts up with IT. And then, it is critical to discover why. Feelings for or against the PMO or IT may or may not be personal, and this is where the politics of an organization come sharply into focus. In the first part of this chapter, we discussed building the foundation for partnership. However, doing all those things right will not, by itself, lead to trust, respect, and ultimately partnership. Some people's opinions can be changed, some cannot. Know the difference.

Do a realistic assessment of how IT and the PMO are perceived. Using a graphic as illustrated in Figure 6.8 can help. Determine where IT needs to be. Then, plan carefully on how to get there.

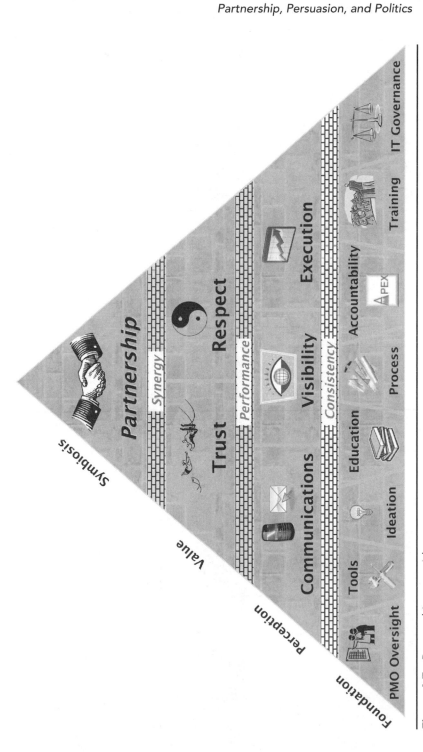

Figure 6.7 Partnership pyramid.

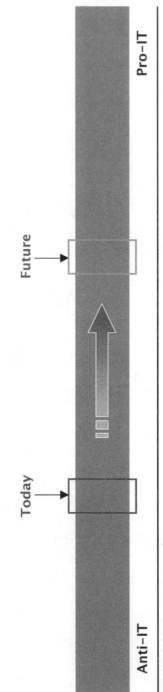

Figure 6.8 Perception scale.

Making Friends, Influencing People, and Avoiding Political Landmines

Everyone in the company will have an opinion of IT and the PMO. People either:

- ...like IT
- ...hate IT
- ...tolerate IT or see it as a necessary evil

Don't waste your time and political capital picking fights or taking on individuals whose opinions are not easy to change. Start with those who are most obviously sympathetic to IT and the PMO.

For example, say an organization has 10 key people you wish to influence. Three love IT. Three hate IT. Four are ambivalent. Since hate is a much stronger emotion than love, the three who dislike IT can rally the rest of the decision makers, be it for budget, resources, or projects. If you start with the three who are most adamantly opposed to your agenda, you will use a lot of resources and are unlikely to get anywhere. But, the three who are sympathetic to your agenda might be willing to use their influence and network to persuade the four who are ambivalent. Having others (particularly in the business areas) advocate for IT is much more influential than trying to advocate for yourself, which can easily be perceived as aggrandizing. If successful, you can change the equation to seven influencers sympathetic to IT and three opposed to IT. The net result being that the three now find themselves in the awkward position of being in a minority among their peers. They might not change their opinions, but they are likely to tone down the rhetoric and stop opposing your agenda as strenuously.

An additional benefit to this approach is that the messenger can be more important than the message. It is one thing to tout the benefits of the PMO. It is quite another to have someone influential in the organization advocate for the PMO. Hearing, "The PMO is a good organization and valuable partner," has some meaning when spoken by the head of the PMO. The same phrase articulated by the vice president of sales or chief marketing officer carries significantly more weight and will resonate much further in the organization.

The head of the PMO should leverage relationships that others have. A common fallacy is that one has to directly influence a decision maker in order to get results. As stated previously, the messenger can be more important than the message, so if you have to deliver a message, find a friend in the organization who has a good relationship with the person you wish to contact and ask the friend to deliver the message. Networking effectively within the organization is critical to success. Not everyone will like you, and that is okay. This is why we have networks.

Persuasion Tactics

It is often said that people are resistant to change. This assumption is often incorrect. People change all the time. They change their cars, jobs, houses, spouses—oftentimes quite frequently and willingly. While unanticipated or unwelcome change can be unsettling and even alarming, people are mostly afraid of the unknown, but they adapt quickly. What people are quite resistant to, however, is control. One need look no further than a newspaper or news website to see numerous references to *freedom*, *liberty*, and *choice*, to name but a few. At work, we assume that there is a certain level of control placed on us, and we accept that as a condition of employment. However, when the level of control changes, or the area of control shifts from the familiar ("My boss", "My department") to the less-familiar ("The PMO", "Someone in IT"), resistance can develop quickly and be quite strong. The nature of a PMO, however, is control. An effective PMO (and PM) controls the project, resources, budget, and communications. Keeping this in mind, how a PMO exerts control over other parts of the organization (and more importantly, how that control is perceived) is the key to success.

Eventually, you will need and want people on your side, both professionally and personally. Here are a few tips:

- Have lunch. A one-on-one lunch is an ideal opportunity to get to know someone. It doesn't have to be fancy or planned. But it is important to get out of the office and onto neutral ground and is a relaxed way to get to know someone.
- Listen for business goals and motivations. As you get to know a person, eventually you will hear the things that really matter—hopes, fears, dreams, and history.
- Strive to politically position the PMO between IT and the business. Being in the middle is often difficult, but it puts the PMO and its leaders in a position to act as arbiters of key initiatives. Also, it is a great place to get visibility into what is happening from a business perspective.
- Be patient. Relationships take time to build.
- Practice what you preach. Communicate clearly, be transparent, execute well.
- Use the pyramid. An illustration goes a long way.
- Seek and incorporate feedback and advice.
- Act like a consultant. Borrow the watch and tell the time.[1]

Keep in mind a few pitfalls. Everyone has a hidden agenda. It may become apparent to you what it is as you network with others in the organization. Then

---

[1]This references the old consulting joke, "What is the definition of a consultant? A consultant is someone who travels a great distance, borrows your watch, tells you the time, and keeps the watch."

again, it may not. Be aware that just because an individual or group appears to support you, it might not be for the reasons you think, or as long-lasting as you would hope.

In organizations of every size, there are often secret alliances. You do not necessarily know who is a friend to whom, inside or outside of work. Or, in some cases, who is related to whom. So be cautious in what you reveal or who and what you criticize. Assume that much of what you say will be repeated or made public at some point, regardless of any promises of confidentiality.

Politics: How to Create Leverage

Getting other areas to come on board can be a challenge. Start inside IT—if IT is not on board, you will not get very far. Sell the ideas to friendly business units. The business units are always looking for ways to make their products more competitive, increase sales, etc. Proactively reaching out to them to ask how technology can assist in solving their business problems puts you squarely on their side. And, by all means, leverage the corporate culture.

Do not go against the grain of the organization. Many good ideas (and people) get rejected outright because they adopt a counter-culture approach. While this may work for a consulting organization brought in from the outside, it rarely works from the inside. The speed, approach, and politics all have to be within the bounds and norms of the organization.

Carrying your own water is necessary from time to time. However, leverage your friends and allies in the organization. Call in a favor. Have other areas (especially business units) advocate for your ideas.

Every individual's motivations and needs are different. Be cognizant of that fact. A one-size-fits-all message will have minimal impact and influence, and will sound contrived. Tailor your message from the perspective of the person whose support you are seeking. Be able to proactively answer, "What is in it for me?" Your ideas and goals will have to be sold one at a time to key stakeholders and influencers.

A CxO (CFO, CEO, COO, etc.) may not know or even care what the PMO is, does, or what value it brings. In some cases, he may know but refuse to acknowledge it. The reason is simple: *politics.* Executives have agendas. The PMO may not fit into that agenda. Say, for example, that a COO is advocating initiative X. He needs two more full-time equivalents (FTEs). Since he does not have the budget to hire more people, he has to make cuts elsewhere. It is much easier to cut people and organizations that one does not understand. So, although an executive's ignorance of PMO value and mission might be unintentional, sometimes it is deliberate. And this does not start or stop at the C-level. Vice presidents and directors can play the game, too. Yes, this does sound a little cynical, but it is the same game that all the other departments play. Marketing, finance, HR, accounting, sales—they all realize that it is not enough to show value and perform well—one must be a smart political player. Initiative X previously mentioned, for example, might be an effort to increase brand awareness, and championed by the vice president of marketing. He is the one who needs the additional head-count. So, when presenting this problem to the COO ("I need more people.") he also presents a solution: "What about that PMO-thing? Do they really need five project managers? And what do they do, anyway?" This situation, or a variant of it, is quite common and can end in one of three results, depending on how the PMO played its politics in the preceding months.

> *Bad*: The COO agrees with the vice president of marketing, since he has no idea what the initials P, M, and O stand for and who those people are, thus, he cuts two FTEs from the PMO staff and gives them to marketing.
>
> *Better*: The COO defends the PMO (having heard from others that they perform well) and looks elsewhere for the cuts.
>
> *Best*: The vice president of marketing never even thinks to bring up the PMO as a place to make cuts—their projects for his area have been successful and he is personally on very good terms with several of them, particularly the director of the PMO, who has made an ef-fort to reach out and understand his area's business needs and con-cerns. He sees the PMO as a partner and vital to his own department's success.

How Long Will This Take?

Naturally, we are anxious to implement these ideas and see results as quickly as possible. However, be aware that this kind of change takes time and patience and must be undertaken at a speed consistent with the rest of the organization. Figure 6.9 identifies the typical speed with which different types of organizations embrace change.

While it is okay to hit the gas pedal from time to time, be aware that attempting any kind of significant change from within the company at a pace faster than that at which change normally occurs will increase resistance. And the faster you at-tempt to go, the greater the resistance. With that in mind, do not go slower than the pace of the organization, either, as you will likely lose momentum. Slightly faster than the organization's natural pace is what you are striving for. Change, especially in regards to perception and relationships, takes time, patience, and persistence.

Conclusion

As stated at the beginning of this chapter, the road to partnership is paved with good intentions. It is within your control to determine where it leads. As with

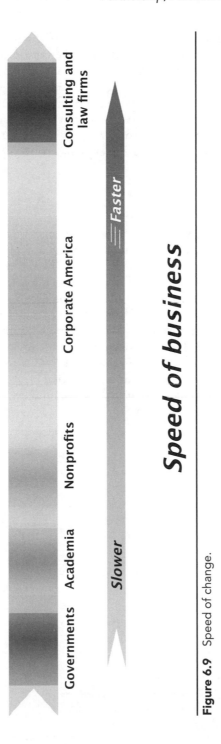

Figure 6.9 Speed of change.

any methodology, politics and persuasion are the guardrails that keep you on the road to partnership. Constructing the pyramid is not an end in and of itself, and establishing relationships is only the beginning. The relationships you build will require maintenance and nurturing. The road can be long and take a few unanticipated twists and turns, but by dedicating yourself and the PMO to building the pyramid block by block by using effective persuasion tactics and paying close attention to corporate and personal politics, the PMO and its leadership can build a solid, fruitful, and mutually beneficial partnership with the rest of the organization.

Author Biography

Paul Risk, PMP, is currently the director of business analysis at the American Medical Association and also an adjunct professor of information systems and operations management at Loyola University, Chicago. He holds a BS in mechanical engineering, an MS in computer engineering, and an MBA, all from the University of Cincinnati. He is a consulting and project management professional with over 20 years of experience in PMO development, IT strategy, methodology development and analysis, organizational change management, and systems integration. He has worked in the consulting industry for Ernst & Young and Deloitte, and has implemented systems, PPM tools, and PMOs for several Fortune 500 corporations. Mr. Risk can also be found presenting seminars and guest speaking on project management subjects that include technology, process, and of course, people.

Web
Added
Value™

This book has free material available for download from the
Web Added Value™ resource center at **www.jrosspub.com**

7

The PMO Revolution—The Strategic COE

Jen L. Skrabak, PMP, MBA

Introduction

Since its initial popularity in the 1990s, project management offices (PMOs) have evolved into bureaucratic organizations viewed as lacking in tactical execution capabilities, but focused primarily on status reporting and tracking. As a result, the average lifespan of a low-performing PMO is 3.5 years (Center for Business Practices, 2007). Although some companies may have a single centralized PMO, it is common for many companies to have multiple PMOs in each function, geographic site, and sometimes each department. They may have various names, with or without *project* or *office* in its title, including business office, operational support, or process support. Whether the *P* in PMO refers to managing projects, programs, or portfolios, only 50 percent of existing PMO respondents view their PMOs as relevant and as adding value (Hobbs, 2007). For the most part, they operate independently of one another without the benefits of standardized processes and without holistically integrating the company vision, current business needs, or capabilities that translate into projects.

Using a nominal IT spend ratio of 25 percent innovation and 75 percent current-state operations as an example, a mere 5 percent reduction in operational costs, when reapplied to innovation, nets a 20 percent increase in the ability of the organization to innovate. Time and effort spent on maintaining the status quo is inherently limited in its net value to the business. Redirecting capacity to engage in more business innovation has an almost unlimited ability to contribute to the success of the enterprise.

A revolution in the traditional concept of PMOs from a reporting and tracking entity is clearly needed in order to achieve its original value proposition and promise: The new model is the center of excellence (COE), where strategy, standards, and services are focused in project, program, and portfolio management excellence (not theory). The revolution in PMOs is to rapidly move away from the traditional policeman and auditor roles, and move into the COE as a product-oriented organization—with services as its chief product that its clients (the organization) want to buy and use. The COE is focused on developing and implementing a multifaceted team that brings cost savings and accelerates innovation for new revenue generation. This includes a new strategic delivery service arm, as well as blending the various independent PMOs into a strategy office that can help deliver the highest impact projects and programs to bridge the overall enterprise multigenerational roadmaps through all core facets—technology, process, and product.

PMO Challenges

Most organizations have trouble finding the right fit, culturally and politically, for their PMO. Based on research sponsored by PMI® on the state of PMOs, there are some alarming facts (Hobbs, 2007):

- Most operate autonomously from other PMOs
- Most have been in existence for two years or less
- Closure and restructuring happens frequently
- Implementation time takes six months to two years

It is a widely held belief that over two-thirds of PMOs fail; it is clear that most models are unsustainable, since most are started without a clear vision or quantifiable results, culminating in many PMOs being disbanded or restructured before they are fully implemented. It is ironic given that if given time for PMOs to mature, "[T]hose with a PMO operating for more than four years reported a 65% increase in project success rate" (Gale, 2009).

Evidence shows that as PMOs mature, they continuously improve on meeting critical success factors, including having effective sponsorship, accountability, competent staff, quality leadership, and demonstrated value. A PMO should be permitted to mature over time, needing to walk before it can run. It is an investment like any other, and takes time to bear its fruit.

Although it is clear that PMOs can and do add value, the majority of the models currently being implemented are fragmented and provide too narrow of a focus. Today, although most of them provide some tools and templates and may have project managers reporting into it, it lacks integrated portfolio and business management. Although it may attempt to integrate various organizational silos, traditional project and program management frequently adds an additional layer of organizational bureaucracy, creating a horizontal silo. An example is shown in Figure 7.1.

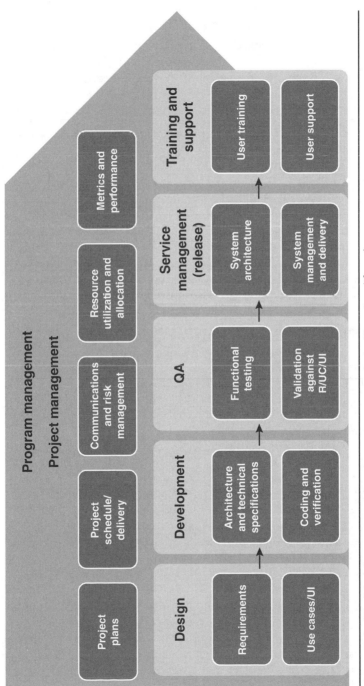

Figure 7.1 Traditional program and project management in an IT project lifecycle.

Why PMOs?

The original value proposition that is often given for creating a PMO is for improvements in project delivery success, repeatable processes, and resource (people, budget, or equipment) management. A survey based on 213 global senior executives and project management experts revealed the following compelling statistics on a PMO's potential and return on investment (Gale, 2009):

- Organizations with PMOs complete twice as many projects as those without PMOs
- Some 76 percent of recently surveyed companies reported that they had created a PMO
- Some 65.8 percent of high performing organizations have enterprise PMOs
- Some 90 percent of global senior executives and project management experts say good project management is the key to delivering successful results and gaining a competitive edge
- Only 33 percent of organizations are good at project management
- Nearly half—49 percent—of organizations follow formal project management practices only on large or complex projects

Overall Project Success Rates Have Dropped Recently . . . But Improved Long Term

The Standish Group, an IT project management research and consulting firm, issued its *CHAOS Summary 2009* report based on a survey of 400 organizations and found a decrease in IT project success rates and an increase in IT project failure rates during the past two years. Only 32 percent of IT projects were considered successful, on time, on budget, and with the required features and functions. Nearly one in four (24 percent) IT projects were considered failures, were cancelled before they were completed, or were delivered but never used. The remaining 44 percent were considered challenged. They were finished late, over budget, or with fewer than the required features and functions.

This is an improvement when compared to 1996 results, where only 16 percent of IT projects were successful, 31 percent failed, and 53 percent were challenged (Standish Group, 2009). Although the 2009 results may seem dismal overall, they demonstrate improvement in project delivery when compared to 13 years earlier in 1996.

It can be argued that from 1996–2009, project success rates doubled, in part attributable to the maturation of project and program management processes. As we also have seen in the research on PMOs, they do add to improvements in project execution by standardizing processes throughout the organization, turning art into science. Just as project management execution and delivery is maturing and gradually improving, COEs are the appropriate vehicle to integrate the disparate practices and transform clouds (fuzzy amorphous concepts) into clocks (standard, repeatable processes).

Evolution or Revolution?

Although revolution and evolution closely resemble one another in the English language, their definitions could not be further apart. A *revolution* can be defined as a fundamental change in an organizational structure that takes place in a short amount of time. In contrast, *evolution* refers to the gradual change over a long period of time. Particularly as it relates to innovation, which most projects promise to deliver, it can be disruptive, and the success of most projects depend on its ability to deliver rapidly, not gradually. Although the iterative approach may sound enticing, sometimes it seems like a constant do-over. The COE is a revolution on two fundamental fronts. First, it delivers radically different services, bringing innovation and creativity. Second, it delivers a new strategic and encompassing portfolio delivery approach. To determine if the organizational culture can support the change, it is crucial to ask the following questions:

- What systems and structures are in place to support or hinder the approach?
- What is the maturity of my current process?
- What is the organizational culture?
- Who will benefit and who will not?
- What is the timeframe?
- What is the end state?
- How big is the delta between *as-is* and *to-be*?

Evaluating the culture will ultimately dictate the sustainability and viability of the revolutionary versus evolutionary approach. The revolution is clearly underway, with many program and portfolio management offices already widening their influence beyond project management to include a more strategic role with an increasing scope of responsibilities. More than 60 percent of the 455 PMOs responding to a survey conducted in 2008 report a wider scope of responsibilities that include all planned work and comprehensive resource management. PMOs are delivering a broad range of business management services, including (Doerscher, 2008):

- Process improvement (82 percent)
- Strategic planning (68 percent)
- IT service and application management (49 percent)
- Management of intellectual assets (47 percent)
- Product management (37 percent)
- Budgeting (40 percent)

Types of PMOs

Most organization's PMOs can be grouped into one of four main types. These can be considered the maturity levels that a PMO may evolve into. However, they are not mutually exclusive and can be defined as the different types of PMOs that can coexist within an organization.

Type 1: Department

The scope of this PMO is within a department or area, typically managing small, routine requests or projects of a limited duration (typically less than six months). Impact is within a department, although may be across multiple sites. The project managers with the department may be part-time project managers with various job titles and include operational or other responsibilities. They may have various titles including business or system analyst, team lead, advisor, programmer, supervisor, or manager.

Type 2: Cross-functional

The cross-functional PMO integrates projects across multiple departments or functional areas. Resources are typically informally matrixed in and are assigned on a part-time basis. Although there may be full-time, dedicated project managers in the PMO, they may be assigned to multiple projects since projects are typically of small-to-medium sized or of limited duration (6–12 months). There may be multiple project managers assigned to large projects, although some of the project managers are on a part-time basis and may have various titles with some operational or support responsibilities.

Type 3: Enterprise

An enterprise PMO is often created in response to a large complex enterprise initiative that a company is undertaking. The organization may realize that there is an unmet need to coordinate across functions, departments, and geographic locations into a standardized and consistent way of managing its individual projects and programs so that it holistically delivers the benefits. There is a focus toward managing interdependencies and resolving issues surrounding resource (people, budget, equipment, etc.) allocation. There may be a need to define and initiate the *right projects*, not just delivering the projects the right way. The project managers will be dedicated project managers with formal project manager titles and certifications.

Type 4: Strategic

The strategic PMO is also the model for the COE. It encompasses portfolio, program, and project management across the organization, driving the strategy and aligning the tactics to that. It is closely aligned with PMI's *PMBOK® Guide's* definition of portfolio management: "centralized management of one or more portfolios, which includes identifying, prioritizing, authorizing, managing and controlling projects, programs, and other related work, to achieve specific strategic business objectives."

COEs Differentiators

In addition to the definition of the strategic PMO, the COE will encompass multidimensional skill sets including business analysis and industry and domain knowledge, as well as project management expertise. The key differentiators of the COE from a traditional PMO include the following:

Focuses on Creating Value

The COE needs to focus on its primary reason for existence—creating value. As a service organization, it must first define the COE's key services and products, which should be broad rather than narrow, and may include managing projects, operations, support, maintenance, resources, and budget.

There is a need to be clear, focused, but expansive when defining the span of projects that will be under its purview. Keep in mind that the critical success factor for the COE, and its core service, is the people and knowledge. Therefore, recruitment and training will be crucial, as will establishing key business partner relationships.

The hub and spoke rather than top-down hierarchy works well for the COE. Although it does not want to, nor can it attempt to manage all projects within an organization, it must roll up and have final accountability over the project in terms of whether it should be initiated, continued, or canceled. The COE is the hub. The department, cross-functional, and enterprise PMOs are its spokes, focused on execution of the results.

It is also critical to scale appropriately—to determine the right fit for the organization's culture, maturity, and vision. Do not get ahead of the capabilities out of the gate, but focus on taking a phased approach to initiating, planning, and progressively maturing the COE.

It is critical that visible, quantifiable value be communicated and validated throughout the organization. The COE should establish key performance indicators (KPI) to measure progress and assess its value to the organization. It is also critical to establish baselines before the COE is implemented so that metrics can be evaluated and published on a regular basis, which publicizes the visible value of the COE. COE KPIs may include:

- Percent of successful projects executed (successful projects can provide a number of key indicators such as ROI or savings achieved from the implementation, resources successfully reallocated due to efficiencies, equipment

redeployed due to reengineering of processes, or the avoidance of additional resources, equipment, or other expenditures)
- Percent of canceled projects (canceled projects can also add ROI in terms of budget dollars or resources saved)
- Percent of challenged projects (overruns prior to the implementation of the COE should be compared to post implementation, where the budget amount and scheduled duration of overruns should be comparably less)

Just as the project manager may spend 90 percent of his time communicating about the project, 90 percent of the COE's time is spent communicating about the COE. This includes constantly measuring and quantifying its value and impact such as time and resources saved or earned.

Ensures that Strategy is Translated into a Single Enterprise Project Plan of Record

Most PMOs do not get involved until the project has been defined, chartered, and budgeted. However, that leaves a significant gap as there is no organized way to assist and drive the business strategy in defining and aligning projects to address gaps in business capabilities or new products or services based on the organization's overall vision and strategy. Or, worse yet, projects are authorized based on IT-driven mandates—system consolidations, infrastructure upgrades, or obsolete hardware or software rather than adding business value. The COE must ensure that the projects and programs are business driven, not IT driven, and while the underlying projects and programs may fulfill IT needs, they must first and foremost add business value based on new or improved capabilities that will be implemented as a result of the project.

Another important role that the COE plays is to ensure a single enterprise project plan of record (typically a three-year horizon). This is the ultimate source of truth for the organization. There is a single funnel and single project prioritization and selection criteria through which all projects must go, eliminating pet projects—or, worse—redundant and overlapping projects. Some Fortune 500 organizations may implement overlapping and competing systems and projects due to the lack of the source of truth of the enterprise project plan of record in initiating the projects. It also ensures that the highest return for the organization's investment is focused on the right projects, defined and aligned according to the business strategy. Sponsorship at the executive management level ensures that senior leaders lead the plan and that they drive the accountabilities and visibility, and redirect needed resources to focus on solving the business capabilities.

The more complex the business situation, the greater the need for a robust design and plan prior to execution. Having a clear business strategy blueprint of the business processes, (*as-is* and *to-be*) helps to ensure the alignment of the right projects to satisfy key gaps in the to-be business process. A blueprint cohesively weaves together multiple strategies and maps them to business capabilities. It catalogs existing system and business capabilities and juxtaposes them with projected need, providing the overall visibility into the path to future state. A single aggregate strategy will drive consensus on decisions with buy-in from all key stakeholders, including business and technology. It allows for efficient sequencing to maximize investments with a clear future state.

In addition, a roadmap that is developed to clearly focus on making blueprint project execution ready—sequencing, technical feasibility, high-level costing, prioritization, and cataloging and phasing projects to deliver future state. The roadmap represents actionable steps to achieve the blueprint over three-to-five years.

Funnels Investments (Budget, People, Equipment)

A fundamental concept that the COE must evangelize is that *fewer* projects will mean that success rates improve and things get done faster. In order to effectively act as a funnel for the organization, it must implement key processes to perform the following (see Figure 7.2):

- Forecast demand as well as manage current demand or allocation of project managers, business analysts, and all key project roles.
- Prioritize the right projects. The COE can deliver a return in three-to-six months by providing the visibility needed to cancel, postpone, or scale back unnecessary or less strategic projects.
- Ensure the right mix of investments; 25 percent strategic and 75 percent sustaining.
- Resolve resource conflicts. A lack of available or skilled resources when needed on a project is a major barrier and contributes to schedule or budget delays.
- Constrain or eliminate pet projects or non-value-added activities.
- Manage key project risk categories including complexity, external factors, operational, organization culture (fit), schedule, and technology.

Delivers Results Through Project Management Discipline

The COE does not have to execute every project in the organization, but must be fully accountable for and own the standardization of project management execution across the enterprise. A core responsibility includes establishing lean standards, tools, templates, and methodology—not becoming a paperwork and bureaucratic entity focused on templates for everything. Due to the many different types, sizes, and complexities of projects within an organization, there is no one-size-fits-all in terms of process. However, clear guidance and direction must be given for each project to determine how much process is enough. This is where project management consulting, mentoring, and guidance from COE mentors who

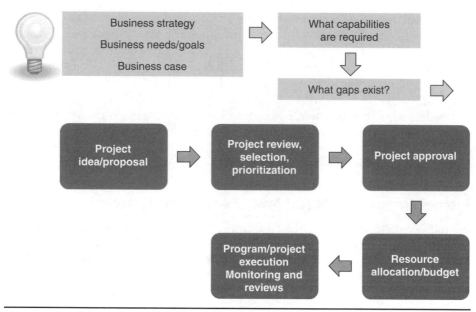

Figure 7.2   COE key processes.

cannot only oversee a project or program execution, but also actively guide and steer the project manager. There is nothing worse than managing a project by template. By assigning a mentor who can consult and guide the execution as well as provide needed direction at critical points to the project manager, it leverages the experience and depth of the COE while also developing the next generation of COE bench strength.

However, the overall focus of the COE must be on strategic, aggregate portfolio success, not on managing the project managers. Project managers must be given the autonomy and empowerment to manage their projects within the guidelines, but can apply their own judgment and experience in ensuring project success. Adopting and instilling risk management—focusing not only on managing project risks that may threaten or have negative consequences, but on the opportunities (those that have positive impacts to exploit) is critical. The COE, by creating structure and processes that will support flawless execution and accountability, will result in a clear line of sight into enterprise priorities.

Transforms the Business

The real value of any project is its ability to fundamentally transform processes and offer true innovation opportunities to develop business capabilities that did not exist before. Do not just focus on automation, but on true transformation in the business to improve or add new capabilities. Some key questions to ask include:

- Are we reinvesting in opportunities as the market evolves?
- Is our performance superior to our major competitors?
- Is our competitive advantage strong enough to leverage more customers and more business from existing customers?
- What gaps exist in current versus desired capabilities?

Figure 7.3 illustrates how the product vision will ultimately transform into the solution.

An Approach to Developing the Business Case

The business case supports defining the business need and may include the following components:

- Executive summary
  - Why are we here?
  - What do we want to get from the sponsors?
  - Do we have approval to move forward with the recommended approach?
  - Other (depending on circumstances).
  - Who is driving this effort (client or sponsor)?
- Opportunity or problem statement
  - What is the current situation or problem?
  - Supplement as appropriate with process graphs or descriptions including *as-is* and *to-be* flowcharts.
  - Why do the sponsors need to take action?
  - What is the impact of inaction?
  - Is this a process issue which can be addressed without a technology-related solution?
- Alternatives and action recommended
  - What alternatives did we consider?
  - Estimate rough cost and the pros and cons for each likely alternative.
  - Use of resources expected (internal versus external consultants).
  - What are any other expected costs (hardware, software, etc.)?
  - Why did we select our recommended course of action?
  - What timing considerations exist?
- Business drivers and value
  - What is the value to the organization for following the recommended course of action?
  - Support your assumptions and cost or benefits estimates including NPV, IRR, and payback period.

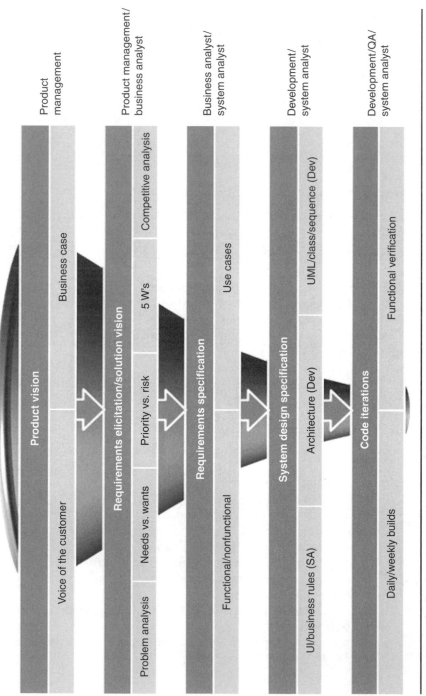

Figure 7.3 The business case and vision of the product.

- Next Steps
  - Any significant next steps and expected timing

Leads Communications and Decision Making Across the Organization

Establishing oversight and governance across multiple regional or departmental PMOs is another differentiator for the COE. Electronic executive dashboards can provide the instant visibility needed to cancel, postpone, or scale back unnecessary or less strategic projects. In addition, a key role of the COE is to facilitate quick decision making and decisive actions (when needed) in order to continue the forward progress of key programs and projects.

Many projects flounder due to a lack of decision making or the pace of the decision making, routing it to multiple levels before it can be resolved. It is important that although collaboration and consensus is needed, it is a highly mature team process, and expert facilitation by the COE is needed to drive the right, collaborative decision making by the right leaders so that it does not lead to stalemate or debate. Table 7.1 provides an illustration of the important components of collaboration and consensus.

Experts in Business Analysis, Domain, and Process

The COE is staffed with not only project managers, but also business analysis and Lean and Six Sigma process experts. Key skills in defining scope and requirement elicitation, analysis, and definition are needed to ensure that the right project foundation is in place prior to project execution.

Table 7.1 Collaboration and consensus

Is	Is not
Results-oriented, positive energy	Brainstorming, free-for-all
Cooperating	Voting
Mutually agreed upon end in mind	Right versus wrong
Worth the effort and highly effective	Easy
Process	Group think
Coming up with the best solution for the company	Coming up with the best solution for the individual or group
Identifying the real issue and creating options	Compromise
Created	Automatic

To mitigate the issue of poorly defined business cases, project discovery and feasibility studies can be powerful COE tools to minimize budget, time, and organizational resource commitments to ensure that projects are fully defined prior to formally committing resources. Typically it takes three-to-six months with a small focused team to prove out key concepts, fully define the business case, and conduct a feasibility study, which will help to mitigate the project risks. In addition, experts in organizational change management are required—understanding, communicating, and leading the organization through key components of sustaining and managing the change:

- What is changing?
- Why is it changing?
- What are the benefits for the organization?

Many projects fail, not due to the system or process not being *installed*, but due to the system or process not being *implemented*. A successful project implementation means that the system or process is understood, used, and part of the new day-to-day life of the organization.

Operational excellence is another trademark of the COE, both in terms of its service offerings and also in terms of its continuous improvement aspect for the COE itself. It is demonstrated by results that reflect (1) sustained improvement over time, (2) improvement in all areas of importance (both performance areas and segments within each area), and (3) performance at a level that is at, or superior to, best-in-class organizations. Common areas of importance for a cost center are safety, quality, people, and cost. The highly advanced COE may actually become a profit center that adds the revenue generation performance area to this mix by having internal consultants that rival the big-four consultants. Common segments within each performance area include employee groups, facilities, departments, and external customer types.

An improvement initiative will not succeed if time is not allocated toward it, or if time, when allocated, is used ineffectively. That said, an organization can allocate this time on paper (in a strategic plan, job description, or expense budget, for example), yet still fail to require each of its leaders to demonstrate the degree to which they are personally using this time to improve the key processes they are responsible for. Most CEOs believe that if they could only change one thing, they would change what is expected from each of their leaders, because most people will find a way to reach a goal if that goal is clearly stated and comes with significant consequences for failing to achieve that goal.

Maintains Knowledge Repository for the Organization

Maintaining the knowledge repository for the organization is much more than simply posting lessons learned. It must ensure that the lessons learned are implemented as preventative techniques and institutionalized as a project management practice in the organization. The lessons learned are translated into processes and instilled through training for the COE and project managers in the organization. Ultimately knowledge management is also about inventory and applying best practices so that each project manager does not have to relearn what another project has already paved the way to do.

In addition, rather than conducting reviews at the end of the project, retrospectives at the end of key milestones or project phases offer the opportunity to course correct and implement needed changes that can have a positive effect on the project, rather than simply waiting until the end.

Since any organization's main asset is its people—or rather its knowledge base of intellectual capital—how that knowledge is captured, maintained, institutionalized, and improved will be critical in sustaining and growing the organization. In addition, many project deliverables fail to make the transition into operational documents where it must outlive the project and continue to sustain the operations.

Manages the Value Chain

Managing the value chain means that the COE's responsibilities do not end when the project or program ends. It stays engaged after the project delivery to perform value capture and to ensure that the ROI originally promised is achieved and the organization can reap its benefits. Most organizations invest a tremendous amount of money after much scrutiny up front. However, no one ever checks to see if the reduction in headcount, redeployment in resources, or money saved was ever actually achieved. Benefit realization—ROI, quality of the product that the project delivered, quality and sustainability of the project deliverables—needs to be used to drive the next set of projects that are selected for execution.

Establishes and Manages Strategic Multisourcing

Even a COE cannot and should not attempt to do everything by itself. The COE must establish and manage key partnerships and vendors that can fill short or midterm skill or resource gaps. A further step is to look at potentially outsourcing low value-added activities that a COE may have to manage, or to establish a shared service pool of contracted resources that is available to all projects in the organization where trained and skilled resources can step into various assignments on the project rather than continuously hunt for outside contracting or consulting resources.

A key component of the COE must be to establish a training and recruitment program. The main purpose of training is to typically develop new knowledge or skill sets that are not currently present. This requires the right recruitment strategies to look at hiring that knowledge or skill set not currently present.

Next Steps: A Four-phase Approach to COE Implementation

Phase 1—Initiation

During the initiation phase, obtain executive sponsorship and ownership of the COE. Key initial steps include:

- Obtaining an inventory of project, program, and other work
- Reviewing, documenting, and sharing all current practices
- Understanding the project manager and supporting resource allocation, and developing a comprehensive project list
- Performing strength, weakness, opportunity, and threat assessments for each PMO in the organization. This will include an assessment of the current needs versus the skill set that may exist in the project management personnel, including short-term plans to fill the gap with outsourced resources, or mid- to long-term plans to recruit and hire those with the appropriate skill sets.

Phase 2—Planning

In the planning phase, identify all projects critical to the enterprise. Determine resource allocations to these subsequent projects and establish a project scoring methodology to establish a consistent criterion that allows project stack ranking across the enterprise. Factors for inclusion in the project scoring typically falls into three general categories: the highest impact projects to help the enterprise find the largest cost savings or attain efficiencies, the best path to accelerate innovation, and to produce new revenue.

Phase 3—Execution

In the execution phase, develop an implementation plan for the COE by determining the best usage of existing resources, identifying gaps in talent, and defining migration plans for one enterprise PMO versus the multiple organizations that exist today.

Phase 4—Iteration

In the iteration phase, mature the COE. Plan retrospectives early and often at key milestones, adjust as necessary, and repeat. The COE must adapt to the needs of the organization and be nimble, which has speed as well as agility, in order to meet the constantly changing business environment.

Author Biography

Jen L. Skrabak, PMP, MBA, is a senior level project executive leading high-profile business transformation project and programs. She brings over 16 years of professional experience in project, program, and portfolio management across broad industries such as healthcare, biotechnology, entertainment, and financial services. Her recent assignments include establishing PMO COEs for a $500 million US and international expansion project portfolio, as well as managing large program execution up to $50 million across multiple sites internationally.

Ms. Skrabak is a distinguished member of the project management community, having served three years as president of the PMI® Los Padres Chapter. In addition, Ms. Skrabak also served as the edit lead for PMI's second edition of the *Project Manager Competency Development Framework*. She is also a member of the UCLA extension Project Management Advisory Board and is a frequent speaker at project management and business analysis conferences.

References

Doerscher, T. 2008. *2008 PMO 2.0 Survey Report: The Continued Evolution of the Project, Program and Portfolio Management Office (PMO)*. Austin, TX: Planview.

Gale, S. F. 2009. *Closing the Gap: The Link between Project Management Excellence and Long-term Success*. Report. Economist Intelligence Unit (August).

Hobbs, B. 2007. *The Multi-Project PMO: A Global Analysis of the Current State of Practice*. White paper. Newton Square, PA: Project Management Institute, 10.

Standish Group, *Chaos Summary 2009*, www.standishgroup.com.

The Center for Business Practices. 2007. *The State of the PMO: 2007–2008*. Executive Summary. The Center for Business Practices.

Web
Added
Value™

8

Restoring Sanity: A Practical Guide to Getting Your PMO on the Right Path

Andrew Williams

Introduction

You may have heard before that the definition of *insanity* is doing the same thing over and over and expecting different results. Despite the popularity of this axiom you would be amazed at the number of companies who do just that when it comes to their approach to establishing and governing project management in their organizations. If this sounds familiar, or if you want to avoid that brand of insanity altogether, then read on!

This chapter is written with two types of people in mind. The first type could be considered the certifiably insane, defined here as those who have willingly agreed—or worse, requested—to be responsible for building or running a program or project management office. The second type I call the *sad sacks*, also known as those who were picked for the role without ever having the chance to turn it down or negotiate any perks. If you have already read my biography at the end of this chapter, you probably have figured out that I have been a proud member of both groups over the years.

Many, including myself, have struggled or failed when attempting to implement a project management office (PMO.) Perhaps it was because the right questions were not asked before starting, or maybe it was because key elements to establishing and growing the effort were missing, or it could be changes in strategy or leadership. Quite possibly, it was some combination of factors that led to a less-than-successful attempt. It is from my own struggles and those of others I have met over the years that I have developed the approach presented here in the hope that it will enhance your chances of success.

As you read, you will be provided with an easy-to-understand approach to establishing or reinvigorating your own PMO initiative. Throughout the chapter, you will read real-world examples of practices that worked and did not work with advice on how to best leverage those experiences during your effort. The chapter will start by helping you gather the critical data needed to correctly align and structure your PMO. Next, the chapter will walk you through a practical approach to help you control the scale and growth of your PMO in a way that will improve your chances for success and adoption. After establishing those fundamentals, you will be introduced to three danger areas, and will be given advice and examples on how to navigate those and come out unscathed. Finally, you will receive tips and best practices on keeping the momentum once you have established a reputation for quality and dependability within your stakeholder community.

Answer These First

Whether you are just starting up a new PMO or are looking to modify an existing one to account for change or growth, there are some key questions that you should first answer with your executive team. And let me be clear on one point, if your executives are not engaged and committed to helping to correctly define the PMO up front, your chances of success are dramatically lower right out of the gate.

Who Are My Executive Sponsors?

Answering this question will help you to understand the types of projects that the PMO may be tasked with and will also define what areas of the organization will be supported. The answer you get may be a committee of executives or one executive representing the best interests of the firm as a whole, but it could just as easily be a single executive representing one department that has recognized a need for change. Many successful PMOs began as a small group embedded within a single operating unit and many of those continue to operate that way. There is nothing that says every one must be an enterprise-wide organization supporting every initiative the firm undertakes, so it is critical to set expectations early on and avoid disappointment later. The answer to this question can also have a big impact on the knowledge and skills that your project managers will need in order to succeed.

A single unit or single subsidiary PMO will likely require a deeper operational knowledge for that unit or subsidiary, can influence how little or how much technical savvy they need, and could be an indicator of how much of a leader or collaborator they need to be to fit in with the group that they will be working together with on projects. A broader-reaching PMO will naturally need a project management team with more diverse skills, more delivery experience, familiarity with resolving cross-functional issues, and a strong aptitude for the facilitation of stakeholders representing different interests of the company.

What Do We Expect to Gain from This PMO?

Once you have identified your sponsors, you need to ask them what it is that they expect the PMO to deliver. You might be surprised at the often vague or unhelpful answers you get in response. For example, a very common answer is that the PMO must provide successfully completed projects. But does that really tell you what you need to know? Let us say you interpret that to mean as long as budget and schedule are both within the original plan, it will be a success. But what if your sponsors really meant that the outcome had to show a measurable impact on revenue, productivity, or profitability, even if cost and schedule had to be adjusted along the way? Or, what if the key measure of success is that regulatory or compliance guidelines are met so the company is not at risk of actions that result in penalties or fines?

You must make sure that you and your sponsors fully understand the business drivers that sparked the creation or modification of your PMO. As the leader, you will be held accountable for its success or failure. You owe it to yourself and your leadership team to keep asking questions until there is no longer room to misinterpret the answers. Then, and only then, will you be sure that the definition of success is agreed to and understood by all parties. Experience shows the most successful PMOs are those that have incorporated the strategic goals of the company into the measurements of success and weighed those against the more traditional project metrics of scope, cost, and time.

Have We Tried This Before?

This might just be the most overlooked question, and it could easily be one of the most critical. If a previous attempt to create or improve a PMO in your company failed, then you will need to perform some additional tasks up front in order to avoid the same fate. Find out who sponsored and who led the failed attempt, and if they are still around, meet with them to get their perspective. Talk to others who were involved to gather as much information as possible before even starting to plan your approach.

Use the information you have collected to formulate a plan of action that is intended to address any lingering issues associated with the previous attempt. Engage those who are most critical of your predecessor and get them involved. Quite often, many people will know how they felt about the earlier initiative, and simply getting them on board and talking positively will bring others along.

Once you are confident that you can answer tough questions about why this effort will succeed where the previous one failed, invite your stakeholders together, acknowledge their concerns, air out the issues, address those that you can, and actively follow up with answers to any that cannot be immediately resolved. You may still encounter individuals along the way who feel that this effort is a waste of time, but they will be much easier to convert if you have won over the majority of your stakeholders before any objections arise.

Start Small and Be Patient

So, now you have some momentum, and you have a lot of good information to get you started. Let us step down a little bit and remember that the tortoise won that race, even though the hare looked like the clear leader early in the event.

Saying No

One of the hardest things in the world to do is to say no to your coworkers, boss, or higher-ups. You must overcome the fear and anxiety associated with using this small but powerful word if you hope to hold off the inevitable flood that is going to come your way. *Why*? Because as soon as people in the company see a way to shift responsibility for delivery of complex and difficult assignments away from themselves, they will make every effort to do just that.

Is there risk in this? Sure. You could be reprimanded, disciplined, demoted, fired, or even promoted out of the way. I have seen all of these things happen to good people because others were impatient and wanted to lighten their own load. But the alternative is even worse. If you do not establish the ability to say no early on, you will end up with more than you and your team can reasonably handle. The PMO will then become the scapegoat for all failed projects, and in many cases, the stress can lead to professional burnout or worse.

The good news is that there are some simple tools you can use to help. The first is to make sure that you communicate early and often that prioritization will be used to determine the order of what will get done. Not everything will get done at once. Then, make the prioritization public knowledge within the organization and publish it on your intranet or in your corporate newsletter—just be sure to get any updates out in a timely manner. A simple list of projects shown in order of priority (based on whatever criteria you have established)—with a clear line between projects being worked on and projects waiting to start—is a very powerful tool.

Next, find a way to show how the resource pool's time is booked over the foreseeable future. Not just on projects, but also on all of those other administrative tasks that everyone always has on their to-do list. This step is a real eye-opener in most organizations and is a key to helping others understand why there are prioritized projects that cannot be started until the right resource completes an assignment, a new resource is provided, or the priorities are changed.

Using this information will give you the power to negotiate with any reasonable person and help you manage the workload for your project resources. This information also comes in handy when dealing with an unreasonable request that escalates to a steering committee or sponsor for resolution. Just be confident in your facts and stand your ground, and you may be surprised at how often the outcome is based on the facts you supplied.

Crawl, Walk, Skip, Jog, Run

Now that you are past the basics, let me give you your first assignment: seek out other PMO leaders and ask them how long it took to get their team fully functional. I bet that the average answer is between three and five years!

The reason I share this with you is to make sure that you set expectations early. You cannot just wave a magic wand and have in place a smoothly running operation in just a matter of weeks. What you can do is quickly show progress and improvement in one or two areas at a time, repeating that approach as often as it takes to ultimately reach the desired level of PMO maturity. Let me explain how by telling you about two common scenarios.

Scenario One—The New PMO

Consider the young lady who was tasked with building her company's PMO from scratch because of her successful track record for delivering projects within her department. She knew she had a huge learning curve to overcome, so she sought out all the qualified advice she could find, spent endless hours on research, took diligent notes, and was lucky enough to set expectations early in the game. She knew that she would never get the funding needed to build the team that was required to support the full scope that her bosses wanted all at once, so she decided to pilot her selected methodology, show that it was superior to the old way of doing things, and then build on that success.

After spending a couple of months to get the basic structure in place, she announced that the PMO was ready for its trial run. She asked for one project, preferably one that had been faltering or was considered behind, so easy comparisons could be made to the prior approach. Her small team was able to apply their techniques and transfer ownership of the selected project in a matter of weeks. They were able to overcome obstacles and make adjustments to their tools and techniques quickly. Ultimately, they delivered the desired results a few months later (not without some bumps along the way, but it was still a positive experience that was recognized as a success).

Upon achieving this success, she went back to her leadership team and told them that the PMO could now take on two concurrent projects, or with the addition of just one more project manager (PM), they could attempt to manage three concurrent projects. Because she had proven her methods, she was given the budget to bring on additional resources so they could deliver results faster, but was challenged to take on four new projects instead of just three. Despite the challenge, she continued to have a high success rate and was able to consistently grow her team in step with the growing portfolio of projects to be managed. It still took a few years to reach the end goal, but the growth was manageable because she was smart in her approach. While this may sound idyllic, it can happen under the right circumstances and with the right amount of forethought, determination, and leadership.

Scenario Two—The Struggling PMO

Then there is the case of the PMO director who was brought into a new company to take their existing PMO to the next level. There had been some effort made prior to his arrival, but there was no standard approach or deliverables, and the project demand pipeline was viewed as a black hole from which most requests never returned. The first thing he did was to define the PMO charter to explain the answers to the types of questions you are reading about here. This took about three months from first draft to steering committee approval due to scheduling conflicts, consensus building, and political infighting—all the normal things one might encounter on a large project.

While that was underway, he and his team developed a standard project delivery methodology and a set of deliverables templates to be used by all PMs on all PMO-managed projects. They also simplified the project request form and educated the company management team on the process that would be followed to submit, approve, fund, schedule, and staff projects going forward. At this point in time, the PMO director was about nine months into his tenure. Between the reviews and approvals needed by the steering committee and compliance department, the lack of trust based on issues with the previous approach, and the resistance to change that had to be overcome, there was significant complexity that had to be managed. And of course, during all of this, business did not stop and they had to continue to deliver projects that had already been approved and budgeted.

He spent three years leading the evolution of this PMO, and when he moved on to another role, the new leader was well positioned to complete the roadmap and achieve their vision. They fought hard to set expectations early and had to constantly remind people along the way that the cultural change associated with their efforts was not a simple feat, but their diligence paid off and progress was steadily made.

In both of these scenarios, you saw how two people with varied degrees of experience and different skills successfully navigated their environment to create a PMO that is producing positive results for their respective companies. This would probably be a good time for a quick reality check. These two people were able to use negotiation and tactics to achieve their strategies without having to significantly modify their original roadmap. But what about when that approach does not work? How do you adjust to try and salvage the initiative?

The first thing I recommend is to double check your approach, frequency, and method of delivering communications. You may have a great message, but if it is too lengthy or is delivered via e-mail to an audience that prefers a phone call or a face-to-face meeting, it will not have the desired impact. This may mean that you have to deliver the same message to various groups in different ways and with a varying frequency, but it is well worth the extra effort.

The other item to consider adjusting is the order in which you evolve the different functional areas of your PMO. Like any major undertaking, regardless of your original plan, if you are bogged down and your initiative is at risk, sometimes a simple change in order can deliver information that wins back your customers. For example, I once had to introduce the basics of portfolio management and value-based prioritization ahead of the resource management and basic reporting functions that I needed to manage the PMO. It caused a delay for the internal PMO needs, but doing so gave the executive team the information they needed to restore confidence and regain momentum.

Hopefully, these lessons learned will give you some insight as you strive for a sense of patient progress in attaining your PMO vision. Keep in mind that no matter how carefully you plan, there will be unexpected events. Having options available to adjust is the key to staying the course.

Under Promise—Over Deliver

I will probably receive a lot of nasty letters, e-mails, and phone calls from consultants around the world for sharing this one, but you have enough challenges ahead without being set up for failure. This simple-but-effective practice is one that you should use wisely in order to help you manage the pace of growth. It simply means giving yourself and your team the opportunity to exceed expectations by setting the expectations yourself. One word of caution, do not over do it (by consistently and significantly padding lead times), or you will build a reputation as a sandbagger!

Inevitably, others in the organization will want to dictate unreasonable deadlines and unfounded priorities to the PMO or the assigned project manager on any given project. Sometimes, by the time you find out about the project, promises have already been made to executives or customers. This should be expected as everyone has deadlines they need to meet, but it can be managed with the right approach.

Start by negotiating the expectations to the point where you are 90 percent confident that you can deliver the completed project in 80-90 percent of the agreed timeline. This could involve reducing scope, staging the delivery, adding resources, increasing budget, or any number of tweaks to the original request to reach consensus. But, if you start with a reasonable target and manage change well along the way, you are much more likely to satisfy the requirements on time and within budget, sometimes even early and under budget.

Practicing the under-promise, over-deliver method can help you in two ways. First, as you and your team repeatedly meet or exceed expectations, you will build a good name for yourselves. People will learn to trust your judgment when your analysis and estimates do not align with their initial goals. Second, if you have followed this approach, you have given yourself some buffer and you might be able to manage smaller changes without impacting resources or the schedule. That may sound like a minor benefit, but by not having to renegotiate every little change, your sponsors and stakeholders will appreciate fewer issues to resolve and will perceive how smoothly the project proceeded.

Market Your Successes

Define Success

Earlier, I alluded to the importance of clearly defining what constitutes the success of a project. Success can mean many things to many people, and on any given project, you may have a multitude of people involved that all need or want something different as a result of the work being done. The same is true of a PMO. Many people will be impacted, influenced, and have something to gain or lose when such a group is first implemented or significantly changed.

One of the best things you can do is to talk to more than just the sponsors, stakeholders, participants, and requestors of projects about what success means. Go beyond that and identify those that will benefit or suffer indirectly to get their input as well.

If you are expected to manage projects to implement new processes, talk to the people who maintain the process, the people who are expected to follow the process, and the people who interact directly with the people who are expected to follow the process. If you expect to be implementing new applications, talk to the people who depend on the potential users of those systems to see what they think is important for success.

Making the extra effort to include peripheral input to your definition of *successful project delivery* will lay the foundation for a more widely accepted PMO. It is much easier to earn the trust of someone by asking for their input before you start delivering projects than it is to try and earn it after you have delivered a project that impacted them negatively.

Do Not Toot Your Own Horn

This one is pretty obvious, but it is necessary to state it, just in case. Nobody likes a braggart, so no matter how well you think something has gone, you need to resist the urge to tell the world. That does not mean that you cannot celebrate with your team or those closely involved—just keep it to a minimum.

A much more effective manner of getting your successes noticed is to let those people who are directly and indirectly impacted do the talking for you. If you heed my earlier advice about expanding the circle of influence in defining success, you will already have a foot in the door. The next step is to keep track of any potential naysayers that you identified earlier when you were getting their input on success, and work hard to overcome their objections. Try to find ways to impress them, and you will be amazed at the results. Not only will you convert some who will happily speak well of your efforts, others who interact with them will see the conversion happen and figure that if they can be convinced, then you must be doing things right.

Get Help Crafting Your Message

While it is good not to toot your own horn, there will be times when a broad announcement is required related to the completion of a large, strategic initiative that the company is counting on to bring significant change of some kind. When this happens, be sure to work closely with your leadership team to understand which key points they want communicated.

Once you have that information, do not try to do it yourself. Unless you have a background in marketing, it may not come across the way you intend. Instead, engage someone from your corporate communications, marketing, or training organization. Not only will they be glad that you asked for their professional help, but if the message is delivered by another group, then you have still managed to avoid bragging on your own success.

Own Your Failures

While I would like to believe that my advice in this chapter has set you on a path to reap nothing but praise and reward, it would be very naïve of me. No matter how prepared you are, there will be times when things just do not go right. Here is some advice on how to drop the shovel and get out of the swamp when you are up to your behind in alligators.

Acceptance and Admission

The first thing you need to do when things do not go as planned is to accept the facts and admit that it did not go as expected. One of the worst things people do is try and manipulate the data and try to claim victory. You will lose credibility so fast if you try to cover up mistakes, that it could completely dismantle everything good you have ever done.

Instead, you should quickly gather the facts and address it head-on with clear, concise communications about what happened, what is being done to remediate the problem, when it is expected to be remediated, and how you are going to keep it from happening again in the future. Do not worry about placing blame. Whatever happened is done and the focus needs to be on overcoming it rather than reliving it over and over.

Accountability

If anything that went wrong is the result of something that you or anyone on your team did, you need to brace yourself and take responsibility. That seems obvious, but here is the hardest part: take the responsibility yourself even if it was one of your team members. As the leader, you are expected to influence the actions of your people, and just as you are given credit for their work when things go well, you will need to step up and take the blame when things go wrong.

Most likely, people outside of your group are going to look at you first anyway, so trying to avoid the blame is only going to lessen their respect for you. When you do the unexpected and welcome accountability, you will accomplish three important goals:

- You will retain much of the respect that those outside your group have for you
- Your team will trust you to not throw them to the wolves if they mess up
- Future issues will be brought to your attention sooner, allowing you to avoid future mishaps

Action

When things do go wrong, speed is of the essence. People love to gossip about any little mistakes that are made by others, so you need to act swiftly and surely to cut off any miscommunication before it happens. You need to get to your sponsors and stakeholders before anyone else can, and let them know something is happening even if you are not prepared to give them all the details of what happened. Assure them that you are managing the situation and will provide more details as soon as you can.

Do anything short of this and you will be in recovery mode. Stakeholders and sponsors are likely to believe the first thing they hear. If someone else does get to them first, be careful not to get defensive about the situation. Stick to the facts as they become available, and try not to discredit any other version of the events unless you can back it up convincingly. One senior executive I worked with once said of his PMO leader, "I hate corporate politics, but I really hate bad corporate politics. He is being stupid and I intend to take him down!"

That is not a battle you want to be in, and it is avoidable if you act decisively.

Keep the Ball Rolling

While the previous sections were written with the intent of giving you some practical advice on implementing or reinvigorating your PMO, this last section contains some tips to keep it healthy and productive over time.

Retaining Interest

An interesting aspect of the PMO is that most people in the organization only think about it when they need something from it or when they have been tasked with helping on a project. The problem this presents is that the same thing can also happen with your leadership team and sponsoring executive. After all the excitement surrounding the initial push to launch and reach a certain velocity, attention can quickly turn to other matters. While it seems like it might be nice to have the limited scrutiny this lack of attention brings, there are risks as well.

If you do not keep your key stakeholders at least marginally involved, reengaging them later will be more difficult and will take longer. Ideally, you will have established some kind of steering committee to regularly evaluate the prioritization and expected business value of your project portfolio and new requests. While this helps tremendously, do pay close attention to members who miss meetings or send a delegate in their place; this is a clear sign that their interest is waning or their understanding of the importance has dropped. Either with or without a steering committee, one way to sustain awareness and interest is to leverage internal channels.

Many companies have an intranet site or newsletter that has a section for announcements or updates. This can be used to publish a small portfolio dashboard that shows key information for the top projects or the projects that are due for completion in the near future—whatever you believe will get people's attention. Do not forget to involve your audience in what they would be interested in seeing, and if possible, get them to participate in creating or selecting the material so they will help to market it to others.

Another possibility is to check with your training group to see if they have or are planning some kind of ongoing company educational series. These usually provide a platform for different business units to explain their role in the company and deliver any key messages they want to get across. Since they tend to be voluntary, the attendees are naturally interested. If they also get credit toward ongoing education and broader organizational knowledge, you may draw quite a crowd. Every once in awhile, you might even find a good candidate to join the team!

In addition to retaining interest, you should also keep an eye out for events that could impact how well integrated the PMO is with the rest of the organization. One such event is during a merger or acquisition. This introduces new people to the organization, and they will need to be made aware of the PMO and how to engage with it when the need arises. Another one to watch for is new job roles being created, people changing roles, or people leaving the company. When this happens, the person filling the new or vacated role and the person leaving may now be in a position that changes their responsibilities as it relates to projects being managed by the PMO. You should be proactive about contacting these individuals and making sure they understand what the PMO has to offer and what is expected of them when they need project work done for their business unit.

These are just a few ideas to get you thinking about how to maximize interest as your operation matures and evolves. Take a look around your own organization and see what other opportunities you may find, and remember to change it up from time to time so that your message does not get stale.

Anticipating Demand

Like most businesses, a PMO will likely see cyclical increases and decreases in the demand for new projects. This could be linked to your company's sales cycle, budget cycle, or marketing campaigns. You will need to familiarize yourself with what drives demand in your company and whether it is seasonal, quarterly, monthly, or occurs with some other frequency.

You will probably also experience off-cycle spikes in demand caused by unusual business events or external factors beyond your control. Most recently, the widespread failures in the financial markets, the subsequent bailout activity, and the wild swings in both directions while we strive for recovery have driven a tremendous demand for projects in almost every industry. Let us hope that this example is rare and focus on some of the more common activities like merger and acquisition activity, changes in the competitive landscape, diversification of product and service offerings, regulatory decisions or actions, territorial expansion, new partnerships, and advances in technology. Regardless of the drivers, you need to be prepared for both expected and unexpected changes in demand.

A sharp increase or decrease in demand requires you to be able to ramp up or down quickly in staff with specialized skills and knowledge of your business. You could request a budget increase to go on a hiring binge or lay people off when things slow down, but you might not want to deal with the headache of constantly bringing new people up to speed; the reputation that comes with cycling through people will ultimately result in an inability to attract top talent.

Instead, you should consider partnering with a few staffing agencies, outsourcing companies, independent contractors, and consulting firms. They can each provide specialized resources on relatively short notice to fill the gaps in your teams when demand increases. They can also quickly be removed from the resource pool when demand drops or when their specific attributes are no longer needed. In case you are wondering about the variety, I have listed them all because of the different services they offer—sometimes you might need a consulting firm to provide an entire project team to deliver a specific project. Other times, you may just need an independent contractor who has a specialized talent to fill a role for a while.

No matter how demand fluctuates, recognize that it will happen and plan ahead. If you can demonstrate the ability to consistently anticipate and respond well, you will enjoy continued support and trust within your organization.

Try Not To Overreach

If you follow all the advice, tips, recommendations, and suggestions included in this chapter, then you will no doubt be running an efficient and effective PMO in no time. Do not let your early achievements go to your head or you could easily make a common mistake that can have disastrous results. As mentioned previously, it is critical to the survival of your PMO that you continue to be patient no matter what.

One problem that occurs when you show you can do the job is that more and more things get sent your way. You need to continue to exercise your right to decline unreasonable requests and you need to temper your desire to grow by remembering that long-term sustainability is more important to your business than is short-term glory.

Do not misunderstand me; we all have aspirations, and most people who lead a PMO have visions of an enterprise-wide organization that manages all the projects that are important to the strategic direction and financial health of the company. There is nothing wrong with that. This is just a reminder that if you try to take on too much too soon, you could undermine all the hard work you put in to get things started.

Now get back to work! You have a lot to do and a lot of people are counting on you to do it well. If any of this information helps you on your journey, I am glad that my trials and errors could be used in a way to benefit others. I wish you the best and welcome you to the PMO family.

Author Biography

Andrew Williams is the founder and president of Artisan Strategy Group. Artisan is a management consulting firm that is providing clients with services related to portfolio, program, project management; business process optimization; customer lifecycle management; vendor evaluation, selection and negotiation; and enterprise change management.

Before founding Artisan, Andrew served as the PMO director at Penson Financial Services. At Penson, he drove the implementation of it as a strategic business unit by developing standards and methodologies used to manage the firm-wide portfolio of high-impact programs and projects.

Prior to joining Penson, Andrew served as director of consulting services at CHR Solutions where his team delivered various projects for clients in the high-tech, public utility, consumer goods, and telecommunications industries. Previously, he spent over 14 years in business development and service delivery while with BearingPoint, eLoyalty, Deloitte Consulting, and Price Waterhouse.

9

PMO Building Blocks—A Practical Approach for Implementing PMO Services

Ruth Anne Guerrero, PMP and Claudia Baca, PMP

Introduction

It is well recognized within the project management community that individuals and organizations struggle to implement project management offices that are perceived as successful. This is due in part to the lack of agreement about what constitutes a PMO. The *P* in PMO can stand for *project*, *program*, or *portfolio*. Some are referred to by other names such as *centers of excellence*.

There is even less consensus regarding what constitutes PMO success. Is it the ability to deliver projects on time and within budget? Is it the ability to deliver projects that realize the intended benefits? Is it the ability to determine which projects are the right projects to work on? With such little common agreement about fundamental PMO concepts, it is easy to understand why so many have failed.

Failure is not inevitable, however. Many PMO failures can be attributed to trying to implement a full-service one in a single leap. In fact, organizational change is always difficult, and a higher level of success is more likely if the PMO responsibilities can be selected, phased in, and matured over time. Incremental changes make it easier to determine how successful the results are, and allow for correction and adjustment as needed. Once a solid PMO foundation is set, there is a higher likelihood that the addition of new PMO services will be successful.

It is important to recognize that there is a short timeline for being able to demonstrate PMO improvements that needs to be carefully watched. Organizations are impatient, and will not wait forever to see results indicating it is moving

155

in the right direction. How can the individual practitioner be sure that the PMO will introduce change quickly enough, but not too quickly? In this chapter, you will be introduced to the concept of *PMO building blocks*, discrete services that a PMO can choose to implement to varying levels of degree and in any desired sequence. Just as many different types of structures can be built from a single a set of building blocks, so too can many different types of PMOs be built using a set of common building blocks.

You will also be introduced to two defining concepts that can further assure the success of your PMO. The first is how to use the organizational project management business solution to guide you along the path of building your PMO. The second is the importance of leadership. Leadership is truly the glue that holds the concepts together.

PMO Building Blocks—The Concept

Typically when organizations decide to implement a PMO, they expect that a wide range of services will be fully implemented from the beginning. There are several issues with this approach, including the time it takes to develop and document all the supporting tools and processes. While these are under development, the PMO shows little evidence of the progress being made, which further fuels the organization's frustration. Even more importantly, this delay does not provide any incremental organizational improvements. Since the organization's need for a PMO, or a new and improved PMO, results from urgent challenges that the organization is experiencing, it is more effective to develop a strategy that will allow you to develop and deploy incremental improvements in a timely manner than to attempt to deliver too much at one time.

Rather than following a traditional implementation approach, if the services a PMO is expected to provide are thought of as being composed of building blocks, it will be possible to implement targeted services quickly, but not completely. A building block, then, is a specific function that, when constructed with other blocks, leads to a portion of work that strengthens project, program, or portfolio management in support of the organization's goals. For example, if the organization's projects are unexpectedly exceeding their planned budgets, a few simple changes can be made to improve the current situation while also laying a foundation for the inclusion of more enhanced financial controls in the future, as seen in Figure 9.1. The financial building blocks that this PMO might choose to implement could include:

- Gathering all the supporting financial documents for the in-flight and planned projects such as budgets, statements of work, contracts, etc.
- Analyzing deficiencies in the current process
- Developing a streamlined change control process
- Developing and deploying an improved process for approving contracts, capturing invoices and payments, etc.

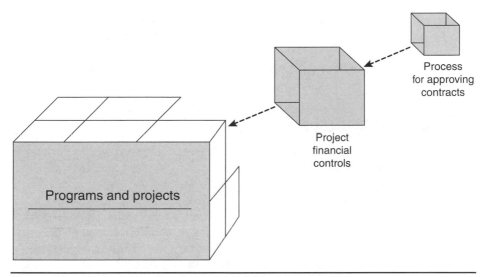

Figure 9.1   Programs' and projects' financial building blocks.

The implementation of these few financial building blocks can hardly be considered a comprehensive financial control function. However, it will serve to address the immediate issues at least on an interim basis. Almost as importantly, it will demonstrate a practical approach to responding to high-priority issues and will show that progress is being made. Using an incremental approach based on a building-block concept will help the PMO gather credibility, as well as yield early benefits. At the same time, these financial building blocks can be enhanced or added upon in the future, after other high-priority needs have been responded to with other building blocks.

The power of the building-block approach is the flexibility it gives to the PMO when trying to decide which functions to implement first, and to what extent. Rather than using a standardized full-service approach, being able to think of what incremental changes are the most needed by a particular organization facilitates the quick implementation of services that will deliver the most benefits. It also provides flexibility so that the implemented functions will be prioritized uniquely based upon organizational needs. If an organization is struggling to obtain consistent and accurate project status information, instead of the financial building blocks discussed above, the PMO could implement some status reporting building blocks. These might include:

- Reviewing all current reporting being done across projects
- Analyzing content, timing, and distribution of the information
- Developing a centralized reporting function
- Creating standard report templates for use across projects and timing the delivery of standard reports to all stakeholders

Again, this is not a robust solution, but should provide a noticeable improvement in the consistency and quality of the project information reported. Future building blocks might enhance the report templates or develop tools to support the capture and reporting of project status information. The building-block concept supports the ability to deliver uniquely creative PMO implementations.

Overview of Typical PMO Services

PMOs are typically implemented because of a perceived need within an organization. This need is usually the result of project management pain that the organization is experiencing. Recent project failures may be the impetus for a PMO to be formed by the orgnization. Most organizations unrealistically think that the mere decision to establish a PMO will prevent all future project failures. Other organizations decide to implement one because of the desire to centralize the functions that may be dispersed across the organization. Again, the expectation is that the establishment of the PMO will serve to harness the project management expertise across the organization and further the project management capabilities of the organization.

Regardless of why an organization decides to form a PMO, trying to implement a full-service one all at once is unlikely to deliver the desired results. Also, trying to use a "typical" blueprint of PMO services to dictate what an individual organization's PMO should be responsible for will result in disappointment. Each organization is unique, and to be successful, its PMO must be a reflection of its own culture.

A PMO may develop its own project management methodology to define a common project structure that defines project phases and deliverables to be produced by each project. It may also provide templates and guidance for their use for the deliverables as part of the methodology. A PMO may be empowered to select the tools that will be used to manage projects. These can include simple spreadsheets, or more comprehensive project management tools. Some PMOs offer project management education and training. Others are responsible for managing one or more programs or portfolios and may need to set up additional services for managing governance of such. Benefit realization or management is another area where the need and importance will vary by organization and its level of maturity.

Overview of PMO Organizational Structures

PMOs may exist within a single functional area of the organization, such as information services. Others are cross-functional and are responsible for managing a wider variety of organizational projects. They may have a small staff and utilize matrix resources for the duration of a project. Others may centralize the organization's project management resources and assign staff to projects as needed.

A PMO may cover a single location or many locations. Today, project resources often reside in other time zones and countries, thus scheduling and conducting project meetings can be a challenge.

There is not a single right PMO organizational structure. There are many success and failure stories for each type of PMO organization. The key to success is to recognize the needs of a particular organization and develop a PMO that meets those needs.

Why Size, Color, and Sequence Do Not Matter

Every PMO must quickly determine why it was formed and what value it needs to continually deliver to the organization. What project challenges were being experienced? What did the organization hope to achieve by forming the PMO? The answers to these questions should be used to guide the selection and sequencing of services or building blocks that the PMO implements, as well as the degree to which they implement the services. If the organization is unhappy with its project results, determining why the results were obtained will enable the PMO to focus on improving the estimation process, improving project communication and status reporting, issue escalation, and methodology. Each organization's needs will be unique, as should the services that they choose to implement. If two PMOs were to implement identical services, the implementation sequence and the extent that the services are implemented would vary between the organizations.

Benefits of Using PMO Building Blocks

Thinking of all the possible services that a PMO could provide as building blocks can help to establish a flexible framework for selecting which blocks to implement, the sequence for implementation, and the extent to which they are implemented. For example, one may choose to focus on project schedule creation and management, while another may focus more on communication.

Recent research into PMOs has found little commonality regarding the services provided and the extent to which they provide the services. The authors here contend that the lack of consistency across PMOs is because successful PMOs can assess their unique organizational needs and respond to them in individual sequences and to varying degrees. Building a PMO is an iterative and ongoing process that seeks to continually improve the level and effectiveness of services provided. Thinking of the PMO services as building blocks, and even thinking of each service as being composed of smaller building blocks provides a flexible framework for the gradual introduction of new services, as well as the enhancement of existing ones.

Project Management Building Blocks

Typical PMO services include the management of individual projects, program management, portfolio management and governance, financial management, change management, project management methodology, and training. Each of these will be looked at individually from a building-block perspective.

There is a wide range of organizational project management capabilities that PMOs attempt to standardize and improve. Developing comprehensive standards, processes, and policies for all aspects at once will be a daunting task. Even if you start with items that have worked in other successful PMOs, tailoring will be needed to ensure that these will work in the culture of the new environment. Instead let us try to break down the major components (building blocks) into smaller pieces (smaller building blocks). This will result in being able to pick and choose first the items that have the highest priority for implementation, and allow more time to develop items that have a lower priority.

Project Management Methodology and Processes

Since organizations form PMOs in response to particular project management challenges, they logically look for improvements to the most painful challenges first. If several high-profile projects have not completed on time, within budget, and delivered the expected results, they are frequently formed to improve the organization's project management ability.

Implementing selected standards that mandate common ways for projects to be managed is one way for a PMO to respond to these challenges. It is essential to quickly determine the most pressing needs and respond accordingly. For example, if there is no project management methodology or processes in use within an organization, it is likely that project results will be inconsistent and largely unfavorable. Putting some structure in place for methodology and process framework will ensure that there is a common approach to project management, and will standardize how projects are managed within an organization.

This need for a project management methodology and accompanying processes does not require hundreds of pages to be authored. Identification of project phase names and agreement as to which deliverables will be produced as part of each phase can be thought of as the first building block. Something as simple as standard phase and deliverable names will enable the organization to think about diverse projects in a consistent manner. It will also enable the standardization of project-status reporting (a future building block). A project schedule template might be developed as the next building block. These improvements will serve to reinforce the consistency of project management across diverse projects because the phase and deliverable names will be managed and reported on in a consistent manner. These changes are visible to other areas of the organization, and will be viewed favorably only if they result in better project outcomes. So it is important to introduce supporting process improvements (other building blocks) to ensure that the changes deliver real improvements to the projects.

Project Templates

Once there is agreement about the phases and deliverables, the next building block could be the development of templates for a few key deliverables. It is not necessary, nor advisable, to attempt to develop a comprehensive project management methodology (fully documented phases, deliverables, and guidelines) as a first step. This is too ambitious an undertaking and will take too long to complete. The advantage of using the building-block concept is that it enables you to prioritize the most important needs and respond to them in an incremental manner. This building-block approach allows the PMO to demonstrate progress, which is very important because PMOs have a short lifespan if they are not perceived as adding value to an organization. The building-block approach also provides a solid foundation that will support the development of future building blocks or enhancements.

Developing a standard responsible, accountable, supportive, consulted, and informed (RASCI) diagram that will be used for every project can also yield great benefits. These documents identify the individuals who are RASCI for each project deliverable. The expectations of individual team members become consistent across projects through the use of a RASCI diagram, which can in turn improve their level of participation and contribution. As you are building out your project templates, do not forget that a RASCI building block is relatively easy to implement and can deliver a big benefit.

Another advantage that the building-block concept provides is that it will enable you to react quickly to rethink an improvement you made that did not deliver the expected result. Since the building blocks introduce a manageable amount of change, it is relatively easy to redirect efforts that are off target. Not only can you use the building-block concept to test-market project deliverable templates, you can also easily improve project deliverable templates as the PMO's experience grows and there are new improvement ideas developed.

Project Management Tools

Other building blocks that can leverage having a common methodology in place include the ability to show project information in a consistent manner across projects. A simple template can be developed to report weekly on the progress of individual projects. If each project uses the same report template, and the same phases and deliverable names, these reports will become a powerful communication medium that not only depicts individual project progress, but also demonstrates more PMO progress in getting its arms around the management of the organization's projects.

Status colors (e.g., red, yellow, and green) and their associated meanings are building blocks that can be used to further standardize PMO project tracking and reporting. It is important that the use of status colors be standardized and used consistently across projects to clarify the organizational understanding of their use.

Project Schedules

Project schedules are another building block that can be placed upon the common project management methodology foundation. Project schedules can mirror the project phases and deliverables to improve consistency across projects. This is not to say that every project schedule will be identical to all others; each project plan will contain unique tasks. Project phases may repeat iteratively if an agile approach is used. But it is possible to increase the level of standardization across project schedules by building a common project schedule building block on top of the project management methodology building block. A future project schedule building block might provide additional guidelines for supplemental project schedule content such as what views are to be used, how tasks are to be resourced, how baselines will be used, how dependencies will be used, how progress will be determined and reported (i.e., percent complete, earned value, etc.). The sequence of building blocks that are introduced should reflect each organization's prioritized needs, but the intent should be the continued improvement of the organization's project management maturity.

Project Communication

Many organizations are frustrated by what they perceive is a lack of communication about project status until it is too late, and the bad news comes as a surprise. It has been said that communication is what a project manager spends the most of his or her time performing, and a PMO should also communicate on a regular basis to a broad audience. Something as simple as having each project produce a consistent status report on the same day of the week can be used as evidence to demonstrate the contribution the PMO is making to the organization with regard to project reporting.

A broader view of the PMO's need to communicate should be developed as well. A communication plan for the PMO should be developed as a building block. The PMO communication plan building block should identify all PMO stakeholders and group them by the type and frequency of information they need to receive. Not all stakeholders need or want to receive detailed weekly project status reports. It may be more important to produce higher-level information suitable for executives on a regular (monthly or quarterly) basis. Some PMOs only report exceptions—with the assumption that no news is good news. Again, every organization will have its own unique communication needs. The successful PMO will identify a series of communication building blocks that it will use to phase in its communications plan.

Project Management Education and Training

Some PMOs are tasked to provide project management education and training to the organization. This training may be limited to project managers, or may also include project sponsors, executives, or team members. There may be a budget that will allow the PMO to engage professional trainers, or they may have to work with HR to develop a class. Some PMOs do their own training, and some encourage self-study and the use of webinars.

There are no specific requirements or guidelines for PMOs to follow to fulfill these responsibilities. The number and types of building blocks to select from is limited only by your imagination. Consider developing a project management reference library as a low-cost building block that will enable project managers to broaden their knowledge. Encourage project managers to become active in the local PMI® chapter or special interest group so that they can obtain another source of professional and personal enrichment. Many project management training organizations offer low-cost or free lunchtime webcasts. Hosting a quarterly brown bag lunch webcast in a conference room is a creative low-cost project management education building block. These building blocks can be chosen as desired in whatever size is needed, or can be supported by the PMO budget. Thinking of project management training components as building blocks will enable creative approaches to be developed in response to organizational needs.

Program Management Building Blocks

In some organizations, there are well-defined programs in place. In other organizations, however, the PMO may discover that many large, multiyear projects are actually programs or groups of projects. Organizing a large work effort into discrete projects makes it easier to plan, manage, and to show progress over time. It also can be used to provide evidence of project accomplishments as projects complete. The process is iterative throughout the life of the program because as some projects end, others must start.

Program Governance

If a PMO decides to implement some program management building blocks, one of the foundational building blocks to consider is program level governance. This function oversees all the projects within the program regarding the prioritization of the projects, planning and managing the projects, as well as financial and resource planning, monitoring, and controlling. Significant changes to the program will also be controlled by this function.

Projects can be grouped into a program for a variety of reasons. Some programs consist of projects for a common customer. Others utilize a common technology. Although there are diverse reasons for grouping projects into programs, the expectation is that there will be efficiencies realized by creating a program to oversee the projects. The PMO challenge is to identify those expected efficiencies, and to develop a governance process that will clearly manage to, and meet, those expectations.

Program or Project Valuation Assessment

Just as the reasons why organization's group projects vary, so too will the ways in which the individual projects within a program will be valued and prioritized. Let us consider a program that consists of all the project work for a particular customer. The PMO will need to work with the customer to develop criteria that can be used to determine a priority among the projects, identify interproject dependencies, and develop a program schedule that the customer agrees with.

In another scenario, a program may consist of all project work related to a particular technology. This program has a diverse set of stakeholders. The PMO will need to work with all the program stakeholders to develop a way to prioritize and schedule the projects in the program.

It is common for PMOs to be responsible for managing multiple programs at one time, and this is where the program or project valuation assessment building blocks become a powerful tool. It should not attempt to implement rigorous program management across all programs at one time. Instead, remembering the building-blocks concept, target one or two of the programs that have the most challenges. Examine the root causes of the challenges and implement small changes that will address those challenges. The PMO approach should be flexible and scalable based on the size and complexity of the program, as well as the level of risks and issues with the program.

The end vision is to have a formal, comprehensive program management methodology in place that addresses, at least, program governance, project selection, project tracking, and reporting for all programs. However, all program governance items do not need to be implemented at once, nor do they need to be implemented across all programs to the same extent or at the same time. The PMO must be sure to address the most critical needs first, even if this approach causes it to implement many program management building blocks into one program, while not doing much on other programs. Once a working set of program governance building blocks are in place for a single program, they will provide a firm foundation to support deployment of program governance to other programs.

Alternatively if there is a common challenge being faced across programs, the PMO may want to pick a selected group of program governance building blocks to implement across multiple programs at the same time. This approach will be successful if it can improve the performance of the programs, and serves as a foundation for future program building blocks to be introduced across the programs.

Program Progress Tracking and Reporting

The program progress tracking and reporting building block has two components: the need to track individual projects within a program and the need to track overall program progress. Hopefully the PMO will be able to leverage the project tracking and project reporting building blocks to satisfy the first component. That will only leave the program progress tracking and reporting building blocks for it to develop.

To evaluate the program progress, the PMO must examine not only the progress of the individual projects within the program, but also have to evaluate the progress being made toward implementing the program goals. The program tracking building block will need to work with program governance to have them determine what information they will use to assess program progress. This could be a combination of program milestones, program financial performance including benefit realization, and program risks.

Program governance should also provide input to the program communication plan that will identify key program stakeholders and their information needs. Program reporting communication building blocks should be developed and implemented to satisfy those identified needs.

Portfolio Management Building Blocks

For companies that develop strategic plans, the company strategy lays out broad directions and goals. The strategic plan outlines what is to be accomplished with a corresponding timeframe for completion. It does not, however, explain how the organization will implement its strategic vision. That is where projects are needed. Companies identify projects that they will undertake to put their strategy into effect. Most organizations typically identify many projects that will need to be completed. Organizing all of this work into a corporate portfolio to be managed by its PMO can help an organization to manage its projects more effectively. Such a portfolio will contain projects of various types and sizes, which will all compete for resources.

Strategic plans usually cover multiple years, and portfolio management will be ongoing and iterative over this period. Achieving the strategic plan will require that as projects complete, new ones begin. Also, the competitive landscape will continue to change and could identify the need for new projects that may impact the work that was originally planned. The ability to manage change at the portfolio level, as well as at the program and project level, is the key to successful portfolio management.

Portfolio Governance

A portfolio governance function is typically used to ensure the company portfolio will be kept in alignment with the company strategy, and to ensure its strategic goals are reached. PMOs that are responsible for strategic projects may choose to implement a few portfolio governance building blocks so that there will be a group of senior executives providing oversight of the corporate portfolio and making needed decisions. It may be responsible for providing information to the portfolio governance members ensuring that fact-based decisions can be made. It is important to note that the PMO is not a decision maker in this process, but it facilitates decisions by providing required information.

As seen in Figure 9.2, the portfolio governance building blocks that may be implemented first might include:

- Identifying appropriate executives to sit on the portfolio governance committee
- Working with committee members to develop the criteria that will be used to value and prioritize projects in the portfolio
- Holding regular portfolio governance committee meetings to review information about projects in the corporate portfolio
- Providing information to the committee members

How does the concept of building blocks help to develop a portfolio governance function? The size and scope of project portfolios will vary greatly between organizations. Some organizations may have multiple portfolios, each with different

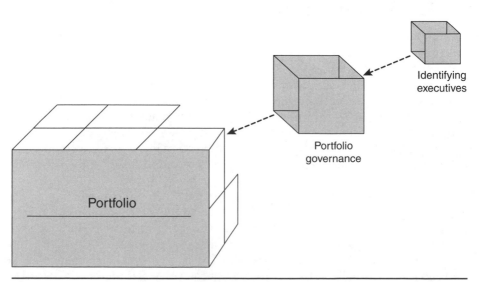

Figure 9.2   Portfolio governance building blocks.

purposes. The governance needs of portfolios will vary, as will the criteria that will be used to prioritize the projects and make decisions. Keeping an open mind, and enabling the PMO to respond in a scalable manner to unique needs, will position it to be more effective in implementing a portfolio governance function that is appropriate for organizational needs.

Project Selection

Every organization is unique, but there are always more good ideas than there is capacity to act on them. It is essential that the PMO work with the portfolio governance function to develop an organizational approach to selecting projects. It is the facilitator of the process, but the portfolio governance function must work within a consistent framework to make decisions. The PMO can assist this process by providing consistent information to the portfolio governance committee so that it can be effective in making decisions. Once the committee members agree to the criteria it wants to see regarding project prioritization, it should maintain the accuracy of these criteria for each project in the portfolio. The PMO will also ensure that the governance committee agrees to meet at predetermined intervals and reviews pertinent information.

Project Valuation Assessment

The PMO should be able to work with the portfolio governance committee members to come to a consensus on the information they will use to value the projects proposed for their portfolio. The project valuation building block does not need to be very sophisticated, especially if organizational project management maturity is low, but it does need to develop a method that will be used consistently. The project valuation may be a composite of various project characteristics, such as the financial value the project is expected to provide, combined with how the project aligns with strategic goals. It may also include risks and any other information the committee members think is important to evaluate.

The goal is to be able to use the project valuation assessments to establish a recommended order of work based on objective measures. These may be adjusted by portfolio governance committee discretion and negotiation, but the idea is that it provides a schema that will compare projects not just against one another, but also within the context of the corporate portfolio that supports the strategic plan. A project valuation assessment building block needs to be able to demonstrate how each project contributes to the company's business success and strategic goals.

Portfolio Benefit Management and Realization

Portfolio management is ongoing and requires information about project progress. The PMO needs to develop a portfolio progress reporting building block to ensure that the agreed-upon criteria are being followed. This function can be very simple at first, and can be added to, over time. Minimally, key information about each project on the portfolio needs to be reported on at regular intervals. This may include schedule and budget information as well as issues and risks. Thinking of portfolio reporting as a function that can be phased in using a building-block approach will quickly enable the PMO to be able to provide support for portfolio management decisions and changes.

OPM—A Practical Framework for Success

You have heard a lot in this chapter about the concepts of building blocks and how you can build a successful PMO using this targeted incremental approach. Step back for just a second and think about the high-level blocks of portfolio, program, and project management. Think about how they need to work in concert with each other to deliver what the PMO has been commissioned to do—add value to the bottom line. When built correctly and completed, those building blocks come together to create a framework that the industry is now calling *organizational project management* (OPM). Organizational project management is formally defined as, "The application of knowledge, skills, tools and techniques to organizational activities and project, program, and portfolio activities to achieve the aims of an organization through projects" (Project Management Institute, 2008).

These elements work together to build a system that creates a strategic delivery mechanism as seen in Figure 9.3. The strategy of the organization is fed to the portfolios, which in turn determine what initiatives should be launched to fulfill the organization's strategy. They make the decisions that deliver the greatest business value. The selected initiatives are then given to the programs and projects that deliver the initiatives the right way, delivering the business value they have been commissioned for, on time and on budget. Once the programs and projects transition the business value to operations, the promised benefits can be realized.

All through this process, the organization monitors market conditions and reviews the results of the programs and projects and adjusts the entire framework accordingly.

The successful PMO must have a vision of where it wants to go—how it will add value and use the building-block approach to incrementally add services to the organization, all while building the framework of a strategic delivery mechanism.

As you build your PMO vision and utilize the building-block approach, you might be wondering if you are on the right track. If this is the case, you might want to stop and analyze what you have accomplished and create a baseline for your organization of what has already been completed to date. The project management industry is seeing that most best-in-class organizations are assessing themselves at a frequency that is tailored to their growth as a PMO. If you are

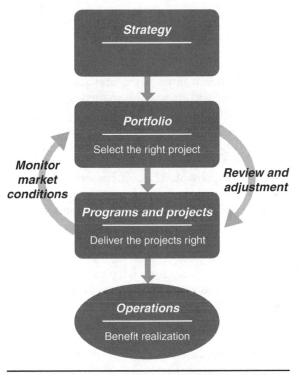

Figure 9.3 Strategic delivery elements.

only able to put a few building blocks in place in a year, you may only need to assess your organization every couple of years. If your PMO is on the fast track, once or twice a year may better suit your needs. This baseline establishes the value you have been putting into place and also gives you a clear picture of what is missing and where your next building blocks should be placed.

How does a PMO assess their approach and accomplishments? A solid model for this analysis is the *Organizational Project Management Maturity Model* developed by PMI. This model was introduced in 2003 and has since been updated to more accurately reflect the best practices of the project management industry. The updated model has a comprehensive listing of industry best practices that reflect what best-in-class organizations do in the arenas of project, program, and portfolio management. There is another arena that it also covers, which is called *organizational enabling best practices*. These best practices are, "structural, cultural, technological and human resource practices that can be leveraged to support the implementation of Best Practices in projects, programs and portfolios in support of strategic goals." (Project Management Institute, 2008). Basically these are the foundational best practices that deal with organization structures, management systems, organizational project management, practices, methodologies, and techniques as well as how the organization supports the entire philosophy of the PMO and organizational project management.

To use this model, you will need to determine the right assessment approach for your organization. There are three paths that you might pursue. The first is to read the OPM3® standard and review the self-assessment that is offered there. This assessment is fairly high level and will give you some indication of what your organization has achieved. The second and third approaches provide more rigor in the assessment, as well as a solid foundation on knowing what to improve. The second approach is to have one or several of the PMO leaders attend classes on organizational project management. These members can be certified by PMI to work in this organizational project management business solution. The last path is to hire an objective third party who has been licensed by PMI as a certified professional working in organizational project management.

Regardless of the approach you use, you will walk away from the assessment knowing exactly (paths 2 and 3) what has been accomplished and what is missing. You use this knowledge to determine what next step building blocks should be implemented to continue to add value to the organization.

It is important that PMOs be able to make and clearly demonstrate improvements that continue over time. Methodologies can be refined and matured through the continued use of additional, more sophisticated building blocks. Tools can be enhanced or replaced as needed. Reports can also become more detailed and eventually lead to the introduction of balanced scorecards.

More importantly, the PMO must continually show how and where it adds value to an organization. The unique organizational challenges that caused the formation of the PMO are important to monitor and report progress. If project budgets were a challenge and early building blocks were successful in implementing controls, later building blocks can focus on developing improved estimates. If post-implementation defects are a challenge, implementing a metrics building-block function to demonstrate improvement in this area will provide transparency into the realized improvements.

Not all improvements will deliver the anticipated outcomes. The PMO should be prepared to knock down some of the building blocks and start over if the results are not as expected. Because the blocks represent small, incremental changes, these are not large setbacks, rather they are small readjustments thanks to the flexibility of the incremental changes referred to as *building blocks*.

Branding the PMO

It is important to communicate the successful outcomes that are being realized. Whether you measure based on size of budget, number of projects managed, decreasing number of change requests, or other characteristics, it is important to be sure that you are making progress, and getting the word out.

Some PMOs develop logos or templates that they use each time they communicate or issue a report. This is a low-effort building block that can help the PMO to forge an identity within an organization. It is also important to emphasize the PMO as the single source of truth for information about its projects. This will prevent organizational confusion and miscommunications.

Some PMOs establish an intranet site and place information about its organization, methodology, training, and other services that they provide. There is no single approach that works for all. The key to PMO success is to determine which building blocks are needed, and to what extent. Implementing those building blocks and measuring the results will not only let you know the good news that can be communicated broadly, but can also give an early warning of additional improvements that are needed.

PMO Leadership—The Glue That Holds It All Together

Leading a PMO is a challenge for many reasons. Organizations frequently have unrealistic expectations of them. They become impatient if it takes too long for a PMO to be able to demonstrate improvements. Projects, budgets, and priorities are typically highly charged politically, and this causes them to be targeted too. The best way to ensure success is to have strong leadership within the PMO. Individuals who have extensive technical, business, and project management backgrounds will be able to successfully meet a variety of challenges. It is also important that they be able to set a vision and get other PMO and organizational resources to achieve the vision.

In this chapter, you have been introduced to the concept of PMO building blocks, discrete services that can be chosen to implement to varying levels of degree and in any desired sequence. Just as many different types of structures can be built from a single a set of building blocks, so too can many different types of PMOs be built using a set of common PMO building blocks.

You also were introduced to two defining concepts that can further assure the success of your PMO. The first was how to use the organizational project management business solution to guide you along the path of building your PMO. The second was the importance of leadership. Leadership is truly the glue that holds the concepts together.

Author Biographies

Ruth Anne Guerrero, MBA, PMP, joined the Amerihealth Mercy Family of Companies in 2007 as vice president of the program management office (PMO). She has a broad background in project management with particular expertise in establishing and managing PMOs. Ruth Anne was a founding member of PMI's Long Island Chapter and served as the chapter's vice president of programs for many years. When her job transferred her to the Philadelphia area in late 2004, she became active in the PMI Delaware Valley Chapter and was subsequently elected to a director at large position, where she is currently serving as president-elect and vice president of programs.

Ruth Anne was the standards manager at PMI, managing thousands of volunteers from around the world, collaborating on virtual teams to develop new and updated project management standards including new editions of the *PMBOK® Guide, Organizational Project Management Maturity Model (OPM3®), The Standard for Program Management,* and *The Standard for Portfolio Management.*

Prior to joining PMI, Ruth Anne worked at JPMorgan Chase Cardmember Services where she served as vice president, responsible for the project management center of excellence, a project office, and a competency development center that supported project managers worldwide. Ruth Anne has also held positions at Cablevision Systems Corporation, the Long Island Lighting Company, and Insurance Services Office.

Ruth Anne has deep experience in standardizing project management processes and promoting ways that the project management discipline can help organizations improve their project execution, thereby enabling the attainment of strategic business goals.

Claudia M. Baca, PMP, OPM3® certified assessor and consultant, has been active in project management since 1984 and has project management experience in multiple industries. During her long and varied career, Claudia has managed multiple mission-critical projects for companies as varied as a major telecommunications company to an Internet start-up. She most recently was the vice-president of consulting services for a nationally known project management consulting firm. Currently, Claudia is an independent consultant focusing on organizational project management consulting and training.

Claudia was a member of the leadership team that produced the standard for project management maturity, OPM3®, and completed delivery of the second edition of that standard in 2007. She has a masters certificate in program management from Denver University and earned her PMP in 1995.

Claudia is also an experienced writer. She coauthored three papers on OPM3®, which were presented at PMI® Global Congresses in 2003, 2004, and 2007. She is the coauthor of the *PMP Project Management Professional Workbook,* and the author of *Project Management Spotlight on Change Management, The PMP Project Management Professional Study Guide Deluxe Edition,* and *Project Management for Mere Mortals.* Claudia now produces video courses. The first is titled *Live Lesson: Project Management for Mere Mortals* based on her book in 2007. The second is *Live Lesson: PMP Exam Prep* produced in June 2008.

Claudia was the first PMI certified OPM3® product suite assessor and consultant. She has assessed and improved organizational project management maturity in organizations ranging in size from an international computer peripheral manu-facturing to a 200-employee mortgage title company.

References

Project Management Institute, *Organizational Project Management Maturity Model (OPM3®)*, 2nd edition, Newtown Square, PA, PMI, 2008.

10

Creating and Proving PMO Value

Matthew Hayes, PMP

Introduction

What is the value of the project management office (PMO) and why should we keep this organization?

This question strikes fear and uncertainty into everyone in the PMO organization and especially the PMO manager. It is a question that not only hints that the business is looking to save costs, but it shows that the organization is improperly executing its mission. But why do companies ask this question? How can the PMO answer this question, and how can it attempt to avoid this question from being asked in the future? The objective of this chapter is to show that a properly aligned PMO can effectively answer this question and possibly avoid it altogether.

Throughout this chapter we will investigate the importance of insuring that the PMO is aligned to the culture of the organization and is focusing on executing projects to meet business needs. These two activities—culture and execution alignments—are the keys to producing and proving value. The ultimate goal is for the PMO to be so tied to the success of the company that it becomes indispensible. When established and managed properly, it will not have an issue proving its value to the company.

Approaches to PMO Justification

Before we move into a discussion on cultures and alignment, it is critical that we understand why the question of PMO value is even asked. Businesses today are constantly looking for ways to improve profitability. Profitability can be obtained through two courses of action: adding new customer revenue or reducing expenses. Although these principles are extremely basic to business, project managers often forget that these two components are the lifeblood of their company. When the PMO is evaluated, senior management does not immediately look at it as a revenue-generating organization, nor does it see the cost savings that the PMO is generating. As a result, senior management begins to question the value of the team and whether the project managers are actually doing anything to reduce cost or increase revenue. The question of value is further complicated by the fact that the PMO does not independently produce any products. On its own, it does not produce software code, additional hardware, new sales opportunities, or ongoing revenue. In the eye of a senior manager who is unfamiliar with what the PMO does on a daily basis, it becomes a line item on a financial statement that should be evaluated for reduction or elimination.

If the PMO has been identified in this way, the questions become more difficult. Senior management and finance begin to ask tough questions such as: *What exactly does the PM do? Why are they doing it?* and *What need is there for a project manager or the PMO?* These questions are aimed at discrediting the project manager and eliminating the PMO. An attempt to justify and explain the daily functions may lead to a discussion of why the functional manager is not addressing the needs of the project. From senior management's point of view, functional managers should be able to manage their business units in a way that not only meets the needs of the business, but also in a way that does not require project managers. However they often do not understand that there can be significant impacts that come from making this type of move. In my experience, when the company moves away from project management to functional manager control, project delivery is not the only item that is impacted. It is also detrimental to the functional department. The functional organization is so focused on its regular activities that it is not able to spend the required time on the overall delivery of the project. In addition, the functional group is not designed to perform cross-functional work, nor is it set up to provide the reporting requirements that senior leadership requires. These items are not looked at when senior leadership looks at cost-saving measures such as a reduction or elimination of the PMO.

Another roadblock to being able to answer the question of PMO value is often caused by its structure. This is especially true for PMO organizations that have been built to police project managers and require that they follow a very rigid project deployment methodology rather than the management of projects. This type of structure does not have a clear connection with successfully executed projects, which prevents it from quickly providing data on the value it is providing. To justify the existence of a PMO, it must be able to answer the value question based on its ability to deliver to the business in an efficient and effective manner.

Many PMOs try to answer the justification question through presentations and persuasion. For example, I have heard many people say something such as, "We are trying to establish a PMO at my organization. However senior management is not buying into following the methodology we have developed."

Attempting to justify a PMO in a company is extremely difficult through theory and documentation alone. It is the same type of selling that is required to move an organization to Six Sigma, TQM, or any other standard methodology that is in the marketplace. Executives may have experience with a given methodology and may have supported it in the past, but it is extremely hard for them to commit to a methodology without proven results. My response to individuals caught in this justification approach is that they must prove the value of project management through execution. Management wants to see that a PMO works and that it provides them something they cannot get through other means. Without hard proof of success in their organization, the likelihood of a senior manager supporting a new group is extremely low. Start with a focus on executing projects, and then move into a more robust project methodology.

This reminds me of what occurs within sporting events. Many teams will show up at the beginning of the game and brag about how many points they will win by, or how much better they are. Time and again we can see that the bigger talkers are often defeated by the teams that simply execute their game plan and work as a unified group. It is not the words of the players that make the difference, it is the fact that they deliver during the game. How many people would rather see someone deliver on their actions than simply talk about their abilities? Unfortunately, many PMOs I have encountered want to go down this path of talking and explaining, rather than just doing. They attempt to justify based on their methodology or their standards. However this shaky ground is not tied to business results, which is the lifeblood of the company. The PMO should focus on delivery, document the success, and then do it again. I am not saying that the PMO should ignore explanations; it simply needs to follow up with action.

Some PMOs have set themselves up for these value questions through their behavior and their requirements. They have drilled methodology into their organization to such a degree that they are actually inhibiting the delivery of a project. In essence, they have become their own worst enemy. In one company I worked for, the PMO had an excellent stage-gate methodology. They followed all the great thinking on project management, including appropriate executive buy in, continual gate reviews, and they established levels of control based on the size and risk of the project. All these things were set up to ensure that a project was delivered successfully. However, they missed one very important function: the function of the project manager to manage in alignment with business needs. Instead, they were relying on the paperwork required by the methodology for a project to succeed, eliminating the critical human interactions. Many times I sat in a gate review for a project, going over the nearly 45 pages of required project management documentation for a gate, and heard the words, "Are you sure this is all the paperwork for this gate? Isn't page X missing from this paperwork?" Or worse yet, "This header on page 35 is not consistent with the other headers. We can't approve this project to move forward without it being correct." The methodology of the PMO was killing the project by focusing attention on the documents rather than on the content and objectives of the project. The lack of business need for the project, not the PMO methodology nor the project manager working the project, should be the determining factor.

As a result of these over-burdened gate reviews, the impression of getting a project manager involved or using project management methodology was that it was not going to help; it was just going to add overhead. Paperwork is important for documentation, status updates, and project organization. However, it should not be the reason for the project manager. This is a sign that value is not being delivered. Value is created, proven, and maintained through meeting a business need in a way that aligns with the company. The best way to ensure that this is occurring is to allow proper focus and attention to be spent on the business needs for a project.

A former boss once told me that, "It is not just if you deliver, but how you deliver that is important." Some individuals are good at doing the specific requirements of their job; others are good at building and maintaining relationships. Few people are good at both. The PMO that learns how to deliver projects without creating collateral damage (e.g., excessive paperwork or extensive project management prodding) will be successful. For example, I have worked with project managers who have been extremely gifted in getting a project completed when others were simply unable to accomplish the tasks. These project managers were very good at forcing a delivery date, holding teams accountable for their delivery dates, and ensuring that scope remained under control. But, these project managers were extremely poor at relationship building and this was the downfall of each of them as they were unable to successfully move from one project to the next due to the bridges burned during the first project. On the other hand, I have seen project managers who were fantastic relationship builders, but did not have the aggressiveness needed to push their project forward. This delicate balance between doing and relationship creation is the same balance the PMO must maintain between project delivery and internal process requirements. Without an appropriate balance, its value will be difficult to create and maintain over time.

Cultural Alignment

A primary key to creating and proving value for the PMO is to ensure that it is properly established within the culture of the company. Not every PMO is the same and there are no magic formulas for setting up a properly formed project management organization. The debate about the proper place for a PMO within the company has been going on for some time and will continue into the future. However where it is placed within the company is not as important as how it functions in relationship to the company's culture. It should then be the objective of PMO management to ensure that they align themselves to the culture of the company. Misalignment will quickly cause conflict. Just as a person would not go to a foreign country and begin insulting the people without anticipating consequences, the PMO should not begin to do things completely contrary to the company's stated practices. For example, I have heard of PMOs that have decided to take it upon themselves to be the determining group on whether to reject or accept a project due to the lack of strategic direction from senior management. This put them in a place of approving business plans, which resulted in immediate conflict with the senior managers who normally would review these proposals. Instead of this radical example, it must fit within the parameters of the company. Because the PMO is an enabling organization, it must be set up to operate as an enabler not a detractor.

As a project manager for a web billing company, I was assigned software deployment projects for telecommunication companies. Some of the companies were large Fortune 500 companies, some were small 100-person companies, and some were international. Each one was unique in how it operated, what it considered important documentation records, and what they required from their vendors. In this role, I could have forced those companies to align with how my company delivered projects, but this would have immediately caused tension during the delivery and there would have been continuing conflict throughout the project. Instead, I focused on how our customers delivered projects, and what they needed from the project manager and from my company as their vendor. By understanding the people that were involved, their personalities, and their goals, the delivery of the projects improved. Success came faster and daily progress became smoother because the companies saw the project manager as the enabler to their end goal. Simply by operating within the boundaries established for that given deployment, while not impacting our internal processes, greater success was obtained. Similarly, the identification of the cultural elements of the company in which project managers deliver projects is the key to ensuring success for the PMO. But how do we identify these areas and what things should be looked at when evaluating the company culture?

In my viewpoint, there are seven unique areas that define any culture, including any company culture. These areas are people, politics, purpose, process, policies, power, and pressures. Our goal as PMO leaders is to identify how these seven items are practiced in our company and apply them to our organization. It should be noted that the findings within these areas can vary vastly from one company to the next and sometimes from one division within the company to the next.

People

People are the key to overall alignment. People, not the projects or the process, will have the biggest impact on the success or failure of how the PMO aligns within the company. Project management is about communication, and communication occurs between people. Understanding the people who are in the company is critical to understanding the cultural makeup of the company. Most people when they leave a company will say something like, "I won't miss the work; I will miss the people." This is because the company is not merely a group of products and services. It is the people that make up the company. It is what causes deliveries to occur and what makes the company move forward. A company could eliminate every process and automate their entire delivery system, but it still would need to have people to make that company move forward. For this reason, it is critical that you understand the makeup of the people in your organization.

A key thing to look for when evaluating the people is how they relate together. Look at how people communicate. Do they spend time at lunch laughing and joking? Do they spend time together discussing anything outside of work, or is it all business all the time? What language is used in the workplace? Is it harsh and critical; or is it open and trusting? Do people communicate passive aggressively or do they communicate directly? Evaluate how they operate in groups and as individuals. During this exercise, focus your attention on those people closest to the PMO and to the projects being delivered.

There are many studies on personality types and how to relate to each type. For the project manager, the gift of identifying a personality and then appropriately reacting to that person is critical to his or her success. This skill is not easily trained in a classroom or by a book. Rather it must be learned through the example of others who are effective at working through other individuals. In my experience, project managers who work as a team can readily assist each other in identifying personality types and provide guidance on how to work with each type. When taking on a new project, spend time learning which individuals will be on the project team and in what capacity each person will operate. Understanding how each person will operate and react on the project will assist the project manager in their communication plan as well as provide indicators to watch for when working through their project. The PMO should encourage project managers to share their *personality* lessons learned just as much as their *project* lessons learned. These personality lessons will be a key to the success or failure of the next project.

After you have completed this evaluation of the people around the PMO, the people within it must come into alignment with the culture of the company or they will continually struggle to deliver. In my organization, we spend a great deal of time evaluating the fit of the individual with the culture. In fact, we have selected project managers to join the company based on this fit rather than on their certifications or project management expertise. I am not suggesting these other elements are not important, only that they are not as important as someone's ability to adapt to the culture of the organization.

Project managers, unlike any other role, must have the soft skills ability to identify the culture of the company and work within it. Without these skills, all the training, certifications, and project manager abilities are useless. If you find that a project manager is not aligning with the culture, but rather is trying to change it, the issue must be addressed quickly. There is nothing more detrimental to the PMO than a project manager who is attempting to change the culture or a PMO that is not properly aligned with the people who it interacts with on a daily basis.

Politics

Next in order of importance is politics. The word *politics* has so many different meanings in our society. As I refer to politics, I refer to the overriding motivations of people that cause them to act in a certain manner, and it typically relates to decisions made to benefit an individual, not the company. Every company has some level of politics, because every company is made up of people. Those who say they have limited or no politics in their company are either oblivious to the realities or they are the drivers of politics. Understand that politics drive the company. They are the core beliefs of people that result in decisions or events. As you look at the politics of your company, look for the person who is really in control. Who is that person who really drives the company, the division, and the team? How are decisions really made, and why are those decisions made? Delve into what makes the events of the company occur the way they do. If you dig hard enough, you are likely to find that they are made because of someone's political agenda to gain something for themselves. This could be a larger bonus, a promotion, greater control of the company, or simply personal bias. For example, look at recent company failures due to corporate greed. In nearly every situation the greed of several individuals resulted in business decisions that were driven by their personal goals and purposes.

Defining the culture of the PMO to align it with the political climate of the company is not an easy task. In this area it is more important to make sure that it does not add to the political underpinnings of the company. It needs to remain neutral in political issues, since siding with a corporate political party will cause the value of the organization to be an issue. If a shared PMO exists across the entire company, it is critical that it does not reside under an organization that consistently conflicts with another organization using its services. I have seen PMOs used by their leadership to push their personal agenda instead of the success of the company. This eventually leads to resentment from other divisions and makes it extremely difficult for the project managers to get work from the other political entity. However if the PMO is aligned with a neutral organization or directly with the chief operating office, that organization can maintain an unbiased view. Neutrality is critical in evaluating incoming projects, performing portfolio reviews, and performing daily functions. It also gives the project managers the ability to accomplish their projects without the political issue of individuals who intentionally do not want to participate in the project due to it being aligned with another organization. In the past I have seen the PMO align to a particular technology division or a particular operational organization. This works when there are multiple PMOs in the company. However this type of alignment does not work when the PMO is responsible for all projects, because this places it into the role of mediator to accomplish its mission.

Once you have identified where the political battles occur and have determined that your group is not aligned with a division that will prevent a neutral state, it is critical to apply that understanding to how projects are managed by the project managers. Doing this is not as easy as just defining a process for how it will be handled. It takes continual communication within the PMO to understand and discuss the elements of the political climate, because political situations change regularly. Each project manager must understand what activities on the project will incur political issues, how to avoid them, and how to use them to the advantage of the project. Effective project managers can use to their advantage the political climate to improve the success of their project through the appropriate use of these motivators. This takes an incredible amount of experience and expertise in understanding the politics of the company and how to effectively position the project to fit within these parameters.

Power

Every company has its power players: those individuals who can quickly destroy a project plan or the PMO. Since the PMO is completely reliant on others in the company for its success, its management must be aware of those people in the company who hold the most power over the PMO and its project portfolio. The power person in your company may not be the individual identified by looking at the hierarchy. Each individual in the company has some degree of power based on their time with the company, the area they are responsible for, or the number of people who report to him. It is critical that all areas of the PMO align with how these power players operate in the company. This includes ensuring that each project manager understands the initiation process that these power players require and the roadblocks they can create. A minor example of effectively managing power players can be seen in project funding approvals. When a PMO started submitting funding requests, the team would have to go through an extensive review process with their chief technology officer. The questions that were asked were always the same and surrounded several basic elements of the requests: *Why do we need it now?* and *What alternatives to this purchase were reviewed?* Tired of constant rework for these questions, the PMO requested that these questions be built into the finance request form. Immediately they saw a reduced number of review meetings to discuss the *why* of the request. This did not eliminate the need to go through reviews, but it dramatically reduced the challenges they faced relating to request justification.

PMO management should spend time with these power players on an ongoing basis so that these players become supporters of the organization. In my career, I have made it a point to spend time with those vice presidents, directors, and managers who play the most significant role in my projects and on my team, even if there is not something specifically required from them. This practice not only allows me to have open communication with these individuals, but also builds a relationship of trust with these key players. A former boss said, "If you always go to someone only when you need something, you create the wrong expectation." Be sure to build the relationship with power players.

Building relationships takes a great deal of time, effort, and persistence. It requires you to pay attention to the likes and dislikes of the other individual. Learn what motivates them and consumes the majority of their time outside of work. These outside interests will be indicators about what is important to them and what drives them in how they respond at work. For example, a person who is very involved with their kids may be focused on getting work done in a way that allows them to spend more time with their kids. Other individuals may be interested in the arts, sports, or world events. Once you understand these interests, take time to educate yourself about these activities so that you can intelligently converse with these individuals. Cutting out a newspaper article that relates to their interest or discussing a recent sporting event creates a stronger bridge. Beyond just the external interests of others, the project manager and PMO manager must understand the work interests of others. Focus on how their team operates, what their intake process is, what their trouble spots are, and what causes them the greatest amount of pain. Understanding these components of their division will build a working relationship with that division and enable the PMO and the project manager to make sure that they operate in a way that fits within the realm of that group. A PMO that can guide their projects to completion while meeting the intangible needs of each division will be extremely successful. PMOs that continually demand from a division simply based on their need to deliver a project will continually destroy these relationship bridges and will hurt their ability to be successful.

Remember you cannot eliminate or change power players. You can, however, learn who they are and what they require, then align your organization to meet their needs. Think about the roadblocks project managers are faced with related to power players in your organization and develop ways to meet those roadblocks more effectively. This could include establishing policies and procedures that prevent the power players from being able to play as strong a role on the delivery of the projects. The end goal is to set up your project managers for success, and power players can either advance the goal or prevent that goal from occurring.

Pressures

Every company is defined by the pressures that are exerted against it. These pressures could be financial, such as quarterly results for Wall Street, or they could be cost-saving goals. They could be driven by others, such as competitive products. All of these pressures play into the success of the PMO as they will be evidenced in the project delivery and will need to be handled by the project managers. Although there are a variety of ways to align the PMO to the pressures the company faces, it is important that the PMO enables the project managers (PMs) to understand what these pressures are and the results that may be experienced by these pressures, so that they can adapt their projects accordingly. Start by identifying what these pressures are, who controls the level of pressure on them, and the triggers. For example, as a company goes through organizational realignment or a buyout, the impact to projects can be extreme. I have seen the mere rumor of organizational realignment result in changed behavior in the affected departments. Consequently the ability to deliver on projects was dramatically impacted as people attempted to show their personal worth through unusually aggressive behavior. It is critical that the project management team is aware of pressures such as these, so that the project team can adapt to this heightened emotional response. Strong communication within the PMO is the primary way of ensuring that the project managers can adapt their projects to changes. There is not a magic solution to pressure points. It is all about interproject manager communication on how to avoid pressure points and how to appropriately use them to assist in meeting the goals of the project.

Policies

Every company must operate under defined policies. These policies dictate to the company and divisions what must occur to be compliant with governmental laws and regulations. Company policies may include: Sarbanes-Oxley (SOX), ISO, and/or employment laws. These policies are the guiding walls in the company that cannot be crossed. It is important that the PMO not only understand what these policies are, but should also be a leader in ensuring that the work of the project teams aligns with these policies.

I have seen project methodologies built that directly conflict with company policy. This puts the project manager in a position of attempting to play two sides of a situation to make sure the project is successful. Avoid this by ensuring that the work of the project manager aligns with the policies of the company. However, the PMO should take it a step further and actually make sure that the project managers are aware of the organization's policies so they can ensure that their projects meet these standards. For example, if company policy requires a security audit of all new code, project managers can build this into their plans. Not only does this help the project manager deliver their project more efficiently; it also allows the PMO's value to be immediately felt since they are making sure policies are met in a timely and effective manner. As awareness of this value increases, different divisions will make an effort to ensure that the PMO is educated on their process so that their work gets incorporated effectively into projects.

Process

The greatest failure area for PMOs in cultural alignment relates to process. Process alignment involves identifying and becoming familiar with the processes that must be followed in the company to implement change. These processes include change management, procurement, funding, provisioning, sales, request for proposal, etc. It is important that the PMO management team clearly understands and communicates the major processes that are used within the company, so that these processes can be properly aligned with the project management methodology. Project managers cannot be rogue and attempt to push things through faster simply because of a project need. They need to understand the processes that must be used for proper completion of their project, the time to get an activity through each process, and how to initiate the process. When there is a lack of a defined process, the PMO can gain value by identifying needed processes and providing feedback for correcting a process in the future. Through project management training and methodology descriptions, it can align with the processes within the company.

Once alignment with company processes has occurred, the PMO must ensure that their own process matches the company culture. Most PMO managers want to move to higher levels of maturity by imposing complex methodology policies and practices upon the project manager. The purpose of applying these processes is to ensure that projects are consistent and successful. However, hiding behind these processes, rather than addressing the individual capabilities of the project managers, can be detrimental to the overall PMO. While the end goal is for consistency and success, these processes can actually have the opposite effect. I have seen a two-inch thick notebook of tools and methodology guidelines used for a Fortune 500 PMO. Because continual methodology changes were occurring, constant retraining was necessary to make sure project managers were following the methodology. All of this training and effort did not improve the success of the projects. It only changed the perception of the PMO from an organization that enabled project success, to an added level of paperwork needed to get something done. It is critical that the team understand that the business need for a project is the reason they exist. Methodology and project management processes should only be established to the level necessary to enable the project managers to effectively manage the project to a successful conclusion.

In the companies that I have been involved with, I have spent a great deal of time ensuring that the PMO methodology and practice remained consistent with the level of process for that company. Wherever possible, I have attempted to keep project management paperwork to the bare minimum and rely on the project manager to perform his duties in a style that is consistent with the project. Every project still requires a set of documents required to meet reporting and regulatory demands. Each document in the methodology should be evaluated for its effectiveness in meeting the goal of enabling the project to satisfy business needs. As a company grows, additional methodology and process documents can be added to ensure all required elements are addressed. However, methodology and process must not distract the project managers from being able to focus on the needs being met by the project they are managing. PMO value is obtained through successful delivery, not on properly completed forms.

Purpose

The final element is purpose. Every organization has a purpose. This purpose is more than the plaque on the wall that states the vision of the company. It is the driving force that causes the company to move in a given direction. It is the end goal that is being pursued. The mission of the PMO should be to ensure that every project selected for inclusion in the portfolio is in line with this purpose. This should be done by establishing gate reviews and tools that require justification of that project against the company's purpose. It should also make sure that each project manager focuses their project on meeting the purpose that has been communicated. This harmony of purpose will ensure that the PMO is in alignment with the vision of the company.

Alignment

As you work toward alignment in these seven areas, you must remember that to be effective the PMO must be considered a neutral organization. It must be an organization that is focused on the good of the overall company. This soft skill must be evidenced in how projects are communicated to senior management, how recommendations are made, and how projects are prioritized. By remaining neutral, a strong trust relationship can be built between the PMO and the other departments within the company. Trust is built through two key items. First, the people in the PMO must use the information being provided to them in an appropriate way. Information provided to the PMO should be used to further the success of the projects, not used as ammunition against the person providing the data. Second, the people in the PMO must be counted on to do what they say they will do. Accomplishing what is promised and using information appropriately are the keys to building trust. Only when the PMO has built enough trust between themselves and the rest of the company will they be able to provide the level of value to the company that is unmatched by other divisions.

Be careful to note that the PMO must align with the culture, not the culture with it. This is where a great number of people make their greatest mistake. They assume that since they have a certification or they have a particular degree, the culture should align with them. This is a recipe for a quick exit from that company, either voluntarily or involuntarily. In my experience, I have seen individuals come into an organization with many excellent ideas and an eagerness to move the PMO forward. These ideas promoted the direction the company needed to go, and were in accordance with what was needed for that particular business area. However these individuals forgot to evaluate the culture around them to determine the best way to implement these ideas. As a result, they began to implement their ideas without any attention to the impact it would cause on downstream divisions. It did not take long for discord to occur, and eventually those individuals had to be removed from the company.

It is important to note that the PMO has little control over changing company culture. As it proves value, it may be able to *influence* the culture, but understand you cannot *change* the culture. If during the process of discovering your company's culture you realize that the company does not align with your core beliefs, you may need to move from that company. It is better to find a company in which you align rather than struggle to fix it.

Culture Conclusion

It is important to note that alignment is not always accomplished through complicated or sophisticated methods. It is about doing the small things to ensure that you are aligning with the needs of the business. When done effectively, alignment with the company allows the PMO to successfully deliver, which in turn increases its value perception. Aligning the PMO with company culture is very similar to a mechanic tuning a car. As the mechanic adjusts the timing of the engine, he must look at the various elements that exist within that engine. He skillfully adjusts the various parameters to ensure that each cylinder is hitting properly and effectively so the car can move forward in the smoothest, most effective way. A properly tuned car not only goes forward effectively, it does so in the most efficient, least expensive manner. The PMO manager is that mechanic making the appropriate adjustments to the overall alignment of the PMO so that the project managers (drivers) can skillfully move the car in the right direction to meet business objectives. The farther the car goes, the more value is created and the more weight can be added to the vehicle.

Importance of Execution

Once the PMO has been appropriately aligned with the company, it can focus on its primary purpose. This purpose is to ensure that projects are executed effectively to meet the needs of the business. Throughout my experiences I have seen the PMO's goals and purpose defined in a variety of different fashions including creators of the process, directors of the portfolio, or a project governance committee. Only those PMOs that maintained a focus on ensuring delivery to meet company strategy have been able to easily prove their value.

In our business world today, successful execution must occur and must be continually measured. Every public company in the United States must provide the financial numbers of their success to Wall Street. It is not enough for them to simply claim that they have been successful. They must show measured proof of their current status and their potential results. This should also be a focus of the PMO. Almost every well-known business methodology teaches that the only way to manage or improve is to measure. This same philosophy needs to be applied to the PMO. You must be able to show numerically what the team has accomplished and what it is currently managing.

Successful project execution is critical, since it is the key metric that will prove PMO value. The success or failure of a project starts with the initiation process. The initiation step is the critical path to success of the entire PMO. Many companies take this process lightly and accept anything as a project. Others belabor the process, thereby limiting the number of projects that are ever started. The initiation process in the PMO must be clearly communicated to the company and defined in a way that is not cumbersome to the company. Do not add multiple steps of justification or extreme levels of paperwork for projects that are small in dollar value or length of delivery time. Rather ensure that the level of effort for initiation matches the project breadth of scope, cost, and control. Overburdening sponsors with meaningless process steps will have a detrimental effect to the result of accomplishing a business benefit to the company. At the same time, not enough process at initiation may result in unnecessary projects being approved or unclear projects being started. A delicate balance must be maintained, and this balance must be established based on the culture of your company.

During the initiation process, the focus should be on the business need for each project and how it aligns with company strategy. Too many times project initiation focuses on the cost and schedule without attention to the business benefit of the project. The project management triple constraint must be applied to the initiation process. This clearly is not new to project management; in fact these components are the most basic element of a project charter. However, ensuring that these three constraints are properly defined at project inception is vital to the success of the project and the PMO.

Sometimes it is impossible to avoid work that does not completely fit the criteria of a project. This is especially true in small to mid-sized companies. Some business owners will initiate a project because the expertise of a project manager is needed to accomplish work that a functional team is not capable of managing. The request to use a project manager for their expertise may sound positive. However, this situation is actually a recipe for disaster. It immediately places the PMO in a precarious position: the project manager's role is not to run an ongoing business, nor is the project manager in a place to define processes for a functional division to correct their shortcomings. As a result, the PMO is faced with unknown success criteria, an unknown end, and an unknown authority level. When taking on these projects, it is important to classify them accordingly and make sure they are clearly known. It is critical that these situations be managed carefully so that the expertise of the project manager is used only to the level absolutely required to get the effort back on track. During the course of these projects, constant monitoring and evaluation are required to determine at what point the project manager can gracefully take themselves out of the work and put it back into the hands of the functional organization. Without this level of constant oversight, these efforts can spin out of control, dramatically impacting the value of the PMO by confusing its objectives.

In new PMOs, it is critical that the company not only understands how to engage its team, but also how to properly write the charter. Depending on the maturity of the company, it may be necessary to accept a reduction in quality of the charter to accommodate the capabilities of those within the company. However it is critical that this document be defined specifically enough that it will allow the project to be successful. In my experience with smaller companies, strong sponsorship of a project has been difficult to obtain due to the number of roles a sponsor plays. To overcome this strong sponsorship issue, the PMO has made sure that the objectives were known up front, were well documented, and were agreed to by the sponsor. At this point it was possible for the project team to be successful. For example, a sponsor once requested four separate initiatives for their organization. As the team evaluated the charters for these initiatives, they quickly realized that the projects had conflicting objectives. In fact, some of them would completely undo work in another effort. Cultural analysis showed that the ability to sort through these charters and resolve these conflicts would likely not occur in a way that would allow the project to be successful. As a result, the PMO accepted the charters with the agreement that it would spend time determining the goals and objectives of that division. Once known, the charters would be revised and sequenced so that the project manager could achieve the business needs of these projects. To reiterate, this clarification of a charter is done for the sole purpose of ensuring that the project is successful in meeting business needs. It is in meeting the business need that the PMO's value is created and proven.

Once the project initiation process is clearly established, the PMO moves to the next area of focus, which is metrics management through portfolio management. As stated previously, value cannot be proven without a measurement of results. Although this discipline can be vast and complicated, the PMO manager must align the focus of this discipline to the culture of the organization. For example, the powerful tool of earned value management would be an ineffective, time-consuming effort for a company that does not know how to interpret and use the numbers. It is not that earned value is meaningless, but rather that the culture of the company inhibits the ability to use these advanced metrics. As a result, the time spent to produce this information is wasted. It is important to evaluate each metric in light of the culture of the company and focus the time spent on metrics to those items that are meaningful to the company. The PMO must then provide that data in ways that are meaningful to the consumers of the data. In some companies, the importance of financial data is not as important as the level of quality of delivery to a defined schedule. As a result, the focus of measurements should be on how well the team delivered to the schedule, and how often the delivery did not meet quality standards. In this scenario, careful attention should be paid to resource availability and how interproject dependencies will impact on-time delivery. This data should then be delivered in visual timeline charts that show how sliding milestones impact other projects. The goal is to provide data that focuses on the needs of the company so that the business can act on the results of the data. Each company will have a different focus, so it is critical to align your metrics with the company. It is important to note that over the course of time, the metrics needs of the company may change due to new management or changes within the company. With this in mind, focus on maintaining the highest-value metrics for your company, but do not forget to anticipate changes and be prepared with metrics that may be requested in the future. Consistently providing metrics about the PMO's portfolio of projects, the amount of money allocated to projects within the portfolio, and the number of projects completed provides senior management with an understanding of its value to the company. Even though senior management may not seem to pay attention to the numbers, they are aware of them.

In metrics-driven companies, it is possible for senior management to run the strategic direction of the organization through the PMO. It is the one organization that has a consolidated view into the highest strategic objectives of the organization. This view gives senior management the ability to take action to ensure that the right projects are being done and the appropriate attention is being spent on the most critical projects for the company. In my experience, I have only heard of this being used effectively once. A new chief operating officer had been hired to manage the company, and within weeks of joining the organization, he went to the PMO for an understanding of the strategic and major initiatives occurring within the company. He was immediately able to cancel projects that did not align with his ongoing objectives, and was able to realign spending to other, higher priority strategic objectives. This not only dramatically impacted the bottom line of the company, but it brought a level of excitement to employees since they could see how his new strategies were being defined and implemented. It also raised the value of the PMO, as they became the focal-point in managing the strategic objectives of the company. Not all companies have seen this value, nor have they learned this power. PMO management's job is to ensure that this capability is available to the company and that they are willing to assist in aligning the projects with the company's strategic direction. The pinnacle of its success is meeting this need when it arises, and then maintaining this level of strategic impact going forward.

Killers of PMO Value and Avoiding Them

All of the work spent to align your organization with company culture and to prove value through execution can be devastated by the following PMO killers. These killers can be external to your company, external to the PMO, or from within the PMO. Beware of these items and take action on them immediately.

Poor Project Execution

The biggest killer of PMO value is poor execution on a critical project. This can quickly devastate the perceived value of the organization. Make sure that proper attention is spent on the critical projects, and wherever possible, ensure that every project is successful. As mentioned before, be sure projects are queued for success at the start. If projects are not started on a path to success, they will not be successful. Naturally, there will be project failures, or projects that need to be cancelled during project execution because the business needs changed. In both cases, it is important that the reason for these challenges is not the project manager or the PMO.

Too Much Process or Methodology

Many sources will attempt to add process and methodology to the PMO. Be extremely careful with these requests. I have seen that excess methodology can actually reduce the PMO to overhead. Careful attention should be spent to prevent the perception that running a project through the PMO will only burden the project with paperwork. The goal of project management methodology should be for consistency, control, and support of the end goal. Find a balance that is in line with your company culture, meets the need of organizational control and regulatory compliance, and does not add more process methodology just because someone believes it is necessary. Carefully evaluate all feedback and the goal of each process that is suggested. Make sure that it adds value, reduces confusion, provides consistency, or provides clarity. If it does not meet one of these objectives, it is likely not worth adding.

No Responsibility for Project Execution

Every company must look to improve profit and enhance results. Without these components, the company fails to exist. PMOs whose entire focus is the creation of methodology and the policing of that methodology run the risk of elimination. There is no way to mathematically prove that PMO work is actually helping the bottom line without responsibility for the projects being executed in the company. When projects are done as part of the PMO, it is easy to prove value through metrics. Value can also be shown in what projects were rejected or stopped because they did not meet the strategies of the company.

Lack of Consistency

In our society, people quickly forget what was accomplished in the past and are constantly looking for what has been done for them lately. This is especially true during times of financial trouble for the company. It is important that you are consistent in initiation, execution, and providing metrics to show your ongoing value. The majority of successful companies are successful because their products are consistently produced. This should be the case for the PMO. The company should be able to receive consistent results in delivery. If the reliability of the organization changes, it will quickly impact the value that has been created.

Company Realignment

When a company goes through an acquisition or a major reorganization, the PMO will be evaluated for its value. During this time, it is critical that the execution of projects remain at the forefront. Changing PMO methodology or processes during this time will only add confusion to the company, and may give further reason to have it reduced or eliminated. I have seen PMOs completely eliminated during reorganizations simply because that team did not have the metrics to show the value it had created. To avoid this killer, keep up with the small things when times are good so that it is easier to weather these major changes. Only those who deliver faithfully over the long term can make it through these difficult times unscathed.

Lack of Neutrality

A PMO that does not maintain neutrality will immediately run into delivery problems on its projects. I have experienced a PMO that was aligned with a particular technical director. As projects came into the workflow, the projects for that individual's department immediately gained the highest level of priority for delivery. Proposed projects from other divisions were severely questioned, and additional justification was required for that work to begin. As a result, the divisions that needed PM assistance stopped requesting projects and began to sabotage the projects of the technical director. These other divisions, by simply not providing resources to projects, were able to impact the delivery of those projects. The result was that its value was destroyed. Managers in the PMO need to continually look for biases in their organization, and evaluate how that bias may impact the PMO's reputation. Without a reputation of neutrality and the good of the company always in mind, it will not achieve a high level of success.

Taking on Nonprojects

As stated previously, evaluation of projects upon initiation is critical to the success of that project and the PMO. It is vital that the PMO be careful of devious projects. These projects are submitted through the paperwork process, not simply because they meet PM criteria, but because of a major failing in another division. These projects can be an attempt to throw blame for the failure on the project organization to avoid retribution on the functional organization. When evaluating the project, ensure that it meets the criteria established for a project and that it is set up for success. If these are not met, stop the project as soon as possible. If stopping the project is not possible due to political pressure, be sure that you set that project up for success through a clearly defined charter and clear objectives. Close out the project as quickly as possible. One example of this type of situation occurred in a company where a new software release was put into production, causing a customer outage. As the teams looked into this issue, it brought to light the many failings of a particular division. In addition, the root cause analysis (RCA) and resolution plan was taking longer than was reasonable. The PMO was brought into this situation to bring the RCA to conclusion and begin the work necessary to resolve the issues on a going-forward basis. Since the PMO had no ongoing operational control of this organization, there was no way to run this as a project because changes to the functional team were required. Therefore, the team quickly focused their attention on a scope of work that could meet the immediate concerns. Acceptance of this scope of work was obtained and monitored closely. As soon as the defined scope items were complete, the effort was handed back to the functional teams with suggestions for ongoing improvement. Always be leery to take on this type of project. It puts the PMO in the place of a functional team that could result in a destroyed relationship with the functional team, and could put them in a place where they are held responsible for something completely unrelated to their core competency.

Initiation Roadblocks

When establishing the initiation process, some PMOs require a great deal of work to prove the need for the project and for the PM. This is appropriate when it is focused on business needs, so that it can be prioritized and funded. However if the PMO starts to add roadblocks to initiation simply to avoid adding work to the PMO organization, the value of the organization will be impacted. I have seen directors attempt to avoid using the PMO due to the rigorous justification process that it required. If the PMO continues to elicit this type of response, the result is not only a lack of projects but a complete reduction of value.

Each of these PMO killers can quickly reduce or eliminate the value that has been, or is being, created through your organization. These items should be evaluated and changes made to avoid the potentially damaging impact on the PMO. Understand that these issues cannot all be addressed or resolved independently, and in some cases, they will be driven by upper management. The PMO needs to be aware that each of these must be managed in an effective way so as to avoid the ultimate effect of each of these killers, which is reduced value and potential elimination of the department.

Conclusion

Throughout this chapter we have looked at the various elements of company culture and the importance of identifying and aligning the PMO to this culture. In addition, we have looked at the importance of execution. We have also discussed how to continually show value through the metrics being produced. In conclusion, the key to creating and proving value is effectively meeting business needs in a way that is in alignment with the cultural structure of the company and showing that this was accomplished. Our world is full of individuals who talk the big talk, but actions speak louder than words, and actions can be proven. Show through action how the PMO is executing to business needs, and you will have no problem proving value.

Author Biography

Matthew Hayes, PMP, is the senior manager of the project management office at TeleCommunication Systems. He has a bachelor of science in communications, holds a certificate in ITIL, and has been trained in Six Sigma. He has spent his 14-year career working in the project management field within the IT and telecommunications industry. Matthew is the current vice president of communications for the Puget Sound Chapter of PMI®, and has been an active participant in the chapter since 2005. He also sits on the board of directors for a large nonprofit organization. His professional experience includes PMO setup and management, multimillion dollar international software release management, and process improvement.

11

Ambassadors, Skits, and Little Blue Books

Bruce Brower, PMP

Introduction

This chapter is about selling project management office (PMO) concepts and gaining acceptance from the unsung heroes who must live and operate under its rules and regulations. If you are unable to sell the concepts to the troops, you are wasting time and money. Your PMO will flounder and die. Presumably, management already bought into the idea of a PMO; that is why you were hired or promoted in the first place. Now you have to convince others that building a PMO makes sense, and they can have fun jumping on the bandwagon. Yes, it can be fun with a little creativity and enthusiasm.

This chapter outlines strategies and tips for gaining acceptance while implementing a PMO from scratch or turning one around. You need the support of those who may not be in the PMO itself, but who must embrace the concepts, use the tools, follow the methodologies, and otherwise be the face of the PMO to the rest of the company. You may not be their boss, but you must lead them. These ideas can be the difference between a willingness to accept it and a decision to reject it. Forced compliance and hollow promises of benefits are deal breakers in many organizations; compliance by trickery will backfire.

Why Worry About Compliance Now?

We all have known what it feels like to have more rules and regulations thrust upon us. Sure, it is for our own good, but it does not feel that way. Unlike the five-stage model for grief (denial, anger, bargaining, depression, and acceptance) where many reach the acceptance stage eventually, there is a reasonable chance that with enough concerted effort, people can ignore the PMO, undermine it, lobby against it, nitpick the details, or just plain refuse to comply. The result is that it will shrivel up and die. As PMO manager, you must be alert to signs of confusion, boredom, laziness, defiance, hesitation, reluctance, and senseless paperwork. Compliance is not something you can just turn on at the end of the build out process—it is important from day one.

Background and Context

Before describing the solutions we developed, I need to give you some background and context. I was hired from the outside to start from scratch a project management office in the information technology (IT) department of a multifacility metropolitan safety net hospital system. The IT department had around 125 employees. Technical specialists acted as project managers, doing the best they could with what they had and what they knew. A few months before I started, the chief information officer (CIO) arranged for in-house project management training by an outside training and consulting company. Twenty students received this training, but no formal methodologies or processes existed at the hospital. The department functioned at the lowest level of the capability maturity model scale. The department was divided into groups by functional or technical specialty and tended to operate within their own silos. I was told that the IT department was not highly regarded within the organization, and in fact, had been criticized for its customer service. What I found was that almost universally employees were smart, capable people who wanted to do good work, develop as professionals, and please their customers. No doubt your situation will be different, but I hope you will find something of value here that will stimulate thinking about your own solutions.

This is not a chapter that talks about setting a build out strategy for the PMO. I assume you will somehow figure out what you need to deliver. You may perform a gap analysis, noting where things stand today, where you want them to be in the future, and how to get there. Since this chapter is about gaining acceptance, let me mention only one aspect of getting started that will help you reach your goal of acceptance.

Current State: Getting a Realistic Assessment

During my job interview, I picked up on the interviewers' vision of the PMO and what was expected of its manager. But I only got a hint of the problems and challenges I might face. As a PMO of one person with a limited budget, I had to get a realistic assessment of the current situation including the real requirements, obstacles, and human factors that could affect progress. To do that, I needed to talk to as many stakeholders as possible. The list included IT management, customers, project managers, project team members and other internal service providers (e.g., network analysts, database administrators, and software developers). Besides being a good way to make introductions and talk about plans for the PMO, one-on-one informal discussions were a valuable source of information about the strengths and weaknesses of the IT department and the organization from their perspective. I set an aggressive goal of meeting every IT department employee and getting to know something about each of them. As it turned out, this was one of the most useful exercises as I formulated plans. In their eyes, I was a neutral third-party without baggage. I was seen as an individual who could eliminate some of their pain and problems. I asked what changes they would like to see and they opened up with candor. The series of interviews gave me insight into the history, politics, attitudes, and aspirations of the IT department and the organization. I felt better connected and better prepared to build the PMO.

Principles Used

What did I learn in my interviews and how did it influence building out the PMO? I realized that change management, influencing techniques, and a home-grown approach would be particularly helpful for successful implementation. In addition to the traditional PMO deliverables shown in Table 11.1, it would need to reinforce a new identity for the IT department, create an identity for the PMO, treat employees with respect, provide opportunities for people to interact, instill pride in their work, teach staff career-resilient skills, and have some fun in the process. Here are some of the guiding principles at work in the solutions:

- Empowered teams are happy, motivated teams
- Two heads are better than one
- Greater involvement leads to greater ownership
- When choosing between carrots and sticks, carrots come before sticks, both alphabetically and at work
- *Warm and fuzzy* is more than just an allergic reaction to the heat—build on it
- Do not take yourself too seriously; no one else does
- Crawl before you walk
- Positive trumps negative every time
- No good effort goes unnoticed
- Practice M.B.E.E. (management by eliminating excuses)
- Make it easy to succeed and hard to fail
- Trying to pin the blame on someone is like gazing through your rearview mirror while driving; it cannot help you to move forward

Table 11.1 PMO deliverables

Significant PMO responsibilities and deliverables	The solutions													
	People		Products				Activities			Incentives				
	Ambassadors	Project leadership council (PLC)	PMO branding	Little blue book of project management	Training delivery	Case studies and examples	Communication	Model the behavior you want	Skits	Rewards	Celebrations	Internal certification program	Assist in gaining PMI certification	Education awards
Project management methodology	X	X	X	X	X	X						X		X
Status reporting		X					X	X		X		X		
Project tracking effort, cost, schedules, deliverables		X			X		X	X			X	X		
Project resource management		X			X		X							
PM-related training	X			X	X	X	X	X		X	X	X	X	X
Portfolio management		X	X		X		X							
Project management software	X				X	X						X		
Budgets and long-range planning							X				X			
Mission, vision, values, and behaviors	X		X		X		X	X	X	X	X		X	
Capitalizing software development effort	X				X	X	X	X		X	X			

The Solutions

When it comes to selling the organization on adopting PMO concepts, sometimes the small things make a huge difference. The success of your PMO does not depend on having perfect templates, although having adequate templates is important. Effective change management is about preparing people to try something new, get comfortable with the differences, and accept the change. This chapter is about some of those little things you can do to make the big changes more acceptable.

I wish I could say that my vision for the PMO was brilliant and innovative, that my solutions were thorough and execution flawless, that acceptance was immediate and compliance was whole-hearted and comprehensive. In fact, I would have been happy if any part of that were 100 percent true. I could present Table 11.1 as a well-planned, integrated set of solutions for some key deliverables. In fact, the table is a look back at what was attempted and what worked.

While I did not use a table like this in my planning, I consciously explored how people, products, activities, and incentives could be used to influence the success of the PMO rollout. For the sake of brevity, solution refers to people, products, activities, and incentives used by the PMO. Keep in mind that the solutions helped to sell its concepts and gain acceptance. Rows in the table represent some of the common and significant deliverables, plus two less-common initiatives that we handled. The columns are solutions we developed. Note that all but one solution affected multiple deliverables.

Ambassadors

Only Robinson Crusoe could have everything done by Friday. It is an old joke, yet contains a grain of truth. Starting a PMO from scratch or turning around a faltering one takes a lot of work; you will need help. Not only will you need help with the volume of work, but with the variety of skills that building a PMO demands. You will need people who are good at communicating, gathering requirements, configuring project management software, designing reports and metrics, paying attention to details, accounting and finance, developing instructional material, teaching, and developing processes to name a few. With a list like that, it is clear that you need people who have the necessary skills, additional hours to contribute, fresh perspectives, and a practitioner's point of view. More importantly, the right people could be the tipping point for PMO acceptance where others fall in line quickly behind significant influencers.

What Will These People Do?

Roles and responsibilities of helpers were pretty broad and unclear at first. As I thought about the vision of the PMO, I simplistically boiled down the work into two parts: building structure and operating within the structure. The first entails concepts, policies, methodologies, processes, templates, reports, and forms of the PMO. The second is performed daily, weekly, and monthly with projects, programs, and portfolios. Both parts depend on the other for success. Ambassadors could help build the structure and then help the entire organization operate effectively within that new structure. On the one hand, ambassadors' roles were visible and structured (e.g., when they actively developed methodology, templates, and processes). On the other hand, their role could be as subtle (e.g., when they offered advice to another project manager or helped set up a project in the project-tracking application). Officially, we defined their role as:

> The role of the ambassadors is to promote the services of the project management office, direct project managers to the various sources of project management knowledge, and serve as points of contact for the PMO within the IT department.

When this statement was first written by the ambassadors, we had no sources of project management knowledge and no services to promote. But this statement became a guiding light for our decisions and a good marketing tool. It became the 30-second elevator speech about ambassadors. Here are some of the activities we had outlined for ambassadors:

- Answer questions about project management
- Participate in training activities
- Participate in department activities involving the PMO
- Review communication materials before distribution
- Help to promote the PMO
- Be the eyes and ears of the PMO; judge the mood and level of acceptance of the PMO
- Understand the goals, tools, processes, and concepts of the PMO

What Kind of People Do You Need?

How do you identify the right people? How many do you need? The challenge is finding those who can become enthusiastic supporters of change and add value in the development effort.

I recommend preparing a job description as if this were a full-time position. You will need to think about an ambassador's activities, required skills, professional characteristics, and work experience. Perhaps even more important is their influence on peers. This can be tricky to assess and even more difficult to have candidates admit that they influence peers.

In my situation, I was fortunate that the chief information officer discussed the topic freely and gave his perspective about individuals. He interacted with department members on a regular basis, so he saw them in action. Plus, he was a good judge of people.

The number of people needed varies by organization. I had twelve. They had a variety of skills and experiences that could be periodically tapped, and they represented most of the major groups within IT, so it helped to break down existing silos. I would not say, "The more, the merrier," because large groups can be hard to manage. However, twelve people with a shared vision, even though part time, can be a formidable body for development and execution.

How Should You Recruit Them?

There were two major options for getting help. First, I could ask for help when I needed it. That meant I would either ask the same people repeatedly or rotate through different people over time. Both approaches had downsides. I would either wear out my welcome with one approach or have to train new people often with the other approach. Instead, I chose a second option. I established the ambassadors as a permanent group. Not only did this minimize ongoing training, but it allowed the people to share a common purpose, learn from one another, and build on the accomplishments of the group. That shared experience was valuable to them and to the development of the PMO.

Shortly after I arrived, the CIO sent an e-mail to the IT department welcoming me aboard and asking staff to give me their cooperation. Memos like that are helpful, but I do not recall a long line of people in my office the next day offering to help. Earning their trust and asking for their cooperation was still up to me.

Instead, I approached people directly, told them my story, and asked for their help. I believe many people respond to a compelling vision that was clearly and passionately stated. I believe the opportunity to contribute to something grand is a great motivator. All I needed to do was invite them to join in this crusade. With apologies to the movie *Field of Dreams*, it was, "I need your help to build it and they will come."

What Training Will They Need?

There were many specific training needs for a group this diverse. Let me just mention two that were beneficial in building the PMO.

Some ambassadors had worked together before, so there were established relationships, both good and strained, as it turns out. Others were virtually unknown to many in the group and had no prior working relationships. I used our first formal team meeting to demonstrate one way to hold a kick-off meeting. It was a time to get to know one another, to understand our purpose, and to establish some expectations about how we would work together.

Influencing skills were important. At first, and for much of my time in the organization, the PMO had no positional authority over any ambassadors or other IT staff. Furthermore, none of the ambassadors had management or supervisory responsibilities. So, it was essential to get work done through others and through the power of influencing. As always in these circumstances, the essential question is, *What is in it for them?* If someone gave me development effort, creative thought, and support, what could I offer in return? I gave them something that many workers valued: respect, empowerment, a creative outlet, positive reinforcement, and rewards that were hard to measure and not readily available elsewhere. This chapter touches more on rewards later.

Why Were They Called Ambassadors?

We thought the term *ambassador* commanded some respect. It conveys a role in the organization without sounding like another formal title from human resources. Ambassadors were not professional PMO staff members. Part of their mission was to spread the word about the PMO and to work with fellow IT staff. One ambassador asked, in the spirit of things, if ambassadors had diplomatic immunity in case someone decided to shoot the messenger after hearing something they did not like.

Oh, yes, and we created a colorful paper nameplate (4″ × 6″) that we inserted in a Plexiglas picture display that could sit on their desks. The nameplate simply read PMO AMBASSADOR. It is surprising how many people looked at the $1.19 display and asked, "What is that?" It was good marketing to tell them about the PMO and their new role as an ambassador.

What is the Advantage of a Group Like This?

In addition to hours of work and valuable ideas, the ambassadors' distinct advantage was that they came from many different silos within IT. The ambassadors had grassroots appeal. Solutions developed by the ambassadors were more readily adopted as being unbiased and supported by the worker bees. At the same time, the ambassadors took on IT department-level tasks and supported the CIO. Once the PMO's focus expanded to include being a swat-team for the CIO, the ambassadors were identified as a can-do team within IT. Of course, each ambassador had to balance this new work with their normal workload, since ambassadors were volunteers for the PMO.

After awhile, the ambassadors not only served as a board of advisors, but also they became sounding boards for various issues on an individual basis. As formal meetings became less frequent, informal discussions became the norm.

Project Leadership Council

Just like projects themselves, project portfolios need structure and coordination. In traditional silo organizations, leadership within a silo approves, prioritizes, and authorizes work for the silo. The degree of coordination with other silos varies. When a PMO exists, it, or a group led by it, frequently assumes the coordination role. We called this group the *project leadership council* (PLC). The value of having a separate group is their independence. The PLC was an independent cross-functional (cross-silo) team with authority to represent the entire IT department. The PLC's primary responsibilities were to:

- Work with project managers to help prepare projects for the approval process
- Evaluate new project ideas and charters
- Coordinate resource assignments across functional and technical groups
- Track project performance throughout the life of the project
- Ensure that status reports and other administrative deliverables were produced on a timely basis
- Rearrange schedules and resource assignments when high-priority projects cause priorities to shift
- Communicate decisions and schedules throughout the organization

Initially, the PLC operated solely within the IT department. Ultimately, the intent was for this group to evolve into a hospital-wide group that administered and oversaw all projects. The goal was to funnel projects through the PLC for approval and prioritizing. The PLC would also oversee project performance and determine whether completed projects had achieved their original goals.

The structure of the PLC was not well-received by traditional silo management in the beginning. Traditional silo leaders were invited but were reluctant to participate in the PLC. They did not accept the decisions of the PLC. Perhaps they felt a loss of responsibility since they previously performed this work. Without silo leadership's participation, the PLC consisted of staff two to three levels below the CIO; people who ordinarily did not have authority to commit resources and approve projects. Eventually, silo leaders joined the PLC, modified it in positive ways, and actively participated. While this may sound like a political blunder on the part of the PMO to try to bypass established department leadership, it was done with the CIO's approval to break down some barriers and encourage department leadership to step up to the plate and join in the changes that were taking place. Forming the PLC accomplished several primary and secondary goals. The PLC:

- Developed and documented procedures and policies. Specifically, it documented the project approval process, the criteria for each decision gate, what documentation was required when a new project was proposed, and what tracking mechanism was appropriate.
- Broke down some of the silo mentality.
- Promoted the coordination of limited resources for the good of the organization.
- Gave some nonmanagement individuals responsibility at the department and organization level that helped them to see a bigger picture.

- Provided individuals with career development opportunities by increasing interaction with upper management.
- Communicated its decisions to the department and customers alike. For the first time, the organization did not have to wonder about the status of a project. Also, there was consistent, formal tracking as new project ideas progressed through each step of the approval process.

The existence of the PLC also addressed a complaint heard throughout the organization that the IT department operated in a vacuum. We heard that IT only worked on projects they wanted, when they wanted, and were not accountable to the organization for results. Sometimes we heard, "I have no idea why my project was rejected and someone else's project was approved." While everyone in the organization understood that you must ration services when you have limited resources, it was not clear to the organization why some projects were approved and others were not. Conversely, IT complained that some projects were started and stopped to the detriment of the organization. IT said there was chaos because someone's pet project did not need justification. They said it jumped ahead of others on a waiting list and was deemed the highest priority (drop everything else). This would consume large amounts of resources and attention. No wonder some projects failed to get done as expected or promised. The PLC, through much improved communication and coordination, helped to address nagging complaints like these.

Creating the PLC's mission and objectives was another example of gaining buy-in through group dynamics and involvement. We have all heard about the power of asking good questions. In the formative stage, the PLC asked itself enlightened questions. This forced members to think beyond their own experiences to consider the bigger picture. The PLC asked questions such as these:

- What does this organization value?
- What information is important for administrators and senior leadership to have in order to run this organization?
- Where can we add value in the critical functions of selecting, approving, and running projects?
- What is the PLC's purpose?

It was through these discussions that the PLC formed guiding principles that helped it to fulfill its mission and become an owner of critical responsibilities.

The Little Blue Book of Project Management

We have learned that the IT department was filled with good people who were doing the best they could with what they had and what they knew. Unfortunately, the work was inconsistent. There is little debate that an established methodology provides benefits including consistency, thoroughness, predictability, and a teachable approach that will grow the skills of individuals and the maturity of the organization.

Project management training classes were well-attended for a variety of reasons—they were high quality, informative, free (as far as group level budgets were concerned), fun, and a break from a student's normal workday. However, similar to other training events, a great deal of information was compressed into three short days. For most people, the timing of the classes did not coincide with their need for the knowledge. And knowledge tends to fade away if not practiced or reinforced within a reasonable amount of time. We needed some way for people to retain the lessons and have quick access to the essential concepts. Thus was born the idea of *The Little Blue Book of Project Management*. *The Little Blue Book* was something that would capture the essence of our adopted methodology, be readily available, and be used as a marketing tool with its customers.

The Little Blue Book was 53 pages, pocket-sized, and had sections including Project Management Introduction, Charter Your Project, Plan Your Project, Manage Your Project, Close Your Project, and Project Charter Content. There were essential process maps showing the flow and interrelationship of major project tasks. We promoted the PMO and the ambassadors with a logo and a description of an ambassador's role. We also provided a list of the ambassadors' names so the department would know who to contact with questions. It never hurts to advertise!

There are existing pocket-sized booklets about project management that are excellent references. They cover a wide range of topics in a reasonable level of detail. They are generic, however. We wanted to build on the specific training that the staff had received regarding a basic project management methodology that we decided to adopt. With a few changes here and there, we created a small summary of the project management methodology with the help of the outside training and consulting company. A more detailed dive into the methodology was prepared and stored on the PMO website.

We did not wear rose-tinted glasses thinking the majority of people would carry *The Little Blue Book* everywhere they went, refer to it throughout the day, study it in their spare time between meetings, and quote long passages to impress their friends. What we did assume was that the material would be readily available (portable and accessible instead of a shelf-dwelling behemoth with its evil twin residing on the intranet), simplistic in format and focusing only on fundamentals instead of minutia. Calling it *The Little Blue Book of Project Management* personalized it and fit the branding image of the PMO.

The Little Blue Book also served as a marketing and discussion tool for our internal customers. We could sit down with a customer to discuss an upcoming project and point out in the methodology where their participation was particularly important for project success. We would leave a copy of the booklet behind in case they had other questions. In these circumstances, *The Little Blue Book* countered the image of the IT department as mavericks with inconsistent results and no set approach to work. It contributed to improving customer relations and the IT image.

Internal Certification Program

We set up an internal project manager (PM) certification program to encourage IT staff to learn and apply project management skills. The certification program combined classroom training with a practical application of learned skills. It was also structured to provide constructive feedback to applicants to enhance the learning process and contribute to their career development. Finally, the program offered both incentive and recognition for individuals developing a competency in project management.

We created an 18-page booklet describing the program. The booklet had sections entitled Steps to Project Management Certification, Evaluation Criteria, Evaluation Process—Roles and Responsibilities, Frequently Asked Questions, and an Appendix with supporting material for each of the groups involved in the program. The program was structured to include the ambassadors, the IT marketing committee, and customers. Each of these groups could assist the applicant throughout the process as well as participate in a final review board. During the final review, involved groups questioned project managers about their use of project management principles using questions similar to those provided in the booklet. We had a web application to simplify the registration process.

The steps to certification followed the natural sequence of a project manager's job *according to the methodology*. There were a few administrative steps to enroll in the certification program and to prepare for the final review, but generally no additional work was required of project managers. At the end of the process, with completed project in hand, the applicant appeared before peer reviewers who asked questions about their experiences and lessons learned. It was intended to be a supportive, learning experience.

I think it is human nature for professionals to seek personal and professional improvement. The project management certification program provided structure and goals for interested individuals. One of the simplest ways to develop professionally is to set goals and work toward them. From the PMO perspective, the number of applicants was another way to see if IT department staff was buying into the PMO concepts and program.

Education Award

We used an outside training and consulting firm to deliver one, two, and three-day training classes. The firm taught soft skills to technical organizations. They had great teachers with real-world experience. Filling the classes was never a problem. And although the training had been a part of the IT department practice prior to the PMO, the training was not part of a structured program with an end goal in mind. When it was established, we started administering the training program and soon had responsibility for most training in the department. We wanted to elevate the importance of training so that people knew it was worthwhile and not just another day away from their job. We identified four core courses that were important for good project management. The four courses taught basic project management, marketing the IT organization internally, becoming a service organization, and politics. These courses were required for one step of the internal PM certification program.

People who completed any single class were given a certificate from the outside training organization. Their names also appeared in internal communication and were recognized at a monthly department meeting. We tracked each individual's training history and posted it on the PMO Web site. We made sure training was available to all and not reserved for a select few.

We established the education award for those who completed the four core training courses. Recipients were announced in a department-wide communication and honored at a monthly department meeting. They also received a desktop clock with the PMO logo and reference to the education award. And better yet, no assembly was required, and batteries were included.

The clocks were not expensive, but they made a statement that training was important to us and their participation was appreciated. Most displayed their clocks in their work areas. More free advertising.

PMO Branding

Have you ever wanted to know more about something but did not know who to ask? We did not want that to happen to the PMO. We wanted everyone to know exactly what we produced and that the product adhered to PMO quality standards.

Brands can be powerful statements about identity—who we are, what we stand for, and what we are trying to accomplish. We felt it was important for the PMO to be associated with the new IT department, but to also have its own distinct identity. In our case, there was some historic baggage to overcome before the IT department could be seen in a favorable new light. A new brand signals a change, but buyers may be skeptical until they see proof. Balancing all those factors was part of the challenge in creating a PMO logo and brand.

The IT department had gone through a similar branding experience shortly before the PMO started. The IT marketing committee created a logo that was becoming readily identifiable within the hospital. The idea of piggybacking on their work helped the PMO move from a lot of words and graphs to a more marketable professional image. It also tapped the talents of the IT marketing committee and created goodwill with the committee. The IT marketing committee consisted of a few individuals who took responsibility for most of the public communication efforts of the department. It provided another outlet for their creativity and validation of their services.

One nice thing about a logo is that merely displaying it will often trigger recognition and reaction. We wanted to ensure that it was a positive reaction. If we were successful running the PMO, completing projects, and training people, then linking the logo to it made it easier to sell the entire set of services. The ambassadors and others could take pride in their work and display the logo appropriately as needed.

Case Studies and Examples

How can case studies and examples help sell the PMO? A case study that is both real and personal can be an effective teaching aid. Case studies do not have to be elaborate presentations. They can be simple examples that illustrate an important teaching point. If the outcome of the event was unfavorable, you can almost see students wince as they remember the pain and frustration they may have felt at the time. On the other hand, if the outcome was favorable, they take pride in how they handled it and are much more likely to engage in classroom discussion. It is a win-win for a teacher. The trifecta of case studies occurs when a student learns something in your class, applies it successfully, and talks about it later in the form of a testimonial. That is a win-win-win.

You may already know the history of project management within your organization. But if not, you can draw upon the collective memories of the class. Ask students to contribute their thoughts and experiences in the classroom. As you hear more stories, you can file them away as future training material and lessons learned. You may even consider having people submit short write-ups of selected experiences for publishing on the PMO Web site or circulating to the entire department.

If you want students to share freely, set a ground rule that the classroom is a judgment-free zone. Then encourage students to share their successes and setbacks. Challenge other students to offer alternative ways to handle situations. I would like to think that successful students who receive valuable support or knowledge in the classroom may attribute part of their success to the supportive atmosphere the PMO tries to encourage.

We periodically held brownbag lunches with subjects announced in advance. There were both formal presentations and informal discussions among peers. Soft skills and noncore project management skills were some of the more popular topics, including:

- Politics
- Working with stakeholders who have conflicting goals
- Communication and status reporting when things go wrong

- Change management
- Negotiation
- Influencing others

As individuals begin to adopt PMO concepts and principles, you may notice that they start to share your mission of developing the organization. They may take a more active role in training others even if it is only sharing stories in class. This grassroots acceptance and unsolicited assistance is welcomed and encouraged.

Training Delivery

The challenge of most training is presenting the right material in the right quantity to the right audience at the right level of detail at the right time and in an effective style for that audience. With those qualifiers it would seem that only one-on-one, fully-customized training could ever work. However, another fact of effective learning is that most people must hear something seven times before they really internalize it. Also from a learning perspective, seeing (visual learning) is generally more effective than hearing (auditory learning). And doing (kinetic learning) is more effective than either seeing or hearing. Thus, one strategy for effective learning is to change the timing and delivery of training material as you repeat the main message multiple times. Keep it fresh. Appeal to different styles of learning.

Technology makes it possible to achieve several of the challenging criteria (right material, quantity, audience, detail, time, and style of learning) but there is no single best solution. There are fans of classroom, case study, webcasts, daily learning topics, brownbag lunches, small-group study experiences, reading assignments, and self-study, to name a few. Each teaching method has pros and cons. For example, some subjects are better suited for instructor-led sessions where interaction and discussion are important. Nothing beats archived webcasts for the right time unless you do not have access to the Internet. Self-study is ideal when the scope is unstructured and the depth of knowledge desired varies greatly by student. If you are putting together a training curriculum, I recommend checking with students for their suggestions. Not only does this earn buy-in, but you are more likely to deliver material that matters to them and is well-received. Also consider consulting a reference book on the effectiveness of various training methods. Learn what works best under different circumstances.

One last thought on training is realizing that effective learning and fun are not mutually exclusive. Keep sessions lively to pique people's interests. Good facilitation skills and knowledge of adult learning habits are important for effective training. When the PMO took over the training responsibilities for the department, we were able to add career-enhancing education without compromising the project management-related training that we needed to provide. For example, the PMO sponsored an effort to have the entire IT department receive individual Myer-Briggs temperament assessments, and then learn more about interpreting the various profiles. This education was fun, helped to provide interaction and rapport-building among IT staff, and had the potential to improve customer relationships through greater understanding of various temperaments.

Communication

Most business books will tell you that you cannot over communicate and that the lack of communication is a primary reason why many projects and relationships fail. I would have to agree—to a point. Just as too little information will starve a person into wanting more, repetitive, lackluster communication will fade into the background and be ignored. Good communication is a selling point for PMOs.

As humans, we are bombarded with signals, stimuli, and messages. We would literally go crazy if we paid attention to every stimulus. The human body is equipped with the reticular activating system, which acts as a filter. The purpose is to let in only those signals that pose a threat or offer pleasure. So how do you get messages across to people who are already bombarded with information and over worked? If there were a perfect answer, every marketing firm in the world would know exactly how to reach you. Instead you can structure your communication to build on the following principles and expect that most people will receive the messages that count:

- Make it timely.
- Give enough information (not a teaser) so that the recipient knows when he or she needs more, and give them a mechanism to retrieve more (e.g., a link, reference, or appendix with details).
- There is no single best way to communicate with everyone on every subject. Instead, there are preferred approaches (yours and theirs). Experiment to find those that work best in certain circumstances.
- Mix up the delivery media for variety and interest. Keep it fresh. You have heard about sticky websites that attract followers and entice them to return frequently. What does *sticky* mean for your PMO?
- Do not cry wolf unless you need an urgent response from everyone, otherwise your messages will lose their urgency in the minds of recipients.
- Follow an escalating pattern if it is imperative to reach someone or a small group of people. For example: you send out a request for status reports and not everyone replies by the deadline. Consider what the appropriate follow-up should be. For some individuals that could be an e-mail reminder, second e-mail reminder, text, phone call, and finally, a personal visit at their desk. If 100 percent compliance is your no-compromise goal, then be prepared to test your patience. Balance the trade-off between what is expedient and what is effective.

- An e-mail sent does not mean an e-mail read. As the sender, it is your responsibility to ensure your message is received. Give people the benefit of the doubt, especially if your e-mail was lengthy or complicated.
- If you can, reach agreement with people about priority communication. Consider putting key words in the subject line when the e-mail is particularly important. Priority flags can be overused unless there are organizational standards about their use. We had a policy that all e-mail would be answered within 24 hours, even if the response was simply, "I got your message and I will reply by Tuesday." Similar to any other worthwhile policy, it takes discipline and repetition until it is ingrained in the culture and becomes the natural way that business is done.

Notifying people in a timely manner does not always mean when *you* think it is timely. Ideally, information should be made available when the recipient wants it. However, unless you are a mind reader, it is impossible to know with certainty when it is needed. When all else fails, ask recipients about what timeliness means for them.

Respond to every e-mail. Even when a response is not required or expected, it is good to let others know that you received it, you will look it over, you appreciate them thinking of you, etc. A response is a courtesy, especially when acknowledging their effort to answer one of your requests. I often used their name in the text response and tried to state something unique to let them know a human being was responding. For example, "That was quick, Paul. Thanks for your prompt reply." It did not take a lot longer to provide the personal touch, and sometimes they let me know it was appreciated.

Model the Behavior You Want

So, why am I talking about behavior? Isn't the PMO focused on filling out forms and getting projects completed on time and within budget? The PMO can play an important role in the transformation of a department or organization as it moves up the capability maturity curve toward continuous improvement. Yes, there are processes and tools to master, but there is also becoming more professional as a department and as an organization. Behaviors are important. Dale Carnegie said, "Act enthusiastic and you will be enthusiastic." Good behaviors lead to changed attitudes and mindsets. Behaving professionally becomes a habit. Okay, I will get off my soapbox for now.

Have you seen the T-shirts that mothers wear that read BECAUSE I SAID SO? It is funny, but only mothers can get away with saying that. In a corporate setting, that behavior would not last long. Do not set yourself apart from others. They will soon learn that there are two sets of rules. If it is a rule for everyone else, then it is a rule for you. If you were promoted into PMO management from inside the organization, it may be difficult to have others see that you have changed in your new role. Nevertheless modeling the behavior you want is a given if you want others to follow.

It may not be typical of PMOs to lead an effort to define the mission, vision, and values of the IT department, but it was a great opportunity for our PMO to get ideas and interaction from so many people within IT. More importantly, it was an opportunity for the department to articulate the values that were important to live by, and then to commit to the behavior that exemplified those values. Duke University Coach Mike Krzyzewski, in his book *The Gold Standard: Building a World Class Team*, attributed part of the 2008 Olympic success of the USA's national basketball team to the standards his team set for themselves. Some of those standards were predictable (great defense, communication, trust, aggressiveness, collective responsibility), but others were unique to the men and their circumstances (intelligence, enthusiasm, pride, poise, respect, and care). What are the standards governing your team?

Another success factor Coach Krzyzewski points out is having the team understand the larger context in which it operates, and that the team goal is bigger than any individual's personal goal. In their case, it was not just a basketball game, it was a chance to represent the United States of America and have American citizens counting on them. You may not be able to evoke the national anthem and flag for your cause, but you can certainly identify a larger context than just the department. Successful projects contribute to the success of the organization, to its customers, and maybe even the community in which it operates.

Skits

The PMO took ownership of a customer-service issue—the perception that IT staff ignored their customers within the hospital by stating, "It is not my job" and then walking away. That led to customers bypassing normal IT procedures for reporting IT-related problems in order to go directly to their favorite IT person who would fix the problem. Bypassing normal procedures leads to an uneven distribution of work, the inability to track problem resolution effectively, and an underground system for getting work done without authorization. Taking ownership of the issue was easy for the PMO, and we could be viewed as part of the solution, not the problem.

The ambassadors quickly discussed the problem, confirmed their understanding with some brief market research, and then brainstormed a simple solution. They developed a desired IT response in circumstances such as this, and then packaged the response in an acronym: ACT, which stood for acknowledge the problem, communicate with empathy ("I'm sorry that problem has caused so much confusion."), and take ownership. Taking ownership meant staying with a problem until it was resolved or handing it off to someone else who then took full ownership. The question was how best to roll out a campaign to change IT behaviors. The group decided to increase awareness through a media blitz. They ordered buttons with the word ACT, printed flyers, and created a skit to introduce the concept to the department. Skits can be quite memorable. In this one an IT staff member was asked by a customer to help with a problem. Appropriately the staff member acknowledged the problem, communicated concern, and took ownership. Then the male staff member said to the female customer, "Your place or mine?" I think it was ad-libbed, but it was the highlight of the skit as the customer blushed and the audience laughed.

The other part of the ACT campaign was to make customers aware of the changes that IT was attempting to make, and to monitor whether IT behaviors actually changed. Invariably IT customers would ask about the buttons. This set up an opportunity for IT staff to discuss the new practice regarding customer service. To reinforce compliance, the ambassadors also set up a feedback mechanism so that anyone in the hospital could report on IT staff who were *caught in the ACT*. These individuals were recognized during department meetings for their exemplary behavior. Often, notes were added to their personnel files. All in all, this was a successful campaign that generated a lot of positives for the department.

This was not the only time that skits were used to introduce an idea or deliver training. Skits are fun to develop and even more fun to perform. They let staff members be creative and enjoy their 15 minutes of fame in front of the department. Skits are a change of pace in an otherwise standard department meeting filled with presentations and monologs.

Assist in Gaining PMI® Certification

Helping department staff become certified by the Project Management Institute (PMI®) is a win for the individual, the organization, and the PMO. It is one thing to be recognized by your own organization as project management savvy. Our internal certification program was built for that purpose. But it is another level of accomplishment to be certified by a leading accredited project management association.

Certification takes time, money and knowledge. As head of the PMO, ask yourself whether you can provide one or more of these to interested staff. Training provided by the PMO often fulfills PMI's education requirement. Many organizations reimburse employees for PMP® certification costs upon successful completion of the final examination. Some organizations even allow study time during normal work days. Other ways to help are to share training materials or provide a spreadsheet to catalogue someone's project management and training hours. The sooner others see your willingness to help them achieve their personal goals, the better the odds of selling the PMO to the organization.

I heard a statistic that people starting in the workforce today will work for an average of ten different companies before they retire. With that daunting statistic in mind, perhaps the best things you can give someone are career-resilient skills that are valued wherever the individual goes. Project management skills are very transferrable.

Some departments fear that a newly certified PMP might seek employment elsewhere because of his or her new credentials. However the exact opposite may also be true. People will tend to stay in organizations that invest in them, even when the organization does not pay top industry wages. A smart boss of mine had three criteria for continuing to work at a company. You must enjoy the work you do, enjoy the people you work with, and feel adequately compensated (and that is not strictly money). As a PMO manager, you can contribute to the organization's goal of attracting and retaining good people by fulfilling their needs for knowledge, career development, advancement, recognition, and respect. That is compensation you cannot find everywhere.

Rewards

One of the first questions asked when someone mentions rewards is, *how much is it going to cost?* That is a legitimate question. Organizations vary widely in their financial support of individual incentives. But focusing on cost alone fails to consider the bigger question of what will motivate employees. Not all people are motivated by the same things. The inexpensive-but-well-suited reward for one individual will have far greater impact than an expensive-but-misguided reward that appeals mostly to the giver. Picture an elegant plaque for your wall (oh, you have a cubicle?) instead of time off with your family that you have been craving.

Maslow's Hierarchy of Needs suggests that humans must satisfy primary, lower-level needs before advancing to the next level of needs. Abraham Maslow identified five levels of need:

1. Physiological needs—Vital to survival. Examples: need for water, air, food and sleep.
2. Security needs—Important for survival, but not as demanding as physiological needs. Examples: need for shelter, safe surroundings, and regular employment.
3. Social needs—Less basic than physiological and security needs. Examples: friendship, acceptance, belonging, love, and affection.
4. Esteem needs—Increasingly important after physiological, security, and social needs are met. Examples: self-esteem, personal worth, and social recognition.
5. Self-actualizing needs—The highest level. Examples: concern for personal growth, reaching your potential, self-awareness, and less concern with others' opinions.

The good news is that many potential rewards are relatively inexpensive—if not free—especially at the higher levels of the hierarchy. Do you have the latitude to let employees pick their own reward from a pool of potential rewards? Perhaps one associate values parking near the building entrance for one month during the winter, whereas another cherishes a public relations article in an industry publication. Just like a well-known company's advertising slogan, *priceless* is in the eyes of the beholder. Try to find something priceless for the individual. Here are some low cost ideas:

- Time off.
- An award that can be put on a resume such as employee of the month, certified PM, PMO build out project manager.
- Name engraved on a plaque that is displayed prominently within the department.
- Name included in published materials, either internal company publications or local or industry magazines.
- Products having the company logo.
- Recognition in front of the entire department, perhaps on a website, or in a company-wide newsletter. Be careful with this one. While most people appreciate acknowledgment of their accomplishments, not everyone wants *public* recognition.
- A letter of commendation in a personnel file.
- Gift card (movies, retail store, restaurant, coffee house).
- Selection from a gift catalog.
- Lunch or dinner with senior department leadership or with a spouse. Remember, it is up to the individual to decide what is *priceless*.
- Attendance at a sporting event using company tickets or prime seating (during working hours is even better).
- Attendance at a conference on a topic that matters to the individual.
- Travel.

Remember, recognizing, and rewarding good performance is important, and the best rewards match the individual's needs and internal sense of value.

Celebration

Celebrations are another form of reward, but with a twist. The dictionary describes celebrating as observing a day or event with ceremonies of respect, festivity, or rejoicing. Generally, celebrations are public. Celebrating an individual's accomplishment makes good sense, and team celebrations can be that much better for the organization. In both cases, you must strike a balance between having too many and too few. Make sure the celebration is deserved and nontrivial. Also, make sure other groups do not feel slighted or jealous and develop he-won-and-I-lost feelings.

At the hospital, monthly department meetings always included directors discussing the accomplishments of their staff for the past month. This tended to be a full laundry list of every activity without singling out any person or group. It was not a celebration. Occasionally, though, an individual was singled out for particular contributions. He or she received the coveted *Geek of the Month* award, a red stapler, and a copy of the movie *Office Space* (I wish I had thought of that). In addition to polite applause during the meeting, recipients were put into a receiving line to serve snacks to the department at the conclusion of the meeting. Does that sound like punishment instead? Not really. The entire department filed past these individuals, received refreshments, and usually made comments to their server. Mostly, the comments were lighthearted, fun, and very forgettable. It may sound trivial, but you would be surprised to know how many people commented on the positive feelings they had while serving their peers.

Addressing Non-PMO Issues—Capitalization

Does your organization capitalize IT development effort? This is a financial technique to allocate the cost of developing an asset (for example, a newly installed computer application) over the taxable life of the asset. Although capitalization is a financial issue, the PMO is the logical place to request help. That is because project details and developer hours are two critical elements in the solution. Tracking hours may be one of the least favorite tasks of project managers. Sometimes, they see it as a necessary evil for their project and fail to see it in the bigger context of helping the organization. But capitalization adds legitimacy to tracking hours. Capitalization is one compelling reason to track hours, since the organization benefits from more accurate accounting and better financial reporting, in this case.

Initially, the hospital's finance department requested that IT develop a paper-based time-tracking system that ran parallel to our own time-tracking system. When we were presented with this idea, I asked the ambassadors to help craft a better solution. They quickly realized the trick for efficiency and acceptance was to develop a solution that required minimal extra work for IT staff yet could stand up to the rigors of an external audit.

I will not get into the intricacies of time entry, reporting, revised or late project reporting, capturing the majority of team member time, tagging projects and line items within project plans to capture qualified data, and combining an individual's hours with his or her salary in a confidential manner. Our solution required one-time configuration changes to our project management software and a special program to merge files before details were sent to finance. Also, each new project needed less than half an hour to determine whether it qualified for capitalization and, if it did, identify project line items that could be capitalized. Beyond that, we followed standard time-keeping methods with one major exception. Individuals had to enter their own time. A project manager could no longer just mark a task as complete. Time keeping was the element needing the greatest sales effort, since it could mean a lot of extra work for the department.

The ambassadors requested modifications in project management training to emphasize the value of capitalization to the organization. They knew that finance was watching monthly results and that IT's budget was based on financial targets with capitalization in place. We stepped up monthly feedback to the IT department and highlighted projects that complied with the new reporting requirements. I would like to think that these efforts made a difference and boosted our compliance to an acceptable level, but I cannot say project managers enjoyed time tracking any better than they did before.

What if the Kinder, Gentler PMO Approach Does Not Work?

Face it, the gentle approach outlined may not work with every individual and every organization. So what can you do?

Resignation is certainly not the answer. Depending on your patience and—more exactly—the patience of your boss and the organization, you can try to wait it out. But if time is working against you, you may need to resort to more stick and less carrot. I suggest two principles when this happens. First, praise in public and criticize in private. Do not publically criticize the department, groups, or individual. Work with individuals to comply. Second, incrementally escalate the response and consequences. Yes, we used both of these principles on occasion. In one case, the escalation was gradual and did not significantly increase compliance until we made compliance a part of selected project manager's annual performance evaluations. No one wants it to reach that point. For those individuals the stick loomed large. Any support they might have had for the PMO and its concepts could have been lost until they realized how their actions affected others.

Limited escalation with individuals can be successful if handled properly. Major decrees and threats that come down from on high rarely work, especially when you are looking for only a few folks to change. Focus on the few who need intervention.

Conclusion

If it were a game, the PMO would be a team sport. Perhaps you would want to put only the best and the brightest on your PMO team. But history shows that the best teams perform well because they play *as* a team. They may not have the most talented individuals, but they win in spite of it. They have shared goals, great teamwork, sound fundamentals, and a collective spirit to improve and to win. This should be the vision of every PMO manager. The success of your PMO does not depend on having the best methodologies, Web site, or training curriculum. It depends on having good people who support the PMO and their peers as they work to improve project management for the organization. It wins when the organization wins.

The PMO manager's challenge is great. There are tools, processes, and systems that can improve an organization if just given a chance. And therein lies the challenge. A few people using PMO concepts will make a difference in their individual projects. But it takes a team effort for the majority of benefits to be realized. Major benefits come only when:

- An organization approaches full compliance using repeatable tools, processes, and systems
- Project managers are effective users of the resources available to them and they use those resources in a cooperative, shared environment
- Management occurs at the portfolio and department level, not just the project level
- It is all about the organization, not the individual

Understanding your audience and what makes them tick is important for moving an organization to greater capability maturity. Implementing change at a pace that the organization embraces is also important. And none of this is possible without enlisting the help and support of the troops; not just during the building phase, but on an ongoing basis. It is then (and only then) that the PMO will be effective and successful. And when it is successful, it will be a feather in everyone's cap.

Author Biography

Bruce Brower, PMP, has more than 30 years of experience helping both large and small organizations improve their internal processes and operational efficiency, establish financial measures and controls that promote growth and reduce risk, achieve program objectives in cost-effective ways, and reduce uncertainty in financial and operational decision making. Bruce has an undergraduate degree in mechanical engineering and mathematics from Duke University and an MBA from the Tepper School of Business at Carnegie-Mellon University. He has held management positions in financial analysis, information technology, and consulting for a variety of companies in several industries. He is on the board of directors of CommunityAmerica Credit Union and teaches in the PMP Exam Preparation Course for the PMI Kansas City Chapter.

References

Krzyzewski, M. with Spatola, J. K. 2009. *The Gold Standard: Building a World-Class Team*. New York: Business Plus.

12

Enhancing PMO Success from the Start

Carol Elzink, PMP

"It ought to be remembered that there is nothing more difficult to take in hand, more perilous to conduct, or more uncertain in its success, than to take the lead in the introduction of a new order of things"—Machiavelli.

Introduction

"If you see a bandwagon, it's too late"—James Goldsmith

Projects can be separated into their delivery of outcomes and operations to support that delivery, similar to the way a company is separated into its delivery of product and business operations. This is why project managers can generally focus on the operational side of the project, or the what-needs-to-be-delivered-when aspect, while technical managers focus on the production of the outcomes, or the how-it-is-delivered aspect. Project managers, along with the project management office (PMO), focus on what and when things are delivered. Executives and line managers in large organizations can set up project managers (and the project) for failure when they expect them to be technical managers or vice versa. A PMO can assist in providing this clarity by either allowing line personnel to focus technically while it manages the project, or it can assist by providing the project management knowledge or assistance to technical managers. In smaller organizations, technical managers and project managers are often a single person, and this can be a difficult individual to find. In larger organizations, technical managers are often asked to be project managers without any previous training.

Given the amount of investment in projects, it is often interesting to observe that they are put in the hands of people who are not experienced in project delivery—especially in large organizations. It is unusual that success is even expected when projects are managed by personnel who are not knowledgeable in the role. Certainly financial management is considered seriously enough to get a chief financial officer (CFO) and an entire organization that specializes in managing finances. Why not projects?

Just as the creation of the chief operating officer (COO) position frees up the chief executive officer (CEO) to focus on corporate strategy, the PMO can free up management to focus on profitability and day-to-day operations. PMOs can take care of all the projects required to translate uncertainty into reality. The PMO can be a permanent structure to manage transient (here today, gone tomorrow) work or a transient structure to support transient work.

The most difficult factor in creating a PMO can be defining it. What is it, what does it do, who runs it, how far is its reach, how long is it needed, and why is it required? There are many definitions in the marketplace.

In the *PMBOK® Guide—Fourth Edition*, the PMO is defined as, "An organizational body or entity assigned various responsibilities related to the centralized and coordinated management of those projects under its domain. The responsibilities of the PMO can range from providing project management support functions to actually being responsible for the direct management of a project" (Project Management Institute, 2008).

At its most basic definition, a PMO is involved in the management or support of transient activity that will result in a permanent effect on an organization. That makes projects sound like a disaster before they have even started! With this in mind, it is important for organizations to acknowledge how well they manage projects.

Setting up a PMO may appear daunting. However, the approach is identical to the approach required for any project or for creating a new department. The functions required of a PMO are often already being performed within an organization or project, and the setup will often just need to identify and locate the functions being performed and identify any gaps, then decide if centralization or providing specialized skills would gain any efficiency. As a minimum, an organization needs to recognize the specialization that is a PMO, and they may not know what they are doing in setting one up.

Common errors in setting up a PMO can be related to functional boundaries and people, and organizations can miss the importance of a change plan to deal with stakeholder issues and the translation of transiency to permanency. Particularly, appropriate expectation management will be important in organizations where the realignment of existing functions is required. PMOs can end up with a bad reputation very quickly, leaving many managers and executives with the impression that they do not work, if these expectations are not addressed. However, they do work because the functions themselves need to be performed anyway. The PMO is often merely just the title to centralize the focus and transactions for project success.

Like many projects, a PMO setup may be doomed to fail from the beginning if it is unsupported and underfunded. When stacked up against the investment in projects, the Low Bid Game (Thomsett, 2002) is a dangerous one if being used to get it started.

Elements of the Implementation Plan

"Failures don't plan to fail, they fail to plan"—Harvey MacKay

When conducting a Google search of "PMO failure," over 200 site references will pop up. Of those web pages that actually have content relating to PMO failure, they will usually reference one or two different reasons. A theme develops that is (for the most part) addressing expectations, roles, and bureaucracy.

The Project Management Institute (PMI®) survey on PMO implementations found that around 50 percent of PMOs were valued—the other half were being questioned (Hobbs, 2007). So if it is 50/50 and the jury is still obviously out, what are the reasons for the lack of definitive success? The following summarizes some observations from various sources:

- Lack of understanding of why one is needed; lack of purpose
- Problem-focused, not value-focused
- Process burdens from too much compliance; overly bureaucratic
- Lack of project management skills; PMO ignored
- Insufficient or inappropriate level of authority
- Roles and responsibilities are unclear
- Lack of independence from business-as-usual groups

Typical project plans or schedules for the implementation of a PMO can often be obtained by searching the Internet. Consulting companies often have free templates to lead you to their services. For example, gantthead.com (an online project management community) has an implementation project plan available in its templates list and various books, such as those included in the references list at the end of this chapter, can provide a task list or be used to develop one.

So what are the main elements for the implementation plan that can be taken from this information? The first element is the identification of a sponsor who can be effective at gaining key stakeholder buy-in and commitment, and can provide conflict resolution if it arises. A sponsor who can assist in the development of benefits and success criteria, can identify key risks, and is clear on the scope.

The second element is answering *why, what, when,* and *how*—in that order. Why is the PMO needed? What is the PMO going to do to deliver that need?

When is it expected to deliver what is needed? And finally, how will the PMO deliver what is needed?

This information is gained through planning, planning, and more planning. And just when you think you can get started, plan again and check the plan. This may seem like overkill, but the message needs to be driven home. A thousand task lists can be reviewed and this message might still be missed. Thorough planning is needed to elicit the many and varied expectations that need to be managed.

In recognizing the answers to just four questions, it is not difficult to understand why there are many different types of PMOs, and consistency amid PMOs is not going to occur and probably ought not be an expectation. Failure can also be linked to many organizations starting with *what* instead of *why*, assuming a quick solution for *when*, and not considering the practical differences in *how* between transient and permanent activity.

Why

Starting to answer *why* a PMO is required will begin the process of setting expectations. It is a key question and the answer will establish the justification or rationale for the PMO. It is this information that can be used to market or gain buy-in from the stakeholders for the development of the PMO. If agreement is not being reached, it could be due to stakeholders not recognizing *why* as being important or assuming that it has no contribution to corporate strategy.

In looking at the reason why various PMOs are set up, it is easy to realize why consistency in PMO structures varies across the industry or even within an organization, and why it is unlikely to be achieved. It may be better to drop this expectation and accept that each PMO needs to be approached individually and not to try to copy something another organization has done. Just as competitors differentiate their products for market share, PMOs are differentiated by the organizations and groups they serve.

The *why* begins with the establishment of a business case or by beginning chapters of a PMO charter. The following list provides a set of key questions to consider when establishing why a PMO is required. Will it:

- Take control of projects on behalf of the business?
- Solve a problem with project delivery?
- Enhance project management capability?
- Improve project delivery capability?
- Provide a consistent project management framework?
- Support delivery lifecycle requirements?
- Centralize resource management?
- Provide training on project management or project delivery approaches?
- Provide governance to a portfolio of projects?

- Select the right projects to proceed?
- Deliver a project management culture?
- Independently audit project status and viability?
- Manage a portfolio of projects balancing investment value and providing strategic alignment?
- Manage a portfolio of projects required to maintain the organization's current position?
- Provide centralized project performance measurement?

Other questions that need answers are:

- Is the PMO temporary or permanent?
- Is it departmental or organization-wide?
- Is it a single structure or department PMO reporting to a central enterprise PMO?
- Is it going to support, manage, or govern?

While this list is not exhaustive, understanding why the PMO is required, because each organization is unique, ensures that PMO setup can focus better on delivering to that requirement. It is appropriate to proceed with root-cause and value-added analysis before understanding *what* the PMO needs to do to ensure that the PMO can be justified and that the expectation at this point is clearly understood. The value of a complete feasibility study cannot be overly recommended. The *why* is the rationale, vision, or mission that is documented in a PMO charter.

What

What the PMO does is intimately related to *why* it exists. For example, the PMO is not necessarily going to be doing centralized resource management if it only needs to be involved in selecting the right projects. The PMO may focus too much on project management frameworks if the problem related to project delivery failure is within the lifecycle.

A good place to start with *what* the PMO is to do is to use PMO reference books, project management or project delivery, and governance frameworks for typical activities and transactions that are needed to directly support, manage, or govern *why* the PMO exists. Then, review other activities in case any auxiliary processes exist that may need to be performed to support the primary functions.

Brainstorming with key stakeholders can help elicit what a PMO is to do and review the listing for what is realistic in relation to why it needs to exist. At times this is useful to elicit contradictory expectations of why from those of the sponsor or those with the idea to setup a PMO. The following example provides an expansion of one of the *why* answers previously mentioned to demonstrate the move to *what* needs to be done:

- Why is the PMO needed?
  - To select the right projects to proceed
- What will it do to select the right projects?
  - Govern a portfolio management framework
  - Manage the portfolio of ideas or initiatives
  - Align ideas and initiatives with the organization strategy
  - Prioritize projects and determine delivery capacity
  - Maintain project selection criteria
  - Mentor the project selection process

In documenting the *what*, the objectives or functions, success factors, and metrics can be established in a PMO charter.

When

For each function or objective of the PMO, *when* delivery of activity is required needs to be considered. This can be *when* in terms of a deadline date or *when* certain conditions or criteria have been met. The following example provides an expansion of one of the *what* answers previously mentioned:

- Why is the PMO needed?
  - To select the right projects to proceed
- What will it do to select the right projects?
  - Maintain project selection criteria
- When will this function be available?
  - End of current financial year
  - When all stakeholders agree to the criteria

The *when* is considered after the *what* as a reality check for an appropriate time-frame, constraints, or criteria required. How the PMO delivers will be affected by when it is expected and when it can be revised, if required, after the *how* is understood.

How

This is the technology; the people and processes required to be developed and decided to deliver what the PMO is doing. Without the appropriate technology, the PMO will need to consider the administrative burden of manual processes. PMOs often do not provide appropriate project management or project delivery skills to the detriment of the PMO. Similarly, processes designed to maintain the current departments may need to be tailored or reviewed for their suitability to deliver functions to transient projects.

The sponsor and stakeholders will be critical to the success of how these functions will be adopted and need to be considered as part of how the PMO will deliver. The PMO can be implemented without a sponsor. However, it may not be as successful and navigation through the stakeholders could be time consuming.

The position of the PMO in the organization and its interaction with other organizations or departments will also factor in the success of how the PMO operates—effectively, its power or support base.

The *how* elements are discussed in more detail in the next part of this chapter.

The following example provides an expansion of one of the *what* answers previously mentioned:

- Why is the PMO needed?
  - To select the right projects to proceed
- What will it do to select the right projects?
  - Maintain project selection criteria
- When will this function be available?
  - When all stakeholders agree to the criteria
- How will this function be delivered to the organization?
  - Criteria will be established and maintained
  - Criteria will include external and internal factors related to strategic alignment, compliance, relative urgency, and market pressures
  - The project administrator will maintain the criteria register
  - Review of criteria for validity and relevance will be completed each quarter

PMO Charter

Table 12.1 outlines a typical table of contents to consider for the development of the PMO charter.

Sponsorship and Stakeholders

> *"Spare me no expense to save me money on this one"—Samuel Goldwyn*

Let's review a list of 10 challenges to project success (Winters, 2002):

1. Inadequately trained or inexperienced project managers
2. Failure to set and manage expectations
3. Poor leadership at any and all levels
4. Failure to adequately identify, document, and track requirements
5. Poor plans and planning processes
6. Poor effort estimation
7. Cultural and ethical misalignment

Table 12.1 PMO charter contents

Table of contents item	Description
Executive summary	Succinct summary of the key points of the PMO Charter. Usually around 10 percent of the final document.
Introduction	Outlines the purpose of the PMO charter and any relevant background to PMOs or the organization.
Rationalization (why)	Provides the justification for why the PMO is required and outlines its value proposition or solution to a key issue.
Vision or mission statement (motivation)	The vision statement is an inspirational or aspiration articulation of the direction of the PMO in alignment with the organization's vision (the *why*). It provides the initial influence for future decision making on PMO activity.
	The mission statement is an expansion of the vision statement. It would broadly describe the capabilities, service focus, and activities of the PMO. It summarizes the *what, how*, and *why* (e.g., providing centralized resource management through specialized skills and technology to support project success and time to market across the organization).
Objectives or functions (what)	A summary of the objectives that the PMO will deliver to a project, department, or organization. A list of what the PMO will do to achieve why it exists from the rationalization.
Critical success factors (what)	A list of the critical success factors that the organization will recognize or agree will determine that the PMO has been a success. These factors need to relate to why the PMO is implemented.
Metrics (what)	A list of the metrics that will be collected to objectively measure the critical success factors of the PMO (not projects) from the previous section of the document.
	An initial baseline of each metric needs to be taken and recorded here so that future measurement can take place. Without the baseline or starting point, measurement cannot take place.
Sponsor (how)	Outlines the role of the sponsor and indicates the individual or group of individuals that is supporting the implementation of the PMO.
	Ideally, this section gets specific as to the activities the sponsor will undertake in relation to PMO activity, during implementation and ongoing.
Stakeholders (how)	This section provides a list of stakeholders that impact or are impacted by the PMO.
	Outlines the stakeholder or stakeholder groups, their relationship to the PMO, and what expectations they have.
	Any priority information in relation to stakeholders can assist in focussing the PMOs initial attention for quick wins.

Organizational structure (how)	An outline of where the PMO is structured in the organization relative to other departments or groups.
	This generally outlines the PMO's level of independence to the other groups responsible for the ongoing management of the organization.
Roles and responsibilities (how)	Provides an outline of the skills required as roles within the PMO to deliver what needs to be done.
	It is critical that these roles be skilled in project management or aspects of project management.
Interaction with existing organization (how)	This section outlines how the PMO interacts with the existing structure of an organization (e.g., what functions are shared, which direction is the relationship in regard to data, who is the customer, etc.).
Objective 1	Detailed outline of the first objective or function, the complete scope of what will be done, when the first initial activity can be expected or when the success criteria is expected to be achieved, what conditions need to exist for the success of this objective and how the PMO will deliver the objective or function through existing or new technology, people, and processes.
	This component becomes the first area of identifying the tasks or work packages that need to be completed. Schedule development, dependency identification, and resource requirements become known for implementation.
Objective 2, etc.	See Objective 1
Appendices as required	Appendices to provide further detail on individual chapters and sections in the document (e.g., glossary, frequent questions, organization charts).

8. Misalignment between the project team and the business or other organization it serves
9. Inadequate or misused methods
10. Inadequate communication, including progress tracking and reporting

Six of these items (2, 3, 4, 7, 8, and 10) have a direct stakeholder component that makes stakeholder management critical to project success. You may already realize that a happy customer generally does not care how much something costs or how long it takes, so ask a project stakeholder and the simple answer might just be, "The project delivered what I needed, so I'm happy." Measure a project's success through the happiness of its stakeholders and you may get more project success without using the metrics related to business as usual.

A PMO implementation is a project until it becomes a permanent structure (even if it is becoming permanent to a transient project) and because it is a new organization structure, it will create corporate political issues as it proceeds. A PMO can be a challenge or change to authority lines already in place or seen as a threat to established practices, in particular those that will manage or govern. With project failure at a high in many organizations, trust in a structure yet to be established is naturally low.

While Rochefoucauld's (1650) contribution that the "only thing constant in life is change" still holds true today, we often do not embrace change before we know for sure about the change. Fear of the unknown is still alive and well and this needs to be remembered when engaging with stakeholders. Ensure that a change management plan exists and provides a clear change road for stakeholders. Consider looking at Prosci's ADKAR (Hiatt, 2006) if unfamiliar with these frameworks.

A sponsor can help offset uncertainty and champion the what's-in-it-for-me messages for the organization, departments, and individuals. An effective sponsor is the "single best predictor" of project success (Thomsett, 2002). If the PMO is to be successful, this will definitely hold true.

Ideal sponsorship is one of empowerment. It is the ability to see the issues, to know the PMO will solve them, to know that it is the right solution, to articulate why, and to be flexible about how the outcome manifests. The sponsor has a stake in its successful outcome and has the authority to make decisions.

When selecting a sponsor for the PMO, the easiest way to identify who is going to be most effective is to identify the senior-most position to whom the PMO will report. Thus, if it is an organization-wide PMO, the sponsor would be the CEO; if departmental, the senior executive of that department, e.g., the CIO if it is an information technology (IT) PMO; and if a project, the steering committee or project sponsor.

Organization Positions

"It's easy to come up with new ideas; the hard part is letting go of what worked for you two years ago, but will soon be out of date" —Roger von Oech

Large corporations spend millions of dollars ensuring that they have a strategy in place to maintain and strengthen their position in the marketplace to provide a return on the investment of those millions. The strategy provides the destination and roadmap for where the company is going and what it does. All activity within the corporation then aligns to guarantee the destination.

In the analogy of a car, if the CEO is the driver with the destination, the CFO, COO, and CIO groups would be the car. Where is the PMO or project world to fit? Answer: a strategic project would be developing the road in front of the car. Other tactical projects are modifying the car or road already developed as the terrain changes. Everyone is involved in attempting to predict the terrain and needs to be able to change as it is confirmed. The project world is one of uncertainty and as it becomes defined, it will be handed to the organization to maintain.

Figure 12.1 outlines a direction that strategy can take through transient projects into permanent organization activity. The PMO and project managers can take the responsibility to deliver the projects—strategic or tactical—and allow other groups to focus on maintaining market position and providing the successful corporate foundation. The projects need to be flexible or removed as direction changes (i.e., are projects really failing, or were they not removed or changed soon enough when the direction changed?). A PMO can help manage this question.

Figure 12.2 illustrates an organization chart representing the potential positioning of different PMOs. Of importance is the independence of the PMO as a specialist organization for governing or supporting project management and project delivery.

When positioning the PMO, the functions that a PMO will perform need to be considered so that the appropriate authority through position can be achieved. For example, if a PMO is intended to select the right projects, it will not be able to achieve this unless it works alongside senior management and executives. If a PMO has too much authority, it may lose its objectivity in balancing the level of compliance to the project size, or become oppressive to project delivery and reduce motivation. The following list provides a typical focus for PMOs based on their position in the organization:

- Organization-wide PMO
  - Reports to CEO, generally referred to as an enterprise PMO
  - Mainly strategic projects, may provide support or project managers for tactical projects
  - Ensures alignment and delegates or authorizes groups to proceed with a project
  - Works with the CFO and COO to prioritize funds and resources
  - Provides governance and framework to lower-level organization PMOs
- Department PMO
  - Reports to senior managers or preferably the enterprise PMO, if it exists
  - Includes a department portfolio of projects aligned to organization strategy
  - Manages a centralized technical resource pool, balancing business as usual with project requirements
  - Could be a department of a project managers
  - Typically found in IT where many tactical projects are ongoing in response to the ongoing business needs
- Project PMO
  - Reports to the steering committee or project sponsor or is part of the steering committee

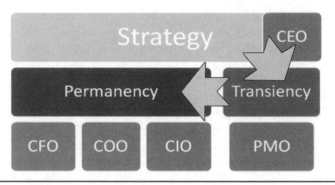

Figure 12.1   Transient strategy projects to organization activity.

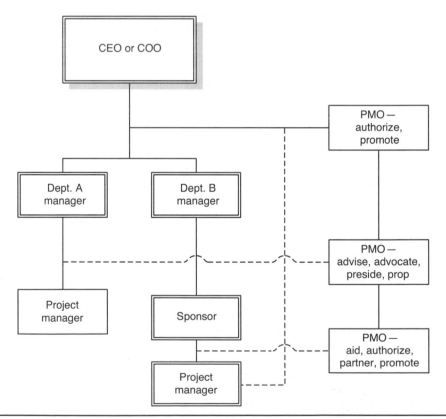

Figure 12.2   The potential positioning of PMOs in an organizational chart.

○ Reports to or provides support to the project manager providing assistance with scheduling, administration, recruitment, and induction (depending on the size of the project)
○ Typically found on larger projects

Personalities and Attitudes

"If I were two faced, would I be wearing this one?" —Abraham Lincoln

After considering the right sponsor and the organizational position of the PMO, the PMO, from the outset, can adopt a personality or attitude for how it will perform by aligning the PMO to the organization's requirements instead of it developing in response to problems.

The PMO personality will be a combination of the functions it needs to provide, its level of compliance or audit involvement, and the organization's project maturity. PMOs often fail when they develop a personality that is in opposition to the organization's project maturity and culture (or lack of it). For example, a PMO is set up to delegate in a low project management maturity environment, or takes a directive stance in a highly mature project management environment when the issue was only one project.

The framework of Situational Leadership® (Hersey, 1992) provides a good view of what personality or attitude a PMO can adopt against the maturity of an organization as it pertains to project management. For example, delegation and descriptive advice generally work well when experienced project managers are available and there is alignment within the organization toward its goals. Perry (2009) also provides some background on this framework in relation to leadership from the PMO.

Figure 12.3 attempts to outline four potential personalities or attitudes that PMOs can adopt from the beginning.

The words within the circle capture the essence of the PMO's attitude toward project management and project delivery. The words outside the circle are overlays from the Situational Leadership®, OPM3®, and CMM® models to align the PMO with an organization's or project managers' project delivery maturity.

The arrows refer to a rotating attitude that may need to be adopted toward single projects or a type of project in consideration of the project management maturity of an individual and an organization as it grows. Figure 12.3 is a transient personality model for a transient project world.

It is important to remember that despite the relative maturity of the organization or project managers in relation to projects, the PMO must be completely mature in its skill sets and processes and preferably have access to many different delivery frameworks to be successful.

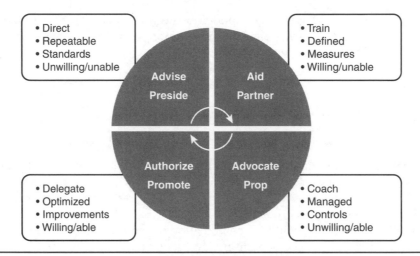

Figure 12.3   Four potential PMO personalities or attitudes.

Advise

The PMO will not be viewed as an advisor if it is not aligned with an organization's strategy, its project managers have insufficient project management knowledge in project delivery, and project managers do not acknowledge the requirement of the project management framework provided by the PMO.

The PMO focuses on advice to the project management (PM) community within the organization and key stakeholders. This PMO fits best in a low maturity PM environment and the advice is generally prescriptive. At its best, this personality can provide trust and a good foundation for an immature project culture. At its worst, it becomes an inflexible, oppressive process controller.

The PMO will necessarily need to focus on compliance to standards, preside over the quality of project outcomes, and will generally focus on creating a repeatable, consistent approach to project management. The PMO can also be the supplier of project management activity when it is absent in the other business departments.

This PMO often fails when attempting to preside over project managers and line managers who are already mature in their practice and do not need to be told what to do, or fails in an immature environment by acting like an unforgiving parent. After a while, the project managers will rebel and actively seek to remove this PMO if it is too aggressive in its approach to compliance without explanation.

Strong sponsorship is required to help this PMO and its approach survive until the organization (or project manager) is more mature. The PMO needs to ensure that the maturity is regularly assessed so that it can adopt another approach better suited to the increased level of maturity.

Aid

The PMO will not be successful in providing aid if it is not aligned with the organization's strategy or if the project manager has insufficient project management knowledge in project delivery and fails to acknowledge the presence and value of a project management framework provided by a PMO.

This PMO focuses on providing assistance to the project managers and is most often a transient organization attached directly to a project. In larger organizations, this PMO may be responsible for maintaining project standards, templates, and delivery artifacts (i.e., a repository) and providing project management training.

On large projects, this PMO may contain a dedicated scheduler, administrator, finance manager, etc. to provide transactional support to the inexperienced project managers or with limited project management resources. In organizations, it may be a senior project manager who can train new project managers on the organization's requirements.

This PMO can fail when incorrectly staffed with people who know nothing about projects. For this PMO to be successful, a project management framework must be defined and consistent across the organization.

Advocate

The PMO will not be viewed as an advocate if it is not aligned with an organization's strategy or if the project manager has insufficient project management knowledge in project delivery and fails to acknowledge the presence and value of a project management framework provided by a PMO.

This PMO, while needed in the right environment, is probably the most difficult to navigate. This PMO will need to respond to knowledgeable project managers by advocating and selling the benefits of a framework that provides a consistent language and approach to project delivery. Generally, this is done by implementing controls that deliver the benefits of good project management. This PMO is most successful when it also supplies the project managers to the rest of the organization.

On projects, this PMO would be a source of descriptive rather than prescriptive advice. The PMO may need to address experienced project managers who are unwilling to adopt a different approach to their own. The PMO also needs to remain flexible to approaches from experienced project managers who may know what has worked well in the past for the organization.

This PMO can fail for the same reasons as the PMO providing aid. Mature project managers will hardly take advice from someone who knows nothing about projects and will respond negatively if the advice or compliance is oppressive or incorrect. Mutual respect needs to be established quickly with strong, ongoing, and open communication.

Authorize

The PMO will not be recognized as having authority if it is not aligned with an organization's strategy or if the project manager has insufficient project management knowledge in project delivery and fails to acknowledge the presence and value of the project management framework provided by a PMO.

This PMO is about delegation. It is about authorizing the work to go ahead and delegating delivery to the project managers. The organization is mature, project managers are trained, and a repeatable, consistent approach to project management exists. The PMO is primarily providing governance. In an organization, this PMO is often doing portfolio management and could be supplying the project managers. In a project, the PMO would be tracking project performance and quality, and would be part of the steering committee.

Failure of this PMO is usually due to a limitation on its decision-making capability and inappropriate positioning in the organization or project. This PMO also has to guard against becoming bureaucratic.

PMO Models and Alignment

> *"Not everything that can be counted counts, and not everything that counts can be counted" —Albert Einstein*

The required functions of the PMO detailing why it exists will determine what PMO model it becomes. Kendall & Rollins (2003) use repository, coaching, and deliver value now. Letavec (2006) uses strong, consulting, and a blended model. Many books and consulting groups provide titles for PMO models, and these descriptions serve as a good foundation for the future direction of the PMO.

What the PMO needs to do stems mainly from why it exists. Read a book on the appropriate model that aligns with the *why*, and *voilà!*, the PMO delivers all the functions. Sounds simple, but many who start with the model forget to develop the *why*. Creating a PMO from a model may cause you to overlook key functions of a different model that are required for success.

While different models develop, what is common among them is that they relate to projects—transient activities that disappear once the projects are completed. The PMO, therefore, does not necessarily need to overlap or repeat any functions already being done in an organization, but can be designed to utilize functions that already exist or centralize them. This is not necessarily an easy task, especially if projects are continually made to report in a similar manner to general management requirements or there are ownership boundary issues. Anyone who has ever had to relate corporate and project accounting requirements can attest to the difficulties in getting information at sufficient granularity from current management systems for efficient project management.

Ongoing, existing business functions have a different management focus for projects, and this needs to be recognized when formulating the processes and performance requirements of the PMO (and even of projects). Ongoing functions tend to focus on unit numbers, money generation, money saved, investments, and inventories, as examples. A PMO and project management:

- Needs to focus on whether projects will achieve their outcomes
- Needs to determine if current project performance will indicate delivery to agreed baselines
- Needs to determine if requirements are changing
- Needs to determine how the organization will need to change without severely impacting business as usual

Table 12.2 PMO requirements

Requirement	Comments and issues
Project management	This is the domain of project managers. They are trained or have experience dealing with uncertainty and know the processes required to manage unknowns. Project managers may not have an appreciation of the impact of projects to permanent activities.
	Technical or line managers are often asked or assume that they will manage projects without any understanding of what is required to manage transient work against permanent work. They can often be unskilled in focusing and reporting on the *what* and *when* aspects of a project.
Tool set	This includes templates, systems, procedures, methodology, and frameworks.
	Quality departments can often own corporate intellectual property. IT often assists with tool or system selection.
	The foundation and bane of any PMO implementation will be the time recording system. Companies may only have this for payroll purposes or not at all, and significant time can be spent implementing one and can create an administrative burden through manual time sheets.
	A PMO implementation needs to consider the maturity of the tools at its disposal. This will reflect on its reputation as the champion of the project management framework.
Competency	Human resource (HR) departments often have a training arm and deal with staff competency. A PMO needs to consider if it is appropriate for HR to continue to provide staff development for project managers.

(Continues)

Table 12.2 *(Continued)*

Finance	This is the domain of the accounts or finance department under the direction of the CFO.
	Projects are more interested in knowing what an activity is going to cost or is costing and not the cost categories provided in a chart of accounts. Knowing labor or materials was charged to a project is great, however the project needs to know how it was used. Often each deliverable needs to be tracked separately and many accounting systems do not provide an easy system for this requirement.
	There can be confusion in the difference between project accounting and job costing with an assumption that job costing will be sufficient to track the project costs without realizing that a project (especially a large one) is essentially made up of several jobs. The job costing system needs to provide a link to a schedule or work breakdown structure (WBS), cost splits by cost categories rather than by deliverables, and outcomes for performance measurement.
Administration	Often the domain of the executive assistants.
	Depending on what activity is being done, this is done throughout a company by various roles.
	PMO setup needs to ensure that it is not duplicating a service provided elsewhere (e.g., travel booking or burdening current service providers with transient requirements).
Scheduling	Generally the domain of the project manager, however, PMOs often provide centralized scheduling support.
	Certainly, large projects that have a transient PMO will often have the PMO do the master scheduling and interproject dependency tracking.
Resource management	There may be an operations role already performing this function or struggling with it. A PMO being setup may need to consider including the role or working with the role already in existence.
Procurement	There may be a department called procurement or contracting that performs this function. Many internal PMOs will work with the other functions to procure items.
	For personnel, this is generally the domain of HR. The PMO may keep track of when assigned contractors are due for contract renewal.

Its future is focused on predicting outcome success, not just on budget versus actual cost, as in many ongoing target measurements. Kendall & Rollins (2003) provide a good discussion on these conflicts.

While there may be conflicts or constraints in report requirements, there will also be constraints and conflicts with other business organizations. Table 12.2 provides a typical set of PMO requirements and provides the overlap or challenges with other business functions.

Table 12.3 provides an example of the primary differences in PMO (or project) focus versus the business function.

Table 12.3 PMO vs. business function

Function	PMO	Business
Finance	Cost account alignment with WBS	Chart of accounts
	WBS cost capture	Profit and loss
	Stages or phase alignment of costs	Balance sheet
	Performance measurement and estimate at completion prediction	Financial year calendar or financial months
		Budget vs. actual
		Spending and funding
Human resources	Recruitment—to the project	Recruitment—to the organization
	Contract tracking	Performance reviews
	Project induction	Attrition
		Training
Project management	Supply project managers	Create design solutions
	Support project management	Assist with project analysis and testing
	Governance of projects	
	May also provide people change management	If IT, coding software, testing, installing, may be doing project management
		People change management

These differences and similarities need to be explored for every department within an organization to ensure that the PMO's role is clearly defined.

Functions and Role Combinations

"If you pay peanuts, you get monkeys" —*James Goldsmith*

In a world short of resources or even a lack of transactions to keep a single person busy, it can be difficult to understand how functions can be combined, or if they are related, to be able to get a resource who has one skill and can transfer the knowledge to another function.

The answer for this lies in a thorough understanding of the transactions, their outcomes, the object focus of the transactions, and how the organization already combines functions. For example, some large organizations combine HR with payroll because of the personnel and privacy focus; other large organizations combine finance with payroll because of the money focus. In smaller companies, HR, finance, and payroll may be a single individual. It is worth looking at small to medium companies to see how functions combine, align, and grow before organizations become large and can dedicate single roles to single functions.

In project management, there are similar alignments between functions because the transactions are the same. The most obvious is the support of risk, issue, and change control management—three different functions that are transactionally similar when providing support through data entry, due date follow up, escalation to technical personnel and executives, documenting outcomes, etc. The following list provides some combinations to consider when short on resources or work volume:

- *Risk and quality management*—both have an outcome-success focus
- *Cost and procurement management*—both have a contract-outcome focus
- *HR and procurement management*—both can have a procurement focus
- *Scope and risk management*—both have an outcome-success and change-control focus
- *Time and cost management*—both have a project performance focus
- *Risk, scope, and integration management*—all have an outcome-success and change-control focus

Hill (2008) in Chapter 7 provides an excellent discussion on the internal organization structure of PMO personnel, while Kendall & Rollins (2003) provide a good starting point for considering position descriptions.

When aligning personnel skills, it is necessary to ensure that an individual has a thorough understanding of at least one domain in detail and has some exposure to the other processes. It will be the senior or more experienced PMO staff who will need to mentor and provide or obtain training in the other process. Large programs or organizations have the luxury of one person per function—smaller projects or organizations may not.

The decision about which function is more important to recruit for is based in negative risk, that is, which function, if it is staffed by someone with no knowledge in the beginning, will have less impact to the project? Or can the function be realistically supported elsewhere until the individual is up to speed across all functions?

The perfect PMO person is someone who has transitioned through nearly every business department, including project management training or exposure and one with a resume that looks like he cannot commit to a long-term career in anything. A career in small PMO management is tailored to the easily bored.

Transaction-driven Recruitment

This is a term usually reserved for agencies that fill the gap when organizations have temporary work or transaction surges that do not justify adding another permanent position.

In the PMO, transaction types, volumes, and combinations can help focus recruitment efforts. Transaction type will drive the underlying skill set for a role in development. Transaction combinations can assist in determining a skill match between the person and the role. Transaction volumes determine the number of people required to fulfill a role or when an additional person is required to split transaction combinations.

Typically, small projects have fewer transactions and will require multiple functions to match with skills. On large programs, it is important not to underestimate the volume of project management transactions that can be achieved by a single project manager. A PMO can provide the additional transactions so that project managers can focus on the management and governance activities.

Summary

> *"If you're not failing every now and again, it's a sign you're not doing anything very innovative"* —Woody Allen

Once the reasons for a PMO are established, PMO implementation success can be enhanced by focusing on sponsorship selection and stakeholder management in alignment with the entire organization. What it needs to do becomes clearer and the PMO can focus on getting the job done.

- Implementation approach
  - Decide the sponsor and manage the stakeholders
  - Establish *why* it is required
  - Determine *what* it will do to address *why* it is required
  - Decide *when* it will address *what* it will do
  - Decide *how* it will do *what* it needs to do

Author Biography

Carol Elzink, PMP, has 20 years of experience designing, developing, and implementing PMO structures across finance, utility, pharmaceutical, government, consulting, and telecommunication industries with personnel numbers ranging from one to 35, covering some or all of the *PMBOK® Guide* functions. PMO types have ranged from administrative support to full governance. Functions have been designed for departments, companies, and projects or programs. Carol holds a Bachelor of Information Systems and a post-graduate diploma in psychology. She has also spent several years educating others in project management and project methodology. Carol currently provides consultation as a planning and estimation subject matter expert and practices as a psychologist part time.

References

Bolles, D. and Hubbard, D. G. 2006. *The Power of Enterprise-Wide Project Management*. New York: Amacom.

Bolles, D. 2002. *Building Project Management Centers of Excellence*. New York: Amacom.

Denison, D. R. 1997. *Corporate Culture and Organizational Effectiveness, 2nd edition*. Atlanta: Denison Consulting.

Hersey, P. 1992. *The Situational Leader, 4th edition*. Escondido, CA: Center for Leadership Studies.

Hiatt, J. M. 2006. *ADKAR: A model for change in business, government and our community*. Loveland, CO: Prosci Research.

Hiatt, J. M. and Creasey, T. J. 2003. *Change Management: the people side of change*. Loveland, CO: Prosci Research.

Hill, G. M. 2007. *The Complete Project Management Office Handbook, 2nd edition*. Boca Raton: CRC Press.

Hobbs, B. and Aubry, M. 2005. *A realistic portrait of PMOs: the results of an empirical investigation*. Newton Square, PA: Project Management Institute.

Hobbs, B. 2007. *The Multi-Project PMO: a global analysis of the current state of practice*. White paper. Newton Square, PA: Project Management Institute.

Kendall, G. I. and Rollins, S. C. 2003. *Advanced Project Portfolio Management and the PMO: Multiplying ROI at Warp Speed*. Fort Lauderdale, FL: J. Ross Publishing.

Letavec, C. J. 2006. *The Program Management Office: Establishing, Managing and Growing the Value of a PMO*. Fort Lauderdale, FL J. Ross Publishing.

Myers, I. B. 1995. *Gifts Differing: understanding personality type*. Boston: Davies-Black Publishing.

Perry, M. P. 2009. *Business Driven PMO Setup*. Fort Lauderdale, FL: J. Ross Publishing.

PM Solutions Research. 2007. *The State of the PMO 2007-2008: a benchmark of current best practices*. Glen Mills, PA: PM Solutions.

Project Management Institute. 2003. *Organizational Project Management Maturity Model: OPM3 Knowledge Foundation*. Newton Square, PA: Project Management Institute.

Project Management Institute. 2008. *A Guide to the Project Management Body of Knowledge (PMBOK® Guide)*, Fourth Edition. Newton Square, PA: Project Management Institute.

Rad, P. F. and Levin, G. 2002. *The Advanced Project Management Office: A Comprehensive Look at Function and Implementation*. Boca Raton: CRC Press.

Thomsett, R. 1989. *Third Wave Project Management*. Upper Saddle River, NJ: Prentice Hall.

Thomsett, R. 2002. *Radical Project Management*. Upper Saddle River, NJ: Prentice Hall.

Winters, F. 2002. *The Top 10 Reasons Projects Fail*. Available at: http://www.gantthead.com/article.cfm?ID=147229

13

How to Implement Project Management Methodologies in a Small Company

Robert Tresente, Jr., PMP, MBA

Introduction

We all know as project management professionals that project management methodologies have greatly assisted large and midsized organizations in achieving business results and because of this, have become very prevalent within these types of organizations. Our purpose here is to recommend strategies that could assist in successfully bringing these proven project management methodologies to small companies or a small division or department within a larger organization. In doing so, it allows these small companies to reap the benefits that project management rigor has been proven to provide to larger and midsized organizations.

To do this we need to be able to address some of the unique challenges and circumstances that small companies present regarding the adoption of project management methodologies. The challenges that will be discussed here have been shown through my professional journey to be the most relevant (or challenges in need of attention) to overcome for the successful implementation of project management methodologies within small companies. The most relevant challenges and circumstances for small companies are that they: have limited resources; emphasize personal interactions over process; focus on the results more than the method; cannot tolerate poor performers; and they are impacted significantly by change.

This chapter will present a series of proven strategies that when employed as outlined here, would assist in overcoming the unique challenges and circumstances that small companies present. These strategies could be used to set up a complete portfolio, program, or project management office, or to just manage one project effort. To make these strategies actionable, each one is accompanied by one or more on-the-ground tools and techniques.

We will get started by first looking at each challenge and circumstance in greater detail.

The Challenges

Let us begin by outlining five challenges and circumstances that a small company presents in the establishment of project management methodologies or the installation of a project management office (PMO):

1. Small number of resources
2. The importance of personal interactions
3. It is all about results
4. No weak links allowed
5. Dramatic impact of change

We will now look at each challenge and circumstance individually.

Challenge 1—Small Number of Resources

In many cases, a small company means a small number of resources (either money or people) that could be available to you. This increases the importance of ensuring that the resources you have are focused on the project tasks at hand. Your project management process should not burden them with complex, administrative activities. Doing so could reduce their likelihood of delivering what needs to get done for their project to be a success and to add value to the company. You need to have a lean administrative process. If a process point is not adding measurable value, it should be eliminated.

Challenge 2—The Importance of Personal Interactions

In a small company, your personal interactions with company staff members and project team members is important. In large organizations, in many cases, the culture of the organization could have more influence over the behaviors of individuals. In small companies, without the strong processes and controls established by large organizations to drive their culture, and to manage their large number of employees, the culture generally does not have the same influence over the employees' behavior. With this in mind, you need to pay more intention to your personal interactions to be able to influence change within the company. Here, utilizing good listening skills and possessing high emotional intelligence will serve you well.

Challenge 3—It Is All About Results

In a small company, having the most elegant and well-documented project management process is not going to mean much to the company's executives if you are not achieving results. In a small company, especially a newer startup, the delivery of expected project results is the key. They may mean life or death to the company. For those leading a PMO, you need to stay close to the project execution process. This would suggest about a 50/50 split between PMO and portfolio management activities and on-the-ground managing project activities.

Challenge 4—No Weak Links Allowed

You cannot afford to have any weak links in your process or on your staff. Every process point and staff member needs to be adding value. If you have a weak link, you need to address it right away. If it is left to linger or not addressed at all, it has the potential of having a dramatic affect on your project outcomes and the performance of the company. Here, you need to be brave and address all performance issues directly and quickly.

Challenge 5—Dramatic Impact of Change

Because change in business environments, organization structure, and staff in many cases, have even a more profound impact on smaller companies, the project management leadership needs to have a degree of flexibility in the way they manage projects. In some cases, you need to be able to bypass process steps or adjust the process to fit the current business challenge. Knowing when to stand tall and be flexible is not always obvious or easily determined. In many cases, this could be the most impactful decision to project delivery that you will be tasked to make as a project manager or PMO leader. The key here is knowing when to stick to the process and when adjustments are necessary. This decision point is probably the greatest ongoing management challenge a project manager or PMO leader in a small company continually faces.

Strategies for Success

Through my experience, the following ten strategies have been successful in addressing, as outlined previously, the unique challenges and circumstances that small companies present when working to establish project management disciplines or a PMO:

1. Obtain and maintain executive support
2. Gather project stakeholders input
3. Establish project metrics to measure success
4. Define and present the project management framework to all project stakeholders
5. Start with a big win
6. Focus on results, not process
7. Develop a great project management team
8. Continually present information that demonstrates effectiveness
9. Use lessons learned and customer feedback to continuously improve
10. Expand responsibilities where possible

We will now review the first six strategies on their own and in detail. Also, to make these strategies actionable, each one is accompanied by one or more on-the-ground tools and techniques.

Strategy 1—Obtain and Maintain Executive Support

You always hear that it is important to obtain executive support when starting a PMO or when attempting to implement project management methodologies to assist some important project. This has even greater importance when you are working to establish project management methodologies or a PMO in a small company. If the leaders of the company do not standup and state the importance of this and that they are behind it 100 percent, you will most likely not be successful. In most cases, staff in a small company is not going to follow a methodology or process unless it is openly supported or mandated by the executive team.

With the above in mind, the first thing you need to do is establish executive support. If you are interviewing with a small company looking to establish project management methodologies or a PMO, be sure you have the opportunity to meet the executives during the interviewing process to obtain an understanding of their opinions regarding project management and the value they believe it could bring to the company. If you do not believe their support is strong enough or if you believe support is lacking considerably, you may not want to accept any possible job offer. The above is also true if you are tapped from within the company to bring this about.

If the executives are supportive at the beginning, that is a good start, but you will need to work continuously to maintain and strengthen their support. A few on-the-ground tools and techniques for achieving initial and ongoing support from the executive team are presented here.

Tools and Techniques for This Strategy

Three actionable tools and techniques to allow you to obtain and maintain executive support include:

1. *Interview with executives*—This is key. You absolutely need to meet with each executive separately and capture their opinions. To maintain executive support, you need to continuously engage with them. An interview is an effective way to start that engagement. Some of the following tools and techniques will ensure that ongoing dialog with the executives is achieved. Be sure to take detailed notes during the interview and to summarize and share your interview notes with each interviewee afterward. Once you have completed interviewing all the executives, you should provide an executive summary report to all the executives. The findings should be written, but it is important to be brief; only one to two pages is sufficient. They are probably not going to read some large dissertation or report. If possible, you should present your findings in a meeting with all the interviewed executives in attendance. This information should be used to assist in determining your proposed project management methodology. We will discuss this topic further under the Gather Project Stakeholders' Input strategy.

2. *State of the PMO report*—As this name indicates, this tool is more relevant for an existing PMO. This tool should be used after the PMO has been in place for a while, preferably after about one year has passed. The state of the PMO report should attempt to obtain a complete and accurate accounting of the state of the PMO within the company. To do this, once per year you should solicit the opinions of the company's business leaders and key project stakeholders from projects delivered over the time being measured. This should be achieved through a series of one-on-one and group interviews. Use these interviews to gather their perspective on how the PMO is performing. After the interview process, a report should be prepared and issued describing all the input received and any associated action items. To assist you in formulating your interview questions, we have provided some examples of possible questions in Table 13.1.

3. *Project portfolio executive steering committee*—To maintain continuous executive engagement, you will need to periodically meet with the executives to review and provide status on the active projects, discuss strategic direction regarding the project portfolio, and review PMO and project management related topics. This meeting's agenda is similar to the PMO planning group, but its purpose is very different. The PMO planning group is largely focused on continuous improvement and on-ground project

Table 13.1 Interview questions for the State of the PMO report

1. Has the implementation of the PMO's new project management process improved on project delivery? Why?
2. Is the weekly status report a useful tool in providing project status information? Why?
3. Is the strategic plan a useful tool in providing a long-term project outlook? Why?
4. How would you rate the performance of the PMO team regarding their project management and business analysis expertise? How would you rate their ability to deliver projects?
5. Tell me about the best experience you have had regarding the PMO team.
6. Tell me about the worst experience you have had regarding the PMO team.
7. What do you believe are the strengths of the PMO team?
8. What do you believe are the weaknesses of the PMO team?
9. What would you like the PMO to address next?
10. Overall, has the PMO team, coupled with the implementation of a new project management process, improved on our ability to deliver projects? Why?
11. Do you have any other comments?

delivery. The project portfolio executive steering committee meeting is to obtain executive direction when you need it and to continue keeping the executives informed of progress on key strategic projects. The added benefits of the steering committee meetings are its ability to ensure continuous support and engagement by the executive team in regards to the value that project management is delivering to facilitate the company's business priorities. Below is a typical meeting agenda:

○ *Active project statuses*—A quick project status review of only projects where (1) executive attention is required to move the project forward, (2) a project is in a yellow or red status, (3) a major milestone has been achieved or (4) the project has been completed. The status should include a brief one- to three-sentence summary, the project achievements since the last status report, the achievement scheduled to occur before the next status report, and any risks or issues that could possibly impede progress regarding the scheduled achievements. When discussing issues and risks, you should focus on any decision points the executives need to make and work to obtain an actionable resolution.

○ *Project portfolio strategic alignment*—This is not an agenda item for every meeting. The frequency of this agenda item depends greatly on the current business environment, but as a general guideline it should be reviewed by the executives at least quarterly. This discussion should review how the projects being undertaken align with the company's strategic objectives. Pie charts are an effective tool for this purpose (see an example of a strategic alignment pie chart in Figure 13.1).

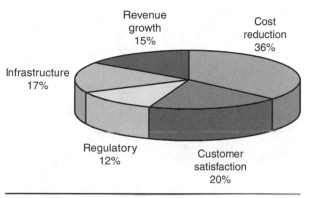

Figure 13.1   Strategic alignment pie chart.

○ *Project portfolio distribution across many different categories (e.g., depart-ments, products, services, processes, sponsors, etc.)*—This is an optional agenda item. The frequency of this agenda item depends greatly on the current business environment, but as a general guideline, it should be reviewed by the executives at least quarterly. This is similar to the stra-tegic alignment agenda item, except here you discuss the distribution of the portfolio based on the example categories outlined above. This topic generally has the effect of stimulating conversation about how well the portfolio is balanced within each category. See Figure 13.2 for an ex-ample of a portfolio distribution report.

○ *Projects not being addressed*—One of the main reasons to perform project portfolio management is to be able to draw the line as to which projects you will work on and which projects you will not work on. If you just continue to discuss the project in execution, you will miss out on valuable input regarding the importance of projects not yet initi-ated. The executives are the people who draw that line, so you need to keep them aware of the line and what is on both sides of it. You con-tinuously need to review the projects on the bench and the value they could bring if undertaken.

○ *Project management methodologies review*—Under this agenda item, you present to the executives any recent changes or proposed changes you plan to make to the current project management methodologies. In some cases, the discussion is just for informational purposes. In others, you will be asking for their approval. Usually, you will be asking only for approval on methodologies related to the portfolio management activities, since they are more directly involved in those processes.

○ *Metrics review*—As any good PMO will do, you will be capturing met-rics that should allow you to measure your performance, and this is one of the forums where those metrics should be reviewed and discussed.

Customer service

Rank	Project name	Status	1Q11			2Q11			3Q11			4Q11		
			Jan	Feb	Mar	Apr	May	Jun	Jul	Aug	Sep	Oct	Nov	Dec
1	CRM system implementation	Active												
2	Call center phone system upgrade	Not started												
3	Customer satisfaction survey system implementation	Not started												

Finance

Rank	Project name	Status	1Q11			2Q11			3Q11			4Q11		
			Jan	Feb	Mar	Apr	May	Jun	Jul	Aug	Sep	Oct	Nov	Dec
1	General ledger system implementation	Active												
2	Standardize financial reporting	Not started												

Human resources

Rank	Project name	Status	1Q11			2Q11			3Q11			4Q11		
			Jan	Feb	Mar	Apr	May	Jun	Jul	Aug	Sep	Oct	Nov	Dec
1	Online candidate recruiting system implementation	Active												
2	Online HR forms system implementation	Not started												
3	Online benefit tracking system implementation	Not started												

Figure 13.2 Portfolio distribution report.

Here, we are not going to suggest what metrics to present, because each company and business environment differs. The frequency of including this agenda item depends on many factors, such as the business environment, project schedules, budget cycles, etc., so you will need to make your own determination about when to include it. In general, biannually or annually should be a sufficient frequency.

Strategy 2—Gather Project Stakeholders' Input

Once executive support has been obtained or confirmed, the next step is to gather input from all the department leaders and key project stakeholders. This could include the following types of project stakeholders:

- Project sponsors
- Department heads
- Business leaders
- Team members
- Project managers
- External customers and clients

Your purpose here is to gather valuable information to be used to formulate your proposed project management frameworks and processes. To be successful you must ensure that you include their feedback in your frameworks and processes. This is a very important point; you need to demonstrate that you have listened to their input and have taken it into account in the way the company is going to manage its projects going forward. Just putting on a good front in collecting the information will not be enough to gain project stakeholders' support and it may even have a worse impact than not interviewing the project stakeholders at all.

Tools and Techniques for This Strategy

These are some tools and techniques to allow you to gather and maintain project stakeholder support, along with information on how to utilize it to create your project management methodologies or PMO:

1. *Project stakeholder interviews*—When you solicit information from these project stakeholders, your purpose is to try to obtain the following information:
   o What do they know about project management?
   o Do they see project management either assisting or obstructing them in achieving the company's business objectives?
   o What has worked well and what could be improved regarding project delivery?
   o What would be the first thing they would like to see change?

○ What project management processes do they believe are currently in place?
○ How would they rate the company's current ability to deliver projects?
○ What types of things (metrics or information) would they like to see measured?

This information will be used to formulate your proposed project management frameworks and processes.

2. *PMO planning group*—The main purpose of this meeting, in regards to this strategy, is to ensure that the gathering of input is not a one-time affair, rather an ongoing activity. As the name indicates, this tool is more relevant for the establishment of a PMO. This group should be made up of department leaders and key project stakeholders. Operationally, the PMO planning group is to continually review the project portfolio to ensure that the right projects are getting addressed in the right way and that the PMO processes have been and are continuing to be effective and efficient. The PMO planning group should meet periodically. The frequency depends on the risk level the company is willing to tolerate in regarding the ongoing review of the portfolio by its company leaders. In most cases, a monthly meeting is usually sufficient. During these meetings, the group should review the current project portfolio performance and alignment with the company's strategic objectives. The group should also discuss many other items; here is a typical meeting agenda that lists other important discussion items:

○ *Active project statuses*—You should use the same status format as outlined previously under the project portfolio executive steering committee to perform a quick status review of all open projects. If there are more than twenty projects, you should only review the most important projects. To determine a project's importance, you could base it on the size of the project's budget, alignment with key business objectives, etc. When discussing issues and risks, you should focus on any decision points the group needs to make and work to obtain an actionable resolution.
○ *Project portfolio strategic alignment*—The description of this agenda item is the same as described above. This is not an agenda item for every meeting, but on some periodic basis, you should review how the projects being undertaken align with the company's strategic objectives. This discussion should probably occur at least quarterly.
○ *Project portfolio distribution across many different categories (e.g., departments, products, services, processes, sponsors, etc.)*—This is an optional agenda item. As with the project portfolio strategic alignment agenda item, the description of this agenda item is the same as described under the project portfolio executive steering committee. Again, this topic

generally has the effect of stimulating conversation about how well the portfolio is balanced within each category.

o *Projects not being addressed*—As stated before, one of the main reasons to perform project portfolio management is to be able to draw the line as to which projects you will work on and which projects you will not work on. If you continue to discuss only the project in execution, you will miss out on valuable input regarding the importance of projects not yet initiated.

o *Effectiveness of project management methodologies*—Under this agenda item, you should continuously be reviewing the current project management methodologies to ensure they are effective and efficient in facilitating the expected delivery of the company's projects. It is a good idea to select one component of your methodology and perform an in-depth review of each process step with the group, the purpose being to fine tune the procedures to be as lean and effective as possible. A good amount of the feedback will be based on the recent experiences the group members have had using the methodology and the lessons they have learned. In some cases, this agenda item could also be combined with the lessons-learned review agenda item we will discuss soon.

o *Metrics review*—This agenda item is the same as detailed for the project portfolio executive steering committee.

o *Lessons learned review*—Regardless of whether a company is small or large, reviewing lessons learned is important. Your process should require that the project team performs a lessons-learned session at the end of all project efforts. You need to have flexibility within your methodologies and, in a small company, there will be projects that, because of their size, resourcing, and importance, would not receive enough value from a lessons-learned session to warrant the investment of time. In the spirit of efficiency, here is an easy and effective way to capture lessons learned; after the project objectives have been delivered, the project team and key project stakeholders should meet for no more than an hour. During the meeting, there should be two rounds of discussion. In the first round, give each participant a turn to speak, uninterrupted, and have them express only that thing that they felt went well with the project. As this is occurring the project manager should be leading the discussion and writing each participant's items on a whiteboard for all to see. In the second round, the participants again—one at a time—present what they believed the team could have done better, again with the project manager noting the information on a whiteboard for all to view. Once everyone has had a turn to speak, the meeting can be opened to a general discussion concerning all the items identified. The meeting should conclude with the project manager crafting a list of what the team believes went well and what could be improved. At the beginning of the meeting, the project manager should lay out the meeting structure, ground rules, and tell everyone that this will be a safe environment to express opinions. After the meeting, the project manager should document the team's finding in a standard template. See Table 13.2 for a lessons-learned standard template example. This template should include a section to capture action items based on the lessons identified. Capturing these action items is the critical component in relation to a small company. These action items could be used to facilitate continuous improvement. Remember, small companies are more focused on results than on administrative activities, so by crafting the lessons into actionable items that will improve their effectiveness at delivering projects, you are relating this administrative activity directly to delivering results. By doing this, we have greatly enhanced the value of this important project management activity in the eyes of the executives and project stakeholders.

Strategy 3—Establish Project Metrics to Measure Success

You want to establish project metrics to measure success from day one. This is the best way to prove that utilizing project management methodologies has been having a positive effect on the ability to deliver projects.

Tools and Techniques for This Strategy

Post-project assessment survey—The post-project assessment survey should be administered right after the project objectives have been delivered. The survey

Table 13.2 Sample lessons-learned template

#	Lessons learned/ stakeholder feedback	What can be done differently next time?	Action items	Assigned to	Target completion date	Comments
	List lessons learned captured during the lessons-learned sessions with the project stakeholders	List the answer(s) to the question above	List any action items required to address the lessons learned	List an owner of each action item	List a targeted completion date for each action item	List any comments regarding the lessons learned

participants should include the project team, project sponsors, and key project stakeholders. The project manager should not participate in the survey. Since he or she led the project effort, they do have a bias regarding the survey results. To assist you in formulating your questions for the survey, a sample survey is provided in Table 13.3. To turn the survey results into metrics, which would allow you to assess project delivery, you should establish a scoring model. This scoring model could be as simple as assigning a score level (e.g., 1 through 5; 1 being low-performing and 5 being high-performing) to each answer option. To illustrate this further, please see Table 13.3. There are two types of reporting to be addressed. The first is reporting the results to the survey participants. The second is reporting the results to senior management. Let us start with the reporting to survey participants. This could be achieved with a simple e-mail sent to the survey participants showing the score received on each question, a total score received for the project, and a brief summary of some of the written comments received. It is very important here not to give away who said what. Be sure to restate and summarize all results, so no one could attempt to predict who said what. The project manager should then utilize the survey results as talking points during the lessons-learned session, which should be scheduled right after survey results have been distributed. For reporting to senior management, you should summarize the results by questions and total score across all the projects. The purpose here is to show what is working well and where improvement is needed. The frequency of this discussion with the executives depends on many factors, such as the business environment, project schedules, budget cycles, etc., so you will need to make your own determination as to when to present this information to senior management. In general, biannually or annually should be a sufficient frequency. One last item: this information should be presented in person to senior management. This way you could frame the discussion and address any discussion points in real time. This approach, versus e-mailing the report, could save much back and forth with the senior management.

Strategy 4—Define and Present the Project Management Framework to All Project Stakeholders

Notice how the word *framework* was used in the title of this strategy. The word *process* was not used on purpose. In a small company, you will have an easier time initially establishing your project management methodologies or PMO if you describe what you are proposing to implement as more of a framework to work within than a process which must be adhered to in regards to managing project efforts going forward. At least initially, this will soften the impact of the changes you are trying to implement and present it as a more flexible methodology.

Table 13.3 Sample questions for the post-project assessment survey

1. Did the project's outcome meet the customer's expectations?	
Selections	Score
• Outcome met 90% to 100% of expectations	5
• Outcome met 80% to 89% of expectations	4
• Outcome met 70% to 79% of expectations	3
• Outcome met 60% to 69% of expectations	2
• Outcome met 59% or less of expectations	1
• Do not know	0
Comments:	

2. How clearly were requirements defined and communicated?	
Selections	Score
• All requirements were clearly defined and communicated	5
• Most requirements were clearly defined and communicated	4
• Some requirements were clearly defined and communicated	3
• Few requirements were clearly defined and communicated	2
• No requirements were clearly defined and communicated	1
• Do not know	0
Comments:	

3. Did the project manager identify, manage, and escalate project issues throughout the project lifecycle?	
Selections	Score
• Always	5
• Mostly	4
• Sometimes	3
• Rarely	2
• Never	1
• Do not know	0
Comments:	

At the same time, you want to ensure that you are communicating to your project stakeholders that this framework would establish a set of practices to follow to assist them in achieving project success, and that there is also some flexibility within these practices.

After you have established executive support and engaged all the appropriate stakeholders to understand what they would like from a project management methodology or PMO, you need to take all this input and draft your proposed project management framework or PMO charter. No project management methodologies will be presented here, but the following section describes a number of tools and techniques which could assist you in determining what your methodology or PMO should look like.

Tools and Techniques for This Strategy

The tools and techniques are here to assist you in taking what you have identified and learned through your executive and stakeholder analyses and bringing this new knowledge together to formulate, present, and sell your plan to establish project management methodologies or PMO in your small company:

- Flowchart
- Formal presentation
- Roles and responsibilities matrix

Strategy 5—Start With a Big Win

If you are leading the PMO, you may want the PMO to manage projects as well. The purpose of this is to do your best to ensure project success right from the start. To do this, try to take on a project that has been troubled and use your new framework and experience to get the project back on track. The most powerful way in a small company to get people to buy in to the value that project management brings is by achieving success out of past failures.

Tools and Techniques for This Strategy

- Project management practices and experience

Strategy 6—Focus on Results Not Process

Limit administration activities and focus on project delivery activities. You cannot hide behind process in a small company. If a project fails or does not go right, everyone knows. Results are there for all to see. The fact that the project's documents have all been completed as required and nicely stored in the share folder does not mean much to the senior management team if the project did not deliver as expected.

Those of you who are leading a PMO should be spending at least half of your time working on ensuring that the active projects are on track. The other half should be dedicated to portfolio management, process improvement, and staff management and development.

Tools and Techniques for This Strategy

- Weekly status reports
- One-on-one staff meetings
- Project plan walkthrough
- Project portfolio review meeting

Author Biography

Robert J. Tresente, Jr., PMP, MBA, currently serves as the director of the project management office at The Harry Fox Agency (HFA). HFA is the foremost mechanical licensing, collection, and distribution agency for music publishers in the United States. In this role, Robert manages a team of eight project managers and business systems analysts. Under his direction, the PMO group develops and maintains corporate strategy, processes, tools, and methodologies to support ongoing project management activities. The PMO group is also responsible for the development of business requirements and quality assurance testing activities required to ensure successful completion and delivery of solutions. Robert reports to the senior vice president and chief information officer.

In 2009, HFA was recognized as among the top American technology innovation leaders in the *InformationWeek 500*. HFA ranked number 182 and was the only music industry company to appear on the list.

Robert joined HFA in 2006 as a senior project manager in the project management office. Prior to joining HFA, Robert was a program manager at Horizon Blue Cross Blue Shield of New Jersey, where he managed the enhancement and maintenance of all systems supporting the sales and marketing division. This included online quotes and proposals, online group enrollment, online member maintenance, document management, and CRM.

14

Building a Ship at Sea: How to Set Up PMOs in the Dynamic Business Environments of Emerging Markets

Olga Nadskakula

Introduction

Research shows that almost 42 percent of project management offices (PMOs) do not meet the expectations of the organizations that they support (Hobbs, 2006). With the increased pressure to complete more and more projects, there is a real need to revisit the original purpose and essence of a PMO. In business, the successful implementation of a PMO has become the hallmark of efficient change management in that:

- The successful adoption of a PMO is a change to all processes that determine how the organization performs.
- An implementation of a PMO suggests that an organization is committed to the implementation of changes (projects) in a structured and more efficient way.
- In dynamic business environments, the objectives of a PMO are to actively respond to changes in an organization.

PMOs continuously face changes due to the dynamic nature of the business environment. To sustain a permanent alignment between corporate strategy and projects, changes to the PMO's scope should be perceived as the norm. Furthermore if an organization desires business growth, it should allow the PMO to evolve.

A successful PMO can be described in a relatively straightforward way: *it provides benefits to the organization*. However this might be difficult to define and measure. Difficulties in justifying PMO success can be linked to the intangible nature of the benefits it promises: improved coordination between projects, the enhanced competitive advantage of the company, and better market timing. In order to overcome these difficulties, it is helpful to ensure that a PMO is founded on a well-defined and solid business case. When changes in the business occur, a PMO business case and definition of success have to be altered.

The PMO lifecycle in an organization could be divided into two significant phases: implementation and maintenance.

- PMO implementation is based on a project approach. Consequently it should be managed as a project.
- PMO maintenance is based on a process approach. It is related to process maintenance, optimization, and development. However, if changes in PMO processes occur, they again can be managed with a project approach.

The early stages of bringing a PMO into operation are crucial to the further development of the PMO in the organization. Its successful implementation creates a foundation for future maintenance. A PMO implementation exhibits many of the unique traits of a project. Among these traits are that it has a start and end date, defined goals, described scope, stakeholder engagement, projection of investment, and the risk involved. These common traits show that a PMO can be implemented as any other project.

As mentioned previously, a significant percentage of PMOs fail to meet the expectations of the organizations they support. PMOs are frequently closed or restructured and their value is frequently questioned. This observation poses questions regarding the quality of a PMO business case and the entire design phase. No PMO, nor its implementation, is the same because of its unique organizational context and traits. Consequently there is no such thing as a universal PMO that when successfully implemented in one organization can be easily embedded into another.

It seems that there is a need for an improved understanding of the design phase of PMO deployment. A major challenge encountered in that phase is to develop the framework of functions and services in a manner that is sufficiently generic and easy to change when required. However, it should be detailed enough to provide effective guidance for those who actually implement the PMO and fund it. This chapter proposes a simple balanced framework of services useful for PMO implementation and concentrates on the preparation of PMO implementation in an organization. The chapter is organized as:

- The PMO identification process
- The details of the PMO definition
- The classification of PMO functions and services based on research
- A case study

The PMO Identification Phase

When developing a PMO with the aim of making a company more agile in a competitive environment, it is crucial to scrutinize the organizational capabilities to adopt such a significant change as a PMO deployment. Prior to detailed analytical work with stakeholder groups (described in the following section in this chapter), it is important that those engaged with PMO implementation are sufficiently aware of the policies, standards, corporate strategy, and organizational culture. The scope and depth of this identification phase depends on how much information is easily available and to what extent people are willing to share their knowledge. The PMO head should evaluate existing information and ensure that the concept of a PMO takes into account elements of the organizational environment. This is why the identification phase focuses primarily on researching the organization's project management awareness and maturity. These findings help determine what type of PMO is needed for a particular organization. Best practices and international standards are useful to follow, but knowledge of organization-specific traits is of paramount importance for successful PMO implementation.

In the PMO identification phase, it is also important to develop a thorough understanding of project definition, PMO sponsorship, people in the PMO, and organizational culture and processes.

Project Definition

While thinking about a project, professionals tend to focus on, "a temporary endeavor undertaken to create a unique product, service or result" (Project Management Institute, 2009).

However, it is often the case that organizations in day-to-day operations call projects any endeavor which has a defined start and end date. The PMO implementation teams need to be able to acknowledge which of the company's activities are projects and therefore of interest to the PMO.

There are several different approaches to determine what a project is. Typically, activities are divided based on its budget and planned duration, e.g., those endeavors that have a budget less than $100,000 may not be defined as projects and could be performed within a department and funded with a local budget. Most organizations tend to exert control over all endeavors that engage critical resource pools (e.g., developers), so that even small changes in IT systems can be treated as a project (with all documentation on business requirements and tests reports). In the process of defining projects, common sense is helpful. It may be the case that some activities previously called *projects* can be arranged into processes, particularly when similar changes are repetitive.

If there is an alignment on what activities fulfill the definition of a project, then information on the number of projects, their size, and their complexity should be collected. With this knowledge, it is easier to build up support for project managers who face particular and repetitive project challenges. Of course, the findings may be different. For example, if a company manages a small number of large projects, it might indicate that there is a long process of business analysis and project planning. In this instance, the support should be focused on those phases. It might show that a company faces issues with project execution and, consequently, the project duration is prolonged because of delays.

The number of projects and their size directly determines the size of the project portfolio that the PMO will support. The project complexity and size can indicate key project challenges that should be handled by the PMO support team.

The PMO Sponsor

According to the broadly accepted definition, a sponsor is, "a person or group that provides financial resources, in cash or in kind, for the project" (Project Management Institute, 2009).

Consequently the PMO sponsor is one of the most crucial PMO stakeholders. It is essential to get commitment from the sponsor on the PMO's scope and structure. Without it, there is a considerable risk of a lack of mutual understanding between the PMO head and the sponsor. This buy-in drives the relationship forward toward a common goal of PMO growth. Determining the needs of a PMO sponsor is the first step in the continuous process of expectations management. Sponsor expectations dictate where the PMO should focus first.

Identifying the political environment surrounding the PMO is equally important to determining PMO sponsor requirements. The PMO is a tool of the organizational politics, particularly politics of the sponsor. According to Walumbwa, organizational politics refer to "those activities taken from within organizations to acquire, develop and use power and other resources to obtain one's preferred outcomes in a situation in which there is uncertainty" (Walumbwa, 1999).

It is important to underline the relationship between organizational politics and the PMO. The PMO establishes rules and standards for project selection, prioritization, evaluation, and reporting. It is common to have pressure from various interest groups, which occurs outside the regular decision-making process. The PMO provides necessary information and recommendations to decision makers. Consequently, the PMO enters the area of politics. There is no possibility of eliminating organizational politics; that is why it should be considered while implementing the PMO. It seems that the greater the level of uncertainty associated with projects, the greater the potential pressure. The sponsor and his or her political involvement will influence the future scope of PMO activities.

The position of the PMO sponsor in an organization's structure can also be viewed from another angle. If the PMO sponsor is the CIO or IT director, the PMO consequently tends to focus on IT projects or IT parts of business projects. Therefore the organizational structure of the PMO determines the potential project portfolio. The departmental PMO has to consider the authority and power of this particular department in the organization. PMOs in IT departments seem to have various negotiating positions depending on what industry the organization operates. When IT is only a supporting function, the IT PMO might be perceived as a supplier of information on IT projects only and not as business partner or adviser.

The position of an IT PMO is much stronger in organizations operating in high-tech industries. In such circumstances, it could be viewed by stakeholders as a source of competitive advantage and an important generator of market value.

People in the PMO

The strength of the PMO lies in its people. In this context, PMO people refer to the PMO team (implementers and maintenance) and project managers, regardless of their reporting lines. The PMO team consists of individuals with relevant competencies who are in a position to support not only a single project but also the whole portfolio. The urgent need to recruit professionals to the PMO seems to be constantly underestimated. There is a clear link between competencies of PMO employees and services that the PMO can offer. It seems that it is a common approach that vacancies in a newly established PMO are filled internally. As a result, people with various professional backgrounds become members of a PMO team. In such situations, proper on-boarding and trainings play a crucial role. This is especially true when it comes to complex services such as project prioritization or workload balancing. To have a successful PMO and deliver business value, it is essential to assure the proper balance between staff on the support side and on the business side. The employees on the support side of the PMO are those operating within supporting services such as reporting or documentation. On the business side are those employees operating within services, such as consulting on project business cases, and advising project managers and the business.

While establishing the PMO, there is a tendency of the PMO sponsor and other stakeholders to inflate the scope of work and raise expectations. As a result, even though much is expected, the initial sizing of PMO staff might turn out to be insufficient to accommodate the workload. It is the role of the PMO manager to address such challenges in an adequate way. As in any project, if we lack resources, the quality of delivery or the ability to meet deadlines may be jeopardized. Especially during its early days, the PMO is vulnerable to failure from insufficient resources. If increasingly high expectations are not matched with an increase in staffing requirements, it is likely that PMO employees' morale, and consequently PMO delivery will be affected. This can generate a great deal of disappointment among the sponsor and other stakeholders, which might ultimately result in the termination of the PMO. So, it is essential to closely evaluate the number and competencies of PMO employees while creating the scope of the PMO activities.

Project managers may be located within a PMO. The PMO head's knowledge of the project managers' competencies and skills should be used to outline the type of support that they will require in everyday project management. The PMO is responsible for the project portfolio, so it directly depends on project managers' effectiveness. This simple bond between the PMO and project managers requires that support from and for project managers cannot be neglected. The PMO's goals cannot be achieved without the commitment and engagement of project managers. The more educated and experienced the project manager, the greater the involvement in the PMO that is expected. They can play the role of change ambassadors, so if they reject the PMO's plan of changes, other stakeholders and the organization may tend to act accordingly. The less educated and experienced the project manager, the greater the involvement that is required from the PMO. It should offer them various supporting activities (e.g., guidance in planning workshops, proper training, or coaching).

Organizational Culture and Existing Processes

When building a PMO in an organization, it is important to remember that the organization existed before the PMO and will likely continue to exist longer than the PMO. That is why a PMO should adjust to the organizational culture and the way business is conducted. The standards and documentation, which the PMO plans to introduce to the organization, should follow existing rules of management.

The organizational culture determines how much work the PMO needs to do to embed some project management techniques and methodologies. If functional managers use some project approaches in day-to-day business operations, the organization may require less effort from the PMO. If the PMO desires quick wins to prove its value, it should not plan activities against the organizational culture. Increasing project awareness and persuading people to do their business differently takes lots of time and requires a great deal of determination. It is hardly a quick win for a PMO. When investigating organizational culture, you should focus some of your time on communication methods and channels, and the decision-making processes. The communication standards represent tools and techniques that can be used to reach PMO stakeholders. The communication of PMO activities and sharing of successes should follow communication channels already established in the company. Otherwise there is a risk that the message from the PMO will not reach the target audience. The use of tools that are atypical of the organizational culture does not build rapport and may generate confusion. Effective communication ensures that people perceive PMO activities as a part of the regular business of the organization. However, knowledge of the organizational culture not only determines the scope of activities—what to do now and what can be done next—but also suggests how the PMO should promote itself in the company.

Moreover, it is valuable to collect the information regarding the decision-making processes in projects. Projects and project portfolio management require the art of decision making and there should be a dedicated committee to make these important project and portfolio choices. Neither a project manager nor a PMO is responsible for making strategic project decisions. With the absence of a proper decision-making committee, the PMO's goals are to create and implement structured project and portfolio processes in the organization. Without an appropriate organizational committee, the project performance reporting does not bring much value. The information should reach someone who is accountable for the decision making.

The next organizational factor to be evaluated is reporting standards. Those processes include financial reporting, risk and quality monitoring, strategic planning, and/or HR development. It is often the case that those processes are already structured and commonly used. The existing process of financial reporting is likely to cover projects. Perhaps the project finance reporting needs to be revised, but if it exists and works, it is not the responsibility of the PMO to change it. If risk and quality assurance monitoring already exist in the organization, it might only require adaptation for PMO purposes.

It is crucial to examine the pre-implementation awareness level regarding a PMO in the organization. Broadly speaking, there are two extreme attitudes. The first one is that hardly anyone appreciates the new PMO and there is a tendency to deny that it will exist. The second one is that everybody anticipates it. These two attitudes largely depend on organizational culture. If the first case proves to be valid, the PMO should focus on promoting itself within the organization and increasing the level of knowledge of the benefits it will bring to the organization. If a majority of stakeholders are aware of the PMO and look forward to it, the challenge is to prioritize expectations and deliver proposed benefits on time.

The next factor regarding organizational process is project-level maturity, which has a direct influence on the scope of PMO activities. To assess project maturity, it is not always necessary to purchase an external, specialized audit on this subject. Usually, it is clearly visible whether the organization is at the lowest level of maturity or at a fairly mature level. It is typically either brand new or well-established. PMO services cover three main areas: project management, program management, and portfolio management. To influence the portfolio management area, it is essential to standardize and achieve fluency in services in the project and program management areas as a prerequisite. Only after this accomplishment is it advisable to move to the area of portfolio management. It is important to understand when the PMO should be able to roll out more complex services. The schematic diagram summarizing the relationships between areas of service and organizational project maturity is shown in Figure 14.1.

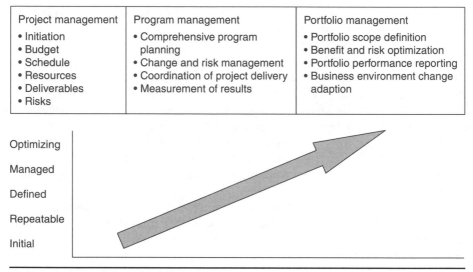

Project management	Program management	Portfolio management

• Initiation
• Budget
• Schedule
• Resources
• Deliverables
• Risks
	• Comprehensive program
	  planning
	• Change and risk management
	• Coordination of project delivery
	• Measurement of results
		• Portfolio scope definition
		• Benefit and risk optimization
		• Portfolio performance reporting
		• Business environment change
		  adaption

Optimizing

Managed

Defined

Repeatable

Initial

Figure 14.1   PMO services with project management maturity.

The PMO Definition

This part of the chapter requires an understanding of the PMO environment (three Ws):

- Why is the PMO being implemented?
- What needs are addressed?
- Who it is realized for?

To fully address these questions, the PMO definition phase begins with stakeholder analysis, which provides a summary of the most important groups with an interest in the PMO. It is followed by an analysis of the organizational challenges to indentify key areas for improvement within the company. The third analysis focuses on the development of solutions to address these areas in line with stakeholders' expectations and concludes with a statement of the PMO objectives.

Stakeholder Analysis

PMO stakeholders include not only the PMO sponsor mentioned in the previous section, but any individuals or groups of people that may have a significant interest in the success or failure of the PMO. A basic assumption behind stakeholder analysis is to realize that different groups or individuals have different concerns, capacities, and interests which may impact PMO deployment. The aim of this analysis is to describe a real (although usually informal) hierarchy of power in the organization. It is the first action required to plan and manage stakeholder expectations effectively.

The findings are a base to analyze the different set of PMO services. They are also used to forecast the magnitude and direction of potential stakeholder reactions to proposed functions. It is essential to determine what actions will be undertaken to manage individuals or groups of stakeholders. When negative stakeholder reactions are foreseen, a plan to mitigate the impact of those reactions should be created. The first step in this analysis is to identify various groups of stakeholders which:

- Are influenced by the PMO
- May influence the PMO
- Can support the PMO even when they do not have a direct interest in the PMO

Not all stakeholders have the same power in the organization. Consequently the next step is to investigate roles, interests, relative power, and capacity of participation. At this stage, it is advisable to determine the stakeholder's hierarchy (e.g., primary, secondary, etc.). Primary stakeholders are those whose interests determine the PMO goal such as sponsors, department directors, board members, and senior managers. Secondary stakeholders are usually engaged in the PMO in roles such as project managers, the PMO team, and business benefit owners. Other stakeholders may not play a major role, but their opinions cannot be neglected. When the PMO services are introduced, a particular stakeholder may become more active as his or her area is influenced.

After both identifying and grouping stakeholders, there is a need to determine potential conflicts in the relationship between stakeholders. The scope and depth of this analysis depends on the resources and information available. The last step in this analysis is to interpret findings and incorporate relevant information into the PMO design document.

Case Study—Stakeholder Analysis

I had the opportunity to develop a PMO for the IT department of a company operating in the energy industry. Simultaneous to implementation of the PMO, the IT department was undergoing a major reorganization. This case study is presented as a picture of the relationship dynamics between various groups of stakeholders. The initial organizational structure is shown in Figure 14.2. The new organizational structure is presented in Figure 14.3. Differences in those organizational structures are shown in Figure 14.4.

We collected information on stakeholder interests and created a matrix that shows who was affected by the creation of the PMO and how. This is illustrated in Table 14.1. The stakeholder analysis matrix shows how people may be affected

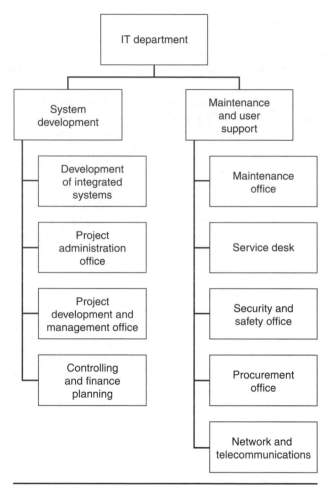

Figure 14.2   Initial organization structure.

by the implementation of a PMO. This type of information can be analyzed in various ways when special needs or circumstances occur.

Problem Analysis

The next analysis described is known as *problem analysis*. Stakeholder analysis and problem analysis are tightly connected, and at least in practice, they could be conducted in tandem rather than in turn. Problem analysis uncovers the negative aspects of an existing situation and establishes the cause and effect relationships between the identified problems. Problem analysis provides a strong foundation

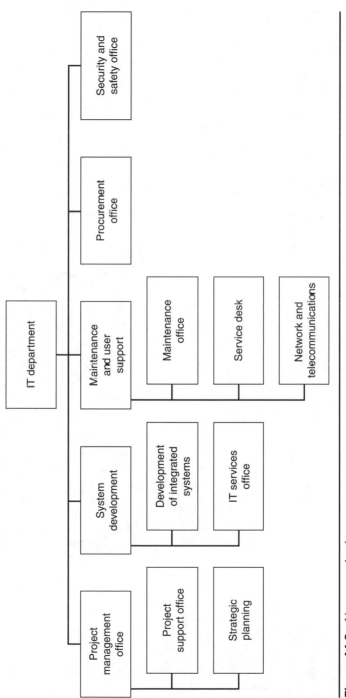

Figure 14.3 New organization structure.

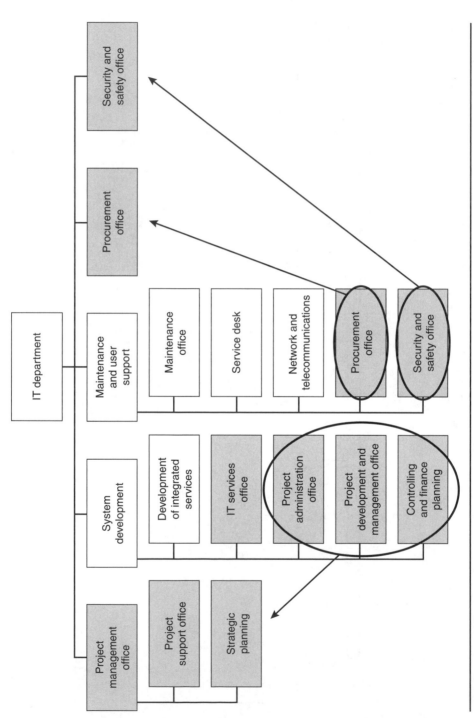

Figure 14.4 Differences between organizational structures.

Table 14.1 Stakeholder analysis

Stakeholder and basic characteristics	Interests and how affected by PMO	Strengths (S) and weaknesses (W)	Possible actions to address stakeholder interests
Head of project development and management office—new in the organization, his desire is to set up one office to coordinate a project portfolio with him in charge			New PMO head
PMO sponsor, CIO—he is new in the organization and changes in organization's structure are one of the first priorities	Direct reporting hierarchy and better access to the project portfolio information	**S:** The commitment to have one PMO headed by one person and receive condensed information on projects. Motivation to show change as a success. **W:** He is a new person in the organization, not personally engaged in the concept and design of the PMO.	Get to know stakeholder expectations of the PMO and plan what actions need to be undertaken to meet them.
Director of the system development department—he has been with the organization for a long time and appreciates the idea of a single place for project portfolio coordination	His department is going to concentrate on system development; other administrative functions are moved to the PMO.	**S:** The commitment to the idea to have one PMO responsible for all projects in the organization. New unit is going to be established within his department. **W:** Decreasing his authority by removing part of the department to the PMO.	Set clear communication channels; his support will be needed because the project managers from the PMO assign people among his employees. Set the process to exchange information on projects and on resource allocation to projects.
IT project managers—only several PMs are professionals (contractors), the rest are dedicated from other IT units depending on the project subject and scope	They are in various units within the IT department. In the new structure they will be placed in the project management office and directly report to head of the PMO.	**S:** The set and formal hierarchy of reporting also to the PMO. **W:** Not all project managers would like to relocate to the PMO. Not all functional managers (heads of units) would be interested in losing project managers.	Difficult negotiations with unit directors to dedicate project managers to the PMO.

(Continues)

Table 14.1 (Continued)

Stakeholder and basic characteristics	Interests and how affected by PMO	Strengths (S) and weaknesses (W)	Possible actions to address stakeholder interests
Head of project administration office—her office aims to support project managers but dedicated to integrated systems and administrative and methodology support	Her entire office will be moved to the PMO and become one with the PMO unit.	**S:** She managed the office with set processes for project manager support and the needed staff is already employed and trained. **W:** She has an ambition to be a chief of the PMO. She does not desire change. Everything can stay as it is. She would be reporting to the new PMO head, which was what she wanted to become.	The most difficult situation to manage. The personal ambition was not fulfilled and a new person in the organization will be heading the PMO. She will challenge all new ideas that are not hers. Careful relationship building is needed. Think about including her to establish new processes in the PMO. The new PMO may have some positions with which she might be interested.
Head of controlling and finance planning office—long time with the organization; desires all project managers to deliver better investment documentation	His entire office is going to be moved to the PMO.	**S:** Very deep knowledge and great support for the PMO head. **W:** He is willing to accept changes, but his interest must be met first.	List all his needs and interests and prioritize with him. Try to reach some compromises and explain why some other actions are also important to undertake. Involve in selecting services and setting schedules.
Heads of other IT offices—various experiences within the PMO	The establishment of the PMO does not affect them directly.	**S:** Changes in the organizational structure will affect them, but they will not deny the need to establish a separate department as the PMO. **W:** Their support and buy-in is crucial to the further development of the PMO. If they are not engaged in this phase of the PMO, they would not be interested in participating in further phases of PMO development.	Difficult negotiations with some of them to assign project managers to the PMO. Depending on which service is planned, close cooperation with setting appropriate processes may be needed. Heads of procurement department and security office now become directors; there is the chance to support them in creating their processes when dealing with projects.

for the set of PMO objectives that are directly connected with the stakeholder's expectations and potential challenges.

Problem analysis can be performed using the *problem tree approach* and begins with brainstorming issues that stakeholders consider a priority to the PMO. The effect of the group synergy concludes in the identification of one major problem (the starter problem) the PMO should face. It is important to determine whether various stakeholders perceive the problem in the same way and if any problem should be reformulated or rephrased. Problems related to the major one should be determined. While drawing a diagram, the following two rules should be followed:

- Problems that are a direct cause of the starter problem should be put below the major problem
- Problems that are direct effects of the starter problem are put above the major problem

When finished, you should review the diagram and verify its completeness. Any further comments and information might be appropriate to include. This problem analysis is visually sorted into a cause and effect relationship diagram as shown in Figure 14.5.

Once completed, the problem tree represents a picture of the existing situation. Consequently, it explicitly shows the purpose of the PMO deployment. Problem analysis is an important stage in the PMO definition process because it provides guidance to the further search for the optimal PMO services.

Analysis of Objectives

The negative situation shown in the problem tree is transformed into solutions, and expressed as a *positive future*. Once again, the analysis of objectives should be undertaken through appropriate workshops with the key stakeholder groups. The knowledge previously gained from the stakeholder analysis and organizational capacities should also be taken into account. This provides support and clarity when setting priorities of defined objectives and assessing how realistic achievements might be. The main steps in this process are:

- Reformulate the negative situations of problem analysis into desirable and realistically achievable situations
- Verify the means and ends relationships (cause and effects relationships are transformed into means and ends linkages)
- If necessary, revise statements, add relevant objectives, or delete unsuitable objectives

Once completed, the objective tree in Figure 14.6 provides a summary of the desired future outcome. The main issue identified in the problem analysis is

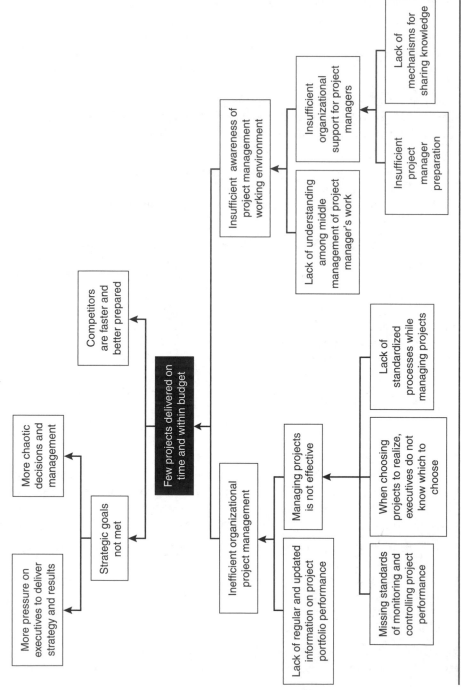

Figure 14.5   Problem tree.

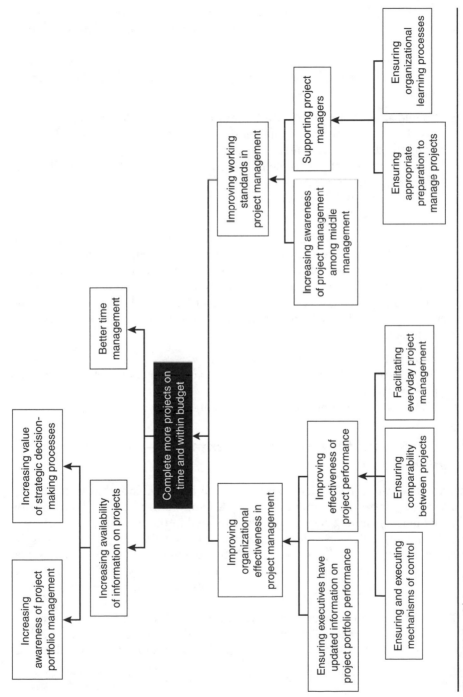

Figure 14.6 Objectives tree.

converted into a key objective for the PMO. The main strength with this activity is that it keeps the analysis of PMO objectives in line with adequately identified problems (problem analysis).

The issues and options identified in the objective tree need to be scrutinized to determine PMO scope before the design work is undertaken. The questions that should be asked at this stage might include:

- Should all identified problems be tackled or only a select few?
- What is the combination of identified objectives that is most likely to bring the desired outcome?
- What are the costs of implementing identified objectives and what can realistically be afforded?
- What strategy will impact organizational needs most positively?
- How can potential negative environmental (corporate) impacts be mitigated?

This analytical step is more challenging than the previous steps because it needs the synthesis of all collected information and makes a complex judgment on the best strategy to be implemented. In practice, a number of compromises have to be made to balance various stakeholders' interests, political demands, and practical constraints (e.g., human and financial resources). It could be helpful to build the set of criteria against which options of chosen strategies would be assessed. Those criteria might include:

- Expected contribution to corporate strategy
- Benefit to target groups such as executives, business benefit owners, and project managers
- Capital and operating costs of implementation

The Framework for PMO Implementation—The PMO Planning Phase

The results of the stakeholder analysis and the problem and objectives analysis are used as input for the planning stage of PMO implementation. All information collected in the planning stage should be finalized in the form of the PMO planning document, which provides a summary of the PMO's design. Finalizing the planning stage requires descriptions of PMO functions and services. The set of functions and services should be defined in collaboration with PMO stakeholders and focus on providing genuine value for both project managers and decision makers.

Since there can be a wide array of possible PMO services, outcomes of the stakeholder problem and objectives analysis provide key input on the best choice of services. The set of services the PMO proposes should satisfy organizational needs and meet the stakeholders' requirements. The important functions are determined by the organizational context as discussed in the Stakeholder Analysis section of this chapter.

Dr. Brian Hobbs, chair of project management research in the Department of Management and Technology of the School of Management Sciences, University of Quebec, Montreal, wrote a research paper entitled, "The Multi-Project PMO: A Global Analysis of the Current State of Practice," published by PMI® in 2006. It includes a list of PMO functions, which are divided into these five groups:

- Monitoring and controlling project performance
- Development of project management competencies and methodologies
- Multi-project management
- Strategic management
- Organizational learning

These groups of functions include services that might be performed by the PMO. The stakeholders' needs should be met by each proposed service. The idea of PMO stakeholder management is to balance the expectations of the three primary groups of PMO stakeholders:

- Executives (including the PMO sponsor)
- Project managers
- Business benefits managers

Each service should meet the needs of one or two groups of stakeholders. After choosing PMO functions and services, it is necessary to verify that these services address, to the same extent, the needs of the identified groups of stakeholders. Table 14.2 shows PMO functions, services, and primary stakeholders for every service.

For example, if you choose these services:

- Report project status to upper management
- Monitor and control project performance
- Implement and operate a project information system
- Identify, select, and prioritize new projects

then look at your stakeholders' distribution diagram as shown in Figure 14.7. The important expectations of project managers are not met as the figure shows a high degree of focus on executives as stakeholders but a very low degree of focus on project managers as stakeholders. Consequently the services should be modified. It is worth remembering that a PMO can serve three to five services. To equalize the stakeholders' needs, you should balance the exact number of services—no more than five. When those services are already embedded in the organization, a PMO can add further services to its range of functions.

Table 14.2 PMO services by function

Services	Objectives	Crucial stakeholder
Monitoring and controlling project performance		
Report project status to upper management	Ensuring the accuracy of information on project and project portfolio performance. Ensuring information regularity and regular updates.	Executives, business benefit managers
Monitor and control project performance	Ensuring control mechanisms. Improving the effectiveness of project performance.	Executives
Implement and operate a project information system	Facilitating everyday project management. Improving the effectiveness of resources usage. Ensuring a common system to manage initiatives and projects.	Executives, business benefit managers
Develop and maintain a project scoreboard	Ensuring comparability between projects. Ensuring an objective process to set priorities. Facilitating the decision-making process.	Executives, business benefit managers
Development of project management competencies and methodologies		
Develop and implement a standard methodology	Facilitating everyday project management. Ensuring comparability between projects.	Executives, project managers
Promote project management within the organization	Increasing awareness of project management among all employees.	Project managers
Develop competency of personnel, including organizing through training	Ensuring appropriate preparation for project management. Improving the effectiveness of project performance. Increasing awareness of project management among all employees.	Project managers
Provide mentoring for project managers	Ensuring appropriate preparation for project management. Improving the effectiveness of project performance. Facilitating everyday project management.	Project managers

Provide a set of tools without an effort to standardize	Ensuring appropriate preparation for project management. Improving the effectiveness of project performance. Facilitating everyday project management.	Project managers
Multi-project management		
Coordinate between projects	Ensuring appropriate flow of information between projects.	Project managers
Identify, select, and prioritize new projects	Supporting executives to build project portfolio.	Executives
Manage one or more portfolios	Supporting business benefit managers to manage project portfolio.	Business benefit managers
Manage one or more programs	Supporting business benefit managers to manage program.	Business benefit managers
Allocate resources between projects	Ensuring forecasts on planned usage of resources. Ensuring information on actual usage of resources.	Executives, project managers
Strategic management		
Provide advice to upper management	Supporting executives in strategic planning. Providing appropriate information for strategic planning. Analyzing the adjustment of the project portfolio to corporate strategy.	Executives
Participate in strategic planning	Supporting executives in strategic planning. Providing appropriate information for strategic planning. Analyzing the adjustment of the project portfolio to corporate strategy.	Executives
Manage benefits	Ensuring the benefits after project implementation. Measuring project benefits.	Business benefit managers
Conduct networking and environmental scanning	Supporting executives in strategic planning. Providing appropriate information for strategic planning. Analyzing the adjustment of the project portfolio to corporate strategy.	Executives

(Continues)

Table 14.2 (Continued)

Services	Objectives	Crucial stakeholder
Organizational learning		
Monitor and control the performance of the PMO	Self-assessment for further development and improvement of service quality and value.	
Manage archives of project documentation	Ensuring the database of project performance history. Ensuring support facilitating works with project documentation.	Project managers
Conduct post-project review	Ensuring information from realized projects and the assessment of closed projects.	Project managers
Conduct project audits	Ensuring information from realized projects and the assessment of closed projects.	Executives
Implement and manage database for lessons learned	Ensuring the organizational learning processes. Improving the effectiveness of project performance.	Project managers
Implement and manage risk database	Ensuring the organizational learning processes. Improving the effectiveness of project performance.	Project managers
Others		
Execute specialized tasks for project managers (e.g., preparing schedules)	Ensuring the administrative support for project managers (e.g., preparing schedules, budget, procure experts, etc.).	Project managers
Manage customer interfaces	Ensuring customer management.	Business benefit managers
Recruit, select, evaluate, and determine salaries for project managers	Ensuring organization has the best project managers.	Business benefit managers

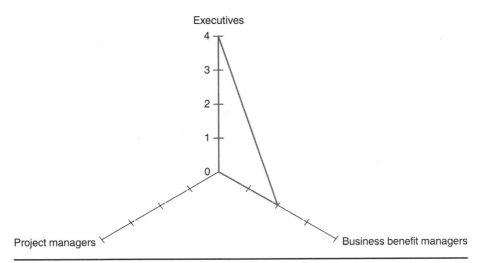

Figure 14.7 Distribution of stakeholders.

An interesting service with no particular stakeholder identified is monitoring the performance of the PMO. Every PMO has to maintain performance measurement indicators and each service should be measured. Only by self-assessment can PMO performance become apparent and further development undertaken.

PMO implementation should be managed in two stages: chosen primary services and chosen secondary services (which often are the target services). Services presented in Table 14.2 can be also divided into those that can be implemented in a straightforward manner when the PMO is set up and others that are followers of primary services.

- *Primary initiatives (short term)*: Services that precede the implementation of long-term initiatives. The purpose of introducing short-term services is to build awareness of the PMO's existence in the organization and to familiarize employees with the approach used to manage the particular type of endeavors in the project. Those initiatives create foundations of a strong PMO that may develop further when the organization requires it. The initiatives cover project manager support, project management standardization, and reporting. Detailed information on what types of services might be implemented in the first stage is presented in Table 14.3.

Do not forget about stakeholder expectations. Check how the chosen services meet stakeholders' needs.

- *Secondary initiatives (long term)*: Follow-up from the implementation of short-term initiatives because they are more complex and usually need more time to become embedded in the organization. Secondary initia-

Table 14.3 Primary PMO services

Functions	Services	Stakeholders
Monitoring and controlling project performance	Report project status to upper management. Monitor and control project performance.	Executives
Development of project management competencies and methodologies	Develop and implement a standard methodology. Promote project management within the organization. Provide a set of tools without an effort to standardize.	Executives, project managers
Organizational learning	Monitor and control the performance of the PMO. Manage archives of project documentation. Conduct post-project review. Implement and manage database for lessons learned. Implement and manage risk database.	Project managers
Other functions	Execute specialized tasks for project managers (e.g., preparing schedules).	Project managers

tives introduce a real change in the way business is conducted. They cover such services as project portfolio management, benefits management, and development of the center of excellence. Moreover, they integrate projects with the business planning lifecycle. Services which might be implemented in further stages of PMO deployment are presented in Table 14.4.

It is worth checking the stakeholder needs distribution. In the first stage of PMO services deployment, it is possible that one group of stakeholders is not included, but a summary of stakeholder needs related to short and long initiatives should be equalized.

The choice of the initiatives that deliver particular services to the organization should be summarized in the PMO design document. The design document includes not only information on the functions and services, but also describes the key performance indicators and the means of measuring them. The PMO benefits, services, and functions should be measured on a regular basis because the quality of the PMO assessment directly affects PMO success. So, the PMO design document requires updates when the PMO business case changes.

Case Study

This case study is intended to outline the role of the PMO head and other critical factors of PMO success. It will describe the PMO environment and indicate

Table 14.4 Secondary PMO services

Functions	Services	Stakeholders
Monitoring and controlling project performance	Implement and operate a project information system. Develop and maintain a project scoreboard.	Executives
Development of project management competencies and methodologies	Develop competency of personnel, including organizing through training. Provide mentoring for project managers.	Project managers
Multi-project management	Coordinate between projects.	Project managers
	Identify, select, and prioritize new projects.	Executives
	Manage one or more portfolios or one or more programs.	Business benefit managers
	Allocate resources between projects.	Executives, project managers
Strategic management	Provide advice to upper management. Participate in strategic planning. Conduct networking and environmental scanning.	Executives
	Manage benefits.	Business benefit managers
Organizational learning	Conduct project audits.	Executives
Other functions	Manage customer interfaces.	Business benefit managers
	Recruit, select, evaluate, and determine salaries for project managers.	Business benefit managers

the first symptoms of PMO failure. This case study refers to a branch of an international banking company with an established position in Central and Eastern Europe. The purpose of implementing the PMO was to build up a strong, centrally located PMO to achieve better market timing with new products. The organization has been restructured and the PMO's location in the organization has been changed. The initial PMO location was in operations and the IT department. After reorganization, the PMO was located in the new area of strategic functions within the board support department.

In this organization, projects are defined as, "every endeavor which engages critical resource pools," such as operations and IT. Every activity that changes processes or includes IT changes is considered a project. The organization manages eight large and 25 small projects a year. Large projects are lead by professional project managers who solely work on these types of projects, while the majority of small ones are directed by project managers from the respective business units who also have operational roles.

Projects, even small projects, have a wide scope of activities that include parts of several different lifecycles: product, software engineering, and processes. Not all initiatives are planned according to implemented standards of project management. Organizational capacity to perform these projects is only generally assessed due to the lack of specific information available. Project priority is measured and set by a project sponsor, depending on his or her political power. There are no scoring models introduced.

PMO Sponsor

In this business environment, it is unclear who the PMO sponsor is. The PMO is located in the board support department and the direct hierarchy is: the head of the PMO reports to the director of the board support department, who reports directly to the company CEO.

The PMO head would like the CEO to act as the PMO sponsor, but this person is hardly engaged in the PMO at all. The director of the board support department is practically a PMO sponsor. The situation of PMO sponsor engagement was dramatically changed when the director of the board support department also became acting operations and IT board member. Since that moment, the PMO lacks a committed sponsor. The board gave the PMO mandate to work, but no scope of the PMO was presented, no problems were identified, and objectives were not set.

People in the PMO

The staff employed within the PMO consists of the PMO head and one expert in project portfolio management who has been recruited externally. There are six professional project managers reporting directly to the PMO head. They usually manage one large project, or at most, two smaller projects. Other project managers are recruited from the business units and divide their time between operational activities and project management. Project management trainings are lead only by the internal resources.

Organizational Culture and Existing Processes

Project management standards were introduced in the organization about two years ago. The current PMO head is the third one since the implementation of the PMO began. Business operations management is tired of permanent trials to implement changes in project approach. The expectations from business operations and other stakeholders are high.

Project management standards and templates were prepared and accepted by the board. They are not broadly used in the organization. A project portfolio management (PPM) tool is implemented and only one crucial resource pool is planned and controlled through the tool.

The execution of the project budget is monitored and reported on by the finance department. There are no standardized processes for risk management, quality assurance, and bringing products into operations. There are processes for reporting key projects to headquarters. The company board is also the project portfolio committee, which decides on project portfolio performance.

The following internal challenges were identified:

- Limited commitment from the PMO sponsor and no support to achieve PMO objectives
- Although the PMO head is newly appointed, previous disappointments with PMO performance tend to overshadow his or her performance
- All changes in processes and systems were considered projects; there was a lack of common understanding of differences between projects and other initiatives
- No established standards to manage initiatives other than projects
- The project management standards were not entirely internalized by the organization
- During the first stage of implementation, there were seven services planned that were recommended for implementation in the second stage of the PMO deployment

The choice of services has been made by the PMO head based on only general and brief consultations with stakeholders. The services that are planned for the first stage of the PMO deployment are:

- Report project status to upper management
- Monitor and control project performance
- Implement and operate a project information system
- Develop and maintain a project scoreboard
- Promote project management within the organization
- Provide mentoring for project managers
- Develop competency of personnel, including organizing through training
- Identify, select, and prioritize new projects
- Allocate resources between projects
- Participate in strategic planning
- Conduct post-project reviews
- Execute specialized tasks for project managers; e.g., prepare schedules

Chosen services regarding PMO team capacity (two people) and the organizational capacity to bring change (three to five services implemented in tandem) was a sign that there is significant risk of PMO underperformance. Not surprisingly, when implementing so many services with insufficient effort and capacity, the results over one year were:

- Stakeholders were not engaged in the PMO; in their perception, the PMO delivered limited value to the organization
- The board was not engaged in project portfolio discussions because it was not engaged in the selection of the projects to the portfolio; the board lacked commitment
- None of the services were fully implemented; there are many services that theoretically the PMO offers, yet cannot deliver in reality because they do not have time to follow new processes
- New initiatives or projects were started even when internal capacity of the PMO (number of project managers and support team) and organizational capacity was too low (key resources pools already engaged in ongoing projects)
- Project managers rejected some of the planned PMO services, so motivation of the whole team decreased

According to the plans of the PMO head, the second stage of PMO implementation should cover:

- Coordination between projects
- Management of one or more portfolios
- Benefits management
- Project audits
- Implementation and management of a database for lessons learned
- Implementation and management of a risk database
- Recruitment, selection, evaluation, and determination of salaries for project managers

In addition to demanding first-stage services, there are planned services that broaden the scope of the PMO. There is a plan to recruit one more person to fulfill the PMO head's expectations.

To summarize this case study, note the critical factors for the PMO's success which were not met:

- There was no strong PMO sponsor. Introduction of the PMO services is an organizational change that poses a considerable challenge for employees engaged in projects. This change considers not only the PMO itself, but also its stakeholders who have their own interests and perceptions. These interests and needs should have been closely analyzed. The PMO needs organizational support, which the PMO sponsor should ensure.
- The PMO head did not have the authority and respect from upper management. Presenting plans that are impossible to achieve is a questionable way to gain respect. Even under pressure, the PMO head should assertively manage stakeholders' expectations on the number of services it can provide.
- The PMO head did not properly allocate the appropriate resources to support planned services. This covers not only the number of employees in the PMO team, but also their expertise.

- A clearly defined scope of work, responsibilities, and benefits are essential in gaining commitment from the team and other stakeholders and were not completed.
- The correct number of PMO services was not undertaken to successfully address the problems pointed out by stakeholders.
- The PMO did not have clearly defined, SMART (specific, measurable, achievable, realistic, and time-bound) objectives to achieve, and indicators to measure its delivery.
- Constant communication between the PMO and the organization was not performed (e.g., communicating decisions from project boards and project committees, sharing information on project successes, etc.).

Conclusion

The PMO lifecycle consists of two main phases: implementation and maintenance. In this chapter, we have focused primarily on PMO implementation, but successful PMO maintenance is also crucial. The decision to implement a PMO generates the need to develop a whole set of processes, which after some time become the operational activities in the PMO. After a successful PMO implementation, those processes cannot be neglected. Every function and service of the PMO described in this chapter needs to be supported with a set of respective processes, enabling the automation and optimization of its activities. All processes and services should be described in detail in the PMO documentation before they are brought into maintenance.

The PMO provides value to internal clients and a thorough analysis of their needs and expectations is crucial for success. An efficient and well-structured PMO can play a significant role in the decision-making process. Consequently, it can directly influence the success or failure of the business enterprise. The quality of delivered information largely depends on the choice of PMO services and the structure of its processes. In order to ensure high-quality services and processes, a great deal of attention should be dedicated to the defining and planning phases. Those phases play a pivotal role in determining the ultimate outcome of PMO implementation and maintenance. Among other crucial conditions, careful scrutiny of organizational needs and business requirements is paramount in the design of a successful PMO.

Author Biography

Olga Nadskakula is a specialist in the area of project management office, particularly in setting up PMOs, project evaluation, project management standards, project portfolio processes, and supporting tools. She is currently working for the Enterprise PMO at AXA Poland.

Olga has worked as a consultant on project management office issues in organizations ranging from the largest companies in Poland and the chancellery of the prime minister to nonprofit organizations and public administration. She is the designer of several training modules on project management and PMOs and of workshop materials for students from the Project Management Postgraduate Studies Program at the Warsaw School of Economics.

Working as a senior consultant, Olga was involved in several projects on the development and improvement of various PMOs in the energy, telecommunication, aircraft, and finance industries. Key areas of these developments included designing the framework of project managers' professional competency, project portfolio workload modeling, setting-up project portfolio indicators, PPM tool implementations, and the building of tailormade project management methodologies.

References

1. Hobbs, B. 2006. *The Multi-Project PMO: A global analysis of the current state of practice.* White paper prepared for the Project Management Institute.
2. Project Management Institute 2008. *A Guide to the Project Management Body of Knowledge (PMBOK® Guide),* Fourth edition, Newtown Square, PA, PMI®.
3. Walumbwa, F. O. 1999. Power and Politics in Organizations: Implications for OD Professional Practice. *Human Resource Development International 2,* 3:205–216.

15

Affording a PMO: An Approach to Establishing a PMO with Limited Resources

Colleen McGraw, PMP

Introduction

Marianne could not contain her excitement. "I've just been offered my dream job!" Excited for her, I pressed for details. "I've been hired to set up a new project management office (PMO) for the enterprise engineering office. I start in two weeks. I cannot wait!" Happy for her and interested when any organization sees the value and benefit of a PMO, I looked forward to following up with her to see how things were going. Three months later, she was bored in a job she hated. "They cancelled the PMO project a month after I got there and moved the budget to another team. They won't even let me try."

Daniel, a manager for a government agency, was resigned. "We implemented the enterprise project management software suite, provided training, and offered assistance and support. However no one used it. Eventually the project was closed and I was moved to a different function." While the cost of the software was money already spent, the lack of adoption led senior executives to withdraw any lingering support for the project, and defund the efforts. The system remained; the money was wasted, because no one used it.

Marianne and Daniel, along with many other well-meaning and talented project managers, have experienced the same fate—the PMO promise unfulfilled. In some cases, sponsors and other well-meaning executives attend seminars and business events or read articles expounding the value of the PMO, then they grasp onto the idea of creating a PMO to expand their programs or to counter recent project failures. Often they reconsider, though, as the cost estimates mount and the pushback from the functional teams and project managers rises. So what approaches can the project manager of the emerging PMO take to nurture the survival of the PMO? How does one find the resources to support its growth, while consistently living up to the value proposition that shows benefits in real time, not just in some distant future? How does one obtain the resources necessary to evolve the PMO while showing returns in this quarter and not just on some future balance sheet?

Successfully launching a PMO in any organization—large or small—and keeping the momentum going can require significant effort. There are many obstacles to a successful launch, with the biggest hurdle often being cost, either real or perceived. One reason is that cost is often the easiest thing for senior executives to focus on. It is concrete, quantifiable, and real. How do we overcome the dreaded phrase, "We just cannot afford it this year," to demonstrate a PMO's true value? We do so by understanding the environment and events that initiated the expressed need for a PMO, identifying a value plan to demonstrate consistent returns to the organization and strategically leveraging resources to drive the value proposition.

Establish the PMO Approach

You have been assigned the task of establishing a PMO for your organization. Congratulations, you have earned a tremendous opportunity. Where do you begin? If you are like many project managers, the first task you have been asked to perform is to establish an estimated budget. So you make some calls, post some questions to your network, look up a few books and articles, get your spreadsheet model ready, and start planning the project.

You lay it all out—the tools you will need, the staffing required, the processes and procedures that will need to be developed, the standards that will be followed, the pilot projects to start with, the rollout plan. Your plan clearly shows the appropriate scale and objectives required to establish a true enterprise PMO. The plan shows monetary and nonmonetary benefits of reduced risk, higher quality, and more efficient use of staff and technology resources. You have clearly shown how the improvement to the company's bottom line will be measurable when the PMO is up and running. You have put this all in a well-researched plan, developed your briefing slides, and presented the business case to the executive sponsors.

What happens next? You did your homework; the initial cost is high, but is well within the averages for your industry. You are confident in your numbers, and you feel you have made the case that this will result in the promised benefits. The sponsors thank you for your presentation and say they will get back to you once they have made the decision. Later that day, the chief sponsor brings you the news: the cost is just too high. The company cannot afford this right now; we will take it under advisement and try again next year. What happened? Was there a better approach?

In a large, mature, or projectized organization, the value proposition for a full-fledged PMO is more established. There are also many organizations that grow and develop, establishing an enterprise PMO as the next step in the growth and process maturity of the organization. In these organizations, budgets, resources, and authorities will be established at the executive level and will become a critical success factor for the company. But what if your organization is not at this point in its lifecycle? What if you do not have an approved budget and senior management sponsorship? Can you still achieve the benefits of a PMO in your organization? And how do you find the resources to achieve this?

In this chapter, we look at another approach to establishing a PMO. It is an evolutionary approach, starting small by identifying key sponsors and stakeholders, targeting key benefits that directly impact those stakeholders, and organically growing the PMO by capturing and leveraging value along the way. The PMO grows with the organization, providing thought leadership and peer support, and focusing on providing value.

What is a PMO? When I asked that question to a group of project managers, they all gave me slightly different definitions. But when I pressed them to describe details, I got very similar answers. They described highly evolved, complex systems of software tools, processes and procedures, rules, support staff, oversight and leverage functions, and other helpful things. Most of the project managers I spoke to viewed the PMO as nirvana—the highest state of project management. They talked a lot about organizational maturity—that a well-developed PMO was an indicator of organizational maturity. They described how it would help a project manager successfully manage their project. However, those same project managers also spoke of how a PMO (usually one they do not control) can impede project progress, increase project costs, and increase the bureaucracy they faced.

Looking back at our earlier scenario, is there anything that could have been done to increase the likelihood of a different outcome? Projects fail for many reasons. Failure to understand the requirements and failure to manage the expectations of the stakeholders are two of the most frequently cited reasons. As we look to initiate and plan the project for establishing the PMO, it will be very important to fully understand the environment in which it will operate and what the requirements and expectations are for the PMO. Before you start planning and budgeting for the PMO (the *what*), take a good look at the *why*. Why a PMO? Why now? Spending the time now to understand the drivers for setting up a PMO is the first step in successfully identifying, planning for, and obtaining the resources needed to launch it.

But why does this matter? As we will see, a detailed understanding of the various drivers, influences, expectations, and obstacles will provide clues on how to approach the development of the PMO. Understanding these drivers will suggest options for accessing the needed resources, while maintaining forward momentum in order to overcome the obstacles of sticker shock and indifference.

Chartering the PMO

This budget estimating exercise, sometimes euphemistically referred to as a feasibility study, should not be the beginning of the exercise. Often, senior management wants to understand the rough magnitude of the internal project cost before making any commitments. Resist this. The beginning must be the PMO charter. Similar to any project, it should be fully initiated prior to planning. In chartering the PMO, we need to look at a number of factors:

- Who are the sponsors and what is their level of commitment?
- What are the motives for launching a PMO now?
- What are the sponsors envisioning when they think of a PMO?
- What benefits do your sponsors expect the PMO to achieve?
- What problems are you trying to solve?
- What obstacles will you face?
- How will success be measured?

In establishing a PMO, it is necessary to examine the stakeholders and the organization culture as a first step. PMO projects can be very political and can challenge the status quo, introduce turf battles, or simply be resisted or ignored. A strong charter will provide the guidance and ground rules for evolving the PMO for the organization. A thorough understanding of the stakeholders and their positions, opinions, and influence in the organization will provide inputs to establishing a detailed charter that will be the foundation of an achievable PMO project. Here are some questions to ask to refine the needs of the stakeholders and uncover the requirements and approach to establishing and growing the PMO.

Who Are the Sponsors and What Is Their Level of Commitment?

The PMO, like any project, will need a sponsor. Multiple sponsors will likely be needed, depending upon the various projects or organizations that will ultimately be in the PMO sphere of influence. The first question to answer is: *who are the sponsors of the PMO?* The obvious starting point is to look at the person who raised the idea of a PMO and who tasked you with planning and executing the PMO project in the first place. What is their level of organizational influence? What budget do they have, and are they willing and able to commit that budget up front—even on a conditional basis? For how long are they able to fund? Why have they decided that the organization needs a PMO, and at what organization level? Are they looking for an enterprise PMO that will exercise governance across the entire organization, or are they looking to develop a PMO for their immediate organization? Conducting detailed conversations with this initial, primary sponsor will elicit clues as to the real expectations and level of commitment that this sponsor is willing and able to offer.

Once you have ascertained the primary sponsor's level of commitment, begin to look for those individuals and organizations that may be influenced or impacted by the PMO. Try to gauge the reactions to this idea among the other stakeholders. Do not be surprised to find that organizational politics arise at this point. Talking about a PMO can initiate fears about losing control and influence. By speaking to a wide array of stakeholders before any plans are in place and by being as neutral and open as possible, you are in the best position to find allies by including as many stakeholders as are willing to be a part of the PMO project. Consider the needs of the various organizations; find a value proposition for each individual stakeholder as well as for the PMO as a whole. Give them a reason to participate. Understand their risks. It is by establishing this coalition of stakeholders and looking for a common benefit that will form the basis for establishing the value plan to sustain the PMO project through its early growth.

Establish a team of stakeholders. Understand their level of influence and authority in the organization, the reach of that influence and authority, and the risks that they face. Try to turn all the stakeholders into sponsors. Now you must seek to understand their motives and what will influence their expectations and decision making.

What Are the Motives for Launching a PMO Now?

Is the drive to establish the PMO part of a larger organizational strategy, or is it a response to a specific need? Is this need based on a realistic understanding of what a PMO can reasonably achieve, or is it a response to organizational frustration or turf battles? Not all motives will be strong drivers for implementing a PMO. Below are a few sample scenarios that may be influencing the demand for a PMO within the organization, but are unlikely to be the foundation for long term success:

> *"I just had lunch with Joe Mitchell over at Amalgamated Widgets, and they've implemented a big new software system for their new PMO. Why don't we have a PMO?"*

> *"I just read on the plane that organizations that have a PMO have more efficient cost control and fewer failed projects."*

> *"We're just not getting the resources from the engineering division for our projects. We need to establish a PMO in order to force engineering to provide the resources identified in the project plans."*

The motives illustrated are not that uncommon. They are natural reactions to information and influences from inside and outside the organization to common needs and problems. As you might guess, they are not sufficient to successfully launch a long-term PMO program. Sometimes potential sponsors do not openly admit these motives, so ask questions carefully and keep a keen eye out for this kind of motive. Do not reject the sponsor or his request out of hand—work to educate them on a more reasonable and realistic expectation of what a PMO can achieve in the organization and what it will take to get there.

Conduct detailed conversations with your sponsors. Try to understand what their motives and expectations are for a PMO. Why are they interested in a PMO? Where and when did they learn about PMOs? What problems or issues do you anticipate the PMO will improve or resolve? Map out their responses, looking for similarities. Look for problems in common, or related issues that could be addressed by a common solution. Also, look for areas of direct opposition. In the third example previously provided, the motive of the project manager is clear. He wants the engineering department to meet his resource demands. But the engineering department in this functionally organized company is also a stakeholder. What challenges are they facing and what constraints do they have in trying to meet the needs of the various project managers as well as the demands of the rest of the organization? How could they benefit from the PMO? What motives might they have for resisting a PMO? By understanding the motives of the various sponsors and stakeholders, we have laid the groundwork for building the case for the PMO. This case—this win-win value proposition—will be the foundation for its charter and will inform the value plan that will drive the evolution of the PMO.

What Are the Sponsors Envisioning When They Think of a PMO?

Understanding the motives is the first step. We must also carefully establish an understanding of the expectations of each of the sponsors and stakeholders. We must ensure that we fully understand the vision of each sponsor and stakeholder, how that vision fits within the organizational functions and goals, and how each vision is similar to or in conflict with the visions of the other sponsors. This critical step requires an understanding of your organization, your customers, and the various business operations and functions. In IT development projects, failure rates can be very high. The most common factors cited for these failures include:

- Unrealistic, unarticulated, or misunderstood project goals
- Poorly defined system requirements
- Stakeholder politics

A PMO project faces similar risks. The goal is to align the PMO charter not to some academic definition of a PMO—a one-size-fits-all approach—but rather to a commonly accepted, shared vision specific to the needs of the individual sponsors. By aligning the PMO vision to the specific needs of the sponsors, the PMO can bring defined benefits to the sponsors as it evolves, promoting increased commitment rather than risking loss of commitment waiting for some future benefit.

In projects, acceptance criteria—conditions which must be met before project deliverables are accepted—must be defined early in the planning process in order to ensure that the project activities are directed toward objectives. Acceptance criteria, also referred to as success criteria, come into play here as well. What will it take to gain the acceptance of the stakeholders? How can we show early success to keep our sponsors attention and commitment? What service can the PMO provide to gain this commitment and acceptance? By answering these questions, we can begin to fashion the value proposition.

In addition to understanding the vision and establishing the success criteria and requirements, we must establish that the stakeholders' visions are realistic and achievable. As the examples at the beginning of this chapter illustrate, often the PMO vision is derived from a very general understanding of a fully realized PMO in a highly mature organization, or worse—an idealized definition that exists only in a textbook or business article. In the process of understanding the expectations and vision, you must influence that vision as well. Ask questions that, rather than change the vision, refine the vision to the specific needs of and benefits to the organization—benefits that can be achieved and measured. Analyze these expectations, visions, identified needs, and opportunities and roughly categorize them into short-term, mid-term, and long-term visions. This exercise will provide insight into short-term objectives and long-term goals. Communicating this analysis back to the sponsors for confirmation will help to confirm your understanding of their needs, while establishing the stakeholders' expectations. This expectation baseline will assist longer term in managing the stakeholders' expectations in order to maintain their commitment to the PMO project.

What Benefits Do Your Sponsors Expect to Achieve? What Problems Are You Trying to Solve?

Now that you have established the short-, mid-, and long-term vision for the PMO, this vision must now be articulated into concrete measurable benefits that can be achieved as the PMO evolves. These benefits will be articulated in the PMO charter and will form the basis for the value proposition. At this point in the process, the benefits will be fairly high level. However, keep them as specific as possible. While the PMO certainly will benefit the enterprise as a whole, that is clearly a long-term vision. Look for short-term and midterm benefits that are specific to the individual or groups of sponsors and stakeholders. Achieving benefits for these groups will allow them to become champions for the PMO across the organization, and they will be able to point to concrete benefits they have achieved.

Another approach to identifying potential benefits of the PMO to the sponsors is to examine their issues, problems, and pain points. What processes are not working? What processes are missing? Do they have miscommunications, conflicts, or coordination challenges that they face? Examining these challenges will yield a goldmine of potential benefits.

In the scenario where the PM wanted to force engineering to provide needed resources, there is clearly a real communication and coordination problem at the root of the project manager's frustration. This problem points to a real benefit, which the PMO can provide. This example demonstrates a common issue in a functional organization—project managers demanding functional resources, functional managers trying to meet all their functional requirements, including but definitely not limited to the project needs. What benefits could a PMO provide to assist each of these managers in meeting their objectives? While it is unlikely that the PMO can force the engineering department to do anything, the PMO may be able to improve communication, understanding, and eventually support coordinated scheduling and planning. This is just one example of how understanding the problems of the organization can identify opportunities for the PMO.

Completing the PMO Charter

Unlike a project where there is a clear scope and defined outcome at the end, initiating a PMO, while the launch itself can be a project, has permanent organizational and operational impacts that can touch on the very roots of an organization. When you are talking about governance, organizational civil wars can break out. Resources—whether money, people, or tools—can become weapons in this war. By taking a gentler lead-from-below approach, the PMO manager can defuse some of these conflicts and focus on the positive services—the benefits—that the PMO can provide.

So how does this exercise—developing a detailed benefits-based charter— contribute to capturing the resources necessary to implement a PMO? It allows us to break free from the all-or-nothing model and provides the raw materials to develop a value based, incremental plan for implementing a PMO that consistently provides measurable value as it evolves and expands over time. This evolutionary approach allows the PMO manager to provide a clear relationship between resource requirements and benefits, utilize indirect methods as well as direct methods to identify and leverage resources, and lead by example to educate the stakeholders into adopting the PMO itself—not just its processes.

Leading from Below

The PMO is traditionally considered a governance function, and there is a distinct tendency to assume that the PMO requires overt authority within the organization to enforce compliance with corporate processes and procedures. While that is certainly one approach (which may be valid for some organizations), the approach discussed here is vastly different. It does not rely on hierarchical authority, and it rejects the control-driven PMO in favor of a more service-driven approach. This service-driven approach is based on the concept of leading from below. One does not have to be in a position of hierarchical authority in order to lead. In fact, simply occupying a position of authority does not make a leader. Anyone within the organization has the capacity and opportunity to lead. This approach to establishing and evolving the PMO relies on leadership, not authority, to be successful. By becoming an asset to the sponsors and stakeholders, and by providing thought leadership and solutions to the organization, you can lead from right where you are. Lead by example, demonstrating the value of the PMO with each completed task.

In order to lead from below, you must focus on influence rather than on control. Forcing someone to do something will certainly provide short-term success, but the success cannot be sustained once the control grip is loosened. If someone is positively influenced to act by seeing and understanding the benefits of his actions, he is then self-motivated to continue without the exertion of control. Consider peer relationships. As the manager of the PMO, look at all of the participants, sponsors, and stakeholders as peers—as team members working together to achieve solutions. Focus on a flat view of the organizational world. Downplay any appearance of exerting authority to prevent conflicts, but also to foster open communications. Establish the PMO as a neutral party designed to serve the needs of all the stakeholders in the organization.

The service-driven, leadership-from-below approach focuses not on directing others, but on removing the obstacles that interfere with the success of others, on solving problems, and on mentoring and supporting the growth of others. Leadership from below means encouraging a broad range of approaches and perspectives, and creating an environment where people can solve their own problems. Become a trusted advisor, someone people come to for help and advice. Provide communication leadership by listening objectively and by being an honest broker of information and assistance. Provide the sustaining vision for achieving the PMO. It is through this leadership, and not through direct authority, that the PMO will evolve into a service-driven asset to the organization.

One specific requirement of PMO leadership is to promote the vision of the PMO and advertise the delivery of value to the organization. It is important that the individuals, including stakeholders and sponsors, be kept aware of the activities of the PMO and the value being created. Success attracts more success. As each success provides further momentum, share that success with others. Ensure that all interested parties are not only aware of the value being created by the PMO, but understand how to access that value for their own projects. This word-of-mouth proliferation is the primary expansion method in the early phases of PMO development.

The Stealth PMO

The reality is that establishing a PMO can be an organization-changing activity. It can result in the alteration of interrelationships of functions and operations, as well as changes in the tools and communication methods of the organization. It can be a very expensive proposition. Like any major organizational change, it has a high potential for failure. Resistance to change can be strong, getting buy-in and agreement across all the functions is daunting, and the risks are high. Capturing all the requirements, issues, and risks across the organization is a highly complex task. Inability to fully capture and manage requirements across the organization is a common risk for projects.

What if you take a step-by-step approach? Test your assumptions. Confirm the requirements. Test and evaluate tools and approaches on real problems. Pilot the various elements of your long-term PMO plan. Can we do all this while providing measurable value? This approach to establishing and evolving the PMO is designed to focus on providing value while incrementally building the PMO. Each increment of growth takes a specific organizational challenge and finds a way to solve the problem using the PMO approach. A number of critical steps to planning the PMO project are highlighted in the following sections.

Formulate the Value Proposition

Generally speaking, the value proposition is the benefit that is offered by an organization's product or service. The value proposition can be seen in a number of ways. It is the value that the stakeholders will accrue related to the costs they incur. It is a promise to deliver an expected experience or result from a product or service, why a product or service is important to the stakeholder, or the unique added value to the stakeholder as a result of the product or service. This value proposition will describe the benefits that the stakeholders will receive as a result of their participation with or from the PMO.

By extensive, detailed examination of the sponsor's needs, challenges, vision, and expectations, you have gathered the raw materials for formulating the value proposition for the PMO charter. If you research the value proposition for the PMO on the Internet, you will find a lot of information. Claims that PMOs reduce delivery times, improve resource management, improve deliverables quality, etc. are all perfectly valid. They are also generic. Take a look at these and define them in specific terms to your organization and to your sponsors and stakeholders. Provide not just the benefits, but also the means to measure these benefits. As you define the value proposition, continue to identify short-term, midterm, and long-term benefits.

Develop the Value Plan

The value plan is a core document in the evolution of the PMO, and it is what makes this approach different from the traditional functional approach to PMO establishment. It is the time-based plan for delivering value to the stakeholders. It identifies PMO deliverables in terms of measurable value to the stakeholders and to the organization in terms of challenges resolved and benefits provided. These benefits are directly derived from the PMO charter work and form the basis for the evolution of the PMO. These value deliverables will drive the PMO task plan.

The value plan identifies each activity that will be conducted in terms of the value that will be provided to a particular stakeholder. The value plan looks at what benefit a stakeholder will accrue, when it will accrue, and what resources will be required to accrue that value. In many cases, multiple stakeholders will accrue the same benefit; other times multiple stakeholders will benefit, but in different ways. Looking at the value proposition, if you have been specific and have identified short-term, mid-term, and long-term benefits, then this will be the foundation of the value plan.

To construct the value plan, instead of listing all the functions of a PMO and constructing a plan to implement all those functions, take the approach of listing problems to be solved and benefits to be met, prioritizing them, and then matching them to the desired ultimate PMO functions. For example, select a problem and define the problem statement. "The project managers and the engineering department are in frequent conflict over scarce engineering resources, resulting in the mutually-perceived lack of cooperation and understanding."

Then describe a general proposed solution: "Establish a mechanism for communicating project engineering requirements to the engineering department and for communicating engineering capacity to the project managers in sufficient time to meet operational and project schedules in order to improve scheduling and prioritization for both groups."

Then, identify a value outcome: "Improved communication and the cross-functional understanding of needs and constraints will result in improved project estimation and scheduling and fewer project schedule or operational delays." This solution aligns with ultimate PMO goals such as integrated scheduling, structured communication, or structured project estimating.

Examine the information gained during the chartering process. At this point, you have cultivated a relationship with your sponsors and stakeholders—a relationship based on understanding their needs, problems, and issues. By taking a service-minded approach, you have developed the trust necessary to begin to provide problem-solving leadership. The value plan organizes all the issues, problems, and benefits and prioritizes them. It identifies what resources will be needed to attack the problem and how to measure the value of the solution.

There are many activities that can produce value. Collecting, collating, and providing access to data can provide value. For example, collecting lessons learned in a structured way and storing them in a way that enables project managers to easily search and access the information will provide measurable value. After hours or lunchtime peer coaching as part of a PMP® preparation project to certify project managers is another example of providing a PMO benefit to the organization. There are many opportunities to demonstrate the value of the PMO—the more you look to your organization for challenges, the more you will find.

The foundation of this evolutionary approach is essentially to use problem solving to consistently pilot the benefits of the PMO in a structured way, with the goal of achieving momentum and buy-in until the organization is committed to formalizing the PMO across the enterprise. This has the added benefit of demonstrating cost-effective solutions, which can be evaluated for scalability and either adopted or re-engineered for the enterprise, rather than starting from scratch.

Develop a Task Plan

For any project, the project manager will establish a project work plan. This plan will include the work breakdown structure (WBS), which describes all the work that must be completed to achieve the scope of the project. The WBS and the WBS dictionary describe in detail the work to be done, what resources will be required, the constraints, and the traceability back to the requirements. The work plan will include the project schedule, showing when each work package will be completed. The PMO project, like any project, will have these elements.

The work packages for this task plan will be identified in relation to the value plan. For each problem, come up with a specific, step-by-step plan to solve that problem (in consultation with the stakeholders). Since this is a pilot, the group may wish to try more than one possible solution. Getting the stakeholders involved in the solution eases resistance and provides an opportunity to build ownership and buy-in to the solution. When building the plan, consider what resources will be needed to implement your solution. Consider resources in terms of effort, skills, tools, and information. What organizational influence or authority would be required? Do not be prescriptive at this point, but simply describe the resources in terms of utility and outcome. Do not name particular tools; rather, identify what capabilities, functions, outcomes, and utilities will be needed to solve this problem or provide the benefit.

Finding the Resources to Establish and Grow the PMO

This approach to piloting a PMO does not begin with the hiring of new staff or permanently reassigning personnel. This approach begins with identifying temporary resources to solve individual problems. As each solution is tested and implemented, even on a small scale at first, measurable value to the organization grows. This approach leverages existing resources within the organization, as well as all the expertise and thought leadership available in the project management community, to build PMO capabilities. This approach incrementally constructs a portfolio of tools and solutions that becomes available to the organization, building momentum and buy-in as it grows. But where do these resources come from? Creativity and flexibility are an important component to finding the needed resources. The availability of specific resources will be unique to each organization. The following discussion highlights some ways to identify the people and tools you need to achieve the PMO objectives.

Human Capital Resources

Find People Affected by the Target Challenge

At first, people may seem the most difficult resource to obtain. But remember, you are not hiring them, you are asking for their help to solve a problem. At the beginning of this process, a lot of time was spent communicating with potential sponsors, understanding their needs and issues, and meeting their teams. The first place to look for help is within the groups that you are trying to assist with their problems. Remember, you are leading from below. They are solving their own problems you are providing assistance, facilitation, negotiation, technical expertise, time, and attention. These are the people who will ultimately gain from the value of the new solution.

Involving the people impacted by the solution works to limit resistance due to territorialism, fostering ownership in the ultimate solution. By encouraging creative solutions and testing them on real problems, the resulting experience will provide valuable insight into the features, functions, and constraints that the ultimate enterprise-level solution requires. In addition, the sense of ownership in the solution can only be increased.

Developing web applications, blogs, wikis, and other tools has become widespread, particularly among younger employees who have grown up professionally with a vast array of IT tools and technologies. Often these people will develop applications and solve problems on their own time if it interests them. Talk with the people on the team—see if anyone has any ideas. Frequently, the best ideas come from the people on the line. They are just waiting for someone to ask.

Homegrown solutions are not always the fastest, most efficient, or most elegant. However the goal is to demonstrate the value of the improved process or tool, gain the support of sponsors and colleagues for the PMO, and to provide a solution that is aligned with the long-term PMO goals. One of the complaints sometimes voiced regarding PMOs is that they are too slow to ramp up. With this approach, that may be a fair description. However, keeping the focus on problem solving that creates measurable value in the short term as well as the long term can initiate the momentum and commitment necessary to speed the evolution.

Find Excess Capacity in Your Organization

In many companies, particularly projectized or matrixed companies, short-term job opportunities are made available to employees who have available time or an interest in trying something new. Often these jobs are in service to internal corporate projects. These special projects may need short-term assistance, such as data entry, file tagging, research—jobs that are too small or too temporary to hire additional staff to the company. This function might be formally organized and managed by internal HR, or managed informally through the employee portal, e-mail, newsletters, or management meetings. Whether informal or formal, this is one option for finding short-term assistance. Look for people who might have a few hours available in their workweek and are willing to try something different. These would generally be activities with straightforward instructions, or where the method to complete is open. I know a number of organizations that maintain a job jar that provides access to sign up for these short-term opportunities. Who would be willing to take on these jobs? Often they are people who are looking to move into another position or to another organization, and will take on these short jobs in order to achieve a new skill, new experience, or face time in the new organization. Not every company will formally make available this type of opportunity, but sometimes informally within your organization, you can seek out those people who have some time or skills you can borrow. If you manage a project or functional team, can you find this capacity by reprioritizing or redefining any activities?

Often these tasks can be assigned as skill-building exercises. In one large program, an employee asked to be assigned activities and training to build her project management experience, as she was interested in becoming a project manager. After reviewing her current position responsibilities and her previous work performance, she was reassigned to the PMO function for one day each week. A few of the functions of her previous job were slightly reengineered and assigned to another employee who was conducting the same activity for another team, with little additional burden.

Meet Rock Stars

Every organization has them. These are the super talented, ambitious folks who love to solve problems and try new things. These people actually gravitate toward change, and are always looking for new opportunities. You probably already know a fair number of these people—you are likely one yourself. Because you are reading this book and trying to learn new ideas and new approaches, you are the kind of person who becomes an organizational rock star.

Does your organization sponsor PMI® chapter meetings? Who else from your organization attends these meetings or other PMI events? Try to find other project managers in your organization who will be interested in supporting the establishment of a PMO. These people will be invaluable to you as you begin to evolve the PMO. They know the company and can provide ideas, expertise, assistance, and support. They will understand the value of the PMO to the organization, and will be able to help you to creatively generate value. They will also help you to market the PMO—talking up the solutions and applying the new tools or processes to their own projects. These project managers will likely be your first customers.

These are a few places to look for human capital resources to leverage the execution of the PMO plan. Remember, you are not appropriating resources permanently, but rather leveraging existing capacity (at least in the beginning). Over time, as you demonstrate value and show that the PMO plan is realistic and successful and that there will be short-term and mid-term returns in addition to long-term returns, you can begin to request limited dedicated funds to access these people on a more formal basis, whether part time or full time.

Tools, Techniques, and Process Assets

In addition to human capital resources, other resources are also needed for the PMO. These include various information technology tools and knowledge resources. This is an area of PMO development that can be particularly challenging. On the one hand, there is a marketplace full of well-positioned, well-developed, well-advertised tools that are well known by project managers. Commitment to a particular tool suite can be political, or simply preferential, and often contentious. In addition, these integrated tools can be very expensive. If implemented and used correctly, they can provide tremendous benefit. But they have some drawbacks, similar to ERP systems, in that they touch so many elements of the organization; failure to adequately understand all the interrelated requirements leads to failure of the implementation and even abandonment of the tool. On the other side of the market, the number of free and low-cost applications is exploding. Open-sourced software, web-based collaboration tools, and new forms of communication media are offering new options to explore. In some cases, with the availability of development tools that can turn anyone with sufficient technology proficiency into his or her own software application developer, the options continue to grow. The risk to these tools can be a lack of security, scalability, and configuration management.

With so many options, it is too easy to just start picking tools. There is an old adage that says, "Do not let the tail wag the dog." In this case, do not let the tools decide the requirements. Just look at the problem you are trying to solve, consider the solution that the team will try, and look into tools specifically to resolve the issue at hand.

There are a number of sources to explore to find resources. Look at adopting existing enterprise software and infrastructure tools.

Check with your IT department. If your organization has already purchased a software tool for use somewhere else, ask if it can be shared, or if the license permits additional installations. Also, ask if the organization has purchased software that is still licensed but is no longer being used for the original purpose. For example, if your enterprise has licensed a document management system for its corporate record keeping, will the licensing permit an additional installation (or a separate database) for tracking project documentation? Many organizations are implementing collaboration tools to aid in internal team communication. Verify with the manager of these tools if a site for the PMO can be initiated. Be creative. The solution might not be ideal in the long term, but if it will do the job, try it for now. Software is not the only resource that can often be found by scavenging in the organization's storage cupboards. Ask the IT department if there are any servers, PCs, or other hardware tools not currently in use that you could borrow. Sometimes equipment is bought for a project, particularly an internal corporate project, and is retired after the project is complete. Some equipment may even survive a technology refresh. It will be older, but it will do the job.

Look on the Web

There are more and more resources being made available on the web each day. One source to consider is free-ware. Many developers put software tools or versions of their tools out on the web for download and installation. Many of these tools are excellent, and many have become the best of breed in their function. Be cautious and research the tools before downloading, to determine the quality of the program and the reliability of the developer or website that provides the software. There are many project management websites, blogs, and online communities that discuss and debate these various tools. This is a good place to start when looking for options. Of course, follow all appropriate precautions to avoid the scourge of malware in the Internet marketplace. Do your homework, but check out some of these tools. Many of them are very good. For example, there are a number of mind-mapping tools in the marketplace that are free for use. These can be excellent aids to planning, capturing and communicating requirements, and organizing thoughts. They can be functional in developing the WBS and in group planning sessions. In addition to downloadable software, consider the web-based tools. These tools store information *in the cloud* (*in the cloud* describes the way information is maintained outside the bounds of your organization). A word of caution—understand your organization's policy on information security as well as the policies of the website you wish to use. Web-based tools are particularly useful in collaboration across locations in that they do not require either co-location or access to common IT infrastructures to communicate.

Some web-based tools can also be hosted on your organization's internal servers. Wikis and blogs are becoming commonplace in organizations. These can be leveraged as tools to apply to the PMO challenges and to document and market the PMO and distribute information to stakeholders and sponsors.

Build Your Own Tools

Building basic tools in spreadsheet, word processing, desktop database, and other available applications is a common approach. It is done every day, but we do not think of it as tool building. There are only a few project managers out there who have not built their own spreadsheet tool to manage the budget for a small project at one time or another, either for professional or personal use. In addition, desktop database applications are relatively straightforward to learn and often come with numerous templates for you to use as a starting point. Consider two very useful tools—the template and the checklist. We use these tools frequently and do not give it much thought. However, templates and checklists are communication tools. Establishing common templates and checklists will lead to a common point of reference, improving communication. Tools can also be built using resources found on the Internet as well. Of course, if you, or one of your colleagues are particularly talented at developing software applications, you could build your own application from scratch. But be wary not to try to take on too much—you may find that a lot of time and effort will be used to build something that is not quite as useful as you envisioned. Keep it simple and flexible. If the application you need is straightforward and the requirements are focused and well understood, custom developing an application may be an interesting option.

Trial Versions

Many software developers make trial versions or limited-use versions of their software available for use. The purpose of these versions is to allow the organization to try the product to see if it is the right fit. These trial versions can be an excellent resource. They can be limited in time of use (30 days), or they can be limited in the number of users, projects, entries, etc. Also, some features may be disabled. Many products even have a free, feature limited version that can be used permanently. If you are interested in a particular product, check their website, or ask the sales representative what options they have for you to try.

These are just some of the tool sources to consider. What is available in the marketplace is really impressive. The freely available functionality can rival the major tool vendors. For example, a software development project team was heavily resisting the software tool suite that management was considering implementing for the program PMO. They felt that they were not only left out of the decision process, but also that the tool in question would limit their flexibility and visibility across all the work they were doing, causing increased workload.

The PMO manager informed them that a control tool must be implemented, and challenged them to present an alternative. With tools available on the web and two rock star senior engineers volunteering to configure the tools, the team built an excellent alternative that met all the requirements as well as providing a few dashboard features that the vendor-provided tool suite did not have. While their solution was not immediately scalable across the organization, it was a stepping stone toward the PMO goal. The PMO management could still monitor progress, code control was excellent, and their tool integrated with the PMO tool that the other projects were using. Eventually, a solution evolved for all projects under the PMO that was a combination of the management-selected tool and the project developed tool—a win-win solution for everyone.

Most of the tools sources described above will generally provide tools to address one function or a limited number of functions. While some of them are best of breed, they typically lack the integration of features of large-scale enterprise software offerings. For this purpose, that is a positive attribute. It allows the PMO solution team to focus on the tool elements critical to the solution being developed. The team can even try out different tools to see which one solves the problem the best.

Do not worry about choosing the wrong tool. You are not selecting the ultimate tool that will be used across the enterprise—you are using the problem-solving challenge to try on tools. These are small pilots for the tools as well as the solutions. Document which features and functions worked and which did not. Which features saved time or resources and which requirements added burdens to the project? What tools did project teams like, and what did they like about them? Trying different tools gives you an opportunity to develop a detailed understanding of what is needed for the PMO in your organization, and what will be the best organizational fit. As it evolves and grows, the time will come when the PMO will need to commit to a tool. Since you have tried out a number of tools, feature by feature, function by function, the teams will have established a detailed requirements set that has been tested on real PMO challenges. These requirements, along with the sponsor commitment that was built, will improve the quality of the decision and support a successful implementation of the organization-wide tools when the time comes.

Techniques and Process Assets

The Internet is an unparalleled resource for the project management practitioner. There are webcasts, blogs, documents, trainings, and sample templates, all available for your use. Many are free. As you research what is available, select information that is acknowledged to be open source and available for anyone to use. Respect the trademarks and copyright of others. Also, ask questions of the project management community. There are numerous blogs, online communities of practice, and other sources where project managers can ask questions of their peers, discuss options and challenges, and request assistance. These resources can provide ideas, insights, risks, and opportunities to help identify and execute solutions. Take full advantage of this resource. Become a part of the online project management community.

Another source of process assets is your organization itself. Search any archives available and talk to long time employees. Is there now, or has there been in the recent past, any templates, deliverables, or plans that you can leverage as a starting point for building new templates and processes? It is always easier to start with something you can adapt and build from the bottom up.

As the PMO evolves, the solution teams can make, borrow, adapt, adopt, repurpose, and recycle available resources as needed to solve the challenges. As solutions are found and tested, tools will evolve. Some tools will become part of the permanent tool set; others will have clear shortcomings that can be documented. These documented shortcomings become requirements as new tools are evaluated.

Evolving the PMO

This approach is not a big-bang approach. Depending on the size of the organization and the ultimate scope and reach of the PMO, this approach will take time and focused effort to achieve its goals. As events occur and organizations change, the PMO program can get lost in the chaos of project demands, imminent deliveries, customer service demands, and other realities of the professional life of project managers. In order for the PMO to be successful, the PMO project must be managed, reported, and controlled as a project. This framework recommends a large investment in initial sponsor development and stakeholder expectation management, followed by value delivery focused planning and using proof of concepts to deliver that initial near-term value to the organization.

As the initial problem-solving efforts are successful and as value is achieved, the momentum for the PMO will grow. Other project managers will see that leveraging the work the sponsors have already done can provide value to their project as well. As new templates, tools, and techniques are made available to the organization, the PMO will attain more visibility. At this point, the PMO project is ready for the next stage in the evolution process. Each evolution stage brings challenges. The challenges include overstepping (or the appearance of overstepping) the authority of the PMO to force or demand change, disputes over the decision-making authority for a project, fear of additional oversight or interference in projects, and conflict over favored tools or solutions. Some managers see a PMO as less of a helping hand and more of a source for additional requirements. Making sponsor development and stakeholder expectation management a key component of your PMO project plan, and sticking to the leading-from-below approach will help to smooth these challenges.

The evolution of the PMO will generally evolve from a proof of concept to an approach, then to an established function, before fully evolving into a separate, permanently established project management office. During the proof of concept stage, the PMO project is launched, focused on communicating with stakeholders, identifying opportunities, and building a value-based plan. As the PMO project gains momentum, organizational culture and identity will begin to influence which problem solutions have traction within the organization. This crowd wisdom provides a clue to the approach that will most resonate with the organization. One of the tasks of the PMO project will be to conduct reviews and lessons learned for each of the activities. These lessons-learned sessions will be one of the ways that the evolution of the recommended PMO approach will be revealed. It is important to also maintain an alignment with the goals of the PMO project as well as the goals and objectives of the organization. Select and adopt those solutions that resonate best with stakeholders while remaining true to the PMO requirements. The approach stage is reached when the proof-of-concept stage has demonstrated the value, benefit, and appropriateness of establishing the PMO.

Once the approach has evolved sufficiently to be recognizable throughout the organization, the next stage to work toward is the establishment of the PMO as a recognized function of the organization. At this point, the PMO project will have identified those activities that are most beneficial to the organization to be performed by the PMO. The goal of this stage is to clearly articulate and disseminate to the organization the tools, techniques, templates, and processes and procedures developed and accepted through the problem-solving stage. The PMO function is defined; however, the actual functions may still be performed by individual project staff. Depending on the organization, the evolution may stop at this point, or may continue on to the last stage where the PMO is a separately staffed office with organizationally recognized authorities separate and distinct from the project teams. At the last stage of evolution, the resource and authority challenges will be resolved and normalized. However, the service mentality, the leading-from-below approach, and the value-based delivery should continue to be the focus to maintain stakeholder commitment.

Conclusion

This approach to developing PMOs will provide benefits and early value returns to any size of organization; however, there are limits to its scalability. This approach is ideal for larger individual programs, small and midsized projectized or matrixed companies, or single organizations within larger enterprises. Very large organizations, particularly those operating at a high level of maturity, may find that the rate of organizational change is too slow to maintain. These organizations may require larger actions to gain and maintain momentum, particularly as the PMO project moves forward. In this case, teams of dedicated resources will be required and will more likely be available to achieve these goals. Regardless of the size of the organization or the ultimate approach selected, the incremental, value-driven method will still provide a framework for demonstrating near-term value while remaining flexible and agile.

For those organizations that do not have the resources to provide dedicated teams or organization maturity to react to a rapid PMO implementation, this approach provides a framework for consistent improvement. For all organizations, focusing on delivering value throughout the PMO development lifecycle and prototyping solutions using pilot projects is an approach that reduces risk and supports sustained sponsor commitment for the PMO.

Developing and establishing a PMO can be a daunting task. Developing the processes and procedures, tools, and training, and building the buy in and commitment to the PMO process throughout the organization takes a tremendous amount of knowledge, effort, and change-management skills. Even with limitless resources, PMOs can take a long time to establish. In that time, momentum can be lost and buy-in falls away. Also like any large project, the further ahead you plan, the less confidence exists that the activities will be completed as planned. The goals and objectives of an organization can shift; rules, guidelines, or constraints may change; and sponsors and stakeholders may change roles. This increases the risks inherent in developing a PMO and can raise the bar for obtaining sponsor commitment and funding.

The incremental, service, and value-based approach discussed here provides an alternative to the big-bang approach. It provides three main benefits. First, it takes a just-in-time approach to resource requirements, providing near-term value and making it a cost-effective option. Second, it also allows the development of the PMO to be flexible and closely aligned with the organization, even as it changes. Last, it reduces the risk by remaining tightly coupled with the real needs of the organization, and prototyping solutions and tools prior to making organization-wide decisions.

Many vendors who sell project management information systems, document management systems, process modeling tools, and other PMO related support systems will present the PMO challenge as a setup problem. Purchase the right tool for your organization, implement it the right way, and this will result in a high-quality PMO. In reality, the greater challenge in the development of a PMO is organizational change management. You cannot buy organizational maturity. This approach provides the opportunity to develop the PMO through organizational development, training, and leading from below in order to affect real, bottom-up organizational change.

In spite of all the established benefits, PMOs can still be a tough sell, particularly in small to medium sized organizations. Fear of high initial cost, with realization of benefits pushed out into the future, is one of many obstacles in achieving and sustaining buy-in for the PMO. This approach allows you to get your immediate house in order and demonstrate value before expanding the scope of the PMO.

Author Biography

Colleen McGraw, PMP, has over 15 years of experience managing programs and teams across a wide variety of domains, including construction, finance, and IT. Ms. McGraw has worked with PMOs in various organizations and has experienced the value that a well-established and effective PMO brings to the successful completion of projects. A speaker and trainer in project management topics, Ms. McGraw has provided project management training for a Fortune 100 company as well as PMP® Exam preparation training courses for various organizations. Areas of practice include program governance, PMOs, and turning around troubled projects.

16

Driving Your PMO in an Operations-driven Organization

Jim Furfari, PMP

The first organizational mission statement I was exposed to was one of the better statements I have seen. "The mission of the United States Air Force is to organize, train, and equip air forces for the conduct of prompt and sustained combat operations in the air."

That statement comprehensively and concisely described the organization's role. But as a young pilot in an operational unit, I heard it expressed even more succinctly, often attributed to flamboyant and controversial Vietnam War-era fighter pilot Colonel Robin Olds:

"The mission of the Air Force is to fly and fight, and don't you forget it!"

Gone are all references to planning and preparation, and that suited the thinking of frontline pilots. We believed that all critical mission work was accomplished in the air, and that the further a support unit was physically located from the flight line, the more disconnected it was from the primary mission. That was not to suggest that the procurement officer or the finance clerk were not performing important tasks, but rather to express the belief that those individuals and their organizations lacked a true understanding of the core mission.

Operational personnel tend to be like that. Theirs is the key work of the organization and all others are, if not superfluous, certainly to be considered noncritical. This obviously presents a challenge to the fledgling project management office (PMO) in an operationally focused organization, and if not addressed can lead to the eventual demise of even an established PMO. Trying to convince operations of the importance of the PMO can be a difficult proposition. Successful operations have existed for decades without the PMO, so why is it needed now? The goal of this chapter is to present an approach for introducing, expanding, and maintaining a project office in a nonprojectized organization or business unit.

The Organizational Focus Challenge

Consider two products: the Grande Café Americano that you ordered this morning, and the software application that allowed you to read the news on your smartphone as you sipped your beverage. What do they have in common? Both resulted from temporary endeavors designed to create unique results—they are each the outcome of a project. That is a parochial outlook, but one that should be expected from a book dealing with project management. Yes, their triple constraint triangles would be quite different, and one could argue that coffee production is perhaps closer to a process, but both meet project criteria.

Now consider the organizations and their staff who performed these projects. The barista undoubtedly has little use for the *PMBOK® Guide*, whereas the software development team is certain to understand and perhaps embrace project management practices. But what about the barista's parent company? Even discounting latte production as a project, that company performs some amount of project work, a quantity that has significantly increased with the advent of the information age. While coffee corporate management is likely to be more open minded toward project management as a necessary practice, they may not accept it to the same degree as the software development organization.

How project work is perceived in an organization ranges from a core business function, as in the case of the smartphone application developer, to a disruption of normal business for remodeling of your local coffee shop. In the development organization, projects are how the primary day-to-day work is done. The organizational structure may or may not be projectized, but employees are routinely members of a team, and the project management profession is likely well represented. Strategic planning, dashboard reporting, and financial management are designed to address projects, programs, and perhaps portfolios. Throughout the organization, there is a project culture not apparent in the coffee shop operation.

The distinction between project-driven and transactional-driven organizations is somewhat less pronounced as one moves from the local franchise to a corporate level where projects become more critical to operating the business. Project work is required to build facilities, develop new markets, upgrade financial systems, and to create business processes. Nevertheless, establishing a successful project management office in a transactional or operationally-driven organization or business unit offers unique challenges beyond those faced by an organization that embraces project management as the core to their enterprise success. The current corporate culture in many organizations, especially in the information technology arena, accepts the concept of a PMO as natural and even necessary to ensure that success. A greater challenge exists in how to try to develop that type of acceptance in an organization that is wary of the value of any entity not directly engaged with daily operations.

Types of Organizations

For purposes of this discussion, organizations are divided into two broad categories as follows:

- Project-driven organizations: Organizations whose primary products or services are project dependent. Examples include software development organizations, construction contractors, and research and new product development-focused concerns. Referred to as a *projectized organization* or as *project centric* throughout this chapter.
- Transactional or operationally-driven organization: Organizations whose primary business involves providing goods or services on a transactional or operational basis. Examples include utility providers, retailers, wholesalers, manufacturers, and most service industry providers. These are referred to as *nonprojectized, operationally driven* or *operationally centric* throughout this chapter.

These distinctions are not exact, nor are the principles addressed throughout the chapter uniquely suited to just operationally oriented organizations. Since all organizations perform projects, have operational aspects, and perform transactions, no precise guidelines can be established even within a given industry. An organization's culture provides many of the most difficult barriers to PMO implementation, and a projectized organization is more likely to have a culture accepting of PMO principles than one that is operationally driven. However similar cultural challenges may be faced by project-centric groups, and the approaches discussed here could have value in overcoming obstacles in those instances.

Degrees of Executive Support

Perhaps more indicative of PMO support than of the type of organization is the level of project office sponsorship. The initial decision to start a PMO requires executive backing to be sure. But there are various degrees of executive backing. Much of what has been written about project management offices deals with software development either as a firm's primary business or within an information technology (IT) department of a corporation. In these cases, the PMO advocate is an executive who understands the nature of project management as a fundamental business function. That individual is more likely to structure the project office as an integral part of their overall organization and will treat it as a natural part of how business is conducted. But with our coffee shop conglomerate, coffee and pastries are its bread and butter. If it recognizes the need for a PMO to attend to the myriad of projects it undertakes, placement of that PMO can be problematic. While it could report through operations, finance, or even IT, none of those are ideal. The obvious place might be as a direct report to the chief executive officer since the function spans all divisions, but the concept of a chief project officer has not caught on extensively. The result in this operationally oriented organization is a project office reporting through an executive whose primary business is not projects. This situation just described addressed an enterprise-level PMO, but the same lack of committed sponsorship can apply for division-level PMOs located within operational groups. Only limited executive support can be counted on unless the PMO is that executive's top priority. The challenge is determining how to build and grow your fledgling project management office without the strong top-level support implied in much of PMO literature. If C-level directives cannot be counted on to direct the necessary changes, the project office lead needs to solve how to transform an organization without possessing the real power to do so. It is an exercise in influencing without authority.

Phase 1—Establishing the New Project Management Office

Once the decision has been made to implement a project management office, the initial steps will be critical to the long-term success of the initiative. Resistance is likely, since establishing a new business unit in the form of a PMO is introducing change, and members of an organization will naturally provide some opposition to just about any change. The more stable the workforce—that is to say the longer they have held their positions—the slower the acceptance will be. The first steps, therefore, are more a matter of determining how to introduce change than they are determining what actions the PMO will take to improve project management. Recognize that the gains certain to result from implementation of a PMO are not apparent from those in the trenches who see only more work directed their way. So, you as the PMO leader are not the bearer of good news.

The Project Management Maturity Assessment

Fortunately, an alternative to alienating the organization is readily available. A safe way to avoid having to announce the bad news is to have a third party do so by means of a project management maturity assessment (PMMA). The PMMA is a method of identifying the strengths and weaknesses of an organization's ability to successfully execute projects by assessing its practices against a defined model.

The advantages of a PMMA are many. It provides benchmarking against industry standards, provides a focal point for addressing project management issues, builds on others' lessons learned, and most importantly, can provide a roadmap for improvement. All-in-all it is a good way to launch your PMO as it can address both the early tactical and strategic maturity challenges as indicated in Table 16.1.

Maturity models have proliferated since Carnegie Mellon University introduced the Capability Maturity Model (CMM®) in 1993, targeting software development processes. Generally, the models can be divided into two major types, continuous and staged. Continuous models identify the universe of goals or best practices associated with the discipline and establish criteria for determining the degree to which those best practices are being accomplished. Staged models group best practices into maturity levels that can only be attained when all practices for that level have been achieved. The CMM was a staged model while the Project Management Institute's Organizational Project Management Maturity Model (OPM3®) is a continuous approach. The United Kingdom's Office of Government and Commerce has published its Portfolio, Programme and Project Management Maturity Model (P3M3®), which started as a staged model but has taken a continuous approach in its latest release. The differences between staged and continuous models are more in the grouping of the practices than in interpretation of what is required for maturity. Staged models cover the entire breadth of project management while continuous models can be more easily applied to targeted areas of an organization's project management practice.

Maturity Model Selection

Several considerations should be examined when determining which model to use for your initial PMMA. First, since the goal is to identify a roadmap to improvement, achievement of a specific maturity level might not be important, especially in an operationally driven organization. Achieving a particular plateau requires a level of effort and financial commitment that may not be supported by the anticipated business benefits of claiming Level 2 or Level 3 maturities. On the other hand, the 600 best practices of the OPM3 may be too daunting in an organization with little formality in their project management methodology. A simpler staged model might help pinpoint the most urgent needs. If your organization's opportunities for improvement are not apparent, the staged approach might be best, whereas continuous models offer more flexibility to target obvious challenges.

Another consideration is selecting a maturity model compatible with other tools the organization has or will employ. If Information Technology Infrastructure Library (ITIL) practices have been deployed, P3M3 may be of interest as both are products of the Office of Government and Commerce. If project managers are familiar with the *PMBOK® Guide* or other PMI® publications, OPM3 might have more value. Maintaining consistency in methods and tools of only one

Table 16.1 Strategic and tactical PMO maturity challenges

	Integrating a PMO in an operational organization			
	Phase 1		Phase 2	Phase 3
	PMO launch		PMO expansion	Next generation
Focus	Tactical	Strategic	Tactical	Strategic
Typical timeframe *(from PMO launch)*	0–2 years	1–3 years	1–3 years	Beyond 3 years
Concept	Baseline the organization through use of a PMMA. Address project management processes identified in the PMMA action plan.	Address supporting processes identified in the PMMA action plan.	Collaborate with finance to attain some organizational leverage. Provide education and mentoring, particularly to sponsors. Build operations relationships.	Build partnerships throughout the organization starting with strategic planning.
Methodology	Assessment	Assessment	Collaboration	Partnership
Tools	PMMA action plan	PMMA action plan	Training Mentoring Direct PM support	Partnering, facilitation, and leadership
Target group	Project managers	Procurement, finance, and operations	Finance personnel, sponsors, and operators	Strategic planning and risk planning

governing body is not a requirement, but can help establish a common framework using a familiar language that will more quickly promote the development of a project management culture.

The last and most important consideration in selecting a maturity assessment tool is the approach to be followed on the PMMA. If it is to be attempted in-house, the native expertise will drive tool selection. If an external group is to be engaged, the assessment tool can be a criterion for their selection. Some consulting groups have adopted the assessment approaches of the governing bodies while others have developed their own (often excellent) assessment approaches. If your organization had developed a positive relationship with an external consultant for other project management services, the best approach is to stick with them regardless of their assessment tool. In your initial assessment, the tool is far less important than the outcome of producing a plan for process improvement.

The Role of a Consultant

If employing a consultant, defining the scope of the assessment is critical. Services range from simply providing an assessment and action plan to providing the expertise and resources to execute the action plan and even provide direct project management to specific projects. Given that the organization has established a PMO, strong consideration should be given to executing the improvement action plan in-house if at all possible. This provides an excellent jump start for establishing PMO credibility. The assessment will poll the organization to identify the areas most in need of improvement, and the project office's ability to address those areas goes a long way in defining the PMO as a valuable business asset.

Before the assessment, the PMO should decide how much they want the consultant to accomplish. While there are clear advantages to having outsiders gather assessment data and report the findings, the resulting process improvement initiatives may be better accepted if done in-house. The determination as to whether the action plan is driven by the PMO or by the consultant depends on a number of factors including the corporate culture, resource considerations, and the level of expertise in the PMO. As with all process-improvement initiatives, beware of an out-of-the-box solution. If your processes are chaotic, automating them with a software tool may only result in automated chaos.

The Assessment Kick-off

The organization implemented a project management office because it recognized the need for improvement, so conducting an assessment is basically acknowledging the elephant in the room. It is an information-gathering exercise of areas already known to be deficient in some way or another. It provides a safe way for project managers, team members, and project stakeholders to express their frustrations with the project work environment. Of course, the assessors must set the right tone in the assessment kick-off by clearly identifying the purpose and methodology. Participants must leave the meeting with an assurance that:

- They can expect a reasonable degree of confidentiality in their interview answers
- The purpose is to fix broken processes, not condemn individual contributors
- Positive actions will be taken as a result of the assessment

Of course, this becomes a balancing act of sorts. By nature, some assessment findings will suggest both the source of the information and the target of the concern. The PMO must work with the assessors and with management to ensure that a proper tone is established. Since the purpose is to fix processes and not people, participants should freely speak their minds with the understanding that every finding may not result in near-term action. The PMMA will produce a plan that allows the critical issues to be addressed within a reasonable amount of time.

The Action Plan

A well-run assessment will result in an action plan identifying the initial steps to improving project management practices. Generally, these will fall into two distinct categories: those that directly impact project managers and the core project management process, and those that deal with supporting processes. What constitutes core versus supporting processes is affected by how the organization views project management. In a projectized organization for instance, resource management is closer to a core project management process than it is in an operationally focused organization where resources are allocated first to operations. Modifying resource allocation processes in the first instance falls directly within the project management process. Changing how resources are allocated in an operational organization involves stakeholders and processes not controlled by the PMO. While all action items in the plan will need to be addressed, not all can be undertaken at the same time, so some prioritization will have to be accomplished. The organization will expect visible improvements in project management, and project managers will be hopeful of having some of the support issues addressed. So both core and supporting processes need consideration. With so many opportunities, where does the project office leader start?

The Tactical and Strategic Aspects of the Action Plan

One characteristic of a nonproject-centric organization is that it is less likely than its project-centric brethren to recognize the strategic aspects of project management. There is a vague understanding that completed projects help advance the company's strategic objectives. But knowing that the outcome of a project has strategic implications is not the same as recognizing the need for corporately ingrained project management. The focus on keeping the shelves stocked or the grid energized overshadows project work, often to the point of projects being tossed over the fence for the PM to deal with. Project management is viewed as a stand-alone process rather than as an integral part of the business. Faced with this challenge, the PMO must address improvement initiatives on both a tactical and strategic front. But not all action plan items can be addressed at once, so there is a proper order to the execution.

Having envisioned the need for a PMO, the operational organization has likely been less than satisfied with its overall project management execution. The PMMA will confirm a low level of maturity due in large part to the lack of repeatable project processes. So the initial efforts should place emphasis on establishing a documented project management process to improve the tactics of project management. This process is primarily directed toward project managers to ensure that they follow certain basic steps from project conception to closeout. It is the process for accomplishing the project lifecycle, not synonymous with the software development lifecycle, construction lifecycle, or the product lifecycle. It is the roadmap that identifies project manager interaction with the project team, stakeholders, and the organization's other business processes. It includes all the steps that the PM is directly responsible for, such as maintaining a work breakdown structure, budget, schedule, project management plan, risk plan, and all the other artifacts of the project plan. The first goal is to make that core project management process repeatable throughout the organization across all projects. Along with refining the process, the PMO must provide the necessary training to ensure that the PMs have the knowledge and skills to execute it.

As with any other process improvement effort, the action plan needs to have measurable goals for each action item. It is best to start modestly since an organization with a low level of maturity is unlikely to have a thriving metrics program in place. Simple measures would be the number of project managers trained in the standard process and the percentage of projects adhering to it. Budget and schedule metrics are easily available, but should be considered suspect and interpreted carefully. Ad hoc project management produces remarkably inaccurate estimates, which an immature organization uses as the definitive basis for the project's cost and schedule. It then wonders why the PM fails to deliver on time and on budget. The time and money metrics will not improve until all the key components of the process improve, especially estimating, baselining, and change control. This will require that the processes are established, documented, taught, and practiced over the course of several projects, which obviously takes some time. Clearly, the PMO should set realistic expectations in what gains management should expect during the execution of the PMMA action plan. Smoother running project teams, higher stakeholder satisfaction, better quality project deliverables, and greater visibility into project performance are the earliest benefits of increasing project management maturity and should be touted by the PMO. Comparisons of current achievements to past failures and anecdotal evidence of improvement are valuable and valid ways of demonstrating success until more objective data are available. Once all of the tactical action items identified by the PMMA have been addressed, the increased effectiveness in executing projects will be obvious. Until, of course, the higher level of performance becomes the new standard and different deficiencies come to light.

Addressing Other Organizational Processes

With a standard process in place, the PMO needs to begin addressing other challenges that directly affect projects. This is the more strategic aspect of Phase 1 in Table 16.1. In a nonproject-centric organization, the thought is often to fix the project managers and their process, and the project performance problem is solved. This stems from the view of projects as stand-alone activities rather than integrated business activities. But projects require the support of the organization's other business practices to succeed. Procurement, finance, risk, marketing, training, and even safety processes are required for project completion. Unfortunately though understandably, the operationally oriented organization has optimized these processes for operations, and consequently they often are not project friendly. The next efforts of the PMO need to be focused more strategically toward the organization's supporting processes.

Identifying project needs to a procurement or finance group that has long been supporting the organization's core business function requires a degree of finesse. The PMO will not be successful if it attempts significant changes to others' processes. The initial steps should involve building awareness of the impact of those processes on successful project management. Too often it may have been a one-way street. Project management processes are expected to support corporate budgeting and accounting, for instance, without regard for the workload being imposed. But finance is a support organization and should meet the needs of project management just as it has for operations units. Having been operationally focused, however, finance may be reluctant to accommodate project management requests.

One of the advantages of having the third-party maturity assessment is the objectivity the consultant provides to the findings. They can reveal how organizational processes affecting project management stack up against industry best practices and will get more traction than the PMO lead in highlighting process problems in other areas of the organization. The action plan proposed by the consultant provides an unbiased look at which items need attention. Having first tackled those tactical processes directly involved with the project management, the PMO can now collaborate with other business units in addressing the strategic findings. Completing the actions from the maturity assessment by building partnerships closes out the initial steps of implementing the project office. The PMO is ready for an expanded role in the organization.

Phase 2—Expanding the Influence of the PMO

Not every project management issue or problem will rise to the level of a *finding* in the PMMA. As we know, project managers serve many stakeholders and are driven by the needs of more than just their project customer. A particular irritation, as suggested above, comes from the seemingly endless demands of finance. This is an area ripe for PMO intervention. As frustrated as the project managers may be with finance personnel, finance is likely just as frustrated with project management. That information may have emerged during the PMMA. If not, the PMO should take it upon itself to interview finance, starting with the CFO and working down. Often, shortcomings of the project managers will be expressed by finance personnel (shortcomings that are more perceived than real), but they should be accepted as valid input to indicate the PMO's desire to address all issues.

Three Challenges and Opportunities

Along with finance, there are two other key groups of stakeholders who hold promise for expanding the PMO's influence. These are project sponsors and operations units. Project sponsors are an interesting group. They know they have concerns about what is happening with the project, but often they are unaware of their role in causing, avoiding, or fixing project problems. The toughest group to win over in a nonprojectized organization will always be the operators. Project work is a distraction to them, so they do not want to be bothered with it. While challenging, all three of these areas offer great opportunities for demonstrating the enhanced value of a project management office.

Finance First

The PMO should take four actions to improve relationships between finance and project management. First, set up meetings between the groups. Requests for information or demands for compliance from finance to project management too often come from impersonal e-mails, phone calls, or manager-to-manager directives. Putting a face to those ivory tower accountants and cowboy project managers can diffuse a lot of animosity. The purpose of the meetings is informational so that each group understands and appreciates the other's needs and challenges. Of course the PMO leader needs to referee and keep things on a professional and process-focused basis. Next, the project office should institute formal training where required. The goal is not to make accountants of project managers or vice versa, but rather to provide an understanding of the basics so that the two groups can collaborate more effectively.

An example of one of the most common finance-related challenges deals with what portions of a project can be capitalized. With enough training and some luck, the project manager may get it right, but why expect that when the organization already has capitalization experts in the finance group. So the third area of PMO focus should be on optimizing processes to ensure that finance support is available when required. One approach is to have a formal review of the project by asset accounting personnel early in the planning phase. Alternatively, they could provide capitalization guidance at project submittal by reviewing all business cases before they are approved. Either method will alleviate the burden from the PM of making financial decisions that could have WorldCom-like implications.

Finally the PMO should examine financial systems to determine if there are disconnects in how they interface with project accounting. Account categories in operational organizations are established to support operations whose logical groupings may differ considerably from project needs. The project manager may be carrying two sets of numbers—one to submit in the appropriate form to accounting, and another with which he manages the project's budget. Obviously two sets of books can lead to all kinds of difficulty, but quite often the organization's accounting system is just not designed with project-cost management in mind. Several major accounting software providers have more recently introduced project management modules that are built for managing projects and interface directly with the organization's accounting software. They may provide a solution if the PMO can secure funding for them, often a challenge in a non-projectized organization. Alternatively homebuilt systems based on spreadsheet or database programs can be the route taken. The PMO should do what it can to ensure that the systems meet project manager needs and minimize the manipulation required to meet accounting requirements. Above all, duplicate data entries should be avoided, as they are both a waste of resource time and an obvious risk.

While the finance organization can present challenges to project managers and hence the PMO, it also provides marvelous opportunities. Once the PMO lead establishes a rapport with the finance organization, that relationship can be used to further PMO goals. By virtue of the regulatory requirements in today's business environment, finance organizations can wield considerable clout within a company. Legislation such as the Sarbanes-Oxley Act has made corporate executives responsible to a greater degree for organizational finances, and they recognize that reliance on their financial group has taken on new proportions. Consequently finance has additional clout, and taken as an ally, can help level the field for a PMO in an operationally driven organization. They may aid the PMO in increasing the priority of a project portfolio management tool or perhaps find funding for critical project management training. Finance can offer the leverage that a project office in a nonprojectized organization may lack.

PMO leaders have an opportunity to establish good relations by their understanding and appreciation of the work of the finance department. Having managed projects, PMO leads are likely to have more firsthand knowledge of that work than do their operational counterparts. Most project managers have learned through experience much more about finance than they had probably ever wanted to know.

Coupled with the comradeship of being another support group, that knowledge can, and should, be used to endear finance from the CFO on down to the PMO. While a clever project office lead will foster partnerships throughout the company, the PMO and finance affiliation should be first and foremost. Developing that relationship is the first step to take in expanding the role of the PMO.

Sponsorship Second

The next area to investigate as an opportunity for raising organizational maturity, improving project delivery, and demonstrating PMO value is project sponsorship. Often a weak area even in projectized organizations, sponsorship faces additional challenges in operationally driven companies. The role does not have a clear counterpart in the operational arena, so it is frequently not well understood. Three major problems are evident in sponsorship in operational organizations. The question of who should be sponsor for a given project provides the first hurdle. Not understanding the role, operations management does not want to fill it. So, the sponsorship vacuum may fall to the PM's functional manager who lacks the essential authorities and organizational positioning to effectively act in the capacity. The result is a weak sponsor who cannot assist the project manager in achieving project goals.

Occasionally, a manager from a support organization such as information technology, marketing, or finance may want to provide project direction or oversight. Intervention of these stakeholders when a project lacks an appropriate operational sponsor leads to the next problem—that of multisponsorship. Now rather than having one ineffective sponsor, the PM must attempt to manage many. Chances are good that even taken together, these individuals lack the knowledge, skills, and attributes of sponsorship to assist the PM in being successful.

When a project manager is fortunate enough to have a single, properly positioned sponsor, that individual often is not well-versed in the role. This is the third major problem in the operationally focused organization. Fortunately the first step to solving each of these challenges is the same. The PMO must undertake a formal education program on the sponsorship role in successful project execution. While building or contracting for sponsor training is not too difficult, convincing those who need to take it can be challenging. Mandating training other than operations training in an operationally focused organization is an uphill fight. In the absence of a mandate, look for a challenged project and a frustrated sponsor who does not know how to perform in the role. As with other change efforts in an organization, demonstrating some successes is an effective way to win converts. Assisting that fledgling sponsor in governing their project can provide the win needed to introduce sponsorship training as a worthwhile endeavor. In many cases, the entire project team might benefit from attending the training as part of their forming process. Understanding roles and responsibilities is more effective when exercised from both above and below.

Sponsor Training

Sponsor training should include some project management fundamentals, roles and responsibilities for all stakeholders, project governance guidelines, project risk management methods, and a comprehensive discussion of phase gate procedures. The extent of project management training in the sponsor course will be dictated by the project maturity of the organization. If corporate-wide, structured project management is just being introduced, the very basics of project management will need to be covered. If some processes have been in place, less emphasis will be required in this area. In all cases, the concept of triple constraints and the sponsor's role in determining priorities and tradeoffs needs to be addressed. To be effective, the prospective sponsor must understand the effects of scope creep, cutting budgets, and moving delivery. A sample sponsor training course outline is shown in Table 16.2.

Table 16.2 Sponsor training course outline

Project management fundamentals
Triple constraint
Project management process groups
Project roles
The sponsor role
Project governance
The business case
The charter
The project plan
Sponsor responsibilities
Initiating activities
Planning activities
Executing activities
Monitoring and controlling activities
Closing activities
The steering committee
Membership
Governance
Role
Tools and techniques of sponsorship
Project metrics
Communication
Stage or phase gates
Cost management

Table 16.3 Sponsor attributes

Strong business knowledge
Operational responsibility
Leadership aptitude
Strategic vision
Communication skills
Mentorship and coaching abilities
Some project management understanding
Seniority
Organizational authority
Standing to express business justification
Have a significant amount at stake in the project

Prior to educating the sponsor, a case needs to be made for operations management to formally assume the sponsorship role. In an operationally oriented organization, managers likely do not see sponsorship as a critical function for themselves. The establishment of a PMO may have actually reinforced that belief. Since resources have been dedicated to build a project office—so the thinking goes—then the overhead associated with projects should be handled by that office. Of course, it is both impractical and undesirable to have the PMO sponsoring all projects. Examining the key attributes of a sponsor listed in Table 16.3 makes it clear that operations must assume that role for many or most of the organization's projects.

The Steering Committee

Once the hurdle of involving operations personnel has been passed, the next challenge is to avoid the sharing of sponsorship duties. Managers who are stakeholders in a project because of resource commitments, related projects, or integration concerns may want to assist in the sponsor role. Organizations sometimes foster this mixing of responsibilities by assigning titles such as executive sponsor, business sponsor, or simply naming co-sponsors. The problem with this approach is the confusing guidance it provides to the project manager. Different perspectives can bring conflicting direction. Trying to serve more than one master cannot possibly improve the PM's ability to deliver scope on time and on budget. That is not to suggest that the other stakeholders should not have input to the project. On the contrary, quality input from all those involved is likely to provide the best project outcome for the time and budget allocated. When dealing with those other individuals, however, the project manager is at a disadvantage, as the *ersatz* sponsors are normally higher in the management chain. They are likely peers of the sponsor. Therefore it is clear that the sponsor needs to provide cover for the PM by filtering input from management-level key stakeholders who try to assert too great an influence. An effective way to accomplish this filtering is by establishing a project steering committee chaired by the sponsor and attended by the project manager as an expert witness rather than as a defendant. The purpose of the steering committee is to allow all stakeholders to provide input through the sponsor, who then directs the PM.

Having a sponsor chair a project steering committee is not always practical due to their availability. When that is impossible, the sponsor must make their role as the decision maker clear in the project governance directives. Along with the change control process, these then become the PM's tools for addressing inputs from other stakeholders. This approach has been proven successful throughout the project management world, but when dealing with an operationally driven organization, the utility of standard project management tools and processes is not self-evident. The PMO needs to educate sponsors to carry the message to their peers.

On to Operations

Success in selecting the right sponsors and having them understand the value of structured project management will go a long way in selling the value of a PMO. But to be completely successful, the rank-and-file operators who play a significant role in executing projects will need to be won over, and they can be a tough crowd. As previously discussed, operations personnel tend to see any work not directly tied to the operational process as a distraction from the real work. Three strategies can be pursued to address this issue of operators' aversion toward project management. These might not make operations immediately enamored with the PMO but will lead to eventual acceptance. The first strategy is the usual course of action when trying to introduce process improvements through change: pursue the low-hanging fruit, or those concerns widely recognizable and relatively easy to address. The PMMA action plan may have identified some fodder, but assessment findings are often not so easily addressed. The key findings are likely linked to the common causes of project failure:

- Misalignment with organizational strategy
- Poor estimation
- Incomplete requirements followed by changing requirements or specifications
- Scope creep
- Lack of change control
- Poor project planning
- Lack of user involvement
- Inadequate coordination of resources or insufficient resources
- Lack of executive support or poor leadership at any and all levels
- Inadequately trained project managers

These are not the quick-hitting wins to establish early PMO credibility, but are addressed over time by the project office's action plan. Major problem areas are not the conduit to engage individual operators as they are too project specific and take too long, and operators expect the PMO to fix project management without their assistance.

Addressing Operations' Concerns

Nevertheless do not overlook the assessment results for opportunities to engage operations. An examination of assessment interviews will reveal numerous statements that did not rise to the level of PMMA finding, but indicate process or communication breakdowns. These isolated comments may represent misunderstandings that do not stem from more pervasive problems, but they offer opportunities to present the PMO to operations personnel as an action-oriented problem solver. This is an opportunity for the project office staff to interface directly and immediately with operators without exerting the same level of effort as required to fix systemic communication problems.

Dealing with these nonfindings obviously should not take precedence over action-plan items. The assessment has identified the most pressing needs and has prioritized them accordingly. Addressing those high needs in a low-maturity organization will usually require building, correcting, or improving what might be considered the mechanics of the project management process. Initially this will look like a project-centric approach, especially to operations. Of course, the goal was to fix project management in the first place, so focusing on project specific processes appears logical to them. However fixing those processes requires operators to eventually participate fully in the relevant project management processes. For that reason, the nonfindings require some degree of attention to break the ice with operations on their issues before you put them to work on yours.

By meeting with operations on their concerns, the PMO is acknowledging the importance of their participation in the PMMA and demonstrating that the project office is an action-oriented organization. That is a good message to send, as operations units are definitely action oriented. Plant workers expect to see action when the assembly line breaks down, for instance. A months-long effort to identify, analyze, and implement a resource management tool will not appear as progress to operations, but quickly addressing a communication concern will.

During meetings with operators, the PMO has an opportunity to educate on the role of the project office beyond addressing assessment findings. The message needs to be skillfully crafted to provide an overview without detracting from the meeting's goal of demonstrating support. This is a time to plant a few seeds, not bulldoze for a new runway. These one-on-one meetings are meant to show that the project office wants to listen. There will be future occasions for presenting the overall plan once the PMO has established itself and addressed the findings from the action item list.

The action item list will provide near-term opportunities for project training throughout the organization by the introduction of improved processes, new tool implementation, or formal project training. The training may be accomplished either by the PMO or a contractor depending upon the PMO resource level and training expertise. In the early phases, though, the project office should avoid the temptation to bring on too much too fast. The assessment results will likely introduce all the organizational change around projects that the organization can handle. Of course, project office leadership needs to be looking at long-term goals to carry the organization beyond the first phase. But sustainable success requires acknowledgement by operations of the value of the PMO as a supporting partner. It all starts with relationship building, which has just begun with our one-on-one PMMA follow-up meetings.

Learning the Business of Operations

The next step in building relations with operations is for project office personnel to go to school. As action items are being worked, the PMO staff must look for opportunities to learn all they can about the business. Some may argue that they already know the business, but unless they were directly involved in operations, project managers on the staff lack the perspective required at the PMO level. By its nature, project management focuses on unique solutions to specific problems. But a successful PMO must consider the universe of problems and opportunities that a business faces. Most project managers are somewhat insular about their projects, fighting for resources because it is *their* project. The project office must eventually become involved in portfolio management and help determine where resources should be committed based on critical business needs. The knowledge to contribute to those decisions comes from understanding all aspects of the business from marketing to accounts receivable. In an operationally focused organization, all processes revolve around the complexities of production, and unless PMO personnel have managed operational units or owned production processes, they have a lot to learn.

The learning process provides a tremendous opportunity to build PMO stature. Operators are not used to ivory tower employees (anyone not directly involved in operations) showing up on the work floor or in the field. Imagine their response to the phrase, "I'm here to learn." It is what they would expect from other operators rather than from the corporate suits. While the PMO is a support organization, it should nevertheless pursue the goal of having operations view them as operationally oriented. Keys to achieving that goal are learning operations' business and meeting operations on their home turf.

Translating for Operations

The third step in building the operations and PMO partnership is to establish the project office as the place to go when operations cannot figure out where to go.

At one time or another, everyone in any type of organization experiences the frustration of struggling to accomplish what should be a routine task. Unfortunately we have come to expect a certain amount of difficulty attributable to red tape or bureaucracy as a fact of corporate life. Some of it is unavoidable in any sizable company where so many complex processes are in play. Interestingly, the primary means of overcoming bureaucracy is to institute formal documented processes and seek to continuously improve them—essentially the same approach used to move beyond Level 1 maturity. This seeming enigma of instituting processes to avoid the obstacles of red-tape actually works and should be a long-term PMO value-add initiative. But problems can also stem from a lack of understanding of what might be rather effective processes. A good example of this is any process that makes any reference to *generally accepted accounting principles* (GAAP). Finance personnel are enamored with the formality of their processes—a good thing since successful corporations and creative accountants do not go together. The problem is that too often the financial processes are not self-evident to the operator (or project manager, for that matter).

In recent years, there has been an increasing emphasis in project management circles on mastering cultural and language idiosyncrasies to operate effectively in the global marketplace. Yet we often overlook the cultural and intellectual differences within our own businesses. The paths to economist, operator, engineer, and human resource manager are quite different, and the practitioners develop a different language, thought process, and value system along the way. Project managers should expect a CFO's staff to view projects in a certain manner and the COO's staff to have a different focus. When they converse, it may not be clear to each exactly why the other is missing the salient points of the discussion. It is an internal language problem that is easier to deal with when working in close proximity than when interacting through e-mail, directives, or infrequent meetings. Hence the need for every PMO project manager to spend extensive face time with operations developing effective communications. But beyond that, the PMO can be the most effective translator for the organization. No other discipline interacts as directly with every unit in an organization as project management. So while building rapport with operations by learning their culture, the PM can show the operator how to work through the bureaucracy of other business entities.

The PMO gains initial standing through its establishment by corporate executives but develops its credibility by building relationships at the working level. Addressing individual concerns, visibly learning the core business by close contact with operations, and demonstrating the ability to problem solve furthers its acceptance. The project office should enjoy good success as it executes the action plan resulting from the maturity assessment. Those initial steps at process improvement address the most visible project-related problems that are sometimes the easiest to tackle. Progress will be demonstrated in the areas identified as needing attention. With careful planning, good relationship building, and the ability to execute, the project office will experience fair skies and favorable winds early in its journey. But there will be stormy weather to come.

Phase 3—Leading the PMO into the Future

Those familiar with Bruce Tuckman's stages of group development might expect a period of storming to follow PMO formation. But Tuckman's model addresses the dynamics of molding a group of individuals so that they can operate effectively as a team. The PMO leader may well have to take the project management office itself through the forming, storming, norming, and performing stages. But of greater concern is the natural resistance the larger organization will demonstrate when faced with changes the PMO is instituting. Organizational change is different than group development and more closely follows the Kübler-Ross grief cycle. The PMMA, resulting action plan, and relationship building are devised to help move the organization as painlessly as possible through the shock, denial, anger, and sadness stages to acceptance and commitment. Eventually the organization will begin comfortably operating at a new level of maturity that can be more or less easily sustained as it is now the norm. At this point, the project office will need to be in a maintenance mode for the realized gains. New hires will require training on project management processes, lessons learned will need to be captured and socialized, and continuous tweaking of the process will be ongoing. But these activities are not sufficient to justify maintaining a resource commitment to the project office. If the organization had gotten by without a PMO when it had poor processes, then certainly it can survive without a PMO once the new and improved processes have been mastered. The project office will always be under scrutiny as a likely candidate for rightsizing, and if it stays in a maintenance mode, that right size may well be below a sustainable level. A certain amount of overhead is required to maintain project and portfolio tools, support project training, and sustain the PM process, but a project office that is only staffed to perform these basic functions will find its value to the organization declining. A successful PMO needs to continually grow in functionality and demonstrate value to be viable in the long term.

Demonstrating Value

Some of the traditional methods of demonstrating value may not be as effective in an operational organization as in one that focuses on projects. Efficient resource management, for instance, is certainly a worthwhile goal that operational managers understand and are themselves pursuing. But since the majority of their workforce hours are devoted to operations, the PMO can at best effectively optimize only the leftovers—those hours that operations leaves for other work. Even that is problematic. Optimizing resources in a projectized organization involves allocating to the highest priority projects in a manner that ensures both project progress and the complete and effective use of a specific resource's time. It is a matter of getting the right person on the right project at the right time. Or more accurately, the right skill set on the right project at the right time. The less available the skill set, the less flexibility in assigning that resource. The optimization process really hinges on the ability to most effectively fill the critical skill sets in the top projects, and then assign all other resources. That suggests a high degree of control over resource assignment. In an operations-oriented organization, the PMO is unlikely to have that much control. Project work for many of the stakeholders is secondary to operational needs, so flexibility is already constrained. Some degree of resource optimization is certainly possible, but the results are not likely to demonstrate the kind of value one might see in companies where the majority of resources are allocated to project work.

Demonstrating significant financial savings may also be difficult. The PMO's claim to bottom-line impacts is challenging in every organization, with some additional hurdles in dealing with operations. The first difficulty stems from the maturity level of the organization. Metric programs are resource intensive, difficult undertakings that are not performed well without good collection and analysis processes and strong management support. Prior to the PMO, project-level metric collection is likely to be incomplete and inconsistent with little meaningful analysis or review. Efficiency claims made by an organization that moves from Level 1 to a higher maturity level are always interesting to ponder. What was the source of the Level 1 data used for comparison? One of the primary reasons an organization is Level 1 is the absence of repeatable processes, making consistent and accurate metric collection improbable. Once the PMO manages to get a metrics program in place, several iterations of project delivery are required before enough standardized data has been collected and analyzed to draw meaningful conclusions. Declaring financial benefits on dubious data can damage rather than enhance the PMO's reputation and raise questions of its true value.

Even when metrics data clearly demonstrate resource, quality, or efficiency gains, the PMO may be unable to claim a financial offset. If a project is more effectively executed because it followed improved processes instituted by the project office, who claims savings?—the PMO or the project funder? The answer "both" often results in double counting. A $500,000 savings reported by a business unit and the same $500,000 claimed by the PMO can leave executives wondering why there is not an additional $1M on the bottom line. Certainly, the PMO has made a significant contribution, but may wish to defer to the project owner. This might seem like forfeiting an opportunity, but actually can have a positive effect on PMO acceptance. Acknowledging operations' claim to the savings presents the PMO as a valued partner rather than a competitor, and lets the senior member of that partnership defend the numbers and impact on the core business. PMO value is confirmed not as a cost center or a losing proposition, but as a critical business function improving operational performance.

One of the real perils of early exaggerated claims of PMO efficiency gains is in setting unrealistic expectations. Those early triumphs following the institution of some key best practices are more easily attainable than successes, once repeatable processes have been established. As project execution becomes more efficient, the PMO will face diminishing returns in terms of cost or schedule savings. As a side note, there is also a possibility of alienating parts of the organization by showing how inefficient they were in managing projects, and how the PMO was required to overcome their ignorance. Although there may be a great deal of truth in those statements, that message needs to be carefully crafted. It might be best to show modest advances that can be reasonably attributed to the PMO, giving due credit to the operational units that embraced the change. The goal should be to show the PMO as a sustainable value to the organization as a full business partner rather than a silver-bullet-fix for obvious inefficiencies. The temptation to claim huge dollar savings is great, but may result in questions about the veracity of the PMO, provoke adversarial views of the PMO, and present challenges to maintaining its value proposition in the long term.

This is not to suggest that financial measures are unimportant. Double-digit efficiency claims and huge dollar savings certainly provide good bullet points for PMO success stories if they can be verified. But justifying project metrics is particularly challenging in an operational organization where measurement of the operational process is normally well established, easily benchmarked, and considerably more straightforward than project metric collection. The very uniqueness of projects as opposed to the repeatability of operational processes explains this reality. Operations rely on their own historical data along with industry or process-specific benchmarks to assess performance. While root cause problems are subject to discussion and analysis, the process can be shown to be in or out of statistical control with little room for controversy. Contrast the certainty of the number of units rolling off a production line in a given period of time with the ambiguity of how long it should take to code a particular module. While cutting a day off the coding process could produce a real and substantial savings, it will always appear to operations personnel as a softer metric than increasing the production line output. In summary, PMO dollar savings should be pursued, documented, and reported, but should not be expected to produce the level of excitement of increased production in an operational organization. Savings alone should not be counted on to justify continuance of a PMO.

How then, does the PMO stay viable in an operationally oriented organization if competing on financial terms with operational units is a losing strategy? Keep in mind that the goal is to demonstrate value, which may be manifested in many ways. An operationally or transactionally driven organization relies on product or service generated by operational units for its revenue flow. In its supporting role, the PMO provides real value in its ability to make those operational units successful rather than being itself a provider of revenue. That ability begins with being accepted as an enabling partner by operations.

The Challenge of Sustaining a PMO

One way in which a project office leader can determine how to keep the PMO viable is by repeating the assessment approach used in the project office's first phase. An assessment of PMO maturity could identify a plan to move to the next level. But although PMO maturity models have emerged in recent years, they themselves are as yet immature. That is understandable considering not just the relative novelty of PMOs compared to the practice of project management, but due to the multitude of roles and responsibilities a project office might embrace. The differences between one PMO and another may outweigh their similarities, which make comparison against a single model somewhat problematic. Beyond that, it will be far more difficult to obtain executive support for a project office assessment than it will be to obtain backing for the initial PMMA. The business case for the PMO assessment is unlikely to show the same degree of organizational benefit that the original promised. So taking the next step to your next-generation PMO will involve a different strategy.

How to Meet the Challenge—and Why

Two questions are worth considering when deliberating an enduring project management office: *how* and *why*. The *how* requires the PMO leader to map out an approach that continues to deliver the current value while engaging in new opportunities. It is a transformation, rather, of the project office, not a renovation. To be successful, the change needs to build on the now imbedded processes, recognized successes, and the solid partnerships that the project office undertook in its initial phases. The organization should see it as a natural progression of the project office function and not a change in direction. As questions are posed as to the value of continuing to financially support a PMO, the unfolding plan provides the answer.

The precise course of action will be determined by specific organizational needs, but there are a few natural alliance opportunities that will provide direction. The most obvious prospect is project office involvement in corporate strategic planning. To be sure, portfolio management has already tied PMO efforts to the strategic plan. But in an operationally focused organization, the project office played a support role rather than being a leading contributor. Operations personnel devise the direction and strategy based on operational needs. But this is one of the interesting paradoxes of a nonproject-centric organization. While operation's day-to-day activities provide the revenue stream, growing the business in a strategic manner only happens as a result of project work. Too often, though, strategic planning is mostly a financial planning exercise. While money is certainly important, spreadsheets do not grow the business. New products need to be developed, assembly lines require expansion, and new markets and outlets must be pursued. These project activities are lengthy undertakings that compete for corporate resources, often in a disjointed manner. Individual business units plan their future direction, which may or may not be guided by some degree of overarching strategy. They then develop project lists that are invariably significantly longer than corporate funding can support. A battle ensues to have a greater share of the overall budget to move their respective cut lines further down their list. The PMO probably helped build the prioritization schema to accomplish this project lottery. But this is a tactical approach to what is supposed to be a strategic plan. The fight occurs over next year's budget rather than over the long-term outlook. Consequently, opportunities are lost, and certainly the project mix is suboptimized. A strong centralized strategic planning function can overcome these problems, but similar to the PMO, a strategic planning office is not always embraced in an operationally centric company. That oversight affords an opening for expanding the reach of the PMO. Without projects of its own (or a very few to support project and portfolio management) the project office can provide unbiased facilitation of long-term planning while developing multiyear prioritization processes.

Another area of PMO opportunity is in the realm of risk management. Here again, the strategic focus of corporations is often confined to financial risk analysis. There are a myriad of operational, contract, and project risks that are not readily recognizable to corporate accountants until after the fact. Addressing risks after the financial impact has occurred is the worst form of risk management. The project office can add value to the financial risk management function by expanding the breadth of risk consideration, or if that function is not currently in place, the PMO can initiate the activity. Here is a further opportunity to draw on the goodwill established between operations and finance. The COO will appreciate the opportunity to share those things that keep her awake at night, just as the CFO will be glad not to be blindsided by operational risks that undermine his financial planning.

A third initiative for sustaining the PMO is to identify ways in which the organization can be more flexible in all that it does. In its initial phase, the PMO concentrated on building project management maturity by instituting repeatable processes. Once those processes are ingrained, opportunities to improve, tailor, and streamline them will arise. While project practitioners will identify many of those opportunities, they will have neither the skills nor the time to institutionalize the process changes. Just as with the basic project management process, more effective processes resulting from increased organizational maturity will need to be documented and trained. The project office should pursue agile methodologies (agile in a generic sense, not merely in terms of agile software development) for all aspects of project management and supporting processes. Because of their process orientation, project office personnel may even find their expertise of value to operational units attempting to optimize their own procedures. This is a leadership role that can naturally fall to the project office.

That leadership opportunity leads to a final thought on how the PMO will continue to show value past its initial charter. As previously discussed, the impetus for a project management office normally results from observing project failures. The goal, then, is for the PMO to fix project management so projects do not fail. Instituting good practices to improve project success is relatively straightforward to a point. However the project management maturity of an organization will be eventually capped by the maturity of its other units and processes. Effective project execution is hampered by poor procurement practices. Inefficient scheduling of operations personnel will make those resources unavailable for project work. Even poor human resource policies can negatively impact project performance. So after fixing project management, the project office needs to help raise the maturity of the other corporate functions. That statement is not as presumptuous as it sounds, and brings us to the *why* of an enduring PMO.

Why Accept the Challenge

The Center for Business Practices study, *The State of the PMO—2007, 2008*, determined that low-performing PMOs only operate for three-and-a-half years before being disbanded. Their demise, presumably, is the result of one of three situations. The project office was either ineffective from the start, it fulfilled its mission of improving project management, or it was unable to show future potential. We can assume that no one reading this book would launch an inept PMO, so we can ignore the first scenario.

The second two, a PMO fulfilling its mission and unable to show continued value, are not necessarily two sides of the same coin. An organization could reap the benefits of initiating a project office, and then once the PM process, methods, tools, and training are institutionalized, determine that maintenance can be accomplished without a project office. The trend in the number of companies embracing the PMO concept seems to contradict that notion on one hand, but the short-lived nature of some PMOs may support it. It is probably safe to assume that a project office that demonstrates value beyond that of fixing project management is more likely to have longevity. But then we must ask, "Should it?" Why should the project office function expand to areas of finance, risk management, operations, strategic planning, and so forth as previously suggested? As project management office leaders we should emphatically answer, "Because we are good at it!"

It is interesting that many organizations recognize project management as a necessary activity yet do not consider it a core function. A primary reason for this may be the relative newness of project management as a profession. Engineering, marketing, operations, and finance have long been recognized as pathways to corporate senior management, while project management was something to dabble in on your way up the ladder. Consequently other than a few CIOs, today's corporate leadership generally does not have much of a serious project management background. That is not to undervalue the experiences of a career in operations, finance, or engineering. It takes remarkable knowledge and judgment to manage a plant or to execute a corporation's financial management plan. But those skills were primarily developed by specializing in engineering or finance responsibilities. Interaction between those various professionals was limited to defined job processes and normally occurred peer to peer. Conversely the young project manager recruiting an engineer and operator to their project team is managing upward through the functional managers in other business units. The PM needs to understand the roles and responsibilities of those team members as defined by their operational or financial processes. When conflict arises between those professionals, the PM becomes the facilitator to work out a suitable solution, without being an expert in either field. In short, the project manager needs to understand everyone else's business and all aspects of the business to successfully lead their project.

When it comes to addressing corporate-level concerns such as risk management or strategic planning, what better than the project manager skill set to draw on? Complex business processes routinely cross divisional boundaries these days, and many of a company's most pressing challenges occur at those interfaces. Visionary strategic planning requires a horizontal effort across an organization rather than a vertical view from each business unit. Risks undertaken in one area of the organization can affect all other areas. Collaboration rather than internal competition is required for optimal resource use. And to change the current organization through its strategic goals to some new state will require numerous projects. Bringing the various elements of an enterprise together into a cohesive team to move the business forward is a natural role for the project office.

Leadership Is the Key

A quality manager once lamented to me that the role of all quality managers was to work themselves out of a job. Her mindset was that the quality department would instill values and systems throughout the organization that would make quality an inherent part of the culture, thus obviating the need for a dedicated quality branch. In essence, every manager—every worker for that matter—becomes a quality manger. That may or may not work in the quality world, but how might that same concept affect the long-term outlook for a PMO? There are certainly parallels. The PMO seeks to build a project management culture across the organization and attempts to establish self-sustaining best practices. But I do take exception to my colleague's perspective, at least in terms of PMO obsolescence. Building project management maturity in an organization should not be a project that eventually faces closeout.

The PMO's pursuit of improving practices, educating stakeholders, managing portfolios, or allocating resources is not temporary, nor does it produce a unique result. Dr. Brian Hobbs' 2007 study on PMOs concluded that "...survey data has not clearly identified the determinants of PMO structures and roles. . . . However, it is very likely that the determinants are largely internal to the organization, related to its internal dynamics, strategies, structures, processes, politics and culture, i.e., its organizational context."

This clearly suggests that each PMO is as distinct from every other PMO as its parent organization is from every other business entity. No single approach, therefore, will work in every situation. The project office must forge the partnerships, enlighten leadership, and grasp the opportunities as they present themselves. It is not just a task for the project office leader, though. The entire PMO staff needs to understand and embrace the expanded role. All of this requires a clear vision from you, the leader. In his keynote address to the 2006 PMI® Mile High Symposium, Rudy Giuliani described an effective leader as a visionary who had the ability to execute. He maintained that a visionary who could not execute was a philosopher, and although the world needs philosophers, they do not make effective leaders. And so it is with leading a PMO. You must be able to plan and execute on that vision you have established.

This chapter has attempted to lay out a vision for a successful and sustainable project management office and has provided some techniques to overcome the challenging situation of belonging to an organization that is not project focused. In such a corporation or business unit, the PMO offers opportunities far beyond just improving the practice or project management. All that is required is a leader with the vision to see the opportunities and the confidence to undertake the challenge. Leadership is the key to executing the PMO mission—and don't you forget it!

Author Biography

Jim Furfari, PMP, is a retired Air Force fighter pilot who attributes his success in project management to the similarities in skills involved in both building and bombing bridges. His project management experience began during his Air Force career where he managed various projects and programs including the air-to-air missile program for continental air defense forces. After retiring from active duty, Jim joined MCI as a project manager, working his way into their PMO as a release manager.

For the past seven years, Jim has developed and led the Enterprise Project Office (EPO) for Colorado Springs Utilities, a four-service community-owned utility that provides natural gas, electric, water, and wastewater services to more than 500,000 customers. Colorado Springs Utilities manages multiple projects including construction, information technology, new product development, and service delivery projects. The EPO met its initial goals of providing a formal project management framework and has expanded over the last six years to provide mentoring and coaching, formal training, portfolio management, and direct project management of selected projects.

Jim holds a BSEE from the United States Air Force Academy. His flying career included time in the F-106 and F-16 fighters, and he was stationed in Canada, Spain, and various sites across the United States.

17

A Methodology Improvement Process to Advance a Corporate-Level PMO

Enrique Sevilla

Introduction

It is not uncommon to learn about companies with an established project management methodology that are under pressure to keep their project management tools updated and perhaps trying to have them more widely used and applied. It is also possible to see how they make decisions to determine the right approach, select a new commercial product, or adapt the product they are used to. These decisions are usually driven by the new trends promoting the creation of some form of project management office to deal with different aspects to increase productivity in the use of shared resources, or to provide commonality in lifecycle development in specific business areas.

We could also say that a significant number of organizations are presently trying to determine if a PMO may be a worthy investment that will give a more substantial momentum to the improvement of their project management practices, thereby improving their efficiency in project management. At the end of the day, they are determining whether it is their project management methodologies or the lack of enough trained project managers that is causing the inefficiency. In summary, many organizations perceive that something needs to be done to improve project management practices in order to increase the efficiency and profitability from their processes, personnel, and systems.

The most efficient way to determine the right course of action in this situation is to look for the solution that best meets the present business objectives in alignment with the relevant strategic business plan. Of course, talking about it is easier than taking action, but a good way to find the best solution is to check for clues in practical examples within your own scenario. This means trying to understand how well reliable project, program, and portfolio managers are adapting themselves to organizational culture and environment effects so their projects achieve business objectives. It may be likely that someone in your own enterprise has already started to apply an acceptable solution, and you only need to focus on that solution and review it from a broader perspective. Find out what model they are adapting, and then decide if it is valid in a wider and more generic context.

A Case Study

A case study of my organization is used to describe how we developed an improved project management methodology process to advance the adoption of a corporate-level PMO.

The challenges presented and described in the case study were initiated by the significant growth of the IT business in the company, closely linked with the acquisition of other companies with different traditions, cultures, and practices in the project management arena. The adaptation process among the different organizations involved in the merging process is ongoing and coincides with the need to keep the business safe during a worldwide economic downturn. In addition, the mergers are also occurring concurrently with a recent increase in other more traditional business directions and markets.

Additionally, the growth in the company size also creates another immediate requirement in the need for explaining the project management methodology to the recently integrated new project managers. They come with their old systems in mind, so specific training is required for them. The training applies not only to the methodology concepts, but also includes the use of the project management tools.

The following paragraphs outline a quick overview of the company business and the project management methodology in place to provide a better understanding of the case we are describing.

Company Business Areas and Business Deployment: An Overview

The company is primarily located in Spain with subsidiaries or associated companies in Latin America, the United States, Eastern Europe, and Asia. By 2009, around 29,000 professionals worked for the company, 2000 of whom were tasked with managing projects.

From a project management point of view, the company manages a regular flow of several thousand concurrently active projects with 80 percent of its business in Europe and the rest in other regions around world. The areas of influence include different markets such as telecom and media, financial services, public administration and healthcare, utilities, transport and traffic control, security, and the defense industry. The company also develops its activity as a first-line IT services provider (outsourcing, consultancy, etc.), making extensive use of a software factory model with labs in 20 different locations. Thirty management units (MUs) accomplish the projects with some of them providing common horizontal execution resources.

The number of projects averages around 500 with a budget above EU 500,000. Projects include development or fabrication of new products, or new versions of existing products, which represent about 75 percent of the budget. The rest includes services and operations, technical assistance, and other jobs. The duration of the projects is highly variable, with projects in the range of several weeks for minor developments in banking services, or several years for big defense contracts.

The contracts are always the responsibility of the business unit in charge that owns the direct relationship with the customer, but a significant number of the projects are executed by horizontal MUs, which require a matrix organization for many project activities.

Project Management Methodology and Information System

The organization's project management information system (PMIS) includes a locally generated main set of tools, initially installed by the late '90s and gradually improving in the following years. The PMIS is built on methodological experience gained from U. S. and European contracts and is formulated using the accuracy and completeness of a work breakdown structure (WBS) and oriented to contract deliverables. This is a mandatory approach to be used by every project in the company.

The set of tools for the PMIS interfaces with another set of either commercial or internally developed products and applications that were designed for full control of project-related organization functions and costs. The PMIS interfaces with the project management planning tool and has other dedicated tools for human resources management, purchasing, and expense accounting applications.

The PMIS offers a wide range of control and reporting capabilities to provide adequate control of the financial status of the project. The associated set of tools and facilities are designed to allow allocating any cost at work-package level. The PMIS supports earned value methodology (EVM) reporting and has been successfully used to comply with standardized U. S. Department of Defense contracts.

The project management methodology is tailored to the *project management lifecycle* itself, and as such, it tries to avoid providing support for any specific *development lifecycle*. This is an intentional feature of the methodology and the associated tooling, so that as much as possible is applicable for any type of project.

Nevertheless, difficulties may arise when it is used for some IT operation's non-development projects where human resources availability management represents a significant complexity of the job. On these occasions, the concept of *deliverable* or *lifecycle* frequently creates the need for additional adaptation effort that sometimes is not as effective as it could be. To help in the process, the methodology includes guidance for WBS preparations and EVM application. The local MUs and business units are encouraged to develop additional instructions in the form of templates or particular procedures to be followed by the projects under their responsibility. The local ruling organization may be a local PMO or the leading area in the business, and in any case, this function is encouraged, promoted, and demanded by the quality assurance organization.

Due to the historical background of the company, the project manager's role has always been considered as a main driving factor for project success. Senior management considers and supports the idea that the project managers should take care of their projects *as if they were running their own business*. Consequently, the set of tools for the PMIS is oriented to provide full support to project managers and full visibility of the project's financial status, as well as facilitate project controls.

The training of the project managers constitutes a major concern of the organization. New project managers are regularly instructed using an internally developed training course that is intended to keep them aware of the goals and the main features of the company's project management methodology. There is no external participation in these courses. A training program has been in place since 2005 to prepare selected project managers for PMP® certification, resulting in 165 certified PMPs currently in the company.

The enterprise project management methodology organizes projects by precontract and contract stages, each with three phases. The precontract stage phases include initiation, proposal preparation, and negotiation. The contract stage includes the planning, execution (monitoring and controlling), and closing phases. At the end of each phase is a stage gate that is closed by an executive decision, thereby allowing the start of the following phase. The methodology includes a set of best practices to ensure that projects stay on the right track in accordance with the contract requirements.

Project Definition and Sponsorship

The case study company is described as:

- A medium-sized company experiencing business growth
- Offering a diversification in products
- Providing value to its customers
- Technologically conforming to be a leading edge company
- Experiencing a multinational deployment process
- Looking forward to being recognized as a leading global company

It should be understood that the company has a demonstrated belief that project management is the source of added value. Having a core belief that the consistent use of project management best practices is an absolute requirement to ensure project success is a cornerstone business objective of the organization.

Nevertheless, the strategic design of diversification, deployment, and growth may not eventually be synchronized with the development of the strategically required changes in methodologies, tools, trainings, etc. And if this is true for any business unit and management area, it is also true for the corporate, control, administrative, financial, or other centralized area.

In this context, the need for some kind of change in the project management field made itself clear through several symptoms when it faced the scenario of a growing number of projects and portfolio diversification, different management practices coming out from merged businesses, and different countries and cultures involved. Some of these symptoms exhibited themselves in the growing number of failing projects: the materialization of the idea that the project management company standards are inadequate to meet the new business needs, the lack of clear direction about how to modify and improve the PMIS, or the belief that the existing methodology may not be applicable to the business in various areas.

The solution to addressing these symptoms was found by exploring the different reactions that were taking place in the leading management and business units. Some of them were creating local PMOs, others were establishing local risk management processes or defining indicators, scoreboards, and dedicated reporting procedures for close project follow-up. At the same time, a very basic corporate PMO (CPMO) was starting to be created whose main responsibilities were to watch over the application of the project management standards and to serve as a reference for the training process of the internal methodology and the preparation for the PMP certification. From an organizational point of view, this CPMO was designed to report to the corporate quality assurance and strategy management department and had very few actual responsibilities in the project execution area except for specific support of projects in the form of consultancy on an as-requested basis.

Senior management began to understand what was driving these symptoms. Namely there was a need to change the attitudes about project management practices to boost an improvement in processes, update the methodology and reinforce its global applicability. One of the actions taken was to modify the organizational dependency of the CPMO, now reporting directly to the corporate control general manager. This new position of the CPMO provided definitive momentum to the role of the project management methodology in the company by defining a new role for the office. This role would allow the office (under the sponsorship of top management) to clearly work as a source of added value to project results through the improvement of tooling and processes in project management practices. It is believed that the positional change of the CPMO should improve the support of the project management methodology by generating an additional source of cost savings and improving the capabilities of the organization to detect candidates for failing projects.

Project Charter

As a result, the project charter for this effort included language to:

- Reinforce the leading role of the CPMO
- Introduce a key improvement in the project management methodology
- Aim to achieve the strategic goal of implementing an early detection mechanism for failing projects
- Have the project management standards adapted and applied at a global level

A project was then initiated to implement, under the CPMO's lead, the required changes in the methodology and the PMIS that would be valid for all management and business units throughout the company. The project itself was also perceived as a good opportunity to review the need for project management practices and to review the adaptation of project management practices to the new requirements of all the business and IT areas. It was further determined that the new features should maintain a basic coherence with the already existent project management tooling and methodology.

Two constraints were immediately identified as strictly associated with whatever solution would be adopted:

- Start producing monthly status reports as soon as possible, showing the evolution of strategic projects to evaluate the efficiency and validity of the action plans
- Require additional staff to execute project monitoring status review and reporting for the new processes or procedures

Furthermore, as another demonstration of the capability of the methodology improvement to increase its payback, it should reduce the effort actually spent on performing tasks associated with monitoring. This was translated by some to mean that the requirement was to provide as much intelligence as possible to an automatic project monitoring capability. Others took this to mean that the existing financial reporting mechanisms were to provide the added value. In other words, the improvements should be valid for their direct use and interpretation by the available control teams, without the need for further elaboration of the results.

As a midterm objective, more methodology and tooling improvements are being seen as immediate candidates for renewal once the possibility of a preplanned improvement became more realistic in the new company situation. In fact, during the development of this action, two other projects were initiated relating to the project management methodology. One of them included upgrading the support tool for the precontract stage of the projects to be more oriented toward the commercial aspects of the process. The other project involved the requirements-gathering phase to prepare a major upgrade of the PMIS to include new features and capabilities concurrently with the foreseen substitution of the existing enterprise resource planning tool.

Design Phase

The design phase of the change project started before the project mission was fully defined. The company decision makers and stakeholders believed there was a need for change. The change process began with interaction between management and its stakeholders to find a solution for a problem that was not yet entirely defined. A significant amount of the initial meeting time was spent clarifying everyone's expectations, priorities, points of view, and concerns. This is a typical problem-resolution approach. You need to understand what is happening under a broader context and try to define the problem before you can identify a relevant solution. Usually this comes with trying to reach the maximum number of agreements with the people involved in the problem-resolution process. For us, a series of discussions and meetings with different management-unit representatives, chaired and organized by the CPMO, took place over several months. The outcome was a basic agreement on the main targets and a preliminary design of the new capabilities to be incorporated into the PMIS. As a result of the process, the following main additions to the PMIS were included:

- A risk management tool
- A milestones status reporting system
- An issues status tracking procedure
- A scope change pending the warning method
- A new project data monitoring system that allows for a quick view of any set or portfolio of projects

A major concern during the process was to maintain compatibility with the existing project management practices and tools. This point of view characterizes the company's understanding of project management and the project manager's role as providing the foundation for the main business control processes. This concern also revealed the need for reviewing and updating the existing project management methodology documentation.

Enterprise Project Management Methodology Update

During the initial phase of the preliminary design of the modifications, the corporate PMO developed a parallel effort to produce a new version of the project management methodology. The need for an overall methodology revision made itself evident while discussing several aspects of the new feature specifications. Some of the topics reviewed in the new version of the company project management methodology included:

- Simplified flow of processes to prepare the WBS.
- Removal of formats and templates from the enterprise project management methodology itself and transferring this responsibility to each management and business unit.
- Introduction of the *development lifecycle* concept as the basis for WBS preparation and as a means to help in the customization process in accordance with the different business needs.
- Preparation of specific guidance for WBS elaboration, EVM application, and risk management plan preparation, including risk concepts and criteria clarification. It also included the definition of a risk breakdown structure that became the company's official risk classification for any risk related to project execution.
- A more detailed analysis of the execution phase (monitoring and control activities) to allow for the incorporation of the foreseen new indicators definition and to allow direct reports produced by the tool and stored in the PMIS.

In summary, a portion of the updates were addressed to allow for a more efficient application of the WBS preparation process, looking to achieve better results in the scope definition processes as a means to facilitate the correct representation of the scope of the projects through the WBS. Another portion was oriented to implement a wider range of applicable earned value methods, so the data provided by project managers would be more reliable. A third major improvement was intended to define the baseline and the concepts related to project risk management to be used throughout the company.

A Common Project Risk Management Process

The most appropriate support process in the prevention of failing projects is probably made up by a comprehensive project risk management process that is clearly oriented to detect project internal risks, sufficiently generic so it may be common to all projects, and capable of calling for management attention when certain boundaries or thresholds are reached. It should serve as a tool to be used by the project managers to manage and report about the perceived project risks in support of the early warning principle: the sooner you see the risk, the easier it will be to deal with it.

To that end, a complete risk management method was defined, taking into account that different local tools were already being used in some business areas. None of the existing tools or procedures were considered valid for every management unit across the different sectors and companies in the enterprise.

Furthermore selecting one of them as the corporate tool could have elicited negative reactions from the non-selected business units (BUs).

The risk management (RM) methodology includes a generic risk taxonomy defining ten categories allowing for a complete coverage of possible risk identification. The first five categories refer to the project's external components including contract, country-related risks, customer, subcontractors or suppliers, and partner-associated risks. The rest of the categories make reference to internal factors, such as project organization, technical risks, resource availability, requirements and processes, or systems risks. All together, a total of 40 risk subcategories are available for use by the project manager.

The procedures defined with the RM processes are fully compatible and coherent with the existing project management method, and it has been integrated into the project management tool set, both at the precontract and contract stages of the project. There is a preliminary identification and evaluation of the risks during the precontract stage, as detailed and required to address proposal-specific needs, followed by a complete risk management plan at the planning and definition phases. During the execution phase of the project, the risk management process includes a set of monitoring and control activities allowing the review of the risk status, the redefinition (if required) of the foreseen impacts, and the identification of new risks as illustrated in Figure 17.1.

The risk evaluation performed before the contract is signed allows for a preliminary classification of the project as requiring special attention during the following project stages, consequently requiring specific supporting documentation. This requirement was developed later for additional monitoring of the project status, as shown during the implementation phase.

Once the contract is signed, a risk management plan is prepared with new risk identification, evaluation, and response planning. A severity value is allocated to the risk depending on the weighted estimated impact percentages in project schedule, cost, and scope with a risk indicator rating allocated to the project. The indicator is a function of the amount of risk with high severity, but in any case, the actual value of the indicator may be tailored by the business unit controller in accordance with the needs and the profile of the unit.

The RM methodology is primarily addressed, in this case, to serve as an internal tool to evaluate project risks that may impact project cost, schedule, or performance. Because it is fully integrated with the company's internal PMIS with full access to internal project data, it is not a process that is shared with the customer. Customers can be informed of project performance through the use of the RM tool to generate the required inputs to customer reports. Sometimes a specific process might be necessary to establish or define an additional risk management procedure that addresses and handles risks that are a common responsibility of both the customer and the contractor.

This new RM design took advantage of the different approaches already in place in some of the business areas and built upon them, and where feasible, added new

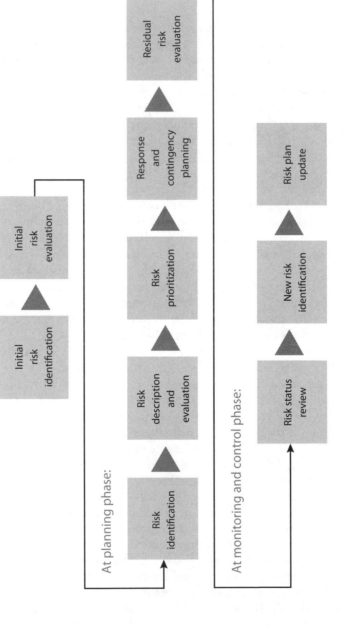

Project risk management

At proposal preparation phase:

At planning phase:

At monitoring and control phase:

Figure 17.1 Project risk management processes.

features and concepts in order to fulfill the requirements of the new mission. Where it was deemed significant, the previous risk management plans were translated to the new risk taxonomy and evaluation criteria.

The RM process allows the creation of different reports as outputs of the tool, such as a project risk management plan document where the user may select different components to be shown. Different reports are available as a set with specific reports related to risk response planning or risk register status. From a project portfolio point of view, summary reports related to the risk plan's status of the portfolio are also available.

Schedule Status Tracking

Schedule status reporting is sometimes exclusively associated, from a purely formal point of view, with the deviation analysis between planned figures and actual numbers. But this approach may not provide enough insight about the delays in a project if the planned value is not as accurate as needed. The classical methodology assumes that cost and schedule deviation analyses and indexes such as the cost performance index (CPI) or schedule performance index (SPI) behavior analyses are the main sources of information on project performance. This is fully true when the WBS has been carefully prepared, documented, and inserted into the PMIS, but sadly this is not always the case. The WBS quality does depend on a variety of factors such as the business area common practices, the project manager experience, the degree of the quality of supervision of the WBS definition process, and many other influences. This necessitates finding a method to eliminate project failure, assuming that the failing project may not have, among other shortfalls, a good WBS. Consequently it is a wise decision to look for additional indicators that can provide further information to complement the classical deviation indexes. Hence, in order to have available additional data on schedule performance tracking, it was decided to include a specific simple milestone status reporting system in the PMIS. This system helps to report, at the planning phase of the project, the foreseen major milestones calendar, including not only the contractual milestones and the invoicing milestones, but also the intermediate milestones that the project manager may consider relevant to recognize the status of the project schedule. The project manager is also asked to input data related to the milestones acceptance method and the actual acceptance date or the negotiated new date. This way, a more complete view of the schedule status is available in the reports provided by the system.

Another good indication of schedule compliance comes from analyzing the difference between the income value recognized in the project and the actual amount invoiced: the bigger this deviation, the greater the chances that the project will be in trouble. Consequently, this figure and its persistence in time constitute a good indication of potential difficulties in fulfilling calendar requirements. Even if the contract or the customer requirements justify an otherwise unjustifiable financial situation, they are still indicators of economic conditions that are not the most advisable for the economic health of the project.

In summary, the milestone accomplishment status and the amount of pending invoices and its persistence in time provide additional indicators of projects potentially in trouble and in this regard, are easier to track. Identifiers are assigned as indicators and their threshold values are assigned by the finance controllers of the business or management units.

Issues Reporting

The risk management process utilizes a very basic issue reporting system. Keep in mind that the risk management issue reporting system was initially considered as a complementary capability to document action plans for issues reporting. Action plans and issues reports may come directly from identified risks becoming actual problems, or they may come from unreported or unknown risks as real problems requiring an action to be taken. Issues are classified as critical or serious, and dates, action plans, and responsible people are allocated. A specific identifier is also assigned to provide insight into the seriousness of unresolved issues at a specific moment in time, as severity is reasonably reduced when an action plan is in place.

This issues reporting feature was also conceived as the appropriate place to summarize and report project manager's specific action plans when their projects had been marked, signifying that additional information needed to be input into the PMIS and stored for follow-up purposes.

A Special Approach for Pending Scope Changes

Another source of headaches for numerous small or medium-sized projects usually involves the need to provide quick answers to customer requests, namely for scope changes while executing a project. Many times, these requests are documented without the desired accuracy, and there may be a time when the project team is performing without the required contractual backup.

Change requests must always be analyzed and documented by the project manager, but it was found useful to provide a method through the PMIS by which the project manager reports requests for changes so the topic may be specifically addressed through the monitoring and reporting activities. The decision was made to include a specific identifier cipher to report projects with scope changes pending negotiation and formal contractual modification. The project manager is required to report and record the estimated cost of the requested change and the amount requested for negotiation. Once the agreement is reached, the agreed amount is included in the PMIS for documentation purposes. In addition to the formal processes required to produce the actual change in the contract, the WBS or the schedule of the project is revised to show the approved change.

Now we want to see all the data and indicators at once to monitor the status of the projects. Once the additional indicators have been defined, the next step was to be able to display all of them in a simplified and efficient view where the principal project data are shown, including the value of the new parameters and indicators. To achieve that, a projects monitor tool was also defined, allowing each user to quickly display results for each project under his or her responsibility in a simple format. Results included general project data (responsible people, customer, project dates, etc.), financial data (margin, income, contract value, etc.) and performance measurement indicators. These indicators include:

- Risks, milestones, scope changes pending, and unresolved issues status indicators
- The performance indexes (CPI, SPI)
- Indicators related to financial performance (invoices pending, payments pending, and margin rate deviation)

All indicators have assigned values (green, yellow, red) in accordance with thresholds defined by the units' financial controllers: green indicates compliance; yellow indicates out of compliance, but still manageable; and red indicates out of compliance and in need of immediate attention. For example:

- Unpaid invoices of the amount of $100K may deserve green, yellow, or red colors, depending on which levels are considered appropriate in that area or business unit
- Projects with one risk with Severity 8 or higher may get the risk indicator in red for a business unit, while a different business unit's project in a similar situation may get a yellow indicator

The CPMO defined a baseline of values for every indicator, but the BU controllers are allowed to modify those. Justification for the deviation from the baseline needs to be available upon request. The projects monitor also included the capability to produce reports with all the information displayed using different filtering features that can facilitate the analysis of the data when big groups of projects are selected.

Reporting the Status of the Project Automatically into the PMIS

Another feature was added to the projects monitoring tool to facilitate the reporting process. If further explanation or additional information about the status of the project indicators is needed, an icon in the projects monitor allows the user to send an automatic message to the project manager requesting that the project manager fill out a form to address project status concerns. The project monitor reports are available online and will be stored in the PMIS for review and historical purposes.

Design Phase Summary

The design phase ended with the full definition of the risk management tool and the projects monitor as well as project milestones, issues, and scope change reporting tools to:

- Help the project manager forecast potential project failures
- Provide a simplified display of the status of the projects to project sponsors
- Facilitate reporting of the project situation by the project manager directly into the PMIS

Project Implementation: Defining Success Criteria and Follow-up Indicators

The actual development of the risk management tool took place while the rest of the features were being designed during the testing phase of the risk tool. At the end, an acceptable package was ready to be implemented and available for general use by the project managers as a new set of improvements to the PMIS.

Once verified, the package was published, and after a series of guidance sessions, the package was officially switched on in the PMIS. Guidance sessions consisted of a series of basic presentations of the new system features to selected groups of project managers and the responsible account. Additionally a specific training package was prepared and added to the regular periodic project managers training courses.

A formal announcement was then issued to every project manager requesting that risk management plans be incorporated into the PMIS for all projects above a specified contract threshold value. The message identified a start date for any project requiring a risk management plan. Projects would not be authorized without fulfilling this requirement. Additionally the project managers were asked to provide milestone plans and use the scope change pending notification and issue reporting as required by the project's evolution.

Reporting of Initial Results

After the first month of using the new features, the projects monitor started to display actual data that the controllers could use to point out and track selected projects. This data showed deviations and warning indicators. Besides the display and the project-filtering capabilities, several types of reports were made available to the users to evaluate the status of the different parameters and to facilitate the preparation of the data to be presented at the BU's steering and governance committees. They were asked to prepare a basic *watch list* of projects requiring special supervision, and based on that list, to prepare the report to be analyzed at the monthly review meetings. Nevertheless, several questions arose right away:

- How well are we doing with the implementation of the improvements?
- How are the different companies and business units reacting?
- Are we reaching every project we should?
- In relation to the controller tasks, how can the system help them in the project selection process for the watch list?

In order to answer these questions, two new sets of indicators were defined and implemented while the system was being used. The first set of indicators identified coverage, estimated cost impact, and exposition related to risk management. The second set addressed the level of attention given to the project selection activity for the watch list.

Risk Coverage, Estimated Cost Impact, and Exposition

A first measure of the risk associated with a set of projects is determining how many of those projects have a project risk plan. What the responsible manager of resources may be more concerned about is how much of their budget has coverage with a risk plan. The answer is determined with a simple straightforward calculation by adding the budget of the projects that actually have a risk plan defined and approved in the PMIS, and expressing it as a percentage of the overall budget. The level of risk coverage required by each BU may depend on several factors and is closely related with the built-in risk associated with the profile of projects the BU deals with. For instance, a business unit generally providing support for banking software with contracts renewed every year does not have the same overall risk in its activity as a BU developing a new air traffic control system. In this regard, every BU should define their target risk coverage figures and issue the appropriate rules over and above the corporate regulations.

Risk management implies following a systematic process for identification, evaluation, response planning, and risk status monitoring. But project risk indicators by themselves may not be sufficient to draw management's attention to the project if they do not provide a clear warning on how much they should be concerned by the project risk plan and risk inventory. Consequently it was decided to use more obvious figures, providing at the same time a tool to objectively compare one project risk against another. This required creating a new indicator based on a figure that clearly identifies the potential risk cost to the project.

Once the project has its risks identified and evaluated and the response plans have been defined, every risk has a residual value and a possible cost impact. This approach conforms to every risk being assigned an estimated cost impact (ECI) based on its probability of occurrence and estimated impact on remaining project costs. This value is supported by a qualitative estimation providing an order of magnitude estimate of which part of the risk impact in cost is not being addressed by a response plan. As a consequence of the plan, there is a residual risk whose estimated value in cost provides an indication of how much the BU manager should be concerned about this risk. In fact, this is a lot of information for the BU director. Of course, a committed manager is also concerned about how well the response plans are being followed, but this is part of the standard responsibilities of the project managers. If they design a project plan, including the plans to mitigate the risks, they are supposed to follow the plans, try to achieve the desired goals, or alternatively, define new action plans. In summary, the ECI is becoming a popular indicator of how well we are managing our risks in a specific project. Going a little bit further, adding all the calculated ECIs in MUs (or in any predefined set of projects) may give us an indication of how well the risks are handled in that specific set. The ECI provides a valid indication of how great the cost impact might be of the risks for which the project manager has no response plans. Consequently, the ECI, expressed as a percentage of the remaining budget of a portfolio of projects, provides a valid indication of the exposure of the portfolio to the identified risks.

The two indicators shown in Figure 17.2 illustrate the degree of implementation of the risk management process in a project portfolio. Acceptable figures should be defined by each BU and reviewed during the portfolio strategic review process beyond the corporate guidelines and in accordance with the business characteristics.

As mentioned earlier, the figures are also available for a predefined set of projects with some features in common, for instance, when sharing the same customer.

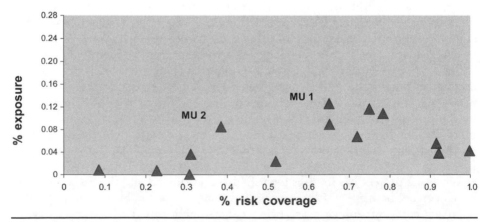

Figure 17.2   Management units (MUs): exposure vs. risk coverage.

Cover and exposure are also available for the surveillance of those sets of projects if required.

In summary, at the project portfolio level, the following indicators were added to the system:

- Coverage—Percentage of the portfolio value covered with a risk plan in the PMIS
- Exposure—Estimated percentage of the overall cost impact in the portfolio

In the end, coverage is supposed to provide a good indication of the level of implementation of the new risk management system in project management practices. It has been showing a progressive growth towards figures close to 100 percent in some business units. Other units are displaying a behavior that appears to be related to the yearly contracting cycle for their type of business. In some of these cases, it looks as if they are reaching a maximum at a certain value, for instance, a 60 percent level of coverage before fluctuating. It is probably due to the fact that as of today, risk plans are not mandatory for all projects and some level of autonomy is left to the units, depending on the type of projects they handle. Therefore a technical assistance contract may not require a risk plan.

The exposure figures will probably evolve toward more stable values, characterizing in some way every management or business unit, and allow a subsequent detailed analysis to look for a further reduction or in support of other management decisions.

A specific report was designed to show to the upper management the evolution of the coverage and the value of other indicators, such as ECI per management unit, coverage, and exposure for each of the business units under their responsibility. The report allows them to prompt the unit managers for further risk management plans, improve the existing plans, and review the exposure figures. The report provides further risk-related information for the strategic decision-making process.

Level of Attention: Preparing the Watch List for the Portfolio Risk Status Report

With the system in place and the data available and ready for analysis by the unit or project managers and the controllers, another fact became clear; preparing the projects watch list required specific additional dedication. This required analyzing data (sometimes for many projects), developing status indicators with a systematic approach and a consistent set of criteria, and efficiently detecting projects in danger. The controllers were assigned a dedicated parameter for each project to mark the level of attention (LOA) that the project deserved. By reviewing the project indicators and the history, they knew about the project and marked the project with a LOA value ranging from *very low* to *very high*, or a special state called *requiring intensive care* (RIC). Every project with an LOA value above *high* was included in the watch list, and the project manager was requested to fill out a situation report in the system.

In order to fulfill the constraint of not creating additional workload for the controllers, it was decided to design a simple tool that would automatically build a portfolio risk status report. The report would be based on output of the risk management processor and would include the following information, with graphical diagrams where feasible:

- Coverage and exposition of the project portfolio
- List of projects under special surveillance, including some basic financial information on each project and the situation report prepared by the project manager
- List of projects without a risk plan
- List of projects with risk plans that have higher values of cost impact estimations (ECI values)

The weakest part of the process was the requirement to prepare the watch list to ensure that no project is disregarded or underestimated. It was clear that with more people looking at the indicators, the probability of missing a failing project would be smaller, but the constraint was to use the people and teams available—basically the financial controllers—for the first phase. It was decided then to add some more intelligence to the projects monitor tool so the system would propose an LOA value that the financial controller could use as as a strating point.

Subsequently, a basic algorithm was defined to provide a suggested assessment for the LOA parameter, taking into account not only the main indicators, but also the absolute figures of the contract. This value was called the *calculated level of attention* (CLOA), and it is mainly intended to provide to each project a parameter from very low to very high. This way, the controllers could look primarily at the CLOA parameter value for each project, and based on that (and on their knowledge of the overall financial status of the project), prepare their monthly project watch list status for later review with the steering committees.

The CLOA algorithm includes a simple formula that calculates what is referred to as *indicators severity*, which is based on the value of the project status indicators. Most of the indicators take into account CPI, risk status, schedule, and issues, with some of them being ignored in order to not weigh too heavily the influence of some aspects of the projects status. In this way, the system estimates an initial LOA from very low to very high. The algorithm then continues with some corrections to this first estimate, taking into account other data such as the progress of the project, the absolute value of the contract, the actual status of invoices pending, etc. At the end, a final CLOA is provided to the controllers for their consideration when preparing the watch list.

Implementation Phase Summary: The New System at Work

By incorporating features such as the CLOA, the portfolio risk status report, and the management report with the evolution of risk coverage and exposures, the system has entered into a phase where data concerning project and portfolio risk performance are being periodically produced and analyzed.

The new capabilities of the system are being widely used throughout the enterprise, although there are still some companies in the group in a preliminary stage of incorporation of the processes. There also are some MUs where the use of the tools is somewhat reduced mainly because of the type of projects they handle. Those cases are specifically being addressed by the CPMO to improve the use of the new system features.

As a mean value, the watch list of projects under close surveillance because their indicators may reach (at this time) 3–4 percent of the total number of projects is shown in Figure 17.3. Periodic situation reports issued by their project managers are being stored for historical purposes.

Every month the business units' controllers analyze the LOA parameter of the project under their responsibility and issue modifications, if required, to the watch list. They select and mark from the list those projects that deserve to be included in the specific automatic risk report that is provided by the PMIS. The MU and BU governance committees include in their regular agenda the review of such reports and the analysis of the action plans that should reduce the chances of failure, and in consequence, should increase the opportunities to achieve their strategic goals.

The local PMOs, where available, are issuing plans oriented to improve the quality of the risk-related data provided to the PMIS so they can also use the new indicators for a better detailed follow-up of the projects portfolio and programs

LOA type	Number of projects
RIC	20
Very high	23
High	66
Medium	441
Low	2442
Very low	166
Not applicable	1332
Pending evaluation	15

Figure 17.3   LOA distribution example.

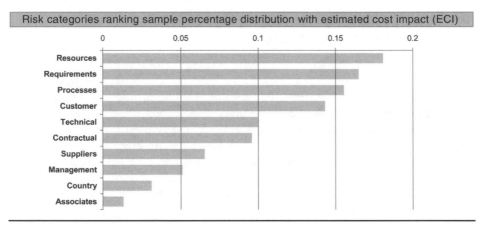

Figure 17.4   Risk impact rating.

under their responsibility. Figure 17.4 is an example of risk-related areas of possible improvement.

The quality assurance groups are reviewing their processes to incorporate checking of the adherence and compliance to the new company risk management standards, and incorporating the specific requirements of the business if required. All of the project's monthly data available from the projects monitor and the risk management processes are stored for historical purposes. It will be possible to track the evolution of specific project indicators and to find out if and when the system detected a possible project failure.

The CPMO watches over the whole process, aiming to promote the correct use of the new features and looking to explain, when required, the new processes and their objectives to new users. Periodically the CPMO analyzes the overall status of the risk management plans and issues recommendations to the project managers to gain efficiency in the use of the tools. In the same way, the CPMO reviews the handling by the business units' controllers of the LOA and CLOA parameters and provides instructions and guidance for its correct application and interpretation.

Lessons Learned and Next Steps

Process Summary

It may be helpful to summarize the main steps in the development of the events so we can highlight the relevant facts and use them for future project improvement. The whole process started with:

- Acknowledgement by senior managers of the need for a change in the project management methodology

This was followed by:

- Defining the scope and direction of the improvement, and deciding who is going to lead the change process

There probably was not explicit and clear evidence that the facts were happening this way, except perhaps to just a few people, but no more is needed. This is what is required to lead the change if the right sponsorship is in place, and of course, as in any other nonspeculative project, if targets and a precise schedule are clearly defined from the beginning. Targets, in this case, eliminate major failure in projects or evidence the need to have an effective risk plan in place for every project of a certain tier.

There came a time when the groups involved, namely the CPMO, the local PMOs with recognized leadership, the PMIS engineering support, and the financial controller's representatives met together to define the functional requirements and a preliminary design of the changes. This process set the stage for the preparation by the CPMO of the formal support of the changes, which updated the methodology to ensure coherence with the existing global enterprise project management methodology.

During the detailed design of the new functionalities, a set of key performance indicators (KPIs) were discussed, clarified, defined, and agreed, then used as pointers or targets that indicated the direction and goals for detailed development. It is very important at this stage to maintain coherence of KPIs with the methodological basis of the system, so they are indicators of the basic processes and not indicators of specific business needs or temporary situations.

Once the new monitoring capabilities were installed, the need for additional indicators of the implementation process was quickly addressed and resolved as it identified a need for going a step further, from just monitoring to actually managing the projects portfolio.

First Results

After the first year of implementation of the enhancements to the PMIS, upper management felt more comfortable with its ability to detect possible project failures.

No new major failing projects have occurred since the start of the process, which formally began when the preparation of a risk management plan was mandatory for projects beyond a certain contract value. We may presume that the early warning system is delivering some positive results, but checking on the stability of the process will be required, as well as monitoring how clearly its advantages are being perceived by the users. Most of all, there will be a need for validating how the project managers are adopting the new set of practices. We will need to verify that the implemented changes are defining, *de facto*, a new level of performance in project management, and this new level implies a higher quality of performance. One outcome that is becoming clear at this time is that the risk management process is now a substantial part of the project management methodology. It has become an asset of the company.

Overall, this process took around two years and the company has entered into a new stage of project management implementation. On one hand, the expected results are being reached, but new needs have been detected, namely related to specific training that is needed to improve the quality of the risk plans and to getting more efficient indicators for portfolio and program management.

Both the risk coverage and the portfolio exposure are becoming broadly adopted concepts to be used as references on how well a portfolio is being governed. They are becoming objective targets to measure portfolio managers' performance.

The ECI value is becoming a good indicator of the level of impact the project manager allocates to the project risks, but it appears it still does not represent a solid value of the seriousness of the residual risks, namely because of the lack of background and experience with systematic risk-prevention reporting and how to evaluate the foreseen positive impact of the mitigation and contingency plans. It is probably a matter of time to validate and consolidate the processes, but in order to further support it, the governance teams are giving instructions to do whatever is required to have strong backup for the residual risk analysis and evaluation in support of the ECI indicator and, consequently, in support of the portfolio exposure figure validation.

As an added value of the data-gathering opportunity created by the projects monitor, another application was defined, although its full use is still pending further development and publishing. It is called *clients monitor*, and it includes a direct global view of customer performance in a single line per management unit. The facility provides general and financial data sorting by customer identification with a direct link to the projects monitor. It allows for a straightforward relationship of the data associated with a specific customer while providing a detailed view of the projects concerned. This feature was considered as a first step in the process of designing a project selection capability when a full portfolio management process is incorporated into the system. Development of sound KPIs is still pending an in-depth requirements gathering phase, but the data are available and it is just a matter of time for project performance and risk-related indicators sorted by customer to become available, providing additional sources of information for the decision-making processes.

With regard to the CPMO, it is becoming the main company-wide reference and authority for any issue related to project management methodology. Requests for PMIS improvements or modifications, questions, and suggestions are being addressed from the management and business units primarily through the corporate PMO.

Things to Improve or Think About

Looking back to the design and the implementation process itself, there are several aspects that will need to be improved:

- Some of the business or management units had their own stable risk management process in place not integrated with the enterprise project management system. The required change process to switch from one system to another was not fully addressed from the beginning and it required specific planning later on. Nevertheless, the most critical aspect was convincing and selling the advantages of the new integrated approach to the representative unit decision makers. We found out that unit managers support corporate decisions and initiatives when it comes to methodological improvements that create added value to their business.
- There was not a good communication plan of the new features in the PMIS, which at the end, meant that the messages were not clearly understood from the beginning. Some time had passed before it was evident that this was not *just another corporate requirement*, and also before it was clear that the need of a requirement risk plan incorporated into the PMIS was something new in the project managers' lives.
- Once the facilities were functioning, the effort required for their maintenance and modifications was higher than foreseen. The consequence was that some features were not as usable as needed, generating inefficiencies in the use of the obtained data.
- Some features (e.g., scope changes pending, milestone planning) are infrequently used, as the focus has initially been on risk management full implementation.
- Some units, businesses, companies, etc. may require other particular KPIs that are not included at the corporate or enterprise level. In the present strategic organizational design, defining, creating, and using those KPIs is a need that must be resolved at the corresponding local level. An example of this is the need for defining specific KPIs to analyze the behavior of projects that are being executed under strongly horizontalized conditions.
- The risk management module is strictly oriented to handle internal impact of risks, and does not attempt to answer the question of how to produce risk-management reports to be shared with the customer or with other organizations. It is possible to take some of the reports produced by the system and use them as inputs to local tools that may be used to manage risks together with the customer, but there is no general approach discussed and implemented yet in this regard.

Next Steps

New upgrades to the PMIS are being considered by the CPMO. The most significant of which are related to the incorporation of the methodology improvement brought by the new PMI® standards in regards to program and portfolio management lifecycles. Those two areas may provide additional value to the organization if they get the benefit of an integrated approach with the standard enterprise project management methodology and if they get an integrated handling within the PMIS. In fact, the incorporation of the projects monitor is evolving to the full development of those two concepts as a natural consequence of the PMIS evolution.

They will probably need a careful analysis of the best practices in place, so a complete definition of the applicable lifecycles may be defined in an acceptable way. Again, as the case described, it will be required to take into account what is already being done in this regard in the different BUs and the concepts that are being used by lead program and portfolio managers to handle their responsibilities. Perhaps one of the first steps will be to formalize in a methodology document the basis of the concepts to be implemented into the PMIS as a result of the preliminary research.

Until now the projects portfolio concept is nearly exclusively dedicated at the PMIS level to provide summary figures of the results of each basic organizational unit pertaining to the strategic targets. This is a major capability of the present system, but it will be useful to improve the concept by adding the lifecycle concept (on a yearly basis) to the organizational unit and to provide the capability to integrate projects being executed with future projects at the PMIS level. This will provide a complete view of the business state and include a project selection or prioritization mechanism to ensure that the right projects are selected to be executed in accordance with each unit's strategic design.

The project portfolio concept used at the organizational level of the company will define the portfolio lifecycle, and, as in the case described here, will be required to review it from the point of view of the PMI standard, deducing any possible contradiction of missing steps in the process. In this regard, one aspect that has already been pointed out is the need for a specific risk management process at the portfolio level. The process will require having the possibility of accepting inputs from the portfolio level itself and also inputs coming out from escalated risk at the project level.

In line with the above, the full integration of the risk management processes from the projects level to the management and units level would allow the consolidation of an efficient enterprise risk management process, thus integrating project data with other risk management plans not strictly associated to projects, but with the organizational units and the businesses themselves.

The full incorporation of the program concept and its lifecycle into the PMIS will be perhaps a little bit more demanding because of the special difficulties of the benefit realization cycle itself, usually on a multiannual basis, which needs to be handled on a different timeline. It will probably only be fully resolved when the projects portfolio management lifecycle is defined and in place.

Whatever is the next set of improvements, it will require strong support and sponsorship from senior management. As seen with the development of the case described, it does constitute a definitive requirement for the success of these kinds of methodology change projects.

Finally, in another direction of improvements, the change implemented into the methodology and the PMIS shall allow for a next stage where those new figures are controlled and analyzed so new process improvements may be defined and implemented to standardize, measure, control, and improve.

Author Biography

Since 2008, Enrique Sevilla has been in charge of the corporate project management office at Indra, a Spanish multinational company with 29,000 employees and subsidiary companies or delegations in many countries. Its business interests include areas such as air traffic control, defense applications, radar systems, and all kinds of IT applications.

While at Indra, Enrique acted as project or program manager from 1985 to 2007 and oversaw a wide variety of contracts, most of them in the defense business. It included a stay from 1985 to 1987 in St. Louis, Missouri, US, for a Spanish F-18 support program.

From 1972 to 1985, Enrique worked for a multinational communications company (an ITT subsidiary at the time), acting first as a real-time software development engineer and then as a technical leader responsible for the development, integration, and installations of different projects. It included stays of two years in Paris and five years in Rio de Janeiro.

18

From Start to Flight Level: Implementing Project Portfolio Management at a Midsized Airline

Ulrich Aigner

Introduction

This case study involves an airline that works as a group and consists of a national carrier that focuses on business travel and long-haul destinations, a regional division that is mainly responsible for regional traffic, and another division that is offering leisure travel and charter operations.

In late 2008, this airline group was acquired by another airline. The deal took effect after final approval of the required governing body at the end of 2009. The carrier maintains its profit and loss responsibility but will be embedded into the larger holding.

Currently, the overall financial situation is not ideal, as the airline was back in the red in 2009. The financial trend has been positive over the past few years; however, fuel prices and the economic crisis have significantly impacted the profitability of the company. In 2010, the trend and forecast are promising, and it is hoped to be profitable again during 2011.

The IT division (corporate project and IT services) has about 120 managers and is the home of the office of corporate project management (CPM), which is comprised of a team of 525 full-time employees (FTEs). IT CPM is responsible for company-wide project management with the following duties:

- Process ownership for project and project portfolio management
- Designing, implementing, and maintaining the project management (PM) and project portfolio management (PPM) methodology
- Offering internal PM training at two levels—one for project managers and one for project owners
- Providing coaching to project managers
- Managing projects and programs that cannot be assigned to a specific division
- Preparing and maintaining the project portfolio
- Owner and user support for PM and PPM tools

Description of the Project Landscape

The company is facing a growing number of projects every year. From 2006 to 2007, there was an increase of 9 percent followed by 12 percent in 2008. Hence the quantity of projects is climbing faster than the yearly increase of passengers. But it is also seen that an increasing number of projects are stopped before reaching their goals or are not fulfilling the project management standards.

From the perspective of CPM, it is necessary to distinguish between two groups. On one side, it is necessary to know how many projects are handled with involvement of the IT department and how many are handled within the business divisions only.

On the other side, starting in early 2007, projects have been split into two categories: smaller projects with a budget of up to EU 50,000 (internal and external costs) and larger projects with a budget of more than EU 50,000. Formerly, projects were divided into small, medium and large sized projects. Classifications were made using seven criteria such as the number of departments involved, number of team members, internal or external partners, and so on. That grouping was skipped in an effort to reduce the complexity and has been switched to the mentioned classification, now influenced only by the project budget.

The distinction between projects with or without IT is important, as CPM is situated in the IT department. Therefore it is possible that some other departments think that they are not concerned with the defined standards of project management and project portfolio management.

The share of projects without IT is steadily increasing. Although IT is an inherent part of daily life, and even if only a computer will be installed (e.g., during a relocation of an office), it is counted as a project with IT involvement. There are certain areas where IT involvement is not noteworthy, such as the phase-in of a new aircraft or technical changes that have to be made to an aircraft.

The project manager has to be a member of the department that either is initiating the project, or is expecting the biggest benefit out of it. Previously, the project manager (who was also the main programmer) was from the IT department because there were no official projects outside IT. This situation created a lot of problems as the projects mostly ran late, overspent the budget, or delivered without the required quality. The next step was *double project managership*, but that also created problems concerning the responsibilities between the project managers from the IT department and the business units. Currently, if IT is involved, an IT coordinator is assigned to the project manager to support him with IT topics.

Since the business units of this company are very functionally oriented, projects are only distinguished between:

- Business unit projects without IT (e.g., setting up a new customer service)
- Business unit projects with IT (e.g., new software for customer handling)
- Projects with building or construction (e.g., office relocation abroad)
- Pure IT projects (e.g., implementing a new operating system on every computer)

The second differentiation is the split into small projects (called *task forces*) and all other projects. The monetary boundary of EU 50,000 has been set up by the controlling department and is arbitrary (equates to the limit that a head of a division is allowed to sign). The big advantage is that task forces face a shorter list of required signatures to get an approved project budget, as they usually are of limited organizational complexity (only one division involved except IT and facility management). The boundary was a compromise between project management and controlling, as the latter required a formal project if the expected budget is higher than EU 10,000. Since it was impossible to start an official project without a budget larger than EU 50,000, the less administrative task force has been accepted to handle the smaller topics.

Task forces were introduced in 2007, and accounted for 50 percent of all projects finished in 2008. But figures of the current running projects show that task forces are now leveling off at about a third, hence reaching the expected share.

All official projects that are currently executed have an average budget of around EU 500,000 (internal and external effort of the top five projects is an average of EU 1.2 million).

From that point of view it shows that we handle rather small projects (compared to other industries) at about 100 projects a year. The annual figures are highly divergent and show no clear trend. Exceptions are common and usually the company faces one to two programs a year that boost the average budget due to their large volume (typically EU 5 to 25 million).

Nevertheless, it is obvious that the company cannot call itself a project-oriented company at all, as only a little more than one percent of the operating revenue is handled through projects, although there are divisions that are very project-oriented such as IT and facility management. All other business units use projects for any implementation, adaption, or change that is handled outside of daily business.

Regarding the magic triangle (deliverables, costs, and schedule) the airline is doing fine in delivering on budget and on quality, but is rather poor in adherence to schedules. For every project or task force that is delivered, the project owner has been faced with an average delay of three calendar months. That is an average delay of one-third regarding the cycle time. Notwithstanding that these figures look bad, it is understandable because the budget is limited and a certain quality of the deliverables has to be reached—therefore, schedules are expanded.

A second reason is justified by the project manager and the project team members themselves. Usually they get their project jobs in addition to their regular duties—companywide, only about five to ten project managers are assigned fully to their projects—and if time is running short, their daily business takes priority.

Start Level: From Starting to Establishing Project Management

Project management practices have been fundamentally implemented since 1998, but in 1999 they were formalized. Once project management in the IT division became formally oriented, this became the driver behind establishing enterprise-wide professional project management. It began with IT management supporting the establishment of a formal requirement to manage all IT investments using project management practices. They began to achieve this objective by designing a project management methodology based on International Project Management Association (IPMA) standards and developing techniques for designing the methodology in-house. It was rather easy to establish project management practices inside IT because the need and advantage of doing so was clearly understood by the staff. The members of the project management office, which was part of the IT development department, received training from a consulting company to pass the certification program of IPMA.

In 2000, the IT project management office was used as a program management office (PMO) to manage a program—the alliance change from the old partner to the new one. A large number of business unit members were involved in the change that had to be done within six months. It soon became obvious to the company that project management is able to provide benefits to the whole organization rather than just the IT division. In 2002, project management was shifted formally to the top management level as a department inside IT. The PMO then earned company-wide responsibility and process ownership for project management.

The next three years focused on training, coaching, and supporting the project managers in the business units. By the end of 2005, the first project management tool was implemented. The tool boosted the quality of project management as it enabled CPM to have a look at all projects, assure a certain level of project management quality, and provide a single source for handling projects by removing the use of templates as well as other project management software tools.

A monthly reporting system was established to list all the currently active projects with consolidated information provided via e-mail to the board of directors and vice presidents. Everyone has access to look up the projects in the report via the Intranet.

For the first time, the annual budget preparation in the summer of 2006 was not only submitted for projects with IT involvement, but also for all other projects, thereby closing the last gap in the project management cycle illustrated in Figure 18.1.

Flight Preparation: Reasons for Implementing Project Portfolio Management

As project management became more accepted within the organization as well as more mature, the PMO assessed itself, comparing the current status quo with the available possibilities to gain maximum benefit.

Project management had been implemented outside the IT division in a missionary style due to limited hierarchical possibilities. By showing the advantages and convincing the persons concerned, project management found its users companywide; some were fans and others simply accepted the benefits.

That missionary effort was good in reaching a certain level and pervasion, but could not develop any further. The three main problems described in the following sections describe the situation before project portfolio management had been implemented (as portfolio management was seen as a possible solution to solving or diminishing these problems).

Uneven Maturity

In an attempt to rank the company using the capability maturity model integration (CMMI®), the company fits on three levels, but does not fulfill them completely.

The main business of the airline is to transport people from Point A to Point B in the most convenient way possible. That is a straight-line business with strictly repeatable processes to trust in. This has been on the minds of the employees for the last decade. Processes are more or less stable, and if certain situations require immediate attention, every effort is made to assure the best travel experience for our customer. That means sometimes unusual or unconventional reactions.

Figure 18.1 Established project management process.

The divisions that have to deal with the customer directly like to follow defined processes but require enough freedom to leave the beaten track.

On the other side, we deal with divisions that are supporting the passenger-handling units and prefer clear decisions about what has to be done, as their daily business is maintaining and delivering new benefits.

The first group views project management as an administrative and bureaucratic hurdle, but as a necessary evil. They are switching between level two and three. The latter group recognizes the advantages of a clearly defined and repeatable project management process. Their maturity is ranked higher and is therefore around a stable three.

Division Blindness

The second main problem is that projects are initiated to solve a specific topic that hurts or hampers the daily business of the particular division. Seldom are the project owners accepting incisions to their intentions in favor of company-wide strategies. That is not caused by ignorance, but by the belief that their projects deliver the highest benefit to the organization. Hence, single-sighted goals are described in an organized way, but without following an enterprise-wide aim. We settled on the term *division blindness* for setting local goals over the company strategy.

Limited Awareness of Top Management

Top management accepted project management as a state-of-the-art methodology to handle complex topics. Where projects are useful (from the project owner's point of view) or required for getting an official budget, the company methodology is used.

By implementing a project overview report in late 2005, management gained its first comprehensive awareness about which projects are running in their single division or department. Furthermore they were able to look outside their division box to get a feeling about which projects are running in the other units and might affect their interests. But the overview was a static view and no central forced action was taken if projects were unsuccessful.

Although the board of directors was officially in support of company-wide project management, they also accepted some projects that were not tracked in the monthly project overview and offered project approval by becoming convinced in meetings rather than by trusting the controlling department.

As a solution to these problems and as the next step in project management evolution, project portfolio management (PPM) seemed to be the right answer. PMI® offered a guide for this with its *Standard for Portfolio Management*.

By coupling different projects into portfolios and networking them, it should prevent being blindsided in any single division, thus keeping the ship on course.

Takeoff: Initiating a PPM-implementation Project

In the summer of 2006, the director of CPM discussed with his team the idea of implementing project portfolio management to get rid of the described problems and support the development of project management maturity. The need to implement PPM was recognized first within the PMO and not by top management. It was therefore necessary to convince upper management to build up PPM and get its support and approval.

The vice president of the IT division was easily convinced, although support was limited because portfolio management was not ranked at the top of his personal action list. On the other hand, he set no boundaries and offered free possibilities to develop PPM and align our ideas directly with the CEO.

As the board of directors was the main focus of the planned efforts, a short meeting was arranged. Luckily a few months prior, a new CEO was appointed. With his personal experience and background, he was amazed that the company had not already installed portfolio management. Thus, an approval was given and the PMO was allowed to implement PPM.

Project Setup and Objectives

To start a project portfolio, it has to be clear what you want and how to do it. Furthermore, certain basic conditions have to be cleared, specified in detail, or installed.

Those clarifications do not seem to be directly linked to project management; rather they are the foundation of project portfolio management. Without them and especially without linking these to the projects, you will develop a project portfolio (merely a listing of certain current projects) but you will be far away from managing it.

To assure that comprehensive project management would help to connect projects directly to the company's benefit, it became necessary to apply more pressure via company hierarchy because CPM had reached its limit in spreading the methodology and ensuring a consistent project management standard. But to gain support from the board of directors, the PMO wanted to offer to them a direct benefit as well. Being mindful of the personal advantages of their work, they should assist and encourage project management voluntarily and honestly.

For this reason, project portfolio management seemed the right solution to address two problems with one initiative. By implementing PPM, the management board should gain advantages through:

1. A better overview of all running projects
2. Better control of the project landscape
3. Assuring focus on the company strategies (avoiding division blindness and ensuring top management attention)

By spreading the word that the board is more concerned with project management, the PM standard should be pushed to all levels and hence eliminate uneven maturity within the company—all of which should benefit the enterprise.

The director of CPM was the project owner, and a member of the team was assigned as project manager. As insisted by the vice president of IT, external consulting had to be used but had to be limited. Due to the experience of the PMO, the design could be developed internally. The consultant was used as a sparring partner; they showed him the ideas and intentions based on the knowledge of the project team and compared them to his external know-how. The strategic objectives of the projects were to:

1. Provide a way to ensure a connection between the company strategy and the projects
2. Install mechanisms to allow optimization of project portfolio results
3. Strengthen company-wide project management

The agreed operative objectives were to:

1. Design and reach agreement regarding project portfolio processes
2. Define reporting
3. Implement project portfolio management with the necessary infrastructure
4. Set up the first project portfolio group meeting

The decision was made not to implement a new software tool, but to use the existing software toolset. This decision was made because the project team wanted to stay focused on the main topic of PPM and not to deviate into a complex toolset implementation. Our existing project management tool, FocusPro (internal name of tool, custom made), built the foundation as a data provider via export of the necessary data into a business data warehouse and furthermore extracting the information and preparing the required reporting tables and charts. On the monetary side, the approved budget accounted for EU 30,000 for internal effort and EU 15,000 for consulting and adaptations of FocusPro.

In the following project WBS shown in Figure 18.2, it is obvious that the design phase (definition) was the most complex and intensive part of the project.

Reflection on Implementation

The basic portfolio process definitions were designed rather quickly. But deciding which metric would allow an easy and fair way to manage the project portfolio was very challenging, time consuming, and required a lot of discussion. There were some very strict ideas about which criteria were required, yet not every criterion could be technically executed into a report. In this matter, our consultant was of great help in sharing his experience.

The second main issue seemed simple but required greater discussion: *who will form the project portfolio group?* Our first thought was to assign all vice presidents

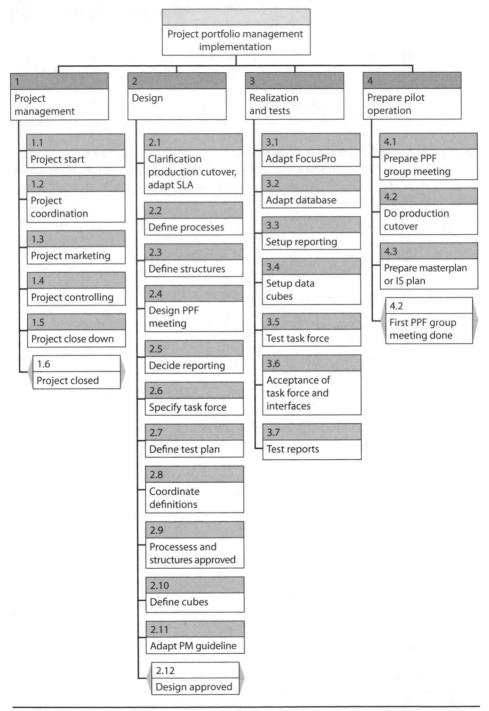

Figure 18.2 Work breakdown structure (WBS) of PPM-implementation project.

and the management board to the group. The VPs should have a deeper overview of the projects and act nearer to the market. But the main challenge would have been to get 23 division heads and two presidents together while handling a large portfolio group meeting and still assure a productive outcome. The next thought was to skip all heads that are not involved in projects. Ten divisions and two presidents would still have remained. Finally, the easy way was chosen: limit the portfolio group to the management board.

With that limitation, it was possible to design a straightforward group meeting and not exceed a reasonable meeting length; the quarterly meeting was set to run for 2.5 hours.

The technical setup (training for the PMO portfolio manager, build data cubes for getting the required information, etc.) had some downsides as not everything that the project team discussed could be implemented because the data handling would have been too complex.

The final results of the report designs were discussed with the head of the IT division instead of discussing it with top management. That was an experience that should not be ignored as this input sometimes brought us back to earth. Due to the enthusiasm of the project work, you get ideas on top of ideas until you have so much to tell or show about what a project portfolio could provide, it would create information overkill for the audience. That overkill could interfere with the objectives of portfolio management.

Another important issue to handle was the project marketing. It was decided to personally sell project portfolio management to every vice president to gain support and hence avoid a blocking risk. The short information meetings were rather surprising as there was no opposition (that had been originally expected) against project portfolio management. The reaction of the VPs had been mostly neutral—sometimes even positive—as they became aware of the benefits for them. That feedback supported our project work and prevented difficulty during the implementation.

Overall, the project was finished on time (within three months), below budget, and with the desired quality range. Only the first project portfolio group meeting had been delayed by one month due to time restrictions of the CEO.

Flight Level: Defined Project Portfolio Processes

The project team had to implement a lean and clear process to avoid misconceptions and help understanding. Thus the core process was designed in three basic steps: assign project, control project portfolio, and assure portfolio synergy (see Figure 18.3).

It was also important that, if possible, we avoid changing the established project management processes. As the project lifecycle is also following portfolio processes, we used the graphic in Figure 18.4 as a sales pitch in discussions

Figure 18.3   Core process of project portfolio management.

and pointed out where portfolio management takes effect and where a project manager or a project owner gets into contact with it.

PPM Step 1: Assign the Project

After a periodic check to see if the corporate strategies had changed or if the defined project portfolio strategy had to be updated (and therefore the portfolio criteria as well), projects have to populate the project portfolio via an assignment. Assigning a project to the portfolio has two steps and two possible methods.

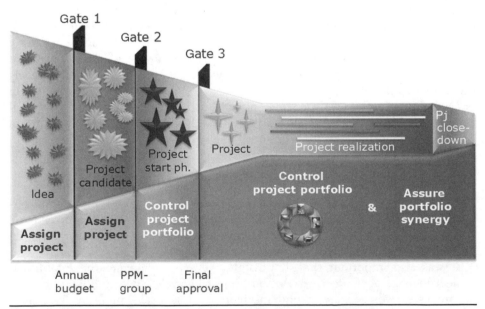

Figure 18.4   Project portfolio process compared to project lifecycle.

One method (the preferred one) is that a project idea is formed, put into the annual budget, and started at a certain time (i.e., planned projects).

Due to the nature of the business, not every project is known ahead of time; you have to react to certain environmental circumstances that require immediate action. In that case, there would be no planned budget and money would have to be withdrawn from other budget items. These are called *ad hoc* projects.

1. Planned projects—By early July, the annual budgeting process is started. Business units and IT are asked to name the planned projects for the following year. This initial planning of the projects is done on a high level (e.g., reason for the project, elementary objectives, total cash out, sum of internal effort, expected start and end date, etc.). After a review phase, controlling the budget is transferred to the enterprise resource planning system and the company's total budget is formed. That corresponds to Gate 1 in Figure 18.4. If the project is started in the budgeted year, it has an easier approval phase.

2. Ad hoc projects—These projects were unknown at the time of budgeting, and therefore have no money reserved for their realization. As it might be useful to start them anyway, they face a tighter check to ensure the project is necessary or beneficial (in general, at the expense of another project that has to be skipped).

The project portfolio group meeting is scheduled quarterly. Hence the project portfolio managers of the PMO visit the head of the divisions quarterly (usually accompanied by the appropriate directors) and compare the budget list with real life: are projects planned to start in the next three months proceeding as expected or are they postponed or cancelled? Furthermore, new (ad hoc) projects are anticipated and they have to provide the same information as is provided during annual budgeting—both types of projects must have verbal justification (description of benefits or why necessary) at that time.

With the aggregated information from the division portfolio meetings, the project portfolio group meeting is started. The group (board of directors) is asked if the listed projects will be allowed to start and prepare detailed planning. The PMO informs the persons concerned about the decisions and the project owner can assign a project manager to start the project.

PPM Step 2: Control the Project Portfolio

The project portfolio group meeting is used as an assignment stage, but also as a controlling meeting to govern the projects and assure that they are supporting the company's strategy (see Figure 18.5).

As a spin-off of project management, the project portfolio group is also informed (by the project manager) about critical projects (projects that are far behind schedule or budget) and decides on action items.

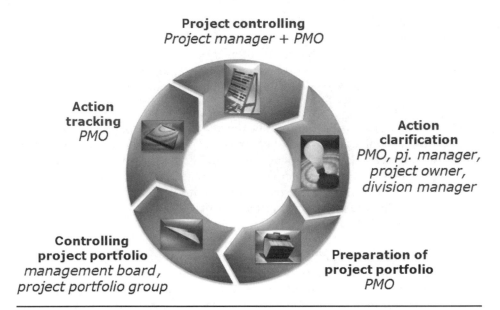

Figure 18.5　Process for controlling the project portfolio.

To get the required information for controlling the portfolio, we use the controlling meetings of the projects. The portfolio managers attend these meetings of the top-ranked projects (ranked by budget). Every project manager also has to update its project methods and plans in our PM tool. That provides the required input to prepare the portfolio group meeting by the PMO. Critical projects are discussed during the monthly division portfolio meetings where suggested action items are offered to get them back on track. If project manager suggestions are in line with the PMO's view, the consensus will be tracked by the PMO without feedback from the portfolio group. If there is dissent (e.g., suggested items were unsuccessful or no offer for improvement is recognizable), then this disagreement will be a topic for the portfolio group.

With the required information from project portfolio meetings and actual information from the PM tool and quarterly division portfolio meetings, we are able to prepare the project portfolio group meetings. The standard agenda for the meeting is:

1.　Information on and discussion of critical projects
2.　Current status of the project portfolio
3.　Approval for beginning project start phase
4.　Controlling of the project portfolio
5.　Any other items concerning the project portfolio or project management

Finally, the decisions of the group meetings are monitored and tracked by the PMO to assure their realizations.

PPM Step 3: Assure Portfolio Synergy

The toughest part is to gain synergy out of the portfolio. The project team focused on the implementation of a functional project portfolio management, assured strategy fitness of the projects, and tried to make the portfolio controllable. However the synergy items were mainly pushed to a further phase that had to be developed.

Nevertheless, quick wins were gained such as starting a light resource management inside IT (delivering core information about planned projects and rechecking availability of technical personnel) or establishing an escalation level to help to get resource alignment based on project category.

A major synergy that is usually gained with PPM is an optimized company-wide resource allocation. It was decided not to account for it due to two reasons:

1. Expected resistance in the line business divisions as they are not used to resource management
2. To avoid risking the goals of the implementation project by discussing or fighting over resource management and limiting complexity

Flight Check: Selection of Project Portfolio Management Criteria

Many new criteria were implemented during the set up of project portfolio management. Subsequently, a few selected criteria being used are:

Project Clustering

Project clustering is used as a primary classification of projects to decide if a business case and return on investment (ROI) has to be calculated. One of the four groups (see Figure 18.6) has to be decided and justified (either verbally or with an ROI).

Project Category

We are distinguishing between four categories from Group A (top, most important) to Group D (basic, necessary). Due to the financial situation, 60 percent of the calculated criterion is justified by the size of the ROI. The other 40 percent is based on the project's strategy fitness. This fitness has to be declared by the project owner who states on a scale of 0 (no support) to 3 (fully supported) at which level the project supports the appropriate strategy. We have a few projects in Group A and many projects in Group D (pyramid-shaped allocation).

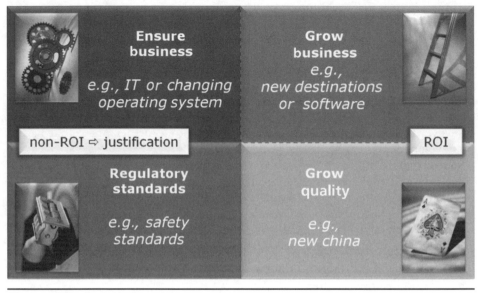

Figure 18.6   Project clustering.

The category is a practical advantage for the project managers because it prioritizes the right to use resources. If two projects are requesting the same resource, or one resource is blocked by another project, the one with the higher category has the right of way automatically. If projects are on the same level, the issue has to be discussed. The PMO can be used for escalation if no solution can be found (seldom necessary).

Value Proposition

The value proposition is the most powerful information provided to control the project portfolio. Figure 18.7 shows (based on the criteria necessary for the project category) the project landscape and where the projects should be.

The upper right quadrant contains the superstars (high strategy relevance, high ROI). The lower left quadrant should include the projects caused by regulatory standards or to ensure business (no strategy relevance and no ROI). For easier reading, a dotted line has been drawn showing the border between ideal projects and subideal projects.

If a new project is up for approval, it is shown on that chart and opens the door for discussion. The current situation of the company determines whether the portfolio group prefers strategic projects over financially attractive projects, or the other way around.

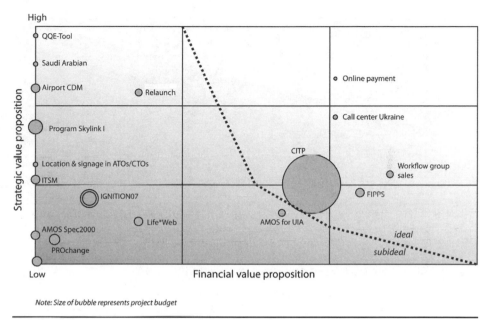

Note: Size of bubble represents project budget

Figure 18.7 Value proposition.

Share of Delayed Projects in the Portfolio

Delay is a major issue in our project landscape. The chart in Figure 18.8 shows how many projects of the current portfolio are delayed (behind approved project closure). Suspended, finished, and projects not approved are excluded. It is obvious that the implementation of PPM brought immediate success as the delay rate dropped in the first year of operations and continued the trend the following years!

Volplane: Current Situation of Project Portfolio Management

Advantages

A major benefit of PPM was that through project portfolio management, project management is not seen as limited to IT topics, but also as relevant for business unit topics. Thus, it strengthened project management and built up pressure in the business units to follow the corporate PM standard.

Furthermore vice presidents saw a big advantage in PPM as the quarterly division portfolio meeting (in addition to the monthly written overview) assures them the best overview of the projects that are handled within their budget. They also appreciate that an independent group is cross-checking the projects and can deliver an outside view and be a neutral unit for escalations.

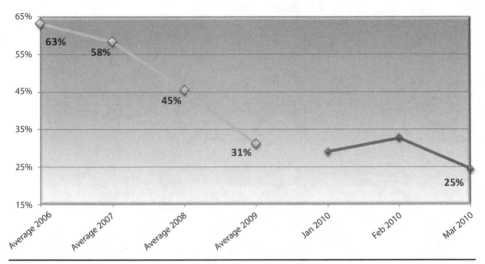

Figure 18.8   Share of delayed projects in portfolio.

As controlling division representatives were involved in the quarterly PPM meetings, they also recognized the advantages of a controlled environment—to know what is going on and act rather than react.

Challenges

The most crucial part is the project portfolio group and therefore the board of directors itself. Two big issues need to be handled appropriately in the near future:

1. The presidents have limited time available, project board meetings are periodically postponed, and one meeting in four is cancelled. Either it shows that the board trusts the PMO to do a good job or it is a sign that project portfolio management is not important to them.
2. More disappointing is when the controlling is not done as expected. The board expects that the controlling division is doing a critical check and therefore is eliminating projects that do not fit into the landscape. But controlling is figure oriented and therefore accepts projects that support no strategy if they have a positive ROI. So, the division blindness in favor of the company's strategy has been reduced but not eliminated.

It also has to be mentioned that the work for preparing the portfolio is higher than expected. A high number of meetings have to be handled, and there is some information chasing that needs to be done (e.g., because the deadline for the monthly status report has been forgotten again).

By early 2009, a new standardized PM tool had been implemented, that, among other things, offered a big help in reducing administrative work.

Furthermore, a few reports had been adjusted, skipped, or changed in their design to make them more understandable. The amount of information had also been reduced (only discussing projects with a budget higher than EU 500,000) to get the right focus.

Landing: Summary

Out of different circumstances (e.g., nonstrategic orientation of projects and uneven maturity regarding project management within the company), the project management office recognized the need for implementing project portfolio management to optimize projects. Support from top management has been assured, and a project has been set up to optimize the implementation. Definition, setup, and realization within the project took about seven months with the design and key figure calculation most laborious.

Although not everything is running as expected and leaves room for improvement, the bottom line is that project portfolio management has been implemented successfully, but some tuning is necessary to get the most out of it.

In early 2007, the first project portfolio group meeting was held, followed by recurrent meetings with the management board once every quarter. The last milestone in the development of project management was the implementation of a new and more advanced PM tool. With that tool (it went live in February 2009) the PMO gained new capabilities within project portfolio management as the new software offers advanced handling facilities and more ways to manipulate the provided data without involving IT specialists. The complete lifecycle of a project is now handled in one single tool and is cross-linked to the central financial data stored and processed in our enterprise resource planning system.

Author Biography

Ulrich Aigner has been practicing project management for 13 years and has developed and managed PMOs in two organizations. He is currently the director of CPM for one of the major European airlines where he is the process owner of project management and project portfolio management, responsible for PM methodology, PM training, PM coaching, PM audits, and preparing the PPM. His team is made up of five project management professionals with a combined 70 years of experience. He has a background in industrial engineering and was among the first in his country to be certified in project management by IPMA. He also has a Masters Degree in project and process management to bridge practice with education.

19

The PMO Maturity Cube: A Project Management Office Maturity Model

Americo Pinto, PMP, MBA;
Marcelo F. de Matheus Cota, PMP, MSc.;
Ginger Levin, PhD., PMP, PgMP

Introduction

In the late '90s through the early 2000s the theme of project management offices was beginning to be widely discussed in various books (Block & Frame, 1998; Dinsmore, 1999; Bolles, 2002; Crawford, 2002; Englund, Graham, & Dinsmore, 2003; Kendall & Rollins, 2003; Hill, 2004; Williams & Parr, 2004; Letavec, 2006). Studies are more recent in academic literature (Dai & Wells, 2004; Hobbs & Aubry, 2007; Aubry, Hobbs, & Thuillier, 2008; Hurt & Thomas, 2009), and their conclusions about the contribution or value of PMOs are ambiguous (Hurt and Thomas, 2009). In addition, one of the discoveries in the first study that presents a "reliable portrait of the population of PMOs" (Hobbs and Aubry, 2007) was that the function of 50 percent of the PMOs studied was to "monitor and control their performance." In other words, PMOs are concerned with assessing and measuring their own performance.

Recent qualitative studies (Aubry, Hobbs, & Thuillier, 2008) indicated that there is a degree of instability in the historical analysis of PMOs. This is a complex phenomenon and one that demands tools for evaluating the performance and constant reinvention of PMOs. Therefore a maturity model, as applied to PMOs, was developed and tested with the objective of helping to take an academic discussion to another level of complexity and making it possible for PMOs to carry out their own self-assessment. On developing the model, the authors came to the conclusion that the better the PMO delivers its services, and only the services related to the needed functions, the more the PMO is perceived as delivering value to its organization.

Since the end of the 1990s, there has been a major movement worldwide toward the creation of PMOs, which grew in intensity throughout the present decade (Dai and Wells, 2004; Hobbs and Aubry, 2007). Despite the common perception that a large number of the major companies in the market have at least one PMO in their organizational structure, Hurt and Thomas (2009) indicated that "the sustainability of PMOs is a tenuous issue."

In fact, PMOs arose because of different needs, but the vast majority had a greater objective in common: to obtain better results in those projects developed by the organization.

Over the last few years, while some of these initiatives have prospered and matured and created noticeable value for the organization, others have lost their vigor and support, and have suffered cuts and reductions or have even been eliminated altogether. Additionally, Hobbs and Aubry (2007) saw that there was a significant variation in the structure, assumed roles, and perceived value of PMOs, demonstrating the instability and the diversity in performance.

Successful PMOs are constantly being challenged to find the best way to ensure that their practices continuously mature. This observation shows that generally speaking, the perception of the value of the PMOs that are not capable of evolving tends to diminish over time, because as the organization itself matures, there is a demand that is aligned with the new needs arising from this process of organizational evolution. Aubry, Hobbs, and Thuillier (2008) analyzed the history of four PMOs and saw that they underwent a complex phenomenon of transformation every two years (on average) and that this came either from the evolution process or from organizational instability. In other qualitative research, Aubry, Hobbs, and Thuillier (2008) concluded that organizational tensions are the primary motivation behind the implementation and reconfiguration of PMOs (i.e., issues of organizational power and politics have to be considered), and these issues further increase the complexity of managing PMOs.

Over the last few years, authors (Crawford, 2002; Hill, 2004; Kerzner, 2005), institutions (Software Engineering Institute [SEI], 2000), and even the Project Management Institute (2008) have developed organizational maturity evaluation models, the objective of which is to facilitate the maturity process in organizations by providing a structured path based on best market practices and to foster continuous improvement. On the other hand, in this same period, if one ignores the fact that the maturing process of the organization as an entity is something different in many aspects from the maturing of a PMO as an organizational unit, no relevant initiative for creating specific points of reference for supporting the evolution of a PMO has been identified. Despite the strong correlation between these two types of maturity, reality shows that it is possible for a little-prepared (i.e., immature) PMO to exist in more mature organizations, given that the maturity of the PMO involves the degree of sophistication with which it is capable of performing its functions and reaching its objectives.

One of the discoveries of the first study that presents a "reliable portrait of the population of PMOs" (Hobbs and Aubry, 2007) was that 50 percent of the PMOs studied have the function of monitoring and controlling their own performance. In other words, PMOs are concerned with evaluating and measuring their own performance. Considering the lack of knowledge that exists about the maturity of PMOs, this article suggests a specific new model for evaluating their maturity. Its objective is to allow a PMO, based on its mission, to objectively evaluate its maturity level, considering the degree of sophistication with which it performs each of the functions for which it is responsible, while also taking into consideration the most common functions of PMOs in the market (Hobbs and Aubry, 2007) and its own specific interests and needs.

The Operating Philosophy of a PMO

But what is a PMO? In literature (Block and Frame, 1998; Dinsmore, 1999; Bolles, 2002; Crawford, 2002; Englund, Graham, & Dinsmore, 2003; Kendall & Rollins, 2003; Hill, 2004; Williams and Parr, 2004; Dai and Wells, 2004; Letavec, 2006; Hobbs and Aubry, 2007; Hurt and Thomas, 2009), there are countless different responses to this question. Generally speaking, they all agree on one thing: it is the area in which certain activities (also called functions) relating to project management are centered, and its objective is to help an organization achieve better results through projects.

Among these activities or functions, we can highlight some (e.g., providing the methodologies and tools needed for managing projects, supporting top management by supplying reports and executive information, lending support when it comes to planning and controlling projects, and taking over altogether by providing project managers from the beginning or helping rescue the management from certain projects) that are considered strategic and are in trouble in terms of meeting objectives and providing benefits. All of these functions were highlighted in a recent study by Hobbs and Aubry (2007), who mapped out the 27 common PMO functions after receiving contributions from 500 professionals involved with PMOs worldwide.

A PMO is often seen as a support area within the organization, in a similar way to the accounting, marketing, or IT areas. In most organizations, these areas are not considered their own *raison d'être*, since their purpose is to support the development of the company's principal activity. However, we see crucial differences that make PMOs somewhat different from a traditional support area.

The requirement that the PMO should generate value is, in fact, something much more critical than the demands normally seen in traditional support areas, the value of which is translated into benefits that are not always noticeable or measurable. Unlike these areas, a PMO is being constantly questioned regarding its contribution to the organization and is often seen as a type of operational overhead. Few people would question the need for the existence of a marketing department or an accounting department. Nevertheless, these same individuals would probably question the need for a PMO if the value generated by the PMO is not clearly perceived.

So in analyzing PMOs from another viewpoint, we can see that it is truly a service provider within the organization, given that an external service provider could have its contract cancelled at any time because it is not adding sufficient value. In the same way, a PMO may also inadvertently lose all the support and backing it has because it is unable to generate value and perceptible benefit that justify maintaining the investment made.

Therefore, a PMO that intends to survive the ups and downs of the organization and the market needs to see itself as a service provider that has customers with needs that must be fully served. It evolves as the organization matures, which means that its customers will have different and generally increasingly sophisticated needs.

In other words, the success of a PMO involves its capacity to understand who its customers are, what their needs are, and how to meet those needs by creating clear and sufficient benefits and generating perceptible and measurable value. Its maturing process involves the skills to meet the new needs arising from the maturing process of the organization and its customers by offering new services, and making the level of service more sophisticated in response to the demands that are made.

Types and Functions of PMOs

The complexity of the PMO phenomenon gives rise to difficulty when it comes to establishing a standard way of typifying them. By observing different PMOs in various organizations, it is possible to notice many significant differences that make the task challenging of summarizing them into just a few.

In considering the extensive literature that exists on the subject, it is possible to identify various attempts that have been made at standardizing the classification of PMOs. Englund, Graham, and Dinsmore (2003), for example, presented five types of PMOs: the single control project office that is more operational and directed toward just one project; the strategic project office that operates strategically and is directed toward the whole of the organization; the business unit project office that operates strategically or tactically and is directed at an area or department; the project support office that has an operational role and is directed toward the whole company; and finally, the project management center of excellence, which focuses on continuous improvement and innovation. The proposal of this PMO maturity model sums up the main standard ways of typifying PMOs in essentially two principal dimensions: scope and approach.

The scope of a PMO comes from how wide-reaching its actions are within the organization. Basically, there are three mutually exclusive possibilities: the project-program PMO, the scope of which covers just one of the organization's projects or programs; the departmental PMO, which covers an area, department, directorship, or business unit, i.e., just a part of the organization; and finally the corporate or enterprise PMO, which covers the organization as a whole.

Approach has to do with how the PMO operates with its customers. This may be strategically, tactically, or operationally, or it may operate with all three simultaneously. In fact, the driver of the approach of a PMO must be its mission, which will define how strategic, tactical, or operational it should be. This approach classification was ratified by Desouza and Evaristo (2006) when they identified that the roles of a PMO could always be classified on three levels: strategic, tactical, and operational. Additionally, Hobbs and Aubry (2007) identified that different authors use different properties to characterize the typology of the PMO. One of these properties is how the PMO provides services from the operational to the strategic approach often associated with a progression from project management to portfolio management.

Common sense might lead us to a simplification of the idea that a PMO that covers the whole organization (enterprise) could be summed up as taking a strategic approach (strategic). However the organizational practice is more complex. It is common to have an enterprise PMO that operates strategically, tactically, and operationally when it respectively provides service to top management, by supporting portfolio management (strategic), providing a common methodology for the organization (tactical), and also managing some important projects (operational). The reality may be a combination of these three approaches in the scope each one provides (organizational, departmental, or project-program) (see Figure 19.1).

Acting in a strategic way involves offering customers services that, in some form or other, have a link with strategic issues of the organization, such as how to manage the organization's portfolio of projects, programs, and other work; provide information to top management for decision-making purposes and to prioritize the portfolio and rebalance it as required; and monitor and implement strategy, etc.

Acting in a tactical way involves offering customers services that serve the needs of a group of projects or individuals, such as developing a project management methodology, providing project management tools, and training for managers and teams, etc.

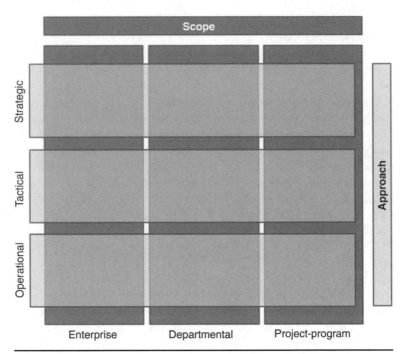

Figure 19.1   The nine quadrants resulting from the relationship between scope and approach.

Finally, acting in an operational way involves offering customers services directed at a project or individual, such as supporting project planning and control, coaching or mentoring, managing a strategic project, and recovering a problembeset project, etc.

From research published by Hobbs and Aubry (2007), the 27 most common functions of PMOs were identified (see Table 19.1). These functions represent the major services provided by PMOs and have become the reference point for the models presented in this paper.

Considering the definitions for strategic, tactical, and operational approaches, and based on the academic and professional experience of the authors, each of these services was evaluated from two aspects: (1) If it was applicable to each and every type of scope of the PMO. In other words, was it valid for enterprise, departmental, and project-program PMOs and (2) was it a service of a strategic, tactical, or operational nature?

It is possible to conclude then that there are 21 possible types of PMOs, considering the three mutually exclusive scopes (enterprise, departmental, project-program) and the seven possible approaches (strategic, strategic-tactical, strategic-operational, tactical, tactical-operational, operational, and strategic-tactical-operational).

Table 19.1 The 27 functions (services) of Hobbs and Aubry (modified slightly), and their relationship with the different types of scope and approach

Services	Scope			Approach		
	Enterprise	Departmental	Project-program	Strategic	Tactical	Operational
1. Report project or program status (information) to senior management	√	√	√			√
2. Develop and implement a standard project management methodology	√	√	√		√	
3. Monitor and control project or program performance	√	√	√			√
4. Develop the competencies (skills) of professionals, including training	√	√	√		√	
5. Implement and operate project management information systems	√	√	√		√	
6. Provide top management with advice	√	√	√	√		
7. Coordinate and integrate the projects in the portfolio; prioritize these projects and rebalance them as required	√	√		√		
8. Develop and maintain a project scoreboard	√	√	√	√		
9. Promote project management awareness within the organization	√	√		√		
10. Monitor and control the performance of the PMO itself	√	√		√		
11. Participate in strategic planning	√	√		√		
12. Provide mentoring for project managers	√	√	√			√
13. Manage one or more portfolios	√	√		√		
14. Identify, select, and prioritize new projects	√	√		√		
15. Manage project files and documentation; set up a knowledge management repository	√	√	√			√
16. Manage one or more programs	√	√	√			√
17. Audit projects and programs	√	√	√			√
18. Manage customer interfaces	√	√	√		√	
19. Provide a set of tools that can be customized to meet the specific needs of programs and projects	√	√	√		√	

(Continues)

Table 19.1 *(Continued)*

Services	Scope			Approach		
	Enterprise	Departmental	Program-project	Strategic	Tactical	Operational
20. Provide specialized tasks (services) for project managers	√	√	√			√
21. Allocate and share resources between projects	√	√	√		√	
22. Carry out post-project management reviews (lessons learned)	√	√	√			√
23. Implement and manage the database of lessons learned or knowledge repository	√	√	√		√	
24. Implement and manage the risk and issues database	√	√	√		√	
25. Manage program benefits	√	√	√	√		
26. Network and environmental scan, map project relationships and environment within the organization and external to it	√	√	√	√		
27. Recruit, select, evaluate, and decide on the salaries of project managers; establish a project management career path	√	√			√	

What defines the type of PMO is a combination of its scope and one of the seven possible different approaches resulting from the services offered to its customers.

The Maturity of the PMO

The degree of maturity of a PMO results from the extent to which it is capable of generating value for its customers and for the organization as a whole. In a first analysis, it might be possible to suppose that the maturity of a PMO might evolve in the sense of operating less operationally and more strategically. However a more careful assessment may provide us with a different view of the process by which it matures.

In a simple analogy that will help us have a better understanding of the issue, we might imagine a company's organizational structure. At the lowest level we have, for example, a cleaner (acting operationally), and at the highest level would be the president (acting strategically).

The question is: What is a mature cleaner? Is he a president? Or is he a professional who is capable of using the best cleaning techniques and practices in order to comply with his operational mission? On the other hand, what is an immature president? Is he a cleaner? Or is he a president with little experience and knowledge, and therefore incapable of fulfilling his strategic mission in the company?

The cleaner has an extremely important operational mission within the organization and may do it in a simple or very sophisticated way, depending on his or her level of maturity. The president also has his strategic mission within the company and, in turn, may carry it out in a trivial or extremely sophisticated way. It all depends on the level of maturity of each one, considering their respective functions and approach (operational or strategic).

Therefore how could we state that in order to mature a PMO with an operational approach the PMO must start adopting a strategic approach? The fact is that if its mission is to be operational, it can be performed in either a mature or immature manner. The same goes for a PMO whose mission is to be strategic; it can perform in a very mature way or one that involves very little sophistication.

This being so, it is possible to have operational or tactical PMOs with a high degree of maturity and extremely immature strategic PMOs. Because a PMO may have multiple approaches (strategic, tactical, or operational) depending on its mission, it would only make sense to analyze its maturity if we focus on what is particular to each of these approaches.

It is therefore possible to conclude that a corporate PMO may have different levels of maturity in each of its possible approaches. It might be very mature from the operational point of view and not very mature from the tactical and strategic points of view. If the mission is to be operational, we can say that it is aligned with its objectives and generating the value expected by the organization.

If we consider, that the PMO generates value through the functions it exercises, which are translated into service for its customers, the maturity may be summed up as being the degree of sophistication with which it provides each service for which it is responsible.

There are different ways of providing a certain service: from the most trivial and simple manner, which adds little value to the organization, to a more sophisticated and complex way, which translates into more noticeable results and provides the organization as a whole with greater value.

To devise the maturity evaluation model that is proposed in this chapter, each of the 27 services (adapted from the most common functions in PMOs, as presented by Hobbs and Aubry, 2007) was analyzed to establish how applicable they were to the three different types of PMO scope: enterprise, departmental, and project-program (see Figure 19.2).

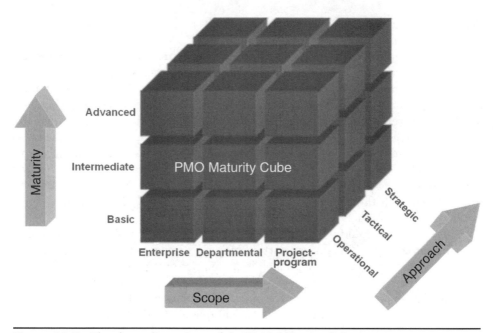

Figure 19.2   The three dimensions of the PMO Maturity Cube.

Each of the services was analyzed as to their possible different levels of sophistication for carrying them out, from the most trivial way to the most complicated. This determines the degree of maturity when carrying it out. Some of the services of an enterprise PMO can be seen in the following:

Service: A.1.7—Managing one or more portfolios (enterprise scope, strategic approach)

Levels of maturity in carrying out the service:

- Level 0—Does not provide this service
- Level 1—Maintains a list of active projects throughout the organization
- Level 2—Maintains a list of active projects and programs throughout the organization and establishes their prioritization but does not follow a structured portfolio management process
- Level 3—Maintains a list of active projects and portfolios, prioritizes them throughout the organization, and establishes formal processes, acting as facilitator in the definition (identification, categorization, evaluation, and selection), development (prioritize, balance,

and commitment) and implementation (monitoring and review and change management) of the portfolio
- Level 4—Maintains a list of active projects and portfolios, prioritizes them throughout the organization, and establishes formal processes, acting as facilitator in the definition (identification, categorization, evaluation, and selection), development (prioritize, balance, and commitment) and implementation (monitoring and review and change management) of the portfolio; the PMO uses an integrated system to automate the organization's portfolio management process

Service: A.2.1—Develop and implement the project management methodology (enterprise scope, tactical approach)

Levels of maturity in carrying out the service:

- Level 0—Does not provide this service
- Level 1—Has developed a basic methodology for the organization, but it is not used consistently on all projects
- Level 2—Has developed a standard methodology for the organization, aligning possible existing methodologies in different areas, and the methodology used in most projects in the organization
- Level 3—Has developed a standard methodology for the organization, and it is used by all projects as it is mandatory unless a specific waiver is requested and approved
- Level 4—Has developed and improved the standard methodology for the organization focusing on best practices and continuous improvement

Service: A.3.3—Monitor and control project-program performance (enterprise scope, operational approach)

Levels of maturity in carrying out the service:

- Level 0—Does not provide this service
- Level 1—Monitors and controls the project or program performance considering time, cost, quality, and customer satisfaction and provides follow-up reports without analysis upon request
- Level 2—Monitors and controls the project or program performance considering time, cost, quality, and customer satisfaction and analyzes the available data
- Level 3—The PMO monitors and controls the project or program performance considering time, cost, quality, and customer satisfaction, analyzes data, and takes preventive and corrective actions working proactively with the project or program manager and senior management

In the proposed model, each of the services offered by a PMO can have up to four levels of maturity according to their scope and approach.

The PMO Maturity Cube

The PMO Maturity Cube results from unifying the concepts presented previously, which have all been consolidated into one specific model for evaluating the maturity of PMOs for any type of organization. The three dimensions that comprise the cube are scope (enterprise, departmental, or project-program), approach (strategic, tactical, or operational) and finally the maturity level (basic, intermediate, or advanced).

Using a specific questionnaire for each PMO scope, the model identifies which services are offered under each approach and determines the level of sophistication of their implementation. Each of the three questionnaires (enterprise, departmental, and project-program) is divided into three parts: assessment of strategic services, assessment of tactical services, and assessment of operational services. When completing the questionnaire, organizations provide information about their current level of maturity in each service provided for that particular scope and the target level of maturity for the PMO that is being analyzed (see Table 19.2).

Table 19.2 Example of a question from the PMO Maturity Cube model questionnaire for an enterprise PMO

Enterprise PMO Questionnaire		
Tactical services assessment		
A.2.1—How does the PMO develop and implement the project management methodology?	**Current level**	**Target level**
Level 0—The PMO does not have this function		
Level 1—The PMO has developed a basic methodology for the organization, but it is not used consistently on all projects	X	
Level 2—The PMO has developed a standard methodology for the organization, aligning possible existing methodologies in different areas, and the methodology used in most projects in the organization		
Level 3—The PMO has developed a standard methodology for the organization, and it is used by all projects, as it is mandatory unless a specific waiver is requested and approved		X
Level 4—The PMO has developed and improved the standard methodology for the organization focusing on best practices and continuous improvement		

Each level corresponds to a specific number of points, and when the questionnaire has been completed, the total points corresponding to the organization's current situation and the situation desired by the organization are obtained and divided into strategic, tactical, and operational approaches. Based on these scores, the current and target maturity levels are calculated.

The current maturity level in each of the approaches is calculated by comparing the points relative to the current situation in the organization with the total possible number of points for the model as a whole. The target maturity level is calculated by comparing the points relative to the desired situation in the organization with the total possible number of points for the model as a whole.

The current and target maturity levels are represented in percentages. The current maturity level represents to what extent the PMO provides all the possible services when it is most mature. The target maturity, on the other hand, represents the level the PMO would like to reach, a situation in which it would fully adhere to its objectives and mission, considering only those services that are really of interest to it in the target maturity levels.

Maturity levels with percentages between 0 and 33 percent are considered basic. Levels between 34 and 66 percent are considered intermediate. Finally, maturity levels between 67 and 100 percent are considered advanced.

To illustrate this approach, we present real case studies where the PMO Maturity Cube model has been applied. All these companies were invited to participate and the authors coordinated the application of the model during a formal meeting. The questions were answered by the PMO's leaders, who were supported by their teams. At the end, the leaders were asked for a quick comment about the experience, including their perception about the strengths and weaknesses of the proposed model. Based on this feedback, the authors promoted adjustments in the model and reapplied the questionnaire in these same companies, obtaining these final numbers and the PMO's leaders comments about the experience of applying the model presented in Table 19.3.

Conclusion

After a detailed assessment of the contribution made by countless books and recent academic literature about PMOs, we were able to confirm the complexity and diversity of the phenomenon. We can see that there is still a need to provide a self-assessment tool in view of the wide range of possible PMO functions. This maturity assessment model provides the required comparison between the functions already existing in it and the whole model and, at the same time, allows the PMO to identify only the target functions, thereby producing an assessment relative to existing and perceived needs. On developing the model, the authors came to the conclusion that the better the PMO delivers its services, and only those

Table 19.3 Results of the application of the PMO Maturity Cube

Company	Sector	Scope of the PMO	Maturity		Approach of the PMO		
					Strategic assessment	Tactical assessment	Operational assessment
A	Consumer goods	Enterprise		Current level	33% Basic	41% Intermediate	57% Intermediate
				Target level	53% Intermediate	62% Intermediate	65% Intermediate

Comments:

The mission of the enterprise PMO is to serve the needs of project managers, line managers, and top management. Today, the main operating focus of the PMO is still concentrated on operational support services and project planning and control. However, the PMO wants to assume more tactical and strategic functions.

Perception of the model by the evaluated company: "The model is useful for providing an overview of how our PMO can evolve in the right direction."—Manager of the PMO

Company	Sector	Scope of the PMO	Maturity		Approach of the PMO		
					Strategic assessment	Tactical assessment	Operational assessment
B	Financial services	Enterprise		Current level	48% Intermediate	44% Intermediate	25% Basic
				Target level	59% Intermediate	57% Intermediate	29% Basic

Comments:

This enterprise PMO has been operating since 2004 and is strategic and tactical in nature, with few operational functions. Its objectives are to evolve more strongly in functions relating to portfolio management in addition to continuing to evolve and spread project management practices to all the organization's corporate projects.

Perception of the model by the evaluated company: "An excellent instrument for self-assessing the maturity of the PMO. The model allowed us to see more clearly exactly where we are and where we can get to."—Executive Manager of the PMO

Company	Sector	Scope of the PMO	Maturity		Approach of the PMO		
					Strategic assessment	Tactical assessment	Operational assessment
C	Telecommunications	Enterprise		Current level	53% Intermediate	65% Intermediate	15% Basic
				Target level	83% Advanced	75% Advanced	25% Basic

Comments:

The mission of this enterprise PMO is to meet the needs of top management, and provide methods, standards, and resources that can be used by projects in the organization. The main objective of this PMO over the next few months is mainly to increase its maturity in the strategic area.

Perception of the evaluated company: "A very good model. Practical, objective, and well grounded. It will undoubtedly be valuable for our development."—Manager of the PMO

Company	Sector	Scope of the PMO	Maturity		Approach of the PMO		
					Strategic assessment	Tactical assessment	Operational assessment
D	Insurance	Departmental		Current level	31% Basic	42% Intermediate	53% Intermediate
				Target level	58% Intermediate	63% Intermediate	85% Advanced

Comments:

The mission of this departmental PMO is to provide services for the IT area, particularly in meeting the tactical and operational needs of project managers, as well as the strategic needs of the executive management. There are still some significant tactical and operational gaps in the way this PMO operates with regard to existing needs, mainly with regard to operational services. This PMO is going through a restructuring process, which involves expanding its staff numbers so that it can provide the service it proposes.

Perception of the evaluated company: "The results undoubtedly portray the exact reality of our PMO. It's interesting to have a reference point like this that can help us outline our action plans."—Manager of the PMO

(Continues)

Table 19.3 (Continued)

Company	Sector	Scope of the PMO	Maturity		Approach of the PMO		
					Strategic assessment	Tactical assessment	Operational assessment
E	Financial services in public administration	Departmental		Current level	78% Advanced	44% Intermediate	72% Advanced
				Target level	78% Advanced	50% Intermediate	82% Advanced

Comments:

This departmental PMO was established in 2002, and its mission is to provide services for the financial institutions' supervision area. In the perception of its managers, the PMO already has a consolidated operation that provides services on a strategic level and can advance further in services directed at supporting project managers.

Perception of the evaluated company: "We see the great value of this tool since it allows for self-application, intentions to improve can be immediately registered, and we can carry out a comparison over time of the focus of our operations."—Manager of the PMO

Company	Sector	Scope of the PMO	Maturity		Approach of the PMO		
					Strategic assessment	Tactical assessment	Operational assessment
F	Energy	Departmental		Current level	9% Basic	35% Basic	18% Basic
				Target level	19% Basic	68% Advanced	75% Advanced

Comments:

The mission of this departmental PMO is to provide services to the engineering area, with a focus on tactical and operational aspects.

This PMO was recently set up, but it expects to achieve great results within 12 months. Because of the short time it has been in existence, there are still some big gaps in terms of its current level versus that of its target level, but action plans are being put together and the forecast is for results in the short and medium terms.

Perception of the evaluated company: "As we are just starting out, a reference point like this is valuable. There's no doubt that we will use the model to help us evolve."—Coordinator of the PMO

Company	Sector	Scope of the PMO	Maturity	Approach of the PMO		
				Strategic assessment	Tactical assessment	Operational assessment
G	Retail	Project-program	Current level	15% Basic	49% Intermediate	58% Intermediate
			Target level	0% Basic	49% Intermediate	58% Intermediate

Comments:

The mission of this project-program PMO is to support the organization's SAP implementation project, with a particular focus on operational and tactical aspects.

This is an outsourced PMO, so its functions are predefined in the contract with the customer. So, from the tactical and operational points of view, the PMO's current levels of maturity are fully aligned with the target levels, given that this is necessary in order to comply with the contract's statement of work and terms and conditions.

It is interesting to note that when the model is being applied, this PMO is providing some of the strategic services. However, these do not fall within the scope of the contract and may mean that the PMO is losing focus in its operations. Therefore, we conclude that in the strategic area, the PMO may regress given that the target level is 0 percent, i.e., fully discontinuing any service of this nature. In this way, the PMO will begin to be fully aligned with its mission, which is to provide the tactical and operational services that have been pre-defined by contract. Further, the organization may wish to reevaluate the operation of the PMO and decide to establish a PMO that is staffed by people who work for the corporation in order to perform the strategic mission of a PMO and using contractor support to focus on operational and tactical aspects.

Perception of the evaluated company: "The model helped us see that we were using our resources for activities that were not part of our objective. Our problem was not a lack of resources, but the poor use of those resources. Instead of focusing on our main objective, we've discovered that we are becoming less efficient in other activities that, in fact, are activities that our customer does not expect us to provide."—Director of the consultancy company

(Continues)

Table 19.3 (*Continued*)

Company	Sector	Scope of the PMO		Maturity	Approach of the PMO		
					Strategic assessment	Tactical assessment	Operational assessment
H	Textile	Project-program	Current level		22% Basic	45% Intermediate	43% Intermediate
			Target level		33% Basic	57% Intermediate	57% Intermediate

Comments:

The mission of this project-program PMO is to support the program for implementing a new production line, with a focus on tactical, strategic, and operational aspects.

The program involves various subcontractors, and one of the challenges of the PMO is to ensure that they are integrated. Furthermore, the PMO supplies overall standards for the in-house team and the subcontractors, as well as supplying information to executive management for decision-making purposes.

Generally speaking, this PMO only needs to fill a small gap in terms of its evolution in order to fully comply with its mission and meet the needs of its customers.

Perception of the evaluated company: "The model was useful when it came to giving us an overview of our current situation and in which alternatives we must invest in the future. As our program has an end-date and we have no additional time, we need to ensure that the PMO gets up to cruising speed as soon as possible. I believe the model is fundamental for giving us the speed we need in the decisions we have to make about what is most important to introduce from now on."—Leader of the PMO services related to the needed functions, the more the it is perceived as delivering value to its organization.

In addition, the PMO maturity assessment tool allows the perceived improvement intentions to be recorded when the maturity assessment is being carried out, which helps produce an action plan. The simplicity of the method allows it to be self-applied by PMOs, without the need to hire consultancy services. The PMO Maturity Cube can be freely accessed at: www.pmomaturitycube.org

Author Biographies

Americo Pinto, PMP, MBA, is a project management specialist and researcher with much experience in large projects in Latin America and Europe. He has more than 15 years of experience in portfolio and project management. He worked as a senior executive and project manager in companies such as Arthur Andersen, Deloitte, and Dinsmore Associates. Currently, he is the executive director of international operations of the Compass Research Center, the research arm of Compass International. Formerly, Americo was the head of the project management consulting practice for Brazil and Latin America at Compass International.

Americo works as a professor at Brazil's most prestigious universities teaching various project management courses to MBA students. He is also a doctoral student at SKEMA Business School, ESC Lille, France. For six years he has been vice president at PMI's Rio de Janeiro, Brazil Chapter. In this volunteer position he was in charge of several initiatives on project management development. Americo has two project management books published in Brazil.

Marcelo Cota, PMP, MSc, is a professor at Brazil's most prestigious universities, teaching various project management courses to MBA students. He is also a doctoral candidate in project management at the University of São Paulo. He is the head of the corporate PMO division of Banco Central do Brasil with responsibilities for the corporate maturity efforts in project management.

Ginger Levin, PhD., is a senior consultant and educator in project management. Her specialty areas are portfolio management, the PMO, metrics, and maturity assessments. She is a PMP, PgMP, as well as an OPM3 assessor and consultant. Dr. Levin is an adjunct professor for the University of Wisconsin-Platteville and ESC Lille, a visiting professor for the Royal Melbourne Institute of Technology, and a registered examiner for the University of Technology, Sydney, Australia.

Her project management consulting clients include Bank One, UPS, Citibank, SAP, the FDA, GE, IBM, John Deere, and the USDA. She is a prolific writer and has coauthored numerous books including *Implementing Program Management, Project Portfolio Management, Metrics for Project Management, Achieving Project Management Success Using Virtual Teams, Advanced Project Management Office, Essential People Skills for Project Managers,* and *The Business Development CMM.*

References

Aubry, M., Hobbs, B., and Thuillier, D. 2008a. Organisational project management: An historical approach to the study of PMOs. *International Journal of Project Management*. 26(1): 38–43.

Aubry, M., Hobbs, B., and Thuillier, D. 2008b. The project management office as an organisational innovation. *International Journal of Project Management*. 26(5): 547–555.

Bolles, D. 2002. *Building project management centers of excellence*. New York: Amacom.

Block, T. R. and Frame, J. D. 1998. *The Project Office: a key to managing projects effectively*. Menlo Park, CA: Crisp Publications.

Crawford, K. J. 2002. *The Strategic Project Office*. New York: Marcel Dekker.

Dai, C. X., and Wells, W. G. 2004. An exploration of project management office features and their relationship to project performance. *International Journal of Project Management*. 22:523-532.

Desouza, K. C., and Evaristo, J. R. 2006. Project management offices: A case of knowledge-based archetypes. *International Journal of Information Management*. 26(7): 414–423.

Dinsmore, P. C. 1999. *Winning in Business with Enterprise Project Management*. New York: Amacom.

Englund, R. L., Graham, R. J., and Dinsmore, P. C. 2003. *Creating the Project Office: a manager's guide to leading organizational change*. San Francisco: Jossey-Bass.

Hill, G. M. 2004. *The Complete Project Management Office Handbook*. Boca Raton, FL: Auerbach Publications.

Hobbs, B., and Aubry, M. 2007. A multi-phase research program investigating project management offices (PMOs): The results of phase 1. *Project Management Journal*. 38(1): 74–86.

Hurt, M., and Thomas, J. L. 2009. Building value through sustainable project management offices. *Project Management Journal*. 40(1): 55–72.

Letavec, C. 2006. *Program Management Office*. Fort Lauderdale, FL: J. Ross Publishing.

Kendall, G. I., and Rollins, S. C. 2003. *Advanced Project Portfolio Management and the PMO*. Fort Lauderdale, FL: J. Ross Publishing.

Kerzner, H. 2005. *Using the Project Management Maturity Model*. New York: John Wiley & Sons.

Project Management Institute. 2008. *Organizational Project Management Maturity Model (OPM3®)*, 2nd ed. Newtown Square, PA: Project Management Institute.

Software Engineering Institute. 2000. *CMM—The Capability Maturity Model*. Pittsburgh, PA: Carnegie Mellon Software Engineering Institute.

Williams, D., and Parr, T. 2004. *Enterprise Program Management: delivering value*. Basingstoke, UK: Palgrave Macmillan.

Epilogue[1]

The Role of the PMO as a Portfolio Management Office

Pat Durbin and Terry Doerscher, Planview, Inc.

This chapter discusses why the PMO is an important component in implementing portfolio management. Traditionally the *P* in the acronym PMO has stood for *project* or *program* when used in conjunction with the words *management office*. Its primary focus is dedicated to the tactical execution of formal projects or groups of projects. In that respect, the PMO has always been an important part of managing change, given that projects by definition are changing mechanisms.

Today this acronym is just as likely to stand for *portfolio management office*. We coined the term *PMO 2.0* in 2005 to differentiate between those PMOs that have evolved into a next-generation portfolio services organization and the more traditional project-centric PMO. In this chapter we explore the modern 2.0 version of the PMO that is emerging as a full-service business management and integration center for managing change.

Throughout our book we stress approaching portfolio management with a broad perspective, discussing how to apply this technique to manage markets, strategies, resources, products, and more. The portfolio environment functions as an interdependent ecosystem that employs different perspectives and applications. Whether it is linking strategic direction with work execution or managing the relationships between customer demand and your products and services, significant coordination is necessary to sustain these relationships.

---

[1]The following chapter is an edited excerpt based on Chapter 16 of *Taming Change with Portfolio Management: Unify Your Organization, Sharpen Your Strategy, and Create Measurable Value*, by Pat Durbin and Terry Doerscher (Greenleaf Book Group; July 1, 2010; ISBN: 978-1-60832-038-7) and is used with permission of the authors and copyright holder. Copyright © 2010 Planview, Inc.

In a growing number of organizations the portfolio management office has become that centralized point of coordination. The PMO also serves to establish the array of tools and techniques needed to foster enough consistency across the enterprise so that it can function as a single cohesive ecosystem.

To understand how its role is changing, we will first draw on recent industry data to explore current PMO trends. We will then analyze the underlying reasons why the project or program management office is evolving to become a portfolio management office.

Next we present the case for the corporate PMO to be established as an essential shared services provider similar to how IT, corporate accounting, and HR are viewed. Before that can become a reality, organizations need to address some common roadblocks to PMO success and longevity. We close the chapter with the key elements that you need for success.

PMO Trends

In 2008 we conducted an extensive survey[2] to quantify PMO performance, identify the scope of services that PMOs provide, and ascertain the presence and impact of the issues facing organizations and their PMOs. Over 450 respondents participated, representing a broad cross-section of organizational sizes, types, industries, and maturity levels from massive multinational institutions to government agencies and local businesses. The results yielded several key findings that added to our overall understanding of modern PMOs and the organizations that they serve. We present the findings that are most relevant to the role of the PMO in portfolio management in this chapter.

The Project Management Office Is Now a Minority

The PMO that focuses solely on formal projects is no longer the de facto standard. As shown in Figure E.1, over 60 percent of the PMOs surveyed indicated that they were extending their scope of interest in work and resource management to either include all forms of planned work in the organization except operations (33 percent), or that they were fully engaged in comprehensive work and resource management, including routine operational activities (28 percent).

The PMO Is Reaching Upward and Outward

According to our findings, the majority of PMOs reported directly to the C-level (55 percent) or to a vice president (10 percent), and 26 percent of PMOs operated at an enterprise level, serving across the board as an integration point for

---

[2]"2008 PMO 2.0 Survey," January 15, 2009, available through www.tamingchange.com.

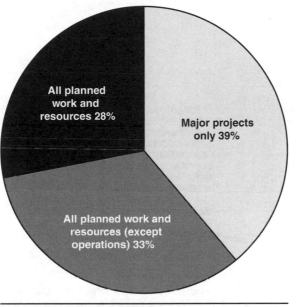

Figure E.1 General PMO work and resource management scope.

different departments, lines of business, or similar divisions. Almost half of all respondents were operating in a multi-PMO environment. Around one third of them were associated with information technology organizations.

The PMO as a Business Management Center

In terms of the services provided by the PMOs, 85 percent of respondents indicated that they were involved in program and portfolio management, which is the highest percentage of any of the 38 functions listed. The next most prevalent functions included process improvement (82 percent), high-level reporting (78 percent), and strategic planning (68 percent). On average, the typical PMO reported involvement with 15 of the 38 activities listed in Figure E.2.

Analyzing the Evolution of the PMO

Before we can discuss how and why the PMO is changing, we must first examine what it is and what it does. Any PMO—large or small, old or new—is generally responsible for:

- Collecting and distributing information
- Managing demand and capacity
- Providing analysis and reporting

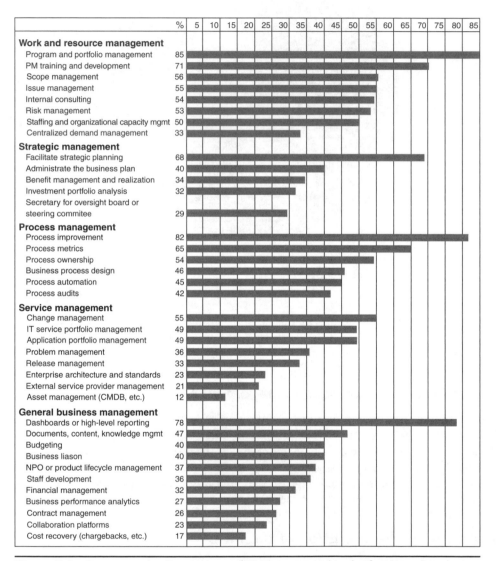

	%	5	10	15	20	25	30	35	40	45	50	55	60	65	70	75	80	85

Work and resource management
- Program and portfolio management — 85
- PM training and development — 71
- Scope management — 56
- Issue management — 55
- Internal consulting — 54
- Risk management — 53
- Staffing and organizational capacity mgmt — 50
- Centralized demand management — 33

Strategic management
- Facilitate strategic planning — 68
- Administrate the business plan — 40
- Benefit management and realization — 34
- Investment portfolio analysis — 32
- Secretary for oversight board or steering commitee — 29

Process management
- Process improvement — 82
- Process metrics — 65
- Process ownership — 54
- Business process design — 46
- Process automation — 45
- Process audits — 42

Service management
- Change management — 55
- IT service portfolio management — 49
- Application portfolio management — 49
- Problem management — 36
- Release management — 33
- Enterprise architecture and standards — 23
- External service provider management — 21
- Asset management (CMDB, etc.) — 12

General business management
- Dashboards or high-level reporting — 78
- Documents, content, knowledge mgmt — 47
- Budgeting — 40
- Business liason — 40
- NPO or product lifecycle management — 37
- Staff development — 36
- Financial management — 32
- Business performance analytics — 27
- Contract management — 26
- Collaboration platforms — 23
- Cost recovery (chargebacks, etc.) — 17

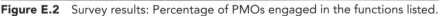

Figure E.2   Survey results: Percentage of PMOs engaged in the functions listed.

- Enabling coordination and communications
- Identifying and addressing opportunities or roadblocks
- Developing, distributing, and maintaining processes and tools
- Providing and promoting specialized skills and expertise

Note that these functions are not exclusive to the PMO; in fact, departments routinely perform these activities as a normal part of general administration and management. What distinguishes the PMO is that it provides these services *across* functional silos and different levels of the organization. The true value proposition of a PMO lies in its ability to effectively traverse departmental and hierarchical boundaries as a mechanism to establish consistency and interoperability. A secondary benefit is the consolidation of specialized business functions to improve quality and take advantage of economies of scale.

The Expanding Role of the PMO

To be clear, when we refer to the evolution of the PMO, the basic *functions* it performs are not necessarily changing. However, the *business processes* that the PMO supports with these functions are changing. As a result, the constituents of those functions and the value they receive from the PMO are shifting as well.

To illustrate this point, consider the traditional PMO that limits its scope to supporting project management; it gathers project proposals and related information, reports on project progress and performance, provides project tracking tools and expertise, addresses project scope and risk issues, and so on. When applying these capabilities to the discipline of project management and related processes, the PMO constituents primarily consist of project managers, project staff, and functional sponsors. The resulting benefit delivered is largely tactical in value.

Referencing the activities in Figure E.2, consider how the PMO constituency changes when it also supports strategic and investment portfolios. Now the PMO is gathering information about proposed strategies, analyzing how potential investments align with those strategies, providing tools and expertise in support of making portfolio trade-off decisions, and reporting on progress toward achieving business objectives. As a result, the constituency served by the PMO shifts to include the leadership team. Equally important, the potential for the PMO to add value to the organization goes up by an order of magnitude.

In both cases the PMO performs essentially the same basic functions and acts as a bridge to coordinate activities across different groups and layers of the organization. However, the target portfolio management processes in its scope of interest have changed. The data suggests this trend has significant momentum behind it. While there are several reasons for this transformation, much of the impetus stems from the issues discussed in the previous section. The complexities that accompany matrix organizational structures, the added difficulty associated with tracking knowledge-based work, and the operational dynamics that we face through constant change have driven the need to *put a head on the monster*.

The PMO as a Portfolio Management Office

As a technique for collectively managing change, portfolio management uses six basic elements:

- A subject change event
- Viable supporting information
- Analytical skills and capabilities
- Decision parameters
- Resulting decisions and actions
- Analysis and decision-support tools

These are universal techniques whether managing a strategic, investment, or execution portfolio, and, regardless of whether the subjects are products, markets, work, or resources. When you compare these elements with the basic functions that any PMO already provides, extending it to be a centralized group that is dedicated to facilitating portfolio management is a completely intuitive and natural step in its evolution; this is what we mean by *PMO 2.0*.

Some people misconstrue the concept of a portfolio management office as a high-level, prescriptive decision-making authority. The very notion can be alarming to senior executives, product managers, and department heads who might view such a group as encroaching on their responsibilities and power. Although a PMO may indeed create, analyze, and make portfolio recommendations in some cases, it is more often intended as a shared central service rather than a center of decision making.

The PMO *can* efficiently provide the underlying information, tools, and process support necessary to enable others. The portfolio management office can also be a practical location in which to concentrate business analytics and reporting skills, coordinate actions across multiple portfolio managers during planning cycles, and provide arbitration and facilitation when making trade-off decisions between competing portfolios. It also provides the necessary administration to keep track of portfolio decisions and the status of portfolio activities.

To the extent that the PMO is actively involved in up-front decision support and back-office functions, it is also well situated to smoothly translate those decisions into actionable work and to facilitate effective execution.

The PMO as a Shared Service Provider

While it is still somewhat uncommon for a PMO to be as firmly embedded in an organization as IT, HR, or accounting, we believe the corporate PMO is on a trajectory to gain just such acceptance in the coming years. This will occur for the same reasons that these other groups were ultimately embraced; the PMO is another example of consolidating essential shared services and specialized competencies to increase effectiveness and reduce costs.

Few would suggest that it would be a wise move to disband your existing corporate technology, HR, or finance groups in favor of dispersing the staff and their functions to individual departments. Besides the inevitable inconsistencies and chaos that such a move would create, you would also need to replicate the processes, tools, and skills within each department. This would greatly distract line organizations from their primary objectives, and the functions themselves would suffer from a predictable loss of focus, effectiveness, and economies of scale.

Contrast this with organizations that have not yet employed a PMO. The need to establish business management processes and tools, manage strategies, make investment decisions, deal with work demand, assign priorities, control capacities, identify and address issues, and track progress are inescapable and ubiquitous. Yet, without a centralized mechanism to establish common approaches and competencies, each department performs these functions independently with responsibilities either divided up or duplicated across that department's management team.

Some organizations have not yet embraced the PMO concept because it has failed in the past or they still consider it a luxury that adds needless administrative overhead to the bottom line. For organizations that have made a long-term commitment to creating a strong, full-service PMO and nurturing it to maturity, actual results suggest otherwise: an investment of less than 2 percent of the total workforce can achieve gains of 20 percent or more in long-term productivity. However, to realize these gains, the cycle of PMO creation, destruction, and resurrection must first be broken.

Improving PMO Continuity and Success

In our own contemporary PMO research, as well as research conducted by leading analyst firms, Hobbs and Aubry,[3] Pennypacker,[4] and others, we consistently find that the average age of a PMO tends to fall somewhere in the 2- to 3-year range. It is a transient entity in many organizations because of perceptions about its role, natural business and economic cycles, and other factors.

The majority of survey respondents view their PMOs as reasonably successful despite their relatively short lifespan; as Figure E.3 shows, 58 percent of PMOs

---

[3]Dr. Brian Hobbs, BASc, MBA, Ph.D, PMP and Dr. Monique Aubry, Ph.D, of the University of Quebec at Montreal; as referenced in the *PM Network Journal*, PMI, Vol. 40, Issue 1, March 2009. Building Value Through Sustainable Project Management Offices, Mimi Hurt, MI2 Consulting, Calgary, Alberta, Canada; Janice L. Thomas, Athabasca University, Athabasca, Alberta, Canada.

[4]James Pennypacker, *The State of the PMO 2007–2008*, The Center for Business Practices, 2007.

were ranked *good* or better. However, a significant minority (42 percent) struggle to meet their mission, usually resulting from a combination of poor execution; low levels of organizational maturity; and inadequate staffing, sponsorship, and support.

Studies also consistently indicate that overall PMO effectiveness increases with time in service; however, there is often a lack of patience or understanding about how long it takes a fledgling PMO to mature into a fully effective contributor and its true role in the organization.

Unfortunately, even PMOs that achieve moderate levels of success are not immune to being purged routinely from their organizations. The reason that PMOs are abandoned is often rooted in why they were initiated. Some have become, in effect, a temporary solution to a permanent problem.

The decision to embark on a PMO initiative is often event triggered. Perhaps it is due to the arrival of a new executive who is a PMO supporter. More likely organizations initiate a PMO in response to a period of high growth and prosperity, or because a new requirement drives the need to improve processes or information. In each case these situations represent a perceived acute need to manage an increasing amount of change.

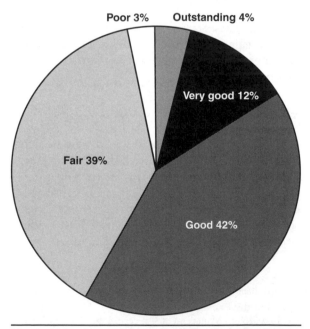

Figure E.3   Survey results: Percentage of PMOs by effectiveness.

In cases where the PMO is not an established shared business service, one of two scenarios typically plays out within the first few years of operation: (1) the initial business drivers for the PMO have subsided or have been substantially satisfied, or (2) it has failed to fully achieve expected improvements.

Either outcome results in the PMO becoming a target of questions about its continued usefulness in the subsequent months and quarters. Organizations abandon their PMOs when these questions coincide with one or more of the following conditions:

- Normal business rhythms reduce the volume of discretionary projects
- Economic pressures drive workforce reductions
- Initial executive sponsorship is lost due to changes in leadership
- Early successes are perceived as a threat and a backlash emerges
- The organization loses focus on the original objectives of the PMO initiative
- The PMO fails to show substantive value

Thus, too often young PMOs suffer a high mortality rate when organizations perceive change itself as a temporary situation. In those cases it may become the phoenix of the organization chart; regularly abandoned after only a few years of operation, it rises again from the ashes when a new cycle of intense change emerges. The biggest obstacle to the long-term success and acceptance of the PMO is overcome once an organization accepts that managing change is a persistent and inevitable part of managing the business thus recognizing that its role is to facilitate change.

PMO Success Factors

Besides recognizing its role in the organization, many other factors go into creating a successful PMO. Several books on PMO development and operation are dedicated to the subject, such as *Business Driven PMO Setup* by Mark Price Perry (J. Ross Publishing, 2009). However, we have identified some general considerations that will go a long way toward establishing the foundation for an effective PMO.

PMO Vision

As the idea of a PMO initiative goes from inception to approval, it needs to be recognized for what it is—the insertion of a specialized support group into the organization. You should approach a PMO as a long-term commitment to create a valuable shared asset. As such, it should be treated no differently than any other programmatic investment as it is refined, analyzed, approved, developed, and deployed. The decision to embark on a PMO program requires a measure of clarity on the part of the primary stakeholders for its basis, purpose, responsibilities, and expected outcomes. These conclusions need to be stated clearly in the business case and charter of the PMO.

Initiation of a PMO in an environment that has had no prior experience with one can be a potentially contentious undertaking. Leaders are naturally wary of any inference that improvements are needed, especially when they are going to be helped by an entity outside of their control that may impose new requirements, demands, and oversight mechanisms. Because of this, to unilaterally initiate a PMO through the brute force of a single executive is likely to invite its prompt destruction as soon as that individual is no longer in a position to protect it. That is not to infer that a strong PMO benefactor cannot be useful—just that it is not enough on its own.

Because the PMO is a group that will serve multiple parts and levels of the organization, it is important that primary recipients of the service understand the business case and have a voice in determining what it will and will not do. While it is unlikely that you will get 100 percent consensus, it will give stakeholders the opportunity to offer their opinions. These insights are invaluable in understanding concerns and areas of sensitivity that need to be addressed during PMO initiation and operations.

PMO Service Span

Before we discuss success elements in more detail, this is a good place to first make some clarifying points regarding the service span of a portfolio management office and about the application of portfolio management in general. Most of our discussion focuses on applying portfolio management at a high level, such as across the entire enterprise, or a largely autonomous organizational unit that has unique markets, strategies, resources, and products. We have done this to illustrate both the wide applicability of the technique and to approach the subject of portfolio management in the broadest sense.

However, the vast majority of the practices and concepts we have offered are applicable at the departmental level as well. For example, an engineering department within a manufacturing environment has defined markets, strategies, resources, and products, even though you may not express them in those exact terms.

There is an element of relativity to consider when discussing portfolios and the PMO. For example, compare the application of portfolio management techniques in these two situations:

- Across an entire company that has $300 million in annual revenue and a staff of 400
- Using portfolios in an information systems department of a global financial services institute that has an annual budget of several billion dollars and 8000 employees

In the latter case it is not unusual to find an *Enterprise IS PMO* in place with several satellite PMOs around the world providing local support, whereas the former might be best served by a single PMO.

When discussing the scope of the PMO, you first need to define its intended span of control and influence. Once you reach agreement concerning those areas, additional discussions can be held in regard to defining its scope.

PMO Scope

Two broad categories need to be addressed when discussing the parameters of a PMO. The first is its general scope of work and resource management interests within the defined service span, and the second is the scope of supporting services and functions that it provides.

We discuss the different types of work and the challenges presented by the technology services organizations environment in earlier chapters of our book. Because of these factors, it is preferable that the PMO's scope of influence create an intersecting set of both the body of work and the resource capacities used to perform that work, as shown in Figure E.4.

The reason for this goes back to one of the early basic concepts for managing demand and capacity. It is difficult, if not impossible, to effectively manage one without the ability to manage the other. The example illustrated in Figure E.4 is representative of a PMO that has within its scope both the workload and workforce of a single department. It does not totally overlap because there will always be some work that relies on the support of external resources and some resource capacity that works outside of the department. The important point is that the

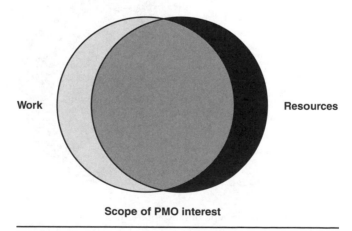

Figure E.4 Managing both work and resources.

PMO has a substantial majority of both demand and capacity within its scope and, thus, can influence how they are co-managed.

Failure to recognize this relationship is part of what limits the success of a PMO in a matrix environment that focuses only on project work—in such a scenario, the PMO does not have the total workload assigned to resources within its span of influence. As a result, the PMO has little control over ensuring resource availability to perform project tasks as scheduled. Figure E.5 illustrates such a scenario.

The second component of PMO scope focuses on the functions and services it provides within its defined span of work and resource influence. The scope of PMO services are defined on two operational planes—the range of its involvement along the continuum of change and how much strategic versus tactical support it provides.

The first consideration of scope includes establishing the points where the PMO begins and ends and its involvement along the portfolio ecosystem. Will it be involved in reporting on current state operations or will it begin its support with providing request management services? Will its involvement end with project completion or will it play an ongoing role in managing the lifecycle of its deliverable or in measuring benefits?

The second consideration is how strategic or tactical the PMO is to be—will its scope of responsibilities include functioning as the secretary for operational planning? What is its role in investment analysis? What should its level of involvement be in financial management and budgeting functions? In tactical terms, more IT

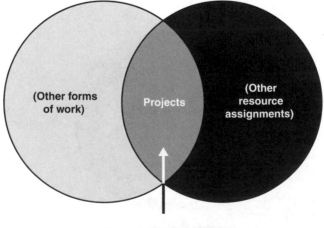

Scope of PMO interest

Figure E.5   Limited intersections of a PMO focused only on projects.

PMOs are getting involved in operational activities such as change management, service level management, managing service catalogs, application portfolio management, and outsourcing and vendor management.

When it comes to defining both PMO span of service and scope, the most important consideration is how its responsibilities intersect with other management roles. Failure to adequately define and communicate the role of the PMO relative to other leadership positions within the organization leads to stressed relationships, turf wars, dropped responsibilities, and unclear expectations. The PMO is but one element in the overall management repertoire, so it is critical that you clearly identify its responsibilities relative to those of line managers, resource managers, project managers, department heads, investment owners, and so on. Use of tools such as a RACI matrix will help you identify in which functions the PMO should be involved. Ensure that there are no gaps or conflicts in responsibilities for core portfolio processes.

Organizational Placement

The PMO must influence without authority and yet have leverage without being seen as a threat or as overbearing. To achieve this delicate balance, the PMO manager should hold a peer-level position relative to the PMO's span of service and the other parts of the organization it supports. For example, a PMO that serves the interests of the entire IT department should report directly to the CIO. If the PMO is expected to operate across the enterprise, it should report to the COO, CFO, chief strategy officer, or other senior executive. If the PMO manager is positioned at the same level as the managers he must work with and influence, then the inherent parity of their positions and the fact that they report to a common superior make it more likely that others will actively engage in collaborative efforts.

Conversely, a PMO placed in a subservient position faces an uphill battle when trying to influence other areas of the organization. Unless an unusually savvy and politically adept manager leads the PMO, chances are it will routinely have to rely on outside authority figures to broker incentives so that other senior positions actively cooperate. A PMO that is perceived as weak or insignificant will find that adoption of its policies and guidance will be more likely considered an optional suggestion rather than an operational imperative. Obviously, it takes much more than a title for the PMO to garner respect. However, the lack of one makes the process that much more difficult, particularly if it is perceived to signal a lack of executive support and commitment.

Executive Sponsorship

Highly visible and consistent sponsorship of the PMO is one of the most important elements of its success. Survey respondents showed a high correlation between the level of active sponsorship they were receiving and the overall effectiveness. As discussed in organizational placement, sponsorship is yet another method of providing the PMO with the authority to influence others. However, too often support for it hinges on the continued presence and benevolence of a single executive.

To ensure that sponsorship is a shared responsibility among executive stakeholders, and that the PMO stays in alignment with expectations, we recommend establishing a PMO steering committee as part of its charter. Holding meetings on a quarterly or semiannual basis to review progress toward objectives and to discuss related issues helps maintain an open line of communication and continued support.

PMO Staffing

Our survey indicated that, on average, PMOs that had achieved an effective level of service usually have a minimum of four or more staff members. Given that modern PMOs are providing a wider range of services, more people are likely to be necessary just to address the diversity of skills required. Based on the scope of services that the PMO is chartered to provide and the size of the constituency it must serve, its staff members must achieve adequate critical mass or risk spreading themselves too thin to be effective. Partially staffing a newly formed PMO with seasoned individuals who are already known and respected in the organization will help garner confidence and acceptance.

While each PMO situation will dictate the appropriate staff quantity, the roles they most often play fall into some general categories and descriptions. Particularly in smaller organizations, individuals who make up the PMO staff should have a broad range of competencies because each person will likely fulfill multiple roles. The following personas suggest the various roles needed to achieve effectiveness:

- *Leader*: The leader must understand the objectives and challenges clearly; not only of the PMO but also the organization it supports. The leader needs to be respected as a team builder, mentor, and internal consultant and to be able to think strategically and to communicate at an executive level. The leader should be politically astute and know the importance of building strong allies across the organization. He or she needs the wisdom to offer sensible alternatives to sticky issues and get everyone back on track. The leader must also be an evangelist to inspire the organization to follow the lead of the PMO.
- *Instructor*: Frequently one of the main functions of the PMO is to educate, which is a deceptively difficult task when dealing with a wide constituency of adult learners. The PMO often needs to build its own curriculums on specialized topics, thus, the instructor needs to be competent and confident on a variety of subjects and administratively adept. As an instructor, he or she must be able to command the respect and attention of the staff

being supported, whether in a formal classroom setting, on a remote web presentation, or during one-on-one mentoring sessions.

- *Mechanic*: Enthusiasm and information has to be backed up with workable solutions; the mechanic of the PMO must be able to disassemble and rebuild processes, configure supporting applications, and generally make sure that PMO solutions work. The mechanic should be able to troubleshoot automated workflows, write documentation, or develop templates equally well.
- *Reporting specialist*: Regardless of the system of origin, disparate information types must be obtained and presented in a number of different ways for varying audiences. Data should be summarized so that it is readily digestible by busy executives or meaty enough to satisfy the needs of working managers. Beyond excellent technical skills to mine information sources, the PMO reporting specialist should also inherently understand the business so as to anticipate what information end users need and how that information will be used.
- *Analyst*: The analyst should be adept at mining actionable information from various data sources, spotting trends, and recognizing emerging issues. To accomplish this, the analyst must have a certain level of intuition about what information is viable and a keen sense of how different types of information are related.
- *Financial specialist*: Everyone wants to know, "What does it really cost?" or "What did we really get?" Every PMO needs someone who can deftly turn labor, time, benefits, and other elements into dollars and sense, as well as act as a liaison with the accounting department. A PMO financial specialist should be as comfortable with a business plan as an accounting ledger, know his or her way around a project schedule, and be adept in various investment valuation techniques.
- *Marketer*: For the PMO to effectively influence without authority it must successfully promote its concepts, information, and processes to an often wary and fickle audience. The marketer constructs internal campaigns to gain buy-in and compliance for process improvements and other alignment initiatives. Do not underrate this skill—sessions in which practitioners relate information on marketing their programs to the organizations with inventive and catchy approaches often draw the largest crowds at user groups and industry forums.

Maintaining PMO Continuity

As we write this the world is slowly emerging from a global recession; many PMOs became a victim to significant cost-cutting measures during the downturn. Current economics aside, most organizations go through business cycles routinely, including periods in which cost control becomes paramount.

Rather than facing the startup of a new PMO while on the path to recovery, there is a strong argument for maintaining continuity of PMO assets and functions in such circumstances, even if it is greatly scaled back. Besides avoiding the loss of your substantial investment in time and intellectual capital, there are certain critical services that the PMO can provide to help reduce costs wisely, keep systems functional through a lean period, and put the organization in a better position to quickly ramp up innovation during revitalization. Being the first mover coming out of an economic downturn has historically proven to be one of the greatest advantages a business can have.

The processes and infrastructure that a PMO puts in place will need to be ready to support new investments if organizations are to get the maximum benefit from a period of growth. If an existing PMO is shut down and all of its staff members are released, it is unlikely that a new manager tasked to restart the PMO later will embrace abandoned systems, tools, and processes. Without PMO continuity, the organization loses its knowledge base and its ability to keep management assets maintained in a functional state. In the end, the cost of missed opportunity and restarting the PMO will far outweigh the additional savings gained by temporarily cutting a few more staff members. Consider retaining a minimum PMO staff during a period of retraction to maintain basic support functions, keep systems operable, provide continuity of intellectual assets, and greatly reduce PMO recovery time and expense.

In the final analysis, the functions performed by a PMO must be done, the effort must be expended, and the results achieved; it is simply a matter of who does the work and at what cost relative to the quality of the outcomes. By concentrating common business management and integration functions into a dedicated center of excellence to improve efficiency and effectiveness, organizations are finding that a well-managed PMO is becoming an increasingly essential element of the overall governance structure.

Key Points

- As the challenges of managing modern dynamic environments continue to increase, the PMO has emerged as a mechanism to foster alignment across a broad footprint in today's organizations.
- For organizations that choose to apply portfolio management, the support of a PMO may make the difference between successfully reaping its value and struggling to make the practice viable.
- The PMO is a valuable resource in helping to identify problems and opportunities; provide information; manage portfolio processes and decision parameters; provide analytical assistance, capabilities, and tools; and ultimately, to help make resulting decisions actionable.

- The PMO can help provide continuity for portfolios, ranging from strategic intent to making investment decisions and executing work.
- The PMO is a logical point to assess the true benefit of products, assets, and services delivered.
- The PMO can ensure that related business processes form a single cohesive network.
- The scope of work and resource management interests of the PMO should span the total demand of the organization it supports and include the workforce needed to accomplish the body of work.
- To be successful, the PMO must have consistent and visible executive sponsorship so that it has the leverage needed to influence the organization and the support for its mission.
- It is critical that the PMO be chartered clearly with objectives and functional responsibilities that facilitate decision making and corrective actions; this keeps the PMO from becoming just a passive reporting function that contributes little value.
- Extra care should be taken to ensure that the PMO is supported as it matures to avoid the trap of constantly setting up, abandoning, and then restarting initiatives.
- PMO staffing needs to address the scope of services it provides, the skills needed to provide those services, and adequate members to deliver those services to its constituency.
- Consider maintaining a minimum PMO staff during periods of economic adversity to ensure change management processes and systems are ready to take advantage of inevitable upswings.

About the Authors

Pat Durbin is CEO and founder of Planview, the award-winning leader in portfolio management solutions. With more than 30 years of experience in business process design and automation, he has designed multiple global management systems including Planview Enterprise. Prior to founding Planview, he served as vice president of research and development and worldwide marketing for Artemis International and has held various positions at McDonnell Douglas and Sun Oil. Pat has a BS in aeronautics from Saint Louis University and an MBA from the University of Illinois.

Terry Doerscher is the chief process architect for Planview. With more than 27 years of experience as a practitioner and consultant, his focus is on innovating world-class management techniques aligned to modern business challenges. Terry is a trusted advisor to many customers and is frequently cited as an industry expert and speaker. He is the primary author of *Planview PRISMS Best Practices*, and drives the PMO 2.0 series of events and research. Prior to joining Planview, Terry served in a number of roles in the public utility industry and received his formal engineering education in the U.S. Navy Nuclear Power Program.

Web
Added
Value™

Index